West of the
Great Divide

FOR KATIE

National Library of Canada Cataloguing in Publication Data

Turner, Robert, D., 1947-
      West of the Great Divide : the Canadian Pacific Railway's first century in British Columbia / Robert D. Turner. –Rev. ed.

      Previous ed. has subtitle: An illustrated history of the Canadian Pacific Railway in British Columbia.
      Includes bibliographical references and index.

      ISBN 1-55039-131-3

      1. Canadian Pacific Railway Company—History. 2. Canadian Pacific Railway Company—History—Pictorial works. 3. Railroads—British Columbia—History. 4. Railroads—British Columbia—History—Pictorial works. I. Title.
HE2810.C2T87 2003   385'.09711   C2003-910443-5

FIRST PRINTING: FEBRUARY 1987
SECOND PRINTING: JUNE 1987
THIRD PRINTING: JANUARY 1988
FOURTH PRINTING: MARCH 1990
SECOND EDITION: MAY 2003

Sono Nis Press most gratefully acknowledges the support for our publishing program provided by the Government of Canada through the Book Publishing Industry Development Program (BPIDP), The Canada Council for the Arts, and the British Columbia Arts Council.

JACKET ILLUSTRATION AND FRONTISPIECE: The climb over the Selkirk Mountains in winter was the toughest section of the main line through British Columbia. The original line over Rogers Pass, depicted in this illustration based on a Byron Harmon photograph, was dominated by extensive snow sheds but even these could not fully protect the line from slides and avalanches.—Robert D. Turner

Published by
Sono Nis Press
PO Box 160
Winlaw, BC V0G 2J0

1-800-370-5228 (North America)
250-226-0077 (International)

sononis@netidea.com
www.sononis.com

Printed and bound in Canada by Houghton Boston Printers.

West of the Great Divide

THE CANADIAN PACIFIC
RAILWAY'S FIRST CENTURY
IN BRITISH COLUMBIA

BY ROBERT D. TURNER

Winlaw, British Columbia

Beyond the CPR's First Century...

The Canadian Pacific Railway, under President Rob Ritchie, embraced its heritage with the repurchase in the United States, and restoration of, its Hudson 2816 which had been retired and sold decades earlier. The locomotive is used as a corporate ambassador for the company. The railway also shed its CP Rail and CP Rail Systems identifications and presented itself, once again, as the Canadian Pacific Railway complete with a modern beaver crest. Meticulously restored at BC Rail's soon to be dismantled steam shop, 2816 and its special train, steams into Mission City in September 2001 on its inaugural tour.
–Robert D. Turner

Canadian Pacific's centennial in 1985-1986 was a milestone in Canadian history and for the railway. The CPR's first century was marked by profound change and since 1986 the pace of change has only accelerated. Growth and technological change have gone on side by side with retrenchment. The railway itself has shrunk dramatically in British Columbia with the abandonment of all of the former Kettle Valley Railway and much of the route across the southern Interior as far east as Castlegar. The branch line from Sicamous to Okanagan which used trackage rights over parts of the CNR to Kelowna, is now the Okanagan Valley Railway operated by OmniTrax, a major owner of short line railroads. On Vancouver Island, the Esquimalt & Nanaimo Railway was taken over by Rail America in a lease and purchase arrangement beginning in 1999 and in the autumn of 2002 is on the verge of abandonment altogether unless a creative and dramatic restructuring occurs. On the positive side, traffic volumes on the mainline have increased and containerization of merchandise shipments has transformed the railway's terminals and rolling stock. The 40-foot boxcar, once the backbone of freight services, carrying everything from furniture and ore to lumber and grain, is as obsolete as the steam locomotive. Intermodal terminals have been built near Port Coquitlam and at Roberts Bank to facilitate container traffic. New third-generation diesel locomotives from General Electric and General Motors have been introduced and have taken over most mainline assignments from the SD40-2s that once dominated nearly all traffic through the Rockies, the Fraser Canyon and the Crowsnest. These powerful engines have reduced the number of units needed on coal and grain trains and have been highly successful. In an operational change in the late 1990s, Canadian Pacific and Canadian National negotiated a joint operating agreement for the Fraser Canyon area making possible more efficient use of both rail lines through this rugged region.

Passenger services on the Canadian Pacific have also changed in unexpected ways. VIA ended its *Canadian* service over the CPR's route through the Rockies in January 1990 and later that year Rocky Mountaineer Railtours began its highly successful *Rocky Mountaineer* tour trains between Vancouver and Calgary. In addition, a service also runs to Jasper over Canadian National. Then, even more surprising, in June 2000, Canadian Pacific re-entered the passenger business with its Royal Canadian Pacific Luxury Rail Tours, using its business car fleet and restored 1950s vintage diesels in a circle tour through the Rockies. Climaxing the railway's heritage accomplishments was the return to operation in 2001 of Canadian Pacific Hudson steam locomotive, No. 2816, named the *Empress*, to act as a corporate ambassador across its system. In 1995, Suburban commuter service, called the *West Coast Express*, began between Mission City in the Fraser Valley and Vancouver. This service is operated by TransLink, the regional transportation authority, under a contract with the Canadian Pacific Railway. At the corporate level, the CPR also moved the headquarters for its railway from Montreal to Calgary and in 2002, Canadian Pacific Limited separated its major components into independent companies. Canadian Pacific Hotels, so long associated with the railway, acquired the Canadian National's hotels and went on to purchase Fairmont Hotels and created Fairmont Hotels and Resorts in 1999.

Preservation activities have been significant with many former CPR stations now serving as community centres, museums, and restaurants or for other uses. The beautiful CPR station in Vancouver has been restored and is a transit terminal. The CPR sternwheeler *Moyie*, the oldest passenger sternwheeler in the world, is beautifully restored and preserved at Kaslo on Kootenay Lake, and the larger *Sicamous* is a prized heritage asset in Penticton along with the steam tug *Naramata*. A section of the Kettle Valley Railway near Summerland was saved and is operated as a steam railway and a steam operation connects Port Alberni with the McLean Mill National Historic Site on Vancouver Island. Dramatic sections of the Kettle Valley and other sections of abandoned CPR right-of-way are now much enjoyed hiking and cycling trails. There is a fine railway museum at Revelstoke and an interpretive centre at Rogers Pass. At Cranbrook the Canadian Museum of Rail Travel presents some of the CPR's finest passenger equipment in an internationally acclaimed collection. Regrettably, the former CPR Royal Hudson 2860 and its service on BC Rail was cancelled in 2002 by the provincial government when extensive repairs were needed for the locomotive and it is now on exhibit, pending a hoped for restoration at the West Coast Railway Museum at Squamish. Finally the venerable 374, the steam locomotive that brought the first passenger train into Vancouver, is on display at the Roundhouse Community Centre, an arts and recreation facility in Vancouver. It is hard to recognize some of the areas where the CPR was once the dominant feature in the urban landscape. Condominiums, shopping areas, recreation facilities and pavilions have replaced the once extensive rail yards around much of Vancouver although the railway still has a presence along Burrard Inlet.

The story of the Canadian Pacific in British Columbia is ever fascinating; its impact on British Columbia is profound, and it will continue to be for many years to come.

Robert Turner
November 2002

A new generation of diesels has come to dominate Canadian Pacific operations in British Columbia dominated by General Electric "Dash 9s" like these at Roberts Bank and near Crowsnest. The changes from the 1880s are almost unimaginable.
–Both Robert D. Turner

PREFACE

The Great Divide at the summit of the Rockies in Kicking Horse Pass, 5332 feet (1625 m) above sea level, was marked by an elaborate wooden sign. A similar monument stood at the summit of Crowsnest Pass. The stone cairn was erected in honour of Sir James Hector, of the Palliser Expedition of 1857-1860, who discovered Kicking Horse Pass.
—BYRON HARMON, AUTHOR'S COLLECTION

The descent from the Great Divide to Field, down the upper canyon of the Kicking Horse River, was known as the Field Hill. It was at once a challenge to the crews and a delight to the tourists. This engraving is from the mid-1880s.
—*THE ILLUSTRATED LONDON NEWS,* JULY 24, 1886, GERALD E. WELLBURN COLLECTION

Work on this book and subsequent volumes began about 1970, before my first book, *Vancouver Island Railroads* was published. At that time, I started seriously collecting the material that ultimately formed the basis for *West of the Great Divide.* However, as the story unfolded in photographs, old documents, newspapers, engineering reports and from discussions with railroaders and travellers, I realized that it was going to take some time to complete the job of describing the history of the CPR in British Columbia, let alone the other railways that operated in the province. I decided to develop the stories of the maritime operations of the CPR first while at the same time pulling together more information and photographs on the rail systems. There was another consideration too. I wanted to familiarize myself more with the province. British Columbia is a large, diverse and complex region of North America and, even though I have spent my life here, it takes time to get to understand its history and geography.

The intervening years have been fascinating, frustrating, intriguing and rewarding—sometimes all at once. In a sense it has been a personal journey—through a beautiful and, at times, daunting landscape and also a journey through time. While I have been able to travel to nearly every area described in this book and gain some insight into it, often the history was more elusive. What was it like to work on the construction of the CPR through the Fraser Canyon? How did the CPR go about dieselizing its operations? What was the impact of the rotary snow plows in keeping the line open through the bitter winters in the Selkirks? There were these questions and hundreds of others. Fortunately, through documents, photographs, newspapers, books and the recollections of many people, the story and the answers to many questions emerged.

The history of the CPR in British Columbia will ultimately require many books ranging from biographies to economic studies. This book is not a corporate history nor a political history. It is directed instead towards examining the construction, equipment and facilities, and day to day operations of this vast and complicated railway system in British Columbia. I felt that the story would be incomplete without including the Great Northern which, along with the CPR, played such an important role along B.C.'s southern boundary. I hope that this book will fill some of the historical gaps, provide an outline of the development and operations of the railway and show how greatly they have changed over the last 100 years. At the same time, I hope it will also give some insights into how this railway has so profoundly influenced the course of British Columbia's history.

I am indebted to many institutions and individuals for their help and encouragement in preparing this book.

Institutions, both public and private, to which I owe my sincere thanks include the following: Archives of the Canadian Rockies (ACR), Banff; R. N. Atkinson Museum, Penticton; Canadian Railway Museum, Delson, Quebec; B.C. Coal, Sparwood; British Columbia Forest Service, Victoria; British

Columbia Legislative Library, Victoria; British Columbia Provincial Museum, Modern History Division (BCPM), Victoria; Burlington Northern Inc., St. Paul; Cominco, Trail; Cranbrook Archives, Museum and Landmark Foundation; Eastern Washington State Historical Society, Spokane; Federal Archives and Records Center, GSA, Seattle; Glenbow-Alberta Institute, Calgary; Interior Photo Bank (IPB), Kelowna; Kamloops Museum; Kelowna Centennial Museum; Kimberley Museum; Maritime Museum of British Columbia, Victoria; Minnesota Historical Society (MHS), St. Paul; Nanaimo Museum; Nelson Centennial Museum; Provincial Archives of British Columbia (PABC), Victoria; Public Archives of Canada (PAC), Ottawa; Revelstoke Museum; Rossland Historical and Museum Association; University of British Columbia Library, Vancouver; Vancouver City Archives (CVA); Vancouver Maritime Museum; Vancouver Public Library, Historic Photograph Section (VPL); and the Vernon Board of Museum, Archives and Art Gallery.

Many, many individuals have helped me out in a multitude of ways. Operating employees of CP Rail from train crews, section men and operators to welders, civil engineers and superintendents have all helped with information about operations, equipment and procedures that have aided photography and research. Retired employees have aided immensely in sharing with me their photographs, papers and personal recollections. Photographers, travellers and collectors have aided greatly by lending their material and relating their own experiences to me for the book. My sincere thanks to: Anne Gloria Alexandria, Donald Bain, the late Earl Barlow, June Barlow, A. G. "Ben" Benning, the late Gerald M. Best, the late H. J. (Bob) Brown, Peter Chapman, Dr. W. B. Chung, Frank Clapp, Paul C. Clegg, Bill Curran, Harry V. Davis, Linda Devore, Arthur Dawe, Albert Farrow, Jack Fawcett, Grant Ferguson, Gordon Fulkerson, Bob Griffin, Dr. Philip R. Hastings, my cousin Mark Horne, Wally Huffman, Adolf Hungry Wolf, Philip C. Johnson, Bob Johnston, Dr. Andrea Laforet, Charles Lillard, Ruth Lomas, Patrick O. Hind, Jack McDonald, the late Perley McPherson, Earl Marsh, E. Ron Matthews, David Mattison, Charles Maxwell, Andre Morin, Pierre Morin, L. S. "Mo" Morrison, Charles Nelles, Ron Nixon, Dean Ogle, Milton Parent, Walter Paffard, C. A. Peterson, David Polster, Doug Richter, Jessie Robson, the late Ted Robson, David Scholes, Lawrence Shawver, Genevieve Singleton, Douglas C. Smith, Pat Stafford, Arthur Stiffe, Lawrence Takkinen, Art Tondini, John Tondini, Bob Townsend, Arthur Urquhart, Bert Ward, Robert Whetham, Michael Wilkie, Michael Woodhead, Annie York, Brian Young, and Ken Young.

While I hesitate to single out individuals, special mention must be made of the contributions of material by Lance Camp, Maurice Chandler, Donald Duke, Norman Gidney, Eric A. Grubb, Jim Hope, John Illman, Gib Kennedy, the late Otto F. Landauer, Ken Merilees, John Newman, Gerry Wellburn,

November 7, 1985 marked the centennial of the driving of the last spike of the Canadian Pacific Railway. The celebrations at Craigellachie, B.C. were a time for reflection. The next year marked the centennial of the opening of scheduled train service to the Pacific. At Vancouver, a featured attraction of *Expo 86* was the Roundhouse pavilion, with its frontispiece of CPR locomotive 374. This locomotive brought the first passenger train into Vancouver in 1887.

Both the Roundhouse pavilion, once the CPR's Drake Street Roundhouse, and the locomotive were extensively restored with great effort and dedication by many people.
—LANCE CAMP; ROBERT D. TURNER

Wilbur C. Whittaker, and Dave Wilkie. Where possible, I have also tried to recognize early commerical photographers in the credits that accompany the illustrations. Two more photographers require special mention. They are the late Albert H. Paull, whom I had the privilege of knowing, and the late Cyril Littlebury. Other examples of their work are in private collections. Their documentation of the height of the steam era on B.C.'s railways during the 1920s and 30s is particularly valuable.

Special thanks must also go to my friends at CPR, particularly Omer Lavallée and Dave Jones of the Corporate Archives in Montreal. Their interest in this project and patience with my many questions is sincerely appreciated. CPR public relations staff in Calgary, particularly Earl Olsen, Steve Morris in Revelstoke and in Vancouver, notably Ed MacPherson, Jack Shave, Harry Atterton, and Don Bower have also been of great help. Photos from CPR Vancouver are credited simply CPR. David Polster, Environmental Supervisor of the Rogers Pass Project was most helpful.

Several friends patiently read all or portions of the manuscript and made numerous helpful suggestions. To Peter Corley-Smith, Walter Paffard, Dave Parker, and Dave Wilkie, a sincere thank you. Jim Finnell provided a lovely painting of the Atlantic Express at Glacier House.

As usual, my friends at Sono Nis Press and the Morriss Printing Company were a pleasure to work with. They made the production of the book interesting and fun with a professionalism that I admire.

Family members contributed in many ways, from providing advice and encouragement to proofreading and photography. It is a particular pleasure to acknowledge their contribution: my mother Isabella and my brother Bill, my older daughters Sarah and Molly and, of course, my wife, Nancy, whose contribution to this book was immense and ran the gammut of editing, photography and determined support.

*　　*　　*

Riding to Craigellachie this morning in a wooden passenger car over 100 years old, pulled by a steam locomotive, I cannot help but reflect on the hundreds of people who worked on or have been affected by the CPR. A century has passed since the railway was completed and so much has changed. Yet in many ways so much remains the same. The railway still serves as a vital link in the transportation system of British Columbia, and it will in the future. The scale of railroad operations has grown tremendously yet the railway's role in carrying passengers has all but vanished. Change has been so much a part of the CPR's history that one cannot but wonder what the nature of the system will be in 50 years.

It is 9:22 a.m. in the overcast cold of Craigellachie near Eagle Pass. Lord Strathcona, great grandson of Donald A. Smith, is driving a spike to commemorate the centennial of the completion of this great railway across Canada...

ROBERT D. TURNER
Craigellachie, British Columbia
November 7, 1985

PROLOGUE

Before the Rails were Laid

John A. Macdonald, the first prime minister of Canada, saw the Canadian Pacific Railway as an essential link across the vast, empty lands of Western Canada. Macdonald's drive and determination saw the CPR through to completion.
—GERALD E. WELLBURN COLLECTION

The miles upon miles of mountains in British Columbia posed many challenges for the surveyors and engineers. Steep, nearly vertical, mountain sides, avalanches, river canyons and deeply cut streams were but a few. The climb up the east face of the Selkirks required numerous bridges, the most noteworthy being Surprise Creek, shown at left, Stoney Creek and Mountain Creek.
—*THE ILLUSTRATED LONDON NEWS*, JULY 24, 1886, GERALD E. WELLBURN COLLECTION

The vision of a transcontinental railway for Canada was the dream of many men, the passion of a few and, to become reality, the toil of many. It was as much an art of political will—sometimes faltering, sometimes steadfast—as it was a great engineering undertaking.

British Columbia agreed to join the young nation of Canada in 1871, enticed by terms of union that promised a Canadian transcontinental railway. It was to be started in two years, operational in ten. The Palliser expedition of 1857-1860 had examined possibilities for new transportation routes across the prairies, and proposals for a transcontinental railway were not new. For example, in 1859 *The Victoria Gazette* editorialized on the merits of a railroad and Governor James Douglas spoke of the desirability of railroads in 1864. Delegates to the Confederation talks argued persistently for one. Across the plains and deserts of the American West, a transcontinental railroad had been in operation since 1869 when the Central Pacific and Union Pacific met at Promontory, Utah. Canada would have no less in its own land. That, at least, was the determination of Sir John A. Macdonald, the first Prime Minister of Canada, and it would dominate his political fortunes for the rest of his life.

The agreement for the union of the Colony of British Columbia with the Dominion of Canada read, in part:

11. The Government of the Dominion undertake to secure the commencement simultaneously, within two years from the date of the Union, of the construction of a Railway from the Pacific towards the Rocky Mountains, and from such point as may be selected, East of the Rocky Mountains, towards the Pacific, to connect the Seaboard of British Columbia with the Railway system of Canada; and further, to secure the completion of such Railway within ten years from the date of Union....

The debate over the wisdom of this commitment by the government of Canada to the new Province of British Columbia seemed endless. To Macdonald's opposition it was the basis of a concerted attack on the government. Meanwhile, the reality of finding a route across the vast expanse of rock, muskeg, prairie and mountain that was western Canada began. In April 1871, Sandford Fleming, an experienced engineer, was given charge of surveys for the railway and the tremendous task of surveying and mapping began. That year and the next, the survey parties crossed the vast wilderness, testing routes, probing mountain passes; Walter Moberley, Marcus Smith, Joseph Hunter, Robert McLennan and others penetrated the vast mountain barriers of British Columbia and gained a permanent place in Canadian history for their exploits. In April 1872, Fleming proposed a route around Lake Superior, across the northern prairies to Yellowhead Pass in the Rockies. From there, the line was to follow the North Thompson, Thompson and Fraser rivers to Burrard Inlet on the Pacific.

However, Victoria, the capital of British Columbia, was on Vancouver Island, and Victoria expected to be the terminus of the railway. Surveys by Marcus Smith suggested an alternate route west of the Yellowhead — across central British Columbia to the rocky, fjord-like Bute Inlet, then by an enormous bridge system or ferry service to Vancouver Island and thence south to Victoria. Complicating the picture, Victoria was rashly, unrealistically, named the terminus in July 1873, by an Order-in-Council but no construction followed.

The government wanted the line built by private interests controlled in Canada. A prospective syndicate was formed, but initially it seemed to be too much dominated by American investors. Later, Sir Hugh Allan, prominent Canadian businessman and head of the Allan Steamship Line, took over the proposal and formed the Canadian Pacific Railway. The situation became more complicated as Macdonald, facing re-election that year, asked for and received funding for Allan. Macdonald was re-elected, only to be forced to resign in November 1873, as the famous "Pacific Scandal" broke. Facing accusations of corruption and patronage for Allan, who was a personal friend of Macdonald's, the government collapsed, and so too did the CPR Company.

Alexander Mackenzie and his Liberals took over from Macdonald and held office until 1878, through a period of economic recession. For Mackenzie, never keen on the railway, the bad times only contributed to his cautious tendencies. The surveys lagged, but continued, often raising as many questions over routing as they answered, and only limited construction was begun in Manitoba. Seeing no progress, British Columbia threatened to leave Confederation, and when the site of the terminal was shifted to Burrard Inlet, petitions were circulated gathering support for Vancouver Island to break away from British Columbia and Canada. Extensive negotiations, arbitration and discussion followed but still little progress was made on the railway.

In the election of 1878 Macdonald's Conservatives were returned to office with promises of building the railway and his strong nationalist policy. Macdonald was personally defeated, but he won in a by-election held in Victoria, and this further strengthened his commitment to the railway. There were still uncertainties over routes and the right syndicate needed to be attracted to finance the venture, but the determination to have a railway to the Pacific was still intact. There would be falterings of will but, with the economy improving, the stage was set for the monumental task of construction to begin.

"It requires but a railroad across the continent, which according to a recent speech of the Duke of Newcastle in the House of Lords, is 'by no means a visionary scheme,' for our ports to be crowded with shipping, our wharves covered with merchandise, and our streets groaning with traffic, and who is there that has thought of the proud future that awaits the city, if this railroad be accomplished?"
— Editorial in *The Victoria Gazette*, December 12, 1859.

"I wish to impress upon your attention that no measure can be more fruitful of prosperous results, than that of improving the thoroughfares, until the Railway and Locomotive supersede the existing cumbrous modes of conveyance on all the main lines of road, from the Coast to Alexandria, whence there is a practicable water communication, through the valley of Fraser River, to the Rocky Mountains; a route which moreover presents so many facilities of ground and general position, that there is every probability of its becoming the main line of overland communication with Canada."
— From a speech by Governor James Douglas, published in the *British Columbia Government Gazette*, February 21, 1864.

CONTENTS

Glacier House in the Selkirks was a welcome respite for weary travellers. It served as a meal stop until 1909 when dining cars began operating over the mountains. The painting, by Jim Finnell, depicts the *Atlantic Express* about 1887, ready to depart. —AUTHOR'S COLLECTION

The Kicking Horse Canyon between Field and Golden
was, and is, a highlight of rail travel through the Rockies.
With the opening of the line to regular service, the
CPR began an active tourist promotion campaign to
increase its passenger revenues and hasten settlement along
the railway. Here, in the 1890s, the crew and passengers
pose beside an immaculate No. 535 (built in 1891 at the
CPR's own shops in Montreal) and a six-car passenger
train. Notable in the train is the open sided observation
car, second from the rear, which afforded travellers
breath-taking views of the mountains. —N. CAPLE, CVA, CANP218

CHAPTER 1

BUILDING A MOUNTAIN RAILWAY

Routes Through the Mountains

Summoning the political will and economic means to build a transcontinental railway was a monumental undertaking in itself, but to build it was even more of a challenge. The distances were so vast and the country so wild, remote and unexplored that few people, whether politicians, engineers, or financiers, really could have appreciated the work and the hardship ahead. Perhaps it is just as well because they might have changed their minds.

To the east of the Continental Divide—the Great Divide—there were the prairies still so little understood that some, seeing them in wet years, visualized an endless granary awaiting the plow, while others saw only drought and semi-desert. Then, between Winnipeg and central Ontario was the rock and muskeg of the Canadian Shield. But to the west, into British Columbia, was the greatest challenge: range upon range of mountains—the Rockies, Selkirks, Monashees, and Coast ranges—running across the path of any railway seeking the Pacific shore.

While in Ottawa endless debate, scandal and dealing dominated the scene and while British Columbians grew increasingly impatient, the surveyors were out in the wilderness of the West mapping, surveying, plotting, struggling to find routes through to the Coast. These men were themselves unique individualists. They had to be to survive months on end with meagre rations in the rain and snow of the mountains. And their surveys led to more and more debate. What was the best route through British Columbia to the Coast? Where should the terminus of the railway be? Despite the years of work and the many reports, the answers remained unclear. Victoria, on Vancouver Island, had been promised the terminus but it was not an easy promise to keep. Georgia Strait separated the Island from the Mainland of British Columbia and even over the narrowest passages at the northern end of the Strait, the necessary bridges would have been enormously costly, if feasible at all.

Sandford Fleming had concluded by the mid-1870s that the Yellowhead Pass was the best route through the Rockies into British Columbia. His detailed reports, submitted regularly, had outlined the easy grades and other advantages of

1

the Yellowhead. But even if the Yellowhead had been accepted, the routes to the west were still difficult to compare. There was also the key consideration of having a deep water port on the Pacific and that port needed to have sufficient land adjacent to it for facility development. Each route, it seemed, had its own vocal advocates, often the surveyors who had discovered the routes. The surveys examined, in addition to the Yellowhead, Howse Pass, Pine Pass and developed routes to the coast via the Nechako and Skeena rivers to Port Simpson near what is now Prince Rupert, through central British Columbia to Bute Inlet and to Dean Inlet (via the Bella Coola Valley) and via the Thompson and Fraser rivers to Burrard Inlet.

Consideration also was given to the problems of taking the line to Vancouver Island via the Bute Inlet route. The reports suggested a ferry service and, when traffic warranted, a bridge system leading to the Island. But it would have taken longer to travel by rail over the extension to the Island than it would have to take a steamer from Esquimalt to Burrard Inlet. Inevitably, the surveys pointed to Burrard Inlet as the terminus. As partial compensation to Islanders, a separate line, the Esquimalt & Nanaimo, described later, would be built.

The other passes and overland routes had distinct drawbacks or they were lacking in port possibilities. The Skeena Route was better, but its north coast terminal was a long way from the American border and the major Canadian population centres of the south coast. Furthermore, it had not been surveyed carefully by the end of the 1878 season and a detailed examination would have resulted in even more delays. By the end of the 1870s, it looked as if the route for the transcontinental railway had been finalized: to the Yellowhead and from there down the Thompson River to the Fraser and on to Burrard Inlet... or was it?

The actual construction of the railway in British Columbia began as two separate undertakings. The western end was built under contract by the government while the eastern sections were built by the CPR itself. In 1879, before the formation of the Canadian Pacific syndicate, the government contracted with a California-based syndicate led by Darius Ogden Mills and managed by Andrew Onderdonk, to begin construction between Yale and Savona (then Savona's Ferry) on Kamloops Lake, a distance of 127 miles (205 km). The price of the contracts was $9,100,000 and the work was to be finished by June 30, 1885.* Onderdonk was an experienced

---

* The four contracts were as follows: Contract 60, Section A, Emory's Bar to Boston Bar, 29 miles (47 km); Contract 61, Section B, Boston Bar to Lytton, 29 miles (47 km); Contract 62, Section C, Lytton to Junction Flat, 28.5 miles (46 km); Contract 63, Section D, Junction Flat to Savona, 40.5 miles (65 km). The later contract for the line between Emory's Bar and Port Moody, 85 miles (137 km), was Contract 92.

Other members of the syndicate were: H. B. L. Laidlaw, banker from New York; L. P. Morton of Morton Bliss & Co., New York; and S. G. Reed, Vice-President of the Oregon Railway & Navigation Company of Portland.

CANADIAN PACIFIC RAILWAY.

Tenders for Grading, Track-laying, &c.

SEALED TENDERS, ADDRESSED TO the undersigned and endorsed "Tender Pacific Railway" will be received at this office up to noon of WEDNESDAY, the 1st day of JANUARY next, for the Grading, Tracklaying and other works of construction required to be executed on the following sections of the Canadian Pacific Railway:—

1. From the westerly end of the 26th contract at English River to Raleigh, a distance of about 50 miles,

2. From Raleigh to Eagle River, a distance of about 68 miles.

8. From Eagle River to the Easterly end of the 15th contract at Keewatin, a distance of about 67 miles.

4. From Yale to Kamloops Lake, in British Columbia, a distance of about 125 miles.

Plans, &c., may be seen, and Specifications, approximate quantities, forms of tender, and other information obtained at the office of the Engineer in Chief at Ottawa.

A bill of quantities will be ready on before December 1st, at the Department of Public Works.

No Tender will be entertained unless on the printed form, and unless the conditions are complied with.

The general Tender for construction of whole line under Railway Act of 1874, covers above sections ; but separate tenders are asked under the ordinary conditions of the Department.

By order,
F. BRAUN,
Secretary.

Department of Public Works,
Ottawa, 18th August, 1878.
August 19, 1878.   H-ao

2

Andrew Onderdonk, the engineer who was to supervise and manage the construction of the Canadian Pacific Railway through the formidable canyons of the Fraser and Thompson rivers. With the backing of prominent Americans, who formed the syndicate that won the contracts from the Canadian government, he was able to complete the western sections of the CPR on schedule. It took the talents and ingenuity of capable surveyors and engineers and the labour of thousands, including many Chinese. —PABC, HP2917

contractor who had worked on the construction of the San Francisco seawall and, with significant financial backers, the government had a reasonable assurance of the work being successfully completed.

The major problem for the government was finding an acceptable group of businessmen to undertake the vast project of construction and operation of the railway. Politics, nationalism, money and personalities all came into the equation but in 1880, an agreement was reached. The principals were financier and Bank of Montreal president, George Stephen; John S. Kennedy, a powerful New York businessman; and James J. Hill and Richard B. Angus of the St. Paul, Minneapolis and Manitoba Railroad (in fact the beginning of what was to become the Great Northern Railway extending all the way to Puget Sound on the Pacific) and affiliates of Stephen. A behind-the-scenes partner of the enterprise was Donald A. Smith, a cousin of Stephen and the same gentleman who would, on November 7, 1885, drive the last spike completing the CPR. But there was an irony in the composition of the syndicate. Donald A. Smith, as an independent member of the House of Commons, had been unable to support Macdonald in the critical debate at the time of the Pacific Scandal. Smith's speech, in which he spoke of "a very grave impropriety" by Macdonald, finished the government's chances of weathering the scandal and the government was forced to resign soon after. That was now history, but still it was politic that Smith was not, at that time, highly visible in the syndicate.

The agreement with the government was signed on October 21, 1880 and ratified by Parliament on February 1, 1881. It was a complex one, the major provisions including a cash subsidy of $25,000,000, a land grant of 25,000,000 acres (10 117 500 ha) in Western Canada† and the promise to turn over the sections of line, once completed, that were already under

† The CPR lands in British Columbia, known as the Railway Belt, were turned over to the Dominion government by the province to assist in the construction of the railway. The Railway Belt comprised a strip of land approximately 20 miles (32 km) wide on both sides of the line as finally located. An additional block of land, the Peace River Block, of 3,500,000 acres (1 417 000 ha), also was transferred to the Dominion government to provide for acreage already alienated. From these lands, the Dominion government granted lands to the CPR as one of the terms of its subsidy agreement. In return, the Dominion government was to pay the province $100,000 annually for the alienation of the land. Lands still owned by the Dominion government were transferred back to the province in 1930.

The amount of the land grant was reduced in 1886 by 6,793,014 acres (2 749 133 ha) when the land was sold back to the Dominion for $1.50 per acre to reduce the CPR's debts to the government. The policy of the CPR was to encourage the settlement and development of these lands. The company maintained that a greater revenues would result, in the long term, by having the land settled and productive, than by realizing high initial return on the lands. The railway lands cannot be dealt with here in detail but other significant holdings added to these original lands included the land grants to the British Columbia Southern Railway (3,775,733 acres, or 1 519 945 ha), the Columbia & Kootenay Railway (188,593 acres, or 76 325 ha), the Columbia & Western (1,315,273 acres, or 532 990 ha), and the Vancouver townsite and Esquimalt & Nanaimo Railway, both discussed later.

contract or government ownership. This included, amongst others, the Onderdonk contracts in British Columbia as well as sections in Manitoba. There were tax concessions and a very controversial clause that gave the CPR a monopoly across the western territories and provinces for 20 years before any other line could be built south of the CPR and connect with American lines.

The Canadian Pacific Railway was incorporated on February 16, 1881, and for its part, it had to finance, build and complete the transcontinental railway within 10 years, to operate it and, finally — critically — to make it pay. These were not simple challenges. Still to be settled was the question of routes and a vast organization had to be built up, staffed, administered and funded. There was little time for mistakes, inexperience or hesitation. In judging that the CPR syndicate was capable of accomplishing the task, John A. Macdonald had been correct. The will, the determination, the ability were all there and they would be tested to the full in the next few years. There was a balance of financial ability, resources, and railroad experience in the syndicate.

Despite all the work of the past years, there were still uncertainties over the routing across the prairies and through the mountains of British Columbia. Even with the apparent advantages of the route through Yellowhead Pass, it was a long way north of the international border and required more trackage, and hence more money, than it appeared a direct route from Winnipeg to the West would have needed. Moreover, the early reports of the southern prairies being little more than desert were being brought into question by new information, notably the enthusiastic reports of persuasive botanist John Macoun, who travelled the western grasslands during years of higher rainfall.

Increasingly, a southern routing seemed advantageous. Moreover and perhaps decisively, there were settlers and speculators already in place across the northern prairies. A southern route would give the railway complete control of its locations, remove its needs from the realm of profiteers and give it an opportunity to maximize its interests in land. Maximizing interests in land did not mean, though, that it would be the company's intention to charge maximum prices for land. Rather, the CPR wanted the land populated with producing farms that would create a steady base of traffic for the railway; that was where the profits would come from. Hill was persuaded and so too eventually were Stephen and Smith. For Hill, there were other advantages. He hoped the CPR would abandon the long, costly diversion around Lake Superior and, instead connect with his St. Paul, Minneapolis and Manitoba before eventually re-entering Canada. As well, the southern route across the prairies would better compete with the new Northern Pacific being built west through the northern states and territories.

Decisively, perhaps imprudently, the choice was made to build west from Winnipeg across the southern prairies towards

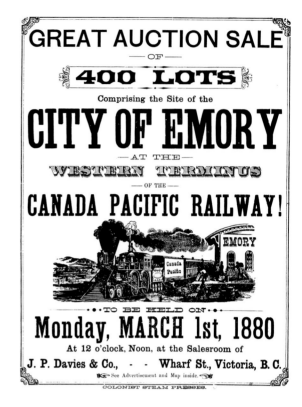

The routing of the CPR would determine the fate of many communities and lead to many settlement schemes and attempts at land speculation. Some towns such as Farwell, adjacent to what became Revelstoke, were bypassed when speculators drove land prices too high for the cash-starved CPR. The "City of Emory" was little more than a steamer landing south of Yale and a supply point for the construction forces when this elaborate land auction was held in Victoria. Emory never was to be an important point on the CPR. Its days as a terminus were limited to a brief period during the construction when navigation to Yale was difficult. It never would develop into the city the advertising promised: "There can be no rival to this the only available townsite, all the surrounding land being locked up in the Government Railway Reservation!" This scheme was not a CPR enterprise; the company was not incorporated until the next year.
—GERALD E. WELLBURN COLLECTION

the Rockies. But while a southern route was chosen, there were still two unresolved problems: finding an acceptable route through the Rockies and locating a pass through the barrier of the Selkirks.

To help resolve this central question of routing through the mountains, more surveys were undertaken. This task Hill gave to Major A. B. Rogers a tough, determined man, intent on his mission. By the end of 1881, Rogers claimed to have found a good route through Kicking Horse Pass but it was not until the fall of 1882 that Rogers found the route through the Selkirks. It was the pass named in his honour. With this discovery, the route of the Canadian Pacific was settled. The Yellowhead would have to await the construction of the Grand Trunk Pacific and the Canadian Northern a generation later.

The decision to relocate the CPR had enormous consequences for the future of the West. The pattern of western development was permanently altered as some new communities would be established and prosper while others would all but disappear. The railroad was that important. The advantages had persuaded the CPR, but the passes through the mountains would be a constant problem for years to come and, for farmers who settled on the southern dry belt hoping to make a living farming the short-grass prairie, there would be heart-breaking cycles of rain and drought, that no railroad, not even the CPR, could control.

Badly needing experienced men to manage the construction and operation of the CPR, Hill brought to the company a man whose influence on the railway would be far-reaching. He was William Cornelius Van Horne, the general superintendent of the Chicago, Milwaukee & St. Paul and a man much like Hill in drive, ambition, ability and temperament. Van Horne, as manager of the CPR, took up his duties in Winnipeg on January 2, 1882. His abilities and personality were soon felt as the pace of construction quickened, and as ineffective or corrupt officials were dismissed. Two of Van Horne's own appointments were particularly important. The first of these was Thomas Shaughnessy, who became general purchasing agent for the company, a position that was vitally important for two reasons: a steady supply of materials was needed to keep the construction crews moving; and the materials had to be acquired at the best possible prices because the resources of the company were being stretched to the limit. The second appointment was John Egan, who became general superintendent for the western lines.

Hill's overriding interest was, however, still with his American railroad and it had been his hope that the CPR would abandon its all-Canadian route around the northern shore of the Great Lakes in favour of connecting to his lines for a faster, cheaper route to the south. But John A. Macdonald was not about to agree to this sort of scheme and Hill realized his logical route from a cost perspective would not outweigh the logic of national interests. His American railroad would need its own trackage to the West. In mid-1883, Hill resigned from the CPR board and devoted his full energies to the expansion of his railroad which, reorganized as the Great Northern, was built through to the the Pacific Coast, reaching Seattle in 1893.

The Onderdonk contracts through the canyons of the Fraser and Thompson rivers were some of the most difficult stretches of railroad construction on the entire CPR. From Yale, at the head of navigation on the lower Fraser River, to Savona on Kamloops Lake, the route traversed an awesome series of gorges, rapids, sheer mountain faces and deep canyons. Tunnelling and bridging were the rules of construction rather than the exceptions. In some areas, the roadbed had to be built up with timber retaining walls, there being no other practical footing for the track. It was an incredible challenge for the engineers and the labourers. It was also extremely dangerous.

Andrew Onderdonk arrived with his family in Victoria on the steamship *Dakota* at the beginning of April 1880, to begin the enormous project ahead of him. Later that month he inspected the route through the canyons and his engineers began laying out the work ahead. Emory City or Emory's Bar, just south of Yale, was to be the point where actual construction started because navigation to Yale could be difficult during some stages of the river. However, Yale was his base of operations, where he established his headquarters and a home for his family. The Onderdonk home became a social centre for visiting dignitaries and people of influence. For the construction workers, it was undoubtedly viewed somewhat differently: a place few ever saw the inside of. At times, at least, it must have been looked upon with resentment or anger.

Yale, a quiet town serving as a trans-shipment point between river steamers and wagons on the Cariboo Road since the flurry of the Cariboo gold rush, took on renewed importance as a headquarters for construction. Here, Onderdonk constructed railroad shops, a small hospital, offices and stores facilities. A sawmill, powder works, nitroglycerine plant, stables, and other businesses related to the construction followed. Some were built for Onderdonk; others were established by suppliers or sub-contractors. Many new businesses were established and the little town boomed with the influx of workers and engineers although the boom was to fade quickly once the line was completed. It was a logical base of operations that could be well supplied from Victoria and New Westminster by sternwheelers which could navigate the Fraser River to Yale throughout most of the year.

To build through this forbidding country, Onderdonk needed a large, reliable labour force. But the local population was too small to provide the needed men; labour would have to be brought in. Some men were recruited locally including

Construction in the Fraser Canyon

Onderdonk's home was occasionally a focus for labour problems as well as a social centre for dignitaries as an 1885 *Colonist* report noted:

Yale, October 5. Four or 500 unpaid men arrived from the front Saturday evening and this morning went to the CPR offices and demanded their pay. The company's books and pay rolls not being made up it was impossible to pay them. The general superintendent being absent, the men agreed to await his arrival. At 5:30 this evening he arrived with the Governor-General who was conveyed direct by train to Onderdonk's private residence, where the men followed, and finding Mr. Haney, demanded their pay. They threatened to tear down the building. Mr. Haney promised to pay them tomorrow morning at 11 o'clock. Severe trouble is anticipated if the men are not paid as promised.

W. H. Holmes recalled the scene at Yale in 1880:

Men were coming in from everywhere by the hundreds — all kinds of good men — as well as roughnecks from San Francisco — Barbary Coast hoodlums. The streets were crowded — saloons doing a roaring business, and fights a daily occurrence; steamboats arriving daily loaded with freight, and no place to put it for although all available teams had been hired, there were not half enough of them to haul it all away. The different camps had to be supplied as soon as constructed; so the company had to buy more horses and wagons, and to build larger stables and warehouses, residences for officials, and a hospital. Hay and grain kept coming in by steamboat loads; also supplies and tools, powder and lumber. Men of all kinds had to be sorted out; stewards, cooks, flunkeys; drillers, carpenters, teamsters, stablemen and blacksmiths; in fact men of all trades, besides the office staff, timekeepers and checkers... It was hammers and drills, picks and shovels, blasting night and day, and work for everybody who wanted it. The wages were not so high as at present [1936], but at that time they were considered fair.

The Chinese found themselves in a distant land with harsh winters and few comforts. These men are typical of the workers whose labour completed the railway through the canyons. Below is a winter camp near North Bend.
—PABC, HP72553; CVA, CANP91

Native Indians and more men came from California. However, they were insufficient in number and often, the men coming up from the south were poor workers. Onderdonk, with the examples of the Central Pacific and Northern Pacific to draw on, looked to the Orient for the men he so desperately needed. Not only were the Chinese good workers, they were cheap to employ. It was an irresistible combination.

Unfortunately, the story of the Chinese workers is at best fragmentary. Few were literate and few spoke English. They lived apart, often in appalling conditions, unused to the climate and the circumstances they found themselves in. Even the numbers of workers involved are difficult to determine but, when construction reached its peak, the total work force numbered about 10,000 men, of whom perhaps 6,500 were Chinese. The average number was certainly lower than this and, as with the White labourers, there was often very rapid turnover. The demanding nature of the work would have tested the strength and endurance of even the most physically fit. Disease was a serious problem in the camps. The Chinese did not like the new foods they were often forced to eat and, particularly during the winter months, because fresh foods were scarce, there were outbreaks of scurvy. Unemployment during the winter months or when construction was slowed made their circumstances bleak. Many spent the winters in Victoria in poverty with little food and meagre shelter. Others lived in camps of log cabins in the Canyon. When construction ended, many were without any funds to return to China and few could find work. How many died from sickness and construction accidents is impossible to say, but the number was considerable. Estimates range from 1,500 published in the *Colonist* to perhaps several thousand noted by Chinese merchants, but these figures reflect those who died in Victoria and other points during the winter months as well as those who died on the construction sites. Whatever the total number, it was a terrible price.

The plight of those Chinese labourers too poor to return to China or unable to find other work after the completion of the railway received considerable attention but little action. The provincial government formed a Committee of the Executive Council (the cabinet) to consider the matter but concluded that the responsibility was the federal government's, noting, in November 1885, that "the Dominion Government insisting that the exigencies of the Canadian Pacific Railway rendered the presence of these Mongolian hordes indispensable, the duty of providing relief for these starving people now fairly devolves upon that Government through whose intervention the unhappy necessity has arisen." But the federal government took no action and what relief there was came from the established Chinese population of merchants and other businessmen. Some Chinese found more railway work with the extension of trackage to Vancouver and New Westminster and on the construction of the Esquimalt & Nanaimo Railway on Vancouver Island. A few moved east, and others returned to China. Others eventually found work in mining, fish canneries, farming or small businesses.

Much of the work and the labour for the railroad was subcontracted. Contracts for ties, food and other supplies were put out for tender to meet the needs of the construction crews. Chinese labour was supplied by contractors who generally brought in the workers from California and southern China. More came from the northern states, having worked on the Northern Pacific which was nearing completion of its transcontinental route through to Portland, Oregon.

The railway through the Fraser and Thompson canyons was built by hand labour with the aid of a limited range of machinery. The railroad itself was important for moving supplies, bridge timbers, powder, rail and ties, and for ballasting as the construction progressed. A steam powered pile driver, a derrick car, and donkey engines (winches) also were used. Ballast cars were evidently emptied by a steam winch which pulled a ballast plow along the decks of the cars from one end of the train to the other. Small tramways with dump cars were used in some excavations for moving the waste rock and overburden.

Rock drilling was done by hand in many situations using hammers and steel drills. Often the men worked from makeshift scaffolding or were lowered down the cliff faces. On the large tunnelling projects, such as the major tunnels between Yale and Boston Bar, steam and air drills were used. These greatly facilitated the work. Steam plants or compressors were located as close to the sites as possible.

For blasting, black powder and nitroglycerine, produced in plants at Yale, were used. The nitroglycerine was a highly dangerous explosive and it took only a small error in judgement or a moment of carelessness to detonate. Even 100 years later, with many improvements to the line, the difficulty of the original construction and the courage of the workers who built it remains obvious.

Nearly all of the numerous bridges were built on site from cut timbers. Some were prefabricated for faster assembly and systems were developed to enable the crews to work from both ends of the structures at once. Sawmills were located at Emory, Yale and near some of the major construction sites. Much of the timber was logged locally, being transported to Yale over the completed sections of the railway. This was, in fact, probably the first use of railroads for logging in British Columbia. The enormous bridges that were required became a problem for both Onderdonk and later the CPR because, no sooner were they completed, than they began a very rapid deterioration.

The original agreement specified that curves should not exceed four degrees but as the work progressed, an increasingly cost-conscious government urged economy and a relaxing of standards seems to have occurred. Building a wooden trestle was cheaper than extensive rock work and certainly cheaper than a steel and masonry structure. Nonetheless, the

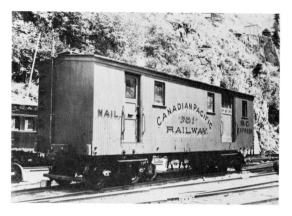

This ornately-decorated car carried mail and express (the latter for the B.C. Express Company) until the line was turned over to the CPR. It appears that the car was built at Yale. In the background is Onderdonk's private car *Eva*. It was used to carry many dignitaries on tours of inspection. The "tool car," shown below, incorporated a derrick for moving rock and other heavy objects.
—PABC, HP74937, HP74959

Track construction, shown here in the Fraser Valley in 1884, was hard, gruelling labour. Supplies were brought by train to the end of track but from that point on all materials were moved by hand. Onto the already graded right-of-way, the men laid out the ties. They were followed by others who put the rails in place. The rails were gauged, spiked in place and finally aligned and ballasted. —CPR

Locomotives were essential to the construction process to keep a steady supply of materials available for the workers and to move men back and forth to the sites. The first locomotives used on the Onderdonk contracts were second-hand machines from the Virginia & Truckee, as in the case of No. 1, the *Yale*, or from other construction projects. No. 2, *Emory*, apparently came from work on the San Francisco sea wall. It soon received the nickname "Curly," denoting the devil, when it nearly killed its engineer in the shops by moving unexpectedly. When construction ended, the locomotive was sold for use as a logging locomotive, eventually being preserved in Vancouver and later moved to Burnaby, as the only surviving locomotive from the Onderdonk contracts. —CVA, CANP123

In contrast to the worn and weary early construction locomotives were the four new Baldwin 4-4-0s ordered by Onderdonk. Of these, No. 9, *Columbia*, is typical. All were built in 1884 and were particularly useful in the train service that was provided over the line before it was taken over by the CPR in 1886. Although the locomotive is lettered "Canadian Pacific Ry" on the tender, it never actually operated for the CPR. —CVA, CANP129

When the first train reached Yale from Emory to the south, it was a cause for real celebration by the citizens of the town. —PABC, HP9745

number of bridges and tunnels seemed endless as the work progressed north of Yale.

In October 1881, the government advertised for bids for a contract to build the railway between Emory and Port Moody, at the head of Burrard Inlet, a distance of about 90 miles (145 km). Onderdonk received the contract in 1882 and work began on this section soon after.

In practice, Onderdonk was in the business of running a railroad as well as building one. In addition to supplying the crews at the end of track, he also carried passengers, freight and mail along the line and, even after the completion of the work, continued to do so until the sections were turned over by the government to the CPR on July 1, 1886. A carshop was established at Yale that produced at least some of the rolling stock required. Other cars were acquired secondhand. Locomotives came from several sources. Four ageing 2-6-0s were bought from the Virginia & Truckee Railroad in Nevada, a line in which Darius Mills was a partner. The first of these, named the *Yale*, arrived at Emory on May 10, 1881, on the steamer *Royal City*.

Landing the machine was not an easy task and it took the efforts of a gang of men and three yoke of oxen using a block and tackle to move the engine up from the river bank to the tracks. The engine crew also came from the V&T. A. J. Minor was engineer and W. S. McDade was fireman and the delivery was supervised by E. M. Luckett of Carson City whose responsibility it was to put the machine in operating condition. The second engine to arrive at Emory was a much smaller machine, a small 0-4-0T named *Emory*, or No. 2.

A second of the former V&T 2-6-0s was brought in the next year and the final two in 1883. As the length of trackage increased, this makeshift roster became quite inadequate for the growing traffic on the line, and Onderdonk ordered four new Baldwin 4-4-0s for delivery in 1884. These were handsome machines, typical of the era, and provided the power for the passenger and freight service on the line for the next two years. Onderdonk also had his own private car, named *Eva*, which was used to carry visiting officials along the line on tours of inspection. After the completion of the line, the car was sold to the Esquimalt & Nanaimo Railway on Vancouver Island for use by Robert Dunsmuir.

The railway reached Yale in June 7, 1881, and the community greeted the train with frontier enthusiasm. As *The Inland Sentinel* reported:

Tuesday at noon it was discovered that the rails would enable the Engine to reach the middle of the town by evening. An impromptu committee consisting of Messrs Mitchell, Leiser and McPhee soon waited upon a few of our inhabitants and raised 'the needful.' Powder and a barrel of beer were procured, and the Engine with a shrill whistle announcing its presence at 6 p.m., the 'little giant' cannon roared out a salute in response, Messrs Ash, Corbitt, Fisher & Carry gunners, while the workmen under Mr. Munro, slaked their thirst in the foaming beverage, and for a few minutes, at least, many were made happy in honor of the long-looked for day, when an Engine would reach Yale.

Construction was more efficient if work could proceed at several locations at once and to accomplish this Onderdonk had to rely on the old Cariboo Road running up the Fraser Canyon. Freighting by this route was time-consuming and expensive, and an alternate method was devised. This involved the use of a sternwheeler on the sections of the river traditionally considered unnavigable. The vessel was built 14 miles (22 km) north of Yale and launched on May 4, 1882. She was named the *Skuzzy*, and was to win the distinction of being the only steamer to navigate Hells Gate Canyon on the Fraser. This difficult task was accomplished only with the help of about 125 Chinese labourers working and pulling lines, literally dragging the vessel through the gorge. With her paddlewheel thrashing at full speed, her steam capstan working lines to the shore through bolts in the canyon wall and the Chinese pulling with all their strength, the *Skuzzy* became one of the most famous of the Fraser River sternwheelers. Onderdonk also acquired the steamer *Myra* for freighting on the lower Fraser.

Sadly, the life of a construction vessel can be short and once the rails had been laid through, the *Skuzzy* was no longer required. Her engines and other machinery were salvaged and incorporated into a new *Skuzzy*, built at Savona to aid in the construction work to the east. She joined a small fleet of sternwheelers operating on Kamloops Lake and the South Thompson River. These vessels, which also played a role in CPR construction, included the *Peerless*, *Spallumcheen*, and *Kamloops* (all owned by James A. Mara) and the *Lady Dufferin* (owned by William Fortune).

One of the major obstacles in the Fraser Canyon was crossing the river itself north of what became the divisional point of North Bend. At Cisco, the tracks were to move from the west bank of the river across a rocky gorge to the east bank before heading on north towards Lytton. Compounding the construction difficulties, the river level fluctuated from 125 feet (38 m) below track level during low water to only 60 feet (18 m) below during spring flood. Building any false works under these circumstances was extremely difficult and the cantilever system, which required none, offered important advantages. The total span of the structure was 525 feet (160 m) comprising two cantilevers each of 210 feet (64 m) which supported a centre span girder of 105 feet (32 m). The centre of each of the cantilevers was supported by a 72-foot (22-m) high masonry pier set on the bed rock of the canyon floor. Masonry abutments were also required at each end of the bridge.

The piers, links, centres and lower chords of the cantilevers of the bridge were of Siemens-Martin steel while the remainder was made from premium quality cast or wrought iron. The total weight of the structure was about 546 tons (554 tonnes). The bridge was prefabricated in England in 1883 by Hawks, Crawshay, and Co., of Gateshead-on-Tyne and shipped to Port Moody aboard the sailing ship *Stormy Petrel*.

The sternwheeler *William Irving* was one of several steamers that took supplies from New Westminster to Emory and Yale. She is shown here at Emory with CPR locomotive 351 soon after the CPR opened. —PABC, HP1473

The iron and steel bridge over the Fraser at Cisco was one of the first cantilever bridges in the world and a significant engineering project in itself. —PABC, HP51761

The awesome canyons of the Fraser and
Thompson rivers were not easily traversed by
the construction crews. Here, during the 1890s,
high above the Thompson, 4-4-0 No. 365 is
stopped in the middle of one of the many
wooden Howe truss spans along the line soon
after the CPR took it over.
—N. CAPLE, VPL, 9556

A track inspector poses next to his velocipede
above a rock retaining wall along the Fraser in
the 1890s. Originally, many of the retaining
walls were timbered. —PABC, HP61402

The delivery voyage took nearly six months and once the bridge components were at Port Moody, their movement to the site was delayed until the railway itself was completed through the Fraser Valley to Yale in January 1884. Erection of the bridge was completed for Onderdonk in June 1884 by the San Francisco Bridge Company. Had the Cisco bridge been erected more quickly — before the Canada Southern's cantilever over the Niagara River — it would have had the distinction of being the first of its type in North America.

Designed to carry a fully loaded, double-headed train, the bridge was to serve at Cisco for nearly 25 years before being dismantled and moved to Vancouver Island for use on the Esquimalt & Nanaimo Railway.

The route through the Fraser Canyon north of Yale was described in the journal *Engineering* in 1884:

At a distance of 23 miles [37 km] south of this bridge [at Cisco] is Boston Bar, a rather celebrated place in the old gold mining days of the province. The work on this section is very heavy through the rocky flanks, and skirting the rugged side of the river which foams and frets below, five large gullies, each from 75 ft. to 100 ft. [20 to 30 m] deep, have to be crossed for lengths of from 400 ft. to 600 ft. [120 to 180 m] each, and an awkward tunnel through a projecting headland. From Boston Bar to Yale, 24 miles [40 km], the work is heavier still, there are altogether fourteen tunnels and three heavy bridges, and the line is exposed in places to slips and land slides that have to be guarded against.

The section of line west of Yale was much easier to construct than the route through the Fraser and Thompson canyons. Between Yale and Hope, there was heavy work, including two tunnels, through the lower reaches of the Fraser Canyon. West of Hope, along the north side of the river, conditions were much better although three tunnels still were required before the flat lands of the Fraser Valley were reached. Some significant bridges were needed across tributary rivers and streams but otherwise there were few obstacles to rapid progress. The line was completed on January 22, 1884 near Nicomen about 40 miles (65 km) east of Port Moody and 50 miles (80 km) west of Yale. With this trackage in place, the complicated problems of supply were simplified since cargoes of rail and other materials could be unloaded directly from deep-sea ships at Port Moody. From there, trains could move the cargoes on to Yale and points beyond. The costly handling of supplies by river boat from New Westminster was eliminated.

Onderdonk's crews completed work on the line to Savona late in 1884 and then proceeded on east, working this time under contract to the CPR itself. Onderdonk was engaged to build through to Eagle Pass in the Gold Range to the east of Sicamous. Compared to the work to the west, this section must have come as a relief because comparatively the work was easy. There were sections of extensive rock work along Kamloops and Shuswap lakes and some major bridges were required but no serious obstacles were encountered and Onderdonk was able to pay off his crews in September 1885.

Extracts from *The Inland Sentinel* during 1884 describe the construction.

August 14, 1884: Tunnel Accident. — A few days since a workman, Mr. Gross, was blown up at Camp Ferguson. His face and hands were considerably injured. When we saw him yesterday he was recovering, but complained at want of medical attendance. It is quite evident that a hospital is required for the Railway employees. The work is now near Kamloops, and for a year or more Kamloops would be a central point. Something should be done promptly.

September 11, 1884:
Railway Progress. — The locomotive now runs to Nicola Bridge [near Spences Bridge]; the track is laid as far as the Bridge; at 8-mile Creek, there are 15 or 20 men at work bridging; Black Canyon Tunnel is pretty near clear of the last cave [in]. The cut this side of the tunnel will be finished in two or three weeks.... Messrs Barnes & Evans, of the Thompson River Hotel, are putting a new steel cable across the river, which in conjunction with a commodious ferry-boat, will be in full running order in a few days; it is anticipated that the steam cars will be up by the end of month, and as it will be a depot for the Cariboo and up country freight, will be an advantage to shippers. A town site has been laid out here and prospects good. The railway station and town site will be called St. Cloud.

September 14, 1884:
Another Railway Smash-up. — On Thursday morning, about 10:30, the regular train from Port Moody came into collision with a working train on the high trestle near Squakum Lake, the engine and nine cars, heavily loaded with iron, attached to the regular train, being thrown a distance of 20 feet. Strange to relate, no one was hurt, though some of the escapes were almost miraculous. It seems that the regular train was running within the limits assigned to the working train, and should have sent a man ahead to flag the latter. This was not done, and in consequence a smash-up involving a loss of $20,000 is the result. The engine 'Nicola' lies bottom-up in the mud, badly damaged, while the report says the cars are totally demolished. The engine of the working train was somewhat damaged, but did not leave the metals. There will no doubt be an investigation, and 'someone that blundered' will lose his head. — *Port Moody Gazette* [reprinted in *The Sentinel*].

September 18, 1884:
Railway Correspondence, Savona, Sept. 14th,
'84. — The track is now laid up to 8-mile Creek;
they are pushing things very rapidly. Black
Canyon Tunnel is now clear. The cut this side of
the Tunnel is about finished; lack of powder
caused some delay at camp 40; but it will be
done on time; everything is now finished up to
camp 42; [past] camp 42 . . . 15 or 20 Chinese
gangs working night and day; 6 gangs of
Chinamen are working right opposite Savona —
some working nights.

Sinclair & Co., employ about 20 white men; 7
men working Chinese gangs. Savona is not very
lively at present; awaiting Paymasters arrival;
Government 'cooler' will soon be ready for use.

Howe truss bridges were the standard design
used on the Onderdonk contracts. Aside from
large quantities of cut timbers, these bridges
required only cast fittings, truss rods, and bolts.
Across the Fraser is the Cariboo Wagon Road.
—CHARLES MACMUNN, PABC, HP19381

The small station at Lytton, photographed in
the early 1890s, was typical of the ones built at
major sidings along the Onderdonk contracts.
—N. CAPLE, VPL, 9557

It now remained for James Ross's crews, working from the east, to complete the track and join the steel together.

Van Horne made an inspection of the work in British Columbia in 1884 and had serious reservations about the quality of the construction on the Onderdonk contracts. While the steel was being pushed ahead at a good pace, much of the work was of a temporary nature. Cuts were insufficiently excavated to stop slumping, timber retaining walls would last only a few years, and he was concerned by the curvature of the line. His concerns were not made public at the time but the issue would be a difficult one to resolve once operations of the railway began.

As Onderdonk's crews toiled up the Fraser Canyon towards Savona, the tracks were slowly reaching across the vastness of the Canadian prairies. The Rockies formed the western horizon ahead of the crews by mid-1883 when the site of Calgary was reached and they pushed on ahead up the Bow River towards Kicking Horse Pass and the Great Divide. Track work came to a halt just east of the Great Divide with the winter's snows and it was not until late in May 1884 that the tracks were laid into British Columbia.

In charge of the work from the east was a capable engineer named James Ross. Still in his thirties, Ross gained the full confidence of Van Horne as he kept the tracks moving ahead, solving numerous logistic and construction problems en route. When there were problems with the workers Ross handled them confidently and with strength. His abilities led him to an exceptional career in business in his later years that left him a wealthy and influential man.

The ascent of the Rockies from the east was comparatively easy all the way to the summit but from the height of the pass, looking westwards, there was a dramatic change. For a short distance, the land sloped gently towards the west, but within a few miles the gap in the mountains narrowed and the waters that had begun at the summit as Divide Creek, joining other tributaries, had turned into the continuous rapids of the Kicking Horse River foaming down the western face of the Rockies to join with the Yoho River in the canyon below. The scenery down the canyon was breathtaking and so too was the task at hand. It was quite true that a railroad could be built down the canyon on a reasonable grade to reach the river flats below the base of Mount Stephen but there was a real difference between the possible and the practical.

It was soon apparent to the engineers that the route proposed by Major Rogers down the face of Mount Stephen would have involved extensive rockwork, tunnelling and a line dangerously exposed to slides. It would have been extremely expensive and time-consuming to construct. For the CPR, increasingly short of funds and needing the revenue from an operating railway, an alternative was essential. The company had agreed not to exceed a maximum grade of 2.2

Construction from the East

The Kicking Horse Canyon presented its own challenges for the engineers and construction workers. Unstable clays made tunnelling work a nightmare. This photograph from 1886 is of Holt's tunnel. Note the truss bridge at right.
—PAC, PA66593

16

Professor G. G. Ramsay, from England, visited the construction sites in fall 1884 and described a ride to end of track:

In a few minutes we are like charcoal burners, covered with thick layers of wood-cinders from the engine. We go rattling and wobbling over fifteen miles [24 km] of new-laid track, through the same glorious scenery of mountain, rock, and forest. The impenetrable forest comes up to the very line: there is no passable foot of ground but the line itself, and the clearance which has been made for forth feet [12 m] on each side of it. The line ahead of us, half laid and unballasted, looks like a pair of wavy ribbons laid down casually on the ground. Here and there comes a swamp or 'musket'... which shakes beneath us; and our nerves are sorely tried as we rush over the bridge which crosses the Otter-tail [sic] Creek. It is 110 feet [33m] high, constructed of light timbers put together on the Howe truss principle... and as we sit on our heap of rails we seem to be shot mysteriously through space. We can see the torrent boiling far below; but the slender woodwork which supports us is invisible.

The work train that Ramsay rode was taking supplies to the end of track camp, recently relocated. He described the scene:

At length we arrive safely at the 'New City,' a city of tent and waggon, fitted to meet all the pressing needs of a community of 4,000 workers. Tents of every shape and form, each with a stove-pipe stuck through somewhere; piles of stores and railway material; hundreds of mules and horses picketed everywhere in the shade; every one on the lookout for the supply of food, the rails and 'ties' which we are bringing, and for want of which the whole army has been brought to a standstill. Some of the grimiest tents have titles in large letters which scarce correspond to their outward appearance. 'Grand Central Hotel' says one; another proclaims itself 'First-class' Restaurant; 'Meals at all hours;' 'Laundry' is on a third, while a fourth announces itself in letters of paint and gold as a 'Tonsorial Palace.'...

The forward gang of men are accommodated in a train composed of large rough vans [boarding cars], fitted up with partitions into sleeping-bunks and eating-places. Each carriage is a sort of human pigeon-box, and the whole constitutes a village on wheels. As the rails are laid, the village is pushed on each day, and so the men are kept always close to their work...

percent but the government approved a new line down the Kicking Horse that would have a maximum grade of 4.5 percent. It was a temporary measure that would last until 1909 and be a source of continuing worry, labour and expense. The line plunged down the upper canyon of the Kicking Horse, crossing the river twice before reaching an area of flat land at what became the helper engine terminal of Field (until December 1884, called Third Siding). A single tunnel and extensive rock work were required to bring the rails down the 1265-foot (385-m) descent and, as a safety measure, three runaway tracks were built to stop any trains that might go out of control.

The engineers knew from the beginning that the steep climb out of the Kicking Horse Valley would require more powerful locomotives than the usual 4-4-0s and orders were placed for the first of many 2-8-0 Consolidations that were to operate on the CPR. Numbered 312 and 313, the first two were delivered by the Baldwin Locomotive Works in 1884 and two more followed in 1886.

One construction train, at least, did have problems on the grade. The story grew very quickly with the re-telling so that later reports were considerably exaggerated, but in August 1884, locomotive 146 was easing down grade with two carloads of construction materials on which 65 or 70 men were riding. The engineer lost control, probably losing air pressure, and the train had to be diverted up one of the safety spurs to prevent a major wreck. Most of the workers jumped off, some were bady injured and one reportedly died. The engine itself was repaired.

West of Field, the tracks were again forced to climb over a low rise called "Muskeg Summit" before winding down through the lower Kicking Horse Canyon to Golden City on the Columbia. To speed the work, a wagon road was put through first so that grading and construction could proceed at several locations at once. This section also proved to be a challenging piece of railroad to build. The steep canyon provided no easy route for the line; four tunnels and six significant bridges were required. The unstable gravel and clay formations of sections of the canyon were a constant source of trouble and one tunnel, the Corry Brothers' Tunnel, or "Mud Tunnel," built through unstable clay, had to be abandoned in 1887 for a sharply curved diversion around the hillside.

As the line advanced, the camps were periodically moved closer to the end of track. Tents, commissary, work equipment, horses and wagons, personal gear, engineering supplies and equipment, were all relocated.

The labour force employed by the contractors for the work through the Rockies and Selkirks comprised a variety of nationalities. Ramsey noted American, English, Canadian, Irish, German, Polish, Swedish, and Russian workers, while another account reported principally Swedes and Italians, many from the eastern United States. Oriental labour was not employed, nor were Native Indians. Wages on the contracts for labourers were about $2.00 per day while board was $5.00 per week.

It took a full season's work to build the line from the summit at the Great Divide down to the Columbia at the Beaver River (later Beavermouth). Before reaching Beavermouth, the Columbia had to be bridged using a 400-foot (120-m) deck truss span, supported in the middle by a wooden pier. Near this point at a place called Donald, headquarters for the next season's work were established. Working ahead of the track-laying crews, surveyors, grading crews, and bridge builders had made some headway to the west but much remained to be done. When track laying stopped in bitterly cold weather for the winter of 1884-85, the men knew that the next season would take them over the final major obstacle, the Selkirks, and on to the West. Some work continued through the winter months but the pace was slow and the conditions extremely difficult. Snow made all work difficult and caused delays, but timber and ties were cut and headway was made on clearing.

As the snow cleared from the mountains in the spring of 1885, the work resumed. The eastern flank of the Selkirks presented an immense barrier, densely forested. Once the grade left the valley floor, it climbed relentlessly upwards towards Rogers Pass. The grade reached a maximum of 2.2 percent and seldom relented. The steep slope of the mountains was cut by several deep stream canyons which required enormous timber bridges to pass over. Working from the east, these were Mountain Creek, Surprise Creek, and Stoney Creek. Smaller structures also were required to bridge the Beaver River and Cascade Creek. Of these bridges, Mountain Creek had the distinction of being the largest bridge on the entire railway while Stoney Creek was the highest and they were within just five and one half miles (9 km) of each other. Mountain Creek measured 1,086 feet (331 m) long and was 164 feet (50 m) high and it included a staggering amount of timber: over 2,000,000 board feet. It included lengthy sections of timber trestles, some incorporating truss sections, and a central truss span over the creek. Stoney Creek bridge was quite different in design. Stoney Creek (sometimes spelled Stony Creek) ran through a deep, rocky gorge, well below track level. To cross this gash in the side of the Selkirks, C.C. Schneider, the engineer responsible, designed a series of truss spans totalling 453 feet (138 m) in length and supported by three timber towers. The central tower was 196 feet (60 m) high to the base of the truss spans which added another 32 feet, 2.5 inches (9.8 m) to the height. The total height from the stream bed to track level was an imposing 292 feet (92 m). It was a spectacular structure and became one of the engineering marvels and scenic attractions of the line. But, like all of the original wooden bridges, it was only a temporary measure. In 1894 it was replaced with a permanent steel arch span.

James Ross had no easy task in 1885 as he worked towards

Stoney Creek Bridge nearly 300 feet (100 m) above the rushing mountain stream. —BCPM

Bridging Mountain Creek required an enormous timber structure; it was 1,086 feet (331 m) long and 164 feet (50 m) high. —CPCA, A341

The descent from the summit of Rogers Pass down the west face of the Selkirks required a series of sweeping loops to keep the grade to a still-rugged 2.2 percent. —PAC, PA66567

The railway rejoined the Columbia River at Farwell (Revelstoke) and crossed to the west bank on a magnificent span composed of deck trusses supported by piers in the river. Locomotive No. 72, a 2-6-0 was stopped with official car No. 1 for the photograph. The view is looking west. —PAC, PA66570

the deadline for completion of the line. In the spring, with deep snow still on the ground, as he tried to proceed with the important and time-consuming bridge projects, the men went on strike. Adding to the problem, merchants, licensed by the provincial government, were allowed to sell liquor near the construction camps. Fueled with liquor and goaded on by some particularly disgruntled employees, the construction workers were angry. The cash position of the CPR had reached serious proportions and the contractors, and hence the men, had not been paid for several months. The situation reached a crisis in late March when about 1,000 of the 2,500 construction workers refused to work. A smaller group tried to stop grading and a confrontation developed. With the aide of Captain Sam Steele of the North West Mounted Police, several men were arrested and sent east by train as the threat of a general riot persisted. Ross, drawing on his own funds and all cash available, was able to pay the men and the work resumed. As more men came in with the accelerating pace of construction, the work force grew to about 5,000.

On the eastern slope of the Selkirks, the major obstacles had been bridging the side canyons, but the surveyed route itself was satisfactory. To the west, there were problems with the route laid out by Major Rogers. During the winter of 1884-85, Ross had men stationed in the pass at several locations to study the snow conditions and the locations of slides. The route was exposed to avalanche danger and would have been expensive to construct. Ross and his engineers, notably James Hogg and Sammy Sykes, had to develop a new line down the western slope of the Selkirks. The result was the famous series of loops that eased the descent down to the Illecillewaet River. As James J. Hill had suspected, Rogers' ego had driven him to find the passes, but his determination had led to unexpectedly impractical, or at least very difficult, routes for the trackage. These specific problems were solved by Ross' construction engineers on site.

The usual process of construction followed. The detailed surveys laid out the work, planned cuts and fills, and engineers designed the site-specific structures needed. A wagon road or "tote road" followed to permit men and supplies to be moved to as many locations along the line as possible. In this way construction of structures, tunnelling where required, grading and tracklaying could all progress simultaneously. Where particularly difficult sections were under construction, temporary tracks were laid around the obstruction. In this way, the summit of the Selkirks was reached on August 17, 1885, and the major bridges to the east were in place. Work progressed slowly down the Illecillewaet and time was running out. But by September, the greatest barriers were already surmounted. Ahead of the end of track, grading and bridging, including the lengthy second crossing of the Columbia at Farwell (later Revelstoke) were proceeding. Supplies were brought in to Farwell from Washington by the steamer *Kootenai*. By October, the end was in sight.

The Last Spike

On November 6, 1885, there remained only the laying of about 3.5 miles (5.5 km) of track left to complete the CPR. While Van Horne and other officials waited in Farwell, just east of the Columbia, the track crews, out since dawn, were rushing the last miles to completion. A correspondent to Victoria's *Daily Colonist* recorded the scene:

At 2 o'clock this afternoon the track-layers had commenced laying the last mile and they put on increased efforts on the home stretch under the direction of Asst. Supt. Brothers and head Track-layer J. Sullivan. . . . First trucks would be drawn quickly down, by horses, loaded with thirty rails and sufficient spikes, bolts and fish-plates. At the end of the track, gangs of men on either side would grasp the rails, run them forward on rollers, and with a precision brought about by practice drop them in their exact place. The rail at the further end would be gauged to its proper width and the truck moved forward to repeat the operation. The men with fish-plates would first bolt up the rails and then spikers would follow in gangs of three and drive the first spikes, followed by others until the rails were spiked and bolted on the ties, ready for the train. Another gang was busy loading the rails on the trucks or unloading the iron band [the rail] from the flat cars, which were run down every once in a while as the last supply was sent down to the front in the trucks. . . . At 3:20, the rails had reached within less than half a mile of the western end; but at this moment work had to be suspended and the gangs and trains run back about twenty miles to get a fresh supply of rails . . .

Donald A. Smith, later Lord Strathcona and Mount Royal, with Van Horne, James Ross and Sandford Fleming looking on, drives the last spike of the Canadian Pacific Railway. It is 9:22 a.m., November 7, 1885 at Craigellachie in Eagle Pass. It had taken the labour of thousands to build and it would take the labour of thousands more to operate. It was really just tne beginning. —ALEX J. ROSS, CPR

By 9:00 p.m., the crew was back with more rails. They worked with lights late into the night and again in the early morning; the last rails were cut and in place for the arrival of the official party.

It was November 7, 1885, and the track-laying crews of James Ross had finally reached the point where Onderdonk's men had run out of rails. It was an unremarked site in the Gold Range of the Monashee Mountains west of Eagle Pass but, symbolically, it would become the most important on the entire line. The spot was named Craigellachie by Van Horne in honour of a gathering place of the Grant Clan in Scotland. Both George Stephen and Donald Smith were related to the Clan and "Craigellachie" had been their rallying cry during the most difficult periods of the CPR's construction. At 9:22 a.m., on a cloudy, cold morning before a small group of dignitaries including Van Horne, Ross, Major Rogers, Sandford Fleming and construction workers, Donald A. Smith, later Lord Strathcona and Mount Royal, drove the last spike. Unaccustomed to the work, he bent the spike on his first attempt and it was removed, but he drove home a second squarely.*

Service from Port Moody to Savona's Ferry was maintained by Onderdonk until July 1886 when the railway was turned over to the CPR. This three-car train carrying mail, baggage, express and passengers is typical of the period before the CPR began full operations in 1886.
—PABC, HP75118

* Later, he was presented with the bent second-to-last spike as a momento of the occasion and it was kept by the family. Some small pieces of the spike were removed and incorporated into decorative pins. This spike survives. On November 7, 1985, the great grandson of Donald A. Smith, also Lord Strathcona and Mount Royal, presented the spike to Canada's National Museum of Science and Technology during centennial ceremonies at Craigellachie. The last spike, a plain iron one, undistinguishable from countless others, has not been preserved.

The modest ceremony lasted only a few minutes. Photographs were taken and Van Horne, brief and to the point stated, "All I can say is that the work has been well done in every way."

Van Horne dispatched a brief but powerful telegram to Sir John A. Macdonald: "Craigellachie, Eagle Pass, Nov. 7. Thanks to your farseeing policy and unwavering support, the Canadian Pacific Railway is completed. The last rail was laid this (Saturday) morning at 9:22. W. C. Van Horne."

For Macdonald, as it was for the men of the CPR, the satisfaction must have been immense. From British Columbia's Premier William Smithe he received the following: "I congratulate you most heartily on the completion of the transcontinental railway on Canadian soil. May it prove a permanent bond of union between the eastern and western provinces of this great Dominion."

The train departed North Bend at 6:50 a.m. on November 8, 1885 and travelled through to Port Moody, the western terminus of the line, arriving at 11:10. The distance of about 120 miles (190 km) was covered in four hours, twenty minutes for an average speed of about 27 miles (45 km) per hour. At Port Moody, the officials boarded the steamer *Princess Louise* and sailed for Victoria, stopping at Coal Harbour and Granville (the future site of Vancouver). Van Horne and the party spent several days on the coast being hosted at dinners and meetings of business groups. They travelled to New Westminster on November 11, and then returned east.

The official train was not the only one operated across the country before the line closed for the winter. Of the other trains, the most noteworthy arrived at Port Moody on November 22, 1885, with the first through freight from Montreal. The shipment was several hundred barrels of oil destined for the Royal Navy at Esquimalt and it was transferred quickly to the steamer *Alexander* for the voyage to Vancouver Island. "The naval supplies," noted Victoria's *Daily Colonist*, "have reached Esquimalt in seven days [actually 6 days, 11 hours], or fifteen days from England, a fact that must be hailed with delight by Englishmen and Canadians. It will also be a startling fact to other European powers, for it proves to them that troops and munitions of war can be landed on the chief Pacific station of the British navy in a little over two weeks time." While the CPR was certainly, and foremost, a link between the West and central Canada, it was also an important component in Imperial defence.

The driving of the last spike at Craigellachie in November 1885, became in some respects an anticlimax when the line was closed through the mountains for the winter. For people along the line west of the Selkirks it was a particular disappointment. However, a weekly service was provided over the Onderdonk sections between Port Moody and Savona but trains did not operate over the CPR trackage east of Savona

Sandford Fleming, described the scene at Craigellachie:

The blows on the spike were repeated until it was driven home. The silence, however, continued unbroken, . . . It seemed as if the act now performed had worked a spell on all present. Each one appeared absorbed in his own reflections . . . Suddenly a cheer spontaneously burst forth, and it was no ordinary cheer. The subdued enthusiasm, the pent-up feelings of men familiar with hard work, now found vent. Cheer upon cheer followed . . . As the shouts subsided, and the exchange of congratulations were being given, a voice was heard, in the most prosaic tones, as of constant daily occurrence: 'All aboard for the Pacific.' . . . in a few minutes the train was in motion. It passed over the newly laid rail and amid renewed cheers sped on its way westward.

Sandford Fleming, at North Bend dispatched the following to Sir John A. Macdonald where the official party spent the night of November 7:

The first through train from Montreal to Vancouver is approaching Yale and within four hours of the Pacific coast. The last spike was driven this morning . . . in Eagle Pass, three hundred and forty miles from Port Moody. On reaching the coast our running time from Montreal, including all ordinary stoppages will be exactly five days, averaging 24 miles per hour. Before long passenger trains may run over the railway from Montreal to Vancouver in four days, and it will be quite possible to travel—especially from Liverpool—to the Pacific Ocean by the Canadian Transcontinental line in ten days. We are especially pleased with the work done. It is impossible to realize the enormous physical and other difficulties that have been overcome with such marvellous rapidity and with results so satisfactory.

Through Trains to the Pacific,
Steamships to the Orient

One traveller, "M.P.," a Kootenay resident who travelled to England in December 1885, recorded his observations in a pamphlet published for distribution to his friends:

Already (in December 1885) the rails and track have been swept away in many places in the Selkirk Range by devastating snow-slides (avalanches). To-day, communication is kept up, and the mail carried by tobogans on this portion of the railway; — sleigh-dogs now replace the locomotive.

... but imagine, if you can, a railway deserted! Hundreds of miles of line abandoned! Signal-boxes, stations, small towns lifeless, and fast being buried beneath the snow, or battered to pieces by fierce mountain storms!

I do not myself think that it will ever be possible to keep the railroad open through the Selkirk Range, certainly never during the winter and spring. The Company may make snow-sheds through the entire Range, but can they make sheds strong enough to withstand the snow-slides, which in these mountains, carry trees, huge rocks, and everything along with them, and sweep bare the whole mountain side?

Passing over a very high wooden trestle, the speed of our train soon fell from fifteen to three or four miles an hour [5 to 6 km an hour], the snorting and puffing of the locomotives shewing with what difficulty the ascent was made. The foremost, one of great size and power, is used solely, I believe, for passing and repassing trains over the summit. Indeed, the grade for eight or ten miles on the western slope, approaching the summit, is steeper far than anything I have ever seen in the way of ordinary railway engineering. After about an hour, a few jerks and tugs threw us all out of our seats, and we came to a standstill. Then followed a few more jerks and tugs, as the locomotives in vain attempted to start us, the wheels slipping round without biting the rails.

After some delay the locomotives started off by themselves, leaving us in the cars. The drivers must have had considerable difficulty in breaking a track through to the summit, as several hours elapsed before they returned to bring us on, although the distance could not have been more than seven or eight miles [about 10 or 12 km]. It was now getting late, and the short winter day fast drawing to a close. The train, however, made better time than I had hoped for, considering the steepness of the ascent; and we arrived at Laggan, four miles [6.5 km] on the eastern side of the summit, before it was quite dark.

to Kamloops and the Shuswap region. As a result, passengers, mail and freight continued to be handled down Kamloops Lake by steamer until the line was opened to the east the following summer. On July 1, 1886, Onderdonk turned over the trackage built under his contracts to the CPR, a relief to the Interior communities which eagerly anticipated lower freight rates and better service once full operation of the railway began.

The railway had not been in condition to permit full winter operation by the fall of 1885, with ballasting, track work, and bridge improvements all required. Many structures — water towers, stations, engine houses, section houses and freight sheds — had to be completed as well. A division point, between the Pacific and Western divisions, eventually located at Donald, had to be established. Moreover, there was an urgent need for the construction of extensive snow sheds (discussed later) throughout the mountain passes. During the winter, a careful watch was kept by engineers in the mountains to determine the optimum locations for the snow sheds.

In the winter of 1885-86, no attempt was made to keep the tracks clear between Savona and Donald to the east of Rogers Pass. Until mid-December occasional trains were operated over the Rockies to Golden and beyond to Donald, but it appears that before Christmas the line was closed until the Spring. One enterprising individual bridged the gap between Donald and Farwell during the spring of 1886 by using a dog team to carry the mails. He made the trip in just two days, weather permitting. Snow accumulated in the cuts, slides came down, and there were earth and mud slides in many locations. There were slides in the Rockies as well. In the spring, crews began the task of clearing the line in preparation for the opening of the railway to regular service. It was not an easy task. Hundreds of labourers, including many Chinese, were employed from late-April through the early summer on the work.

The first scheduled passenger train for the Pacific left Montreal on June 28, 1886 at 8:00 p.m. and, after a journey of 2,892.6 miles (4655.1 km), taking 5 days and 19 hours, the train arrived at Port Moody, at the head of Burrard Inlet on Pacific tide-water. Led by engine 371, and running on time, the *Pacific Express*, with about 150 passengers on board, was met by a large and enthusiastic crowd. It was 12:00 noon, July 4, 1886.

The steamer *Yosemite* of the Canadian Pacific Navigation Company had brought an estimated 750 people from Victoria and Vancouver, 250 travelled over from Nanaimo on the *Amelia* and "several hundred," made their way by foot or buggy from New Westminster. In total, perhaps 1,500 were on hand to witness the arrival of the train from the East. Henry S. Abbott, General Superintendent of the Pacific Division, was the senior CPR official on hand and he was met by the Premier, William Smithe, mayors M. A. McLean of Vancouver and James Fell of Victoria, and civic officials from

CANADIAN PACIFIC RAILWAY.
ARRIVAL OF THE FIRST THROUGH TRAIN AT THE SEABOARD OF BRITISH COLUMBIA.
JULY 4TH, 1886.   T. S. GORE.

24

The arrival of the first scheduled through passenger train at Port Moody on July 4, 1886 was a great event for the citizens of British Columbia. Many travelled to the little community to be a part of the ceremonies. After years of waiting, political fighting, and hope, the CPR was at last an operating railway line across the country. The train consisted of locomotive 371, a baggage car, baggage-mail-express car, colonist car, coach, the sleeping car *Honolulu* and official car No. 78.
—T. S. GORE, PABC, HP61701

The ceremonies are past and No. 371 heads a four-car *Atlantic Express* being readied to leave Port Moody not long after the beginning of regular service. —PABC, HP69163

Port Moody and New Westminster. The civic dignitaries gave lengthy speeches of congratulation and welcome. Mayor McLean probably summarized the optimism of the crowd, and in particular the business community, when he noted:

The day marks an epoch, not only in the history of this province and of the Dominion, but in that of the Empire at large; because the opening of a transcontinental line of such magnitude as this, must be fraught with untold advantages, socially, politically, and commercially to all civilized nations. It is the only line of railway extending from ocean to ocean on this continent. It has opened up to the inhabitants of the Eastern part of the Dominion the magnificent resources of the forests and the mines in the hitherto inaccessible regions...

For the first time, the country had a direct means of rapid communication with the national capital in Ottawa. Not only that, but mails could be transported with relative ease, families could visit, and fashion, news and ideas could spread across the country. No longer was it necessary for British Columbians, far from central Canada, to have to rely on connections through the United States over the Union Pacific and Southern Pacific to San Francisco or, even farther and more indirect, via steamships and the railway across Panama. The CPR did bring a revolutionary change to British Columbia and it would leave its mark on the province for as far into the future as anyone could see.

Meanwhile, far out on the Pacific, a small three-masted sailing vessel was making her way from Yokohama to Port Moody with a cargo of tea from the Orient, destined for shipment over the CPR to eastern markets. The barque *W. B. Flint*, sailing under charter, was the first of seven tea ships that, during the balance of the year, would bring an estimated 7,880,000 pounds (3 574 000 kg) of tea to the rail head. These valuable cargoes and the many more that would follow added significantly to the revenues of the new railway in its early years when traffic was still light. The tea ships were the beginning of the CPR's trans-Pacific shipping services but before new, large steamships could be built, the company had to secure mail contracts and subsidies. After the first voyages by sailing ships, three steamships, the *Abyssinia*, *Parthia* and *Batavia*, were chartered to improve the speed and reliability of the service. These vessels, supplemented by other steamers as traffic required, remained on the route until the arrival in 1891 of the first CPR Empress liners.

Port Moody's moment of glory as the western terminus of the CPR was to be brief. The site, at the head of Burrard Inlet, was too restrictive for the development of facilities and related businesses that the railway would require. In 1871, lands had been transferred from British Columbia to the federal government for the CPR along the shore of Burrard Inlet to English Bay but later, with the official terminus fixed at Port Moody by Ottawa, the lands were returned to British Columbia. Van Horne, appreciating the advantages that the more western location could bring, began negotiations with the province for land grants and in February 1885, the agreements were concluded. For the lands,* the CPR agreed to build a major hotel and also to construct an opera house, both of which would be major features of the new city that would grow around the terminal. The lands, along Burrard Inlet, adjacent to False Creek and in nearby areas suitable for city development, provided the property for terminal facilities and, through sales, the money to extend the line the final 12 miles (19 km) to the west. Just to the west of the quiet sawmilling centre of Hastings Mill, a new city, known as Vancouver, was to be the ultimate terminal of the CPR and eventually, the largest and most important industrial and trade centre in Western Canada.

Excitement on the arrival of the first scheduled train had just abated when news passed up and down the line that on July 8, 1886, the *Atlantic Express*—only the second train to depart since the opening—had been caught in a forest fire and burned. There were extensive fires in the Selkirks as well as the Monashees, and west of Rogers Pass the telegraph lines were down. At 6:00 p.m., as the train reached Beaver, just west of Donald, a large forest fire was burning beside the tracks and also in large piles of firewood stacked near the line. The engineer, after conferring with a section crew who had just passed along the line, believed he could continue safely. But just as the train passed one of the piles of cordwood, it collapsed, derailing the locomotive tender and the baggage car. Flames spread quickly to the cars and the passengers and crew jumped off and hurried clear of the flames. Fortunately, the sleeping car *Tokio*, at the end of the train, had escaped the flames and Conductor Woods and several crew members had the presence of mind to roll it clear of the fire. A crew member was sent to Donald to bring relief for the passengers.

As the flames engulfed the derailed train, J. O. McLeod, the mail clerk, in a classic instance of putting duty ahead of his own safety, ran back to the car to try to save the mails. Quickly, he placed all the letters in a mail sack and jumped off the car but by this time, the cars were in flames. His only route of escape was to crawl under the mail-car and then run along the tracks. But after several hundred yards, he was nearly overcome with heat and smoke. His luck held and he found a small, grassy refuge where he was able to catch his breath. His feet and hands were badly burnt and to give some protection he filled his shoes with damp earth. Then he was off again, down the tracks. After stumbling a further few hundred yards down the line, he was met by one of the train

* Crown grants amounted to 6,245 acres (2527 ha) while private donations of lots increased the total grant to the CPR to approximately 6,458 acres (2614 ha). The crown lands were in two major sections. The first, a former reserve on Coal Harbour, included 480 acres (194 ha) and ran between False Creek and Burrard Inlet including much of what became the business district of the city. The second included 5,795 acres (2345 ha) in a tract south of False Creek much of which eventually became important business and residential districts.

Kamloops became an important centre for the CPR and the location of major shops. This photograph from the 1880s shows the extent of the facilities which included a 12-stall round-house for locomotive servicing.
—LEONARD FRANK COLLECTION

The small wood-burning 4-4-0s were inadequate for the trains in the mountains and the CPR soon acquired heavier power. No. 409 is one of 28 2-6-0s added to the roster in 1888.
—R. H. TRUEMAN, GLENBOW MUSEUM, NA990-4

Crew and passengers pose beside a typical CPR passenger train of the 1880s.
—GLENBOW MUSEUM, NA990-1

Steam shovels were used in the late 1880s for filling and ballasting. This one is at Mountain Creek in 1888. J. H. Currie was identified as the engineer.
—H. T. DEVINE, (J. A. BROCK & CO.), CVA, CANP118

crew, returning to help. Unable to proceed further, McLeod was carried back to the sleeping car. While the mails were saved, the payroll was not, the paymaster apparently being either unable or unwilling to risk the fire to save the $8-10,000 on board.

A locomotive and caboose were dispatched from Donald and after passing other fires retrieved the sleeping car, the stranded passengers and crew, but the rest of the train was destroyed. The fireman, slightly burned, was the only other person injured and McLeod, who lived in New Westminster, recovered from his burns.

The problems of the fires in the mountains continued through the dry summer. While the wreck was being cleared away, news came down the line that the major bridges over Cedar and Surprise creeks were in danger as was the crossing of the Columbia. Snow sheds, under construction in the mountains, also were threatened. The fires could have closed the whole mountain section of the line doing damage that might have taken months to repair. Wisely, preventative clearing around bridges and other structures had been carried out and, with great effort, the crews were able to prevent serious damage. Any lengthy disruptions of service were avoided.

Construction work on the line west of Port Moody was completed in time for the first scheduled train from the East to reach Vancouver on May 23, 1887. The next day was Queen Victoria's official birthday and also marked the celebration of her Golden Jubilee as monarch. The celebration for the arrival of the train was a lavish one and also showed that Vancouver had recovered from the fire that had all but destroyed the new city on June 14, 1886, just two weeks before the first through train had arrived at Port Moody.

At approximately 12:45 p.m., the first train, led by locomotive 374, steamed slowly into the terminal at Vancouver. The locomotive was elaborately decorated with banners, flags, a picture of Queen Victoria and greenery. "From Ocean to Ocean, Our National Highway," and "Montreal — Vancouver," were among the slogans carried by the locomotive. The train passed under a ceremonial archway opposite the station to be welcomed by cheers and speeches. A band played "See the Conquering Hero Comes," and Vancouver's Mayor McLean called for three cheers for the CPR. McLean's welcoming address praised the CPR and noted a bright future for Vancouver. Henry Abbott, General Superintendent of the Pacific Division, representing the CPR at the ceremonies, responded that Vancouver and the CPR would prosper. Immigration would grow and as "proof of the confidence placed in the future of Vancouver, the steamship which left Hong Kong on the 17th for Vancouver had every berth on board booked." This was the *Parthia*, the first of the three chartered steamships. Cheers and speeches followed, the band played; the CPR had reached the western terminal of its main line.

The Field Hill with its 4.5 percent grade was a constant challenge to the crews. Here, a long mixed consist is eased downgrade with a 2-8-0 on the front and a 4-4-0 (slightly cropped by the photographer) behind the passenger cars. This is the Upper Canyon of the Kicking Horse and the first safety switch leads off the main line at right. —PAC, PA66611

Consolidation 315 was the third 2-8-0 acquired from Baldwin for Field Hill service. Originally these engines had sloped-back tenders but when this glass plate photo was exposed about 1890, the tender had been rebuilt.
—TRUEMAN & CAPLE, VPL, 9562

28

The CPR wharf at Vancouver was built along the shore of Burrard Inlet and had to be constructed well out from shore to reach deep water. Later extensive filling was undertaken and the docks and yards were expanded. This photo was taken in 1887, a few days after the arrival of the first passenger train into the city on May 23. —J. A. BROCK & CO., CVA, CANP203

In 1891 the *Empress of India*, first of the CPR's trio of new, twin-screw liners, arrived from the Orient to place the trans-Pacific service on a permanent, reliable basis. The Empresses were to become a critical source of traffic for the railway and an important extension of the CPR system across the Pacific. —BCPM

The next year, George Stephen retired as president of the CPR and his place was taken by Van Horne. Stephen remained on the board of the CPR until 1893. As Baron Mount Stephen he lived to be 92. Van Horne, the tough, practical railroader, was to see the CPR through its next decade of development.

In 1886-87, a branch line was built from Coquitlam on the main line to the long-established city of New Westminster on the Fraser. Further up the valley in 1889, a connection was built from Mission to Huntingdon Junction, B.C. and, just across the border at Sumas, Washington. From there, via the Bellingham Bay and British Columbia Railroad, a connection was made to Whatcom (later Bellingham), and via steamer to Seattle and other Puget Sound points. The only major engineering obstacle in completing the line from Mission was the bridging of the Fraser and the route to Whatcom was opened in June 1891. Rail service to Puget Sound was expanding rapidly during this period. The Northern Pacific had been completed to Tacoma in June 1887, and the Great Northern was building westward, its line due to reach Seattle in 1893. As an interim measure, an agreement was reached permitting Great Northern traffic to be routed to and from Puget Sound via the CPR through Vancouver, and after 1891, over the Mission branch line route to Bellingham.

In 1889 a contract was finally approved which required the CPR to provide a monthly mail service, connecting with the transcontinental trains, from Vancouver to Japan and Hong Kong for an annual subsidy of £60,000, £45,000 of which came from the British government and the balance from Canada. With the contract in hand, orders were soon placed for three modern liners, the *Empress of India*, *Empress of Japan* and *Empress of China*. For their time, the three ships were the most modern and luxurious on the Pacific.

The arrival of the *Empress of India* in Vancouver on April 28, 1891 was met with fanfare almost equal to the celebrations accorded the arrival of the first train from the East. Van Horne was there to greet the ship and civic receptions and a banquet followed. A special train was dispatched to the East that evening to carry the mails and the through passengers. With a gleaming white hull and decked out in flags, the new *Empress* was symbolic of what the port of Vancouver was to become — a rival for San Francisco as a gateway and cross-roads for world trade. In a real sense, the CPR and its new ocean steamships had provided a route for commerce that fulfilled the promise of the elusive northwest passage that had frustrated generations of explorers. The CPR became, as its advertising proclaimed, "The New Highway to the Orient."

At War with Winter

Even before the transcontinental main line was completed, winter snows had plagued the surveyors and construction crews. When the line was officially completed in November, 1885, it was only a matter of days before Rogers Pass had to be abandoned to the snows of winter and the line through the mountains closed until the following summer. Some questioned if the line could ever be kept open all year long.

What they underestimated was the determination and abilities of the company and in particular its engineering and operating crews to face the challenge of keeping the CPR open throughout the mountain winters.

Making the main line through the mountains an all-weather route was a tremendous task but snow sheds could be built to withstand even the tremendous forces of the avalanches in Rogers Pass and with the use of modern snow-fighting equipment and hard labour, keeping the line open all winter was both possible and practical. By the winter of 1886, after months of labour, the defences were in place. Miles of snow sheds had been built, new snow plows were on hand and work gangs were ready for the battles ahead.

The first line of defence against the slides and snow storms was the series of snow sheds that stretched over the most threatened sections of track in Rogers Pass. Sheds were also required in hazardous places in the Kicking Horse Pass and elsewhere on the line. The construction of these sheds was a major engineering achievement in itself. In the first years of operation of the line, 54 sheds were built between a point six miles (9.7 km) to the east of Rogers Pass and Three Valley Lake in Eagle Pass to the west of Revelstoke. Most were concentrated in Rogers Pass, where, to the work crews, it must have seemed that the entire line through the pass would eventually be covered by snow sheds. The work force itself sustained a small town called Summit City that, on its stump-filled main street, featured general stores, hotels, a barber shop and saloons.

The cost of the snow sheds was enormous. CPR *Annual Reports* for the years 1886 and 1887 recorded expenditures of over two million dollars for snow shed construction alone for the main line through British Columbia. In a paper published in 1905, H. B. Muckleston, formerly Assistant Engineer on the Pacific Division, outlined their construction and set the problem against the characteristics of winter in the Selkirks.

Owing to the geographic situation of the Selkirks, coupled with their comparatively great height, these mountains intercept most of the moisture contained by the air currents passing over them. In consequence, there is an extremely large precipitation and correspondingly luxuriant vegetation. As much of the precipitation is in the form of snow, it follows that the annual snow-fall is phenomenal. The average yearly snow-fall at the Glacier House is some thirty-five feet [10.7 metres], which for the winter of 1898-99 reached the enormous total of forty-four [13.5 metres] the fall for the month of January being nine feet two inches [2.8 metres], and even in May of that year, the comparatively large total of two feet four inches [0.7 metres] was recorded. . . . the accumulations at the higher levels must be very great, and as the sides of the mountains are nowhere near the angle of repose for snow, very little is required to start a destroying avalanche. In the spring, as the snow may weigh nearly fifty pounds per cubic foot [245 kg/m³] the tremendous force of one of the slides can be imagined.

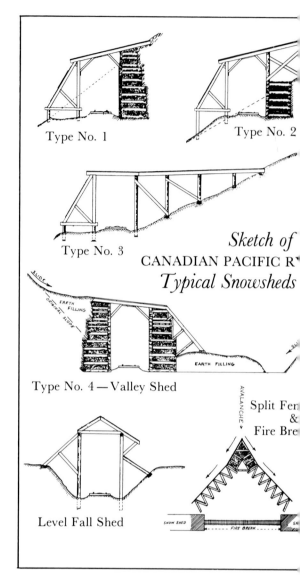

Type No. 1

Type No. 2

Type No. 3

Sketch of
CANADIAN PACIFIC R'
Typical Snowsheds

Type No. 4 — Valley Shed

Level Fall Shed

Split Fen
&
Fire Bre

The loops west of Rogers Pass were a major feature of the ascent to the summit. To protect the line from snow slides, sheds which all but covered long sections of the main line were built. Here, in a Vaux photo of July 29, 1897, the *Atlantic Express*, behind a 2-8-0 assisted by a pusher on the rear, rumbles over the first crossing of the Illecillewaet River having just emerged from 29 Shed and 31 Shed. Originally there was also a 30 Shed but the gap was closed. 29 Shed measured 359 feet (109.5 m) while 31 Shed was 327 feet (100 m) long. Note the snow diversion fences between the sheds and on the left in the distance. Contributing to the problem of slides was the damage done to the forest cover of the Selkirks by the fires that swept the area during the construction period. —ACR, MG4-255

Pilot plows mounted on the locomotives were the first defence against the snows of winter. This upper scene is at Glacier House in the winter of 1890-91. When the drifts got deeper, the wedge snow plows were brought out; this one is at Rogers Pass.
—THOS. MILLS, PABC, HP93990; GLENBOW MUSEUM, NA2216.6

The interiors of the snow sheds were like vast, endless caverns. In the winter, there was no alternative but to use them, but in summer, the trains operated around some of the longer sheds over summer tracks which opened the view of the mountains to travellers and reduced the danger of fires starting in the costly wooden sheds. "The miles and miles of snow sheds are something wonderful," recorded a traveller on September 14, 1891 in her annotated timetable. "The massive timbers look as if they had grown where they are fixed."
—S. J. THOMPSON, CVA, 137

There were five basic designs for the snow sheds and all had to be built solidly. Normally, the bents were placed on five foot (1.5 m) centres but where extra strength was required they were positioned only four feet (1.2 metres) apart. The rafters were enormous 12 x 15-inch (30 x 38 cm) Douglas-fir beams while the plumb and batter posts were 12 x 12s. The sheds were equipped with systems of piping in case of fires and the structures were broken into short lengths, separated by fire-breaks. The breaks were protected by split fences above the shed gaps, made of heavy V-shaped cribbing, to divert the snow slides towards the sheds.

The potential of fires in the show sheds was a serious one particularly considering their cost. As the timbers dried out, the chance of a spark from a locomotive catching in the woodwork became a real concern. Water lines were run the length of the sheds but the summertime diversion of the trains along outside tracks aided significantly in reducing the danger of fires. In a less than serious report, a Swedish watchman at sheds No. 4 and No. 5 wrote: "to prevent the sheds catching fire, I suggest that the engineers be notified to keep their smokestacks shut when passing through them."

Snow plows (or snow ploughs) were the next weapon in the fight against the winter. The simplest were wedges mounted on the pilots of the locomotives. These were useful against light accumulations of snow on the tracks but could do little against a slide. More effective were the wedge plows, or bucker plows. These were specially-built, heavily-constructed cars with reinforced concave blades on the front. Pushed by locomotives, they could clear the tracks effectively but they were unable to cut through deep drifts since they had no means of removing the snow from the tracks. Often, several locomotives were required to push the wedge plows and it was a case of teeth-jarring, sheer brute force as the locomotives charged the snow drifts. In the first winters the CPR was open, 1886-87 and 1887-88, these were all that was available to keep the line clear. Fortunately, better equipment was coming, but it did not arrive until late in 1888.

That first full year of operation and particularly the winter of 1886-1887, was tough, demanding and dangerous for the men working the main line through the mountains and canyons of British Columbia. The snow sheds were still not completed in all locations, there was still much to learn about the nature of weather conditions, operational hazards, and the behaviour of the new equipment in the mountains. Moreover, many new slopes and cuttings were not yet stable and washouts could come unexpectedly. Each train over the line added new experiences for the crews. A slide west of Ashcroft in late September or early October derailed the locomotive and baggage car of the *Pacific Express* and sent them crashing 20 feet (6 m) down the embankment. Further movement of the slide carried the engine another 30 feet (9 m) away from the tracks. The engineer was badly scalded by steam from the boiler of the locomotive but he survived. In the Selkirks, on November 6, 1886, when two trains were ascending the grade to the summit, a drawbar, or the link and pin coupler, on one of the cars in the first train, apparently a work train, failed and the remaining cars began to roll back down the grade. The brakemen were unable to control the cars and they ran into the following train with tragic results. The caboose and a car carrying men and horses telescoped into the engine and three men were killed and 25 other people injured.

The most serious problems came late that winter. In February, heavy snows built up to dangerous depths in the Selkirks. On the 27th, two feet (0.6 m) of snow fell and slides started coming down over the tracks. Plow crews were sent out to clear the line but while the work was underway, a large slide came down and buried the plow train and 16 men near Cascade Camp. Six men were killed including the engine crew of one of the locomotives. It was several weeks before the main line could be reopened. Traffic accumulated, passengers and travellers grew weary of the delays, and no mail went through. By mid-March, some people had gone south to take the Northern Pacific east and communities became increasingly distressed at the lack of mail service. It was not until March 24th that the first trains from the east had cleared the pass and made it as far west as Kamloops. *The Inland Sentinel* reported that about 250 people arrived on the first two trains and that "the amount of mail was enormous." Some people had been en route for over a month.

While the Rogers Pass remained blocked there were other problems to the west further isolating towns in the Interior. Slides and washouts in the Fraser Canyon added to the railway's problems. The same storms that hit the passes caused a slide near Spuzzum that Victoria's *Daily Times* described as being 20 feet (6 m) deep and 300 yards (275 m) long. There were also three washouts between North Bend and Lytton and two between Yale and Harrison's. Very cold and stormy weather was reported from the Canyon.

While the track crews fought valiantly to keep the railway open during the long winter months in the mountains, they really needed more effective and efficient equipment to do the job. Fortunately, a device known as the rotary snow plow had just been developed. It held the promise of easing greatly the task of snow removal.

This machine, a Canadian invention, combined an effective steam-powered cutting wheel and a fan to blow the snow well clear of the tracks. The first rotary plow was built by the Leslie brothers in Ontario, using the designs of Orange Jull, owner of a flour mill in Ontario. The Leslie brothers fabricated many of the parts for the new machine but the final assembly was carried out at the CPR's shops at Parkdale, Ontario, and tests were run on a CPR branch line. The tests suggested improvements which the Leslies developed and

Insights from *The Truth* of Donald, B.C.:

One evening this week telegraph operator Rogers took a young lady friend tricycle riding on the railroad track. As they were approaching a curve just east of town, the lady noticed something ahead of them, and excitedly asked Mr. Rogers what it was. That gentleman looked up and calmy said, 'Sarah, my dear, that is an engine' but he tipped that tricycle over, girl and all, and down a 20-foot embankment in a jiffy, all the same; just in time too, for a big mogul pusher passed on up the road a second later. The young lady says she slid down that embankment just like she used to slide down the cellar door when a little girl, and escaped unhurt, barring a skinned elbow. Mr. Rogers got off without a scratch. Better go walking next time, children; surprises won't come so sudden like. (August 18, 1888)

The boys tell this on J. E. Griffith, engineer-in-chief of this division of the CP. A pressing engagement called him east last week. The evening of the second day out, he ate a hearty supper, partaking liberally of "Welsh rarebit," a favourite dish. At the usual hour he retired to his berth in the sleeper, and soon was dreaming of levels, cross sections, tangents, glance cribs, and 4½ percent grades. Just as he struck the latter subject, he imagined the train was climbing the Big hill; that the train had parted, and the sleeper was taking the back track down the western slope of the Rockies at a rate of a mile a second. He jumped out of his berth, made for the rear platform, and set the brake so tight that it almost stopped the train. While twisting the brake he awoke, only to find the night wind flirting with his shirt tail, and the train speeding slowly over a dead-level Manitoba prairie. (October 20, 1888)

The New Rotary Snow Plows

There were other hazards besides snow. There were also slides, rockfalls and washouts. No. 361 was derailed in the Fraser Canyon about 1890. —PABC, HP61344

Down the line they knew something was wrong when the telegraph went dead. The boiler of this 4-4-0 blew up between Yale and North Bend in 1897. —PABC, HP20045

The tests of the first rotary snow plow—Rotary A—were witnessed by the crew, officials and also by several women, dressed warmly for the Selkirk winter.
—BOORNE & MAY, REVELSTOKE MUSEUM

patented. Seeing good markets for their machine, they contracted, in 1885, for a new, revised plow to be built by the Cooke Locomotive & Machine Works in Paterson, New Jersey.

This first production Leslie rotary was built in 1885 and was then tested on a Chicago & North Western subsidiary between Omaha and the border with Wyoming. Again improvements were made and in 1886 the machine was extensively tested on the Union Pacific. It was a dramatic success. Deep drifts could be cleared with comparative ease and the snow thrown well clear of the tracks. The rotaries were big and expensive to operate. Each rotary had a steam boiler and a two-cylinder engine to power the snow cutting mechanism. Just like a locomotive, each rotary was fitted with its own tender for water and fuel. One or sometimes several locomotives were used to push the plows. When conditions got really bad, trains could operate with a rotary at each end. If a slide came down behind a plow train that was operating with no plow on the back end, the train could be isolated and unable to cut its way back down the line. The crew of a rotary normally consisted of an engineer and fireman, who ran the boiler and engines, and a foreman and two assistants in charge of the plow itself. The foreman handled the signals for the cutting wheel or excavator, ice cutters and flangers. Running all day, a plow would burn three or four tons of coal.

Railroads in the western United States saw the potential of the machines and were quick to order them. The CPR, no less interested, ordered six rotary snow plows which were completed between October and late December 1888. These were designated with letters A through F.

The first of the Canadian Pacific's new rotaries arrived in the West late in 1888 and was tested in the Selkirks. Fortunately, details of the tests survive in a letter from Robert Marpole, superintendent at Donald, to Henry Abbott, general superintendent at Vancouver. Tests were carried out in November 1888, on the summer track on the western side of Rogers Pass. There, in a heavy snow fall, the plow cleared dense, wet drifts averaging two and one half feet (0.75 m) deep at a speed of four miles per hour (6.5 km per hour). Tests at higher speed saw the plow plug up with the wet snow. Later tests in wet compact snow in cuts with depths of six feet (2 metres) caused the machine to "choke itself" when pushed to 10 miles per hour (16 km per hour) but at half that speed, "no trouble whatever was experienced," noted Marpole, "and the machine did effective work. Hereafter the machine was in service at this class of work, and the results were always of the same encouraging character." At higher speeds, as the foreman apparently put it, the machine, "bit off more than it could spit out."

In dry snow, the performance of the new rotary was even more impressive: "In December and January we had several fair tests of the plow in *dry snow*, and I am free to confess that it

The ability of the rotary plows to throw snow well clear of the tracks is demonstrated in this early photo from Rogers Pass. Although the picture is undated it is most likely during the first tests of the machine described in the letter, quoted in the text, from Robert Marpole to Henry Abbott. The plow is clearing the summer track beside one of the snow sheds. Probably, the posed picture on the previous page also was taken on this test. —GLENBOW MUSEUM, NA1608-11

Rotary C was typical of the first CPR plows (spelled "plough" on the letter board). The cutting blades are clearly visible below the headlight. Immediately behind is the fan housing on top of which is a deflector to direct the snow to either side of the tracks. The wooden car body of the plow houses the engines, boiler and operator's controls. The tender has an enclosed fuel bunker to prevent blowing snow from covering the coal. In this view, the locomotive pushing the plow is backed up to the rotary. In this way, if small slides came down behind the outfit, the pilot plow on the locomotive still would be functional. —TRUEMAN & CAPLE, GLENBOW MUSEUM, NA2216-5

fully fulfilled the claims of the Patentee in respect to speed and effectiveness in this class of snow. In level fall or drifted *dry snow* it can be run at a speed of 15 miles per hour, as from close observation I do not think it is possible to choke it with this class of snow."

Abbott reflected on how the rotary would have eased snow clearing problems the previous winter and then described the first use of the rotary in clearing a large slide.

Last season, 1887-88, without the Rotary plow, as you are aware, we were compelled to remove snow from congested through and side-hill cuttings by means of trains and a great number of shovellers, and our difficulties were much enhanced by the fact that dumping ground for such stuff was scarce between Bear Creek and the Loop, as after several small structures were filled up, we were compelled to run our work trains longer distances, entailing great loss of time and constant trouble in backing up over bad flange occasioned by the almost continuous snow-fall, and drifts in that neighbourhood. By the use of a few shovellers and the Rotary Snow Plow all these difficulties are avoided. By shovelling, in fact dragging the compressed slope snow on to the track to a width covered by the scoop of Rotary, and wings of same, the material is thrown far and clear of track, and at the same time, a first class flange is left by the Rotary. In heavy level snow-falls of over twelve inches, we run the Rotary. Snow-falls of less than that, we run the ordinary Wing Plow as speed is the desideratum and the cost of course is far less.

In February, we were afforded a chance to test the Rotary in a snow slide, but it was not of as great a magnitude or cohesiveness, as the majority of the great avalanches over sheds. The slide in question, descended between 19 and 20 sheds, and came from a point 2000 feet above the track and was entirely free from timber ice and rock. It was 300 feet in length and 32 feet in greatest depth over track, was of course very compact, and would in my opinion weigh 30 lbs to the cubic foot, about half the weight of ice. We tackled this slide with the Rotary and two heavy Engines, one Mogul and a Consolidation on a 2% grade, working down hill; the first twenty five feet or so, greatest depth 3 feet, was cleaned out without trouble; after this, the two engines could not propel the shovel into the compact material without backing up and punching at it, the invariable result being, that the machine choked itself so completely that shovels even failed to dislodge the really cemented material, and we were compelled to free it by the use of a steam hose connected with the Engine of Rotary. I put on another Consolidation Engine, and ordered a steady pressure to be maintained against the face of the snow, but as the depth of the slide was more than the height of the Rotary, we have of course to break and shovel the material forward into the cut already made by the shovel; by continued and steady onslaught in this manner, we cleared the whole slide out in five hours from time of commencement, having only eighteen men.

Without the Rotary and with flat cars and all the men we could have covered on its surface, it would have taken at least twelve hours to clear out this slide, so that from every standpoint, the test was satisfactory. Undoubtedly, had this slide contained much timber, the delay would have been greater, but the number of men employed would be about the same.

By the following winter the CPR had its new rotary fleet fully in service. The rotaries were used in other locations beyond the Rockies and Selkirks as they were particularly effective in clearing drifted dry snow, common on the prairies.

Glacier House at Glacier Station west of the summit of Rogers Pass was the first of the CPR's three small hotels to open for meal stops following the completion of the line. Trains stopped for passengers to eat and enjoy a brief walk before proceeding. In this way, it was unnecessary to use dining cars on the passenger trains over the heavy mountain grades. Snows are building up in this scene from 1886 as the staff and a snow clearing gang pose for their photograph. —CVA, CANP203

They also saw service on the Schreiber Division in northern Ontario and elsewhere in eastern Canada. The big rotaries were a great success and made a significant contribution to keeping the CPR open on a reliable all year basis. In a good year the rotaries might only be used once or twice, but if the weather were bad they could be on the move for weeks at a time. Two more rotaries were built for the CPR in 1899, and another was added in each of 1906 and 1907. When the CPR acquired the Kaslo & Slocan Railway in the Kootenays in 1912, it acquired a 3-foot (0.91 m) gauge rotary that had come originally from the Rio Grande Southern in Colorado. This machine was changed to standard gauge and used over the Coquihalla Pass. Finally, two larger machines, which will be described later, completed the roster of this equipment on the railway. The machines proved particularly durable and were used into the 1950s. The rotaries were an expensive, but necessary, form of insurance for the CPR and the other mountain railroads and their contribution to the financial success of the CPR should not be underestimated.

All of the snow fighting equipment depended in the end on the men who operated and maintained it. Moreover, large labour gangs were kept on duty ready to help dig out the line when the inevitable snows hit. Labour gangs, including many Chinese, Japanese or East Indians, worked through the long, freezing, winter nights with shovels and pry-bars to keep the lines clear.

Hotels, Chalets and the National Parks

While the vast, almost insurmountable ranges of the Rockies and Selkirks and the gorges of the Fraser Canyon were a tremendous and apparently never-ending problem to the operating crews on the CPR, it would have taken a person completely lacking in aesthetic senses to ignore their beauty. The scenic qualities of the CPR route through British Columbia were realized even before the line was operational and for the company they were an asset not to be ignored. Even in the 1880s, tourism, particularly for the wealthy, was becoming important and it represented a welcome source of revenue for the struggling railway. The CPR moved quickly to establish a system of hotels and chalets along the line through western Alberta and British Columbia, and it was also no coincidence that Canada's first National Parks were established along the CPR main line.

Three of the hotels that were constructed along the line were built, in part, with the operational problems of the railway in mind. These were Fraser Canyon House at North Bend, Glacier House near the summit of the Selkirks and Mount Stephen House at Field. Their function was to eliminate the need to haul heavy dining cars in the passenger trains operating in the mountains. Passenger trains stopped at the hotels and passengers were given time for a meal and a short walk before the train proceeded. At Field and North Bend, the stops coincided with regular servicing and crew change points as well. For passengers travelling westbound, breakfast would be served at Field, lunch at Glacier and dinner at North Bend. Travelling east, the reverse would be true, assuming, of course, that in both cases, the trains were running on time. From the traveller's point of view, the hotels presented a welcome respite from the long hours on the train. As can be readily imagined, for those travelling with young children, an opportunity to get off the train and have the youngsters get some exercise would have been eagerly anticipated by parents and children alike.

As first built, the three hotels were quite small, being little more than dining halls with half a dozen rooms for overnight guests. However, it was not long before expansion was required, particularly at Glacier House and Mount Stephen House, both of which became major facilities. The new buildings were not ready by the summer of 1886 when service first opened on the CPR and in the interim, dining cars were parked at the sites to serve the train passengers. The three hotels were designed by Thomas Sorby, receiving many suggestions from Van Horne who took a keen interest in the project. Mount Stephen House opened first in the fall of 1886 and the other two were ready the next year.

The scenery in all three locations was spectacular. Fraser Canyon House was situated with an eastern exposure overlooking the Fraser River about half way through the wild and formidable route that had been such a challenge to Onderdonk's construction crews. Glacier House, on the western side of Rogers Pass, was located upgrade from the trestles crossing the Illecillewaet River at the end of the last loop before the tracks turned north to climb steadily along the face of the lower slopes of Eagle Peak and Avalanche Mountain. It was a breathtaking setting for a hotel, with the beautiful valley leading off to the west and the mountains rising up from the valley floor another 6,000 feet (1830 m) to the east in just one mile's (1.6 km) horizontal distance. The peaks of the Sir Donald Range to the east and the Hermit Range to the west were dominated by perennial glaciers and snowfields and in the short alpine summers, the wild flowers bloomed in profusion. As CPR promotional literature from the period noted, the "station and hotel are within thirty minutes' walking distance of the Illecillewaet Glacier, from which at the left, Sir Donald (10,808 ft.) [3294 m] rises a naked and abrupt pyramid..."

Mount Stephen House, in the valley of the Kicking Horse River was situated in another dramatic mountain setting. It was close to Emerald Lake, where the CPR also built a chalet, the Natural Bridges and Takakkaw and Twin falls. In later years, however, its appeal for tourists was overshadowed by the nearby attractions of Banff and Lake Louise to the east just over the summit where the CPR had developed what were to become its most famous resorts: the world famous Banff Springs Hotel and the Chateau Lake Louise. The CPR recognized the business that could be generated from these

North Bend, shown in the early 1890s, was the division point between Vancouver and Kamloops—a turnaround point for crews and equipment. —R. H. TRUEMAN, CVA, CANP195

North Bend's Fraser Canyon House (at left behind the station) gave passengers a pleasant stop while the trains were serviced and crews and locomotives changed. The hotel became a popular weekend destination for the more affluent residents of Vancouver. This summer scene shows the *Pacific Express* at the station. The last car is the sleeping car *Montreal* while the third from the end is one of the open-sided observation cars. —PAC, PA25047

Mount Stephen House at Field, shown here after the completion of a substantial expansion in 1901. The addition to the original structure, at left in the photo, was described in *The Railway and Shipping World* of March 1902 as having "a large and handsome hall and billiard room, with heavy beam and panelled walls and ceiling, and a huge open fireplace for burning logs; there is also a smoking room and a drawing-room commanding views of the Kicking Horse valley. Fifty additional bedrooms are provided most of which have bathrooms attached, with up-to-date plumbing and several have private sitting-rooms en suite." It has "transformed the old building ...into a small but first-class hotel."
—PABC, HP35134

sites and promoted the scenic attractions of all of its hotels with great effectiveness. Mountain climbing in particular was featured and Swiss guides were brought in to provide the necessary expertise. "Experienced Swiss guides are stationed, during the summer season, at the Company's hotels at Field, Lake in the Clouds [Lake Louise], and the Great Glacier [Glacier House]," noted a brochure published in 1903. "Their services are placed at the disposal of guests free of charge to make short trips to points of interest within easy distance of the hotels, when they are not engaged by parties wishing to make difficult ascents or extended explorations, for which the fee is $5.00 per day." At Golden, several chalets for climbers were built as well. A small hotel was also built at Revelstoke, just behind the station, for the accommodation of guests who either wished to stay in the divisional point or travel south into the Kootenays.

The construction of the CPR through the Rockies and Selkirks brought the awesome beauties of these mountain ranges to the attention of people throughout the world. Photographs recorded the natural wonders in often perceptive detail and it was clear that some form of special legal status should be given to these areas. Following the lead of the United States Congress, which established the world's first national park, Yellowstone, in the remote wilderness of Wyoming and Montana, the Canadian government created in 1885, a reserve over 10 square miles (2692 ha) encompassing the hot springs at Banff. The Banff Hot Springs Reserve was established to ensure that the springs would be saved for public benefit and protected against excessive and unrestricted commercial exploitation. These considerations did not exclude development of the hot springs, however, and the active cooperation of the CPR was clearly understood. Van Horne himself had supported the establishment of the reserve which in 1887 was enlarged to 260 square miles (67 392 ha) and established as the Rocky Mountains Park of Canada by act of Parliament. Later renamed Banff National Park, it was expanded over the next several decades.

The system of parks was expanded to include: Yoho (1886) on the western slope of the Rockies including the Field Hill; Glacier (1886) over the summit of the Selkirks; and Mount Revelstoke (1914) just north of the railway division point and Kootenay (1920), south of Yoho and including Radium Hot Springs. Posters, travel booklets, and timetables all featured the parks, in particular Banff with its two major hotels. The scenic qualities of the parks were attractions for all travellers on the railway, whether immigrants or princes, but it was to the more wealthy travellers that the hotel system and much of the advertising was directed. International travellers in particular were sought and encouraged to journey via the CPR.

At Vancouver, a major hotel was built and was in operation in May 1887. The Hotel Vancouver was to provide first class accommodations for businessmen, visitors to Vancouver and also for those travelling on the CPR's Empress liners on the

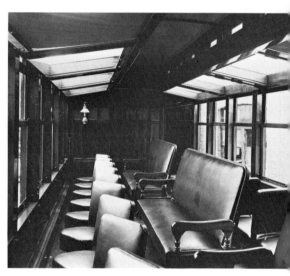

Recognizing the value of tourism from the beginning of service, the CPR operated special cars for sightseeing. The first were the open sided cars illustrated earlier. In 1902 came these enclosed observation cars with caboose-like cupolas at each end. They were, in fact, the first dome cars. —CPCA, 460,9200

The CPR's Revelstoke Hotel, built in 1896 on high ground above the station, was one of the railway's smaller operations. It also served as a meal stop before dining cars operated through the mountains. It was last open in 1927 and demolished in 1928.
—WALTER PAFFARD COLLECTION

The first Hotel Vancouver was in operation in 1887 and was a source of considerable civic pride. This engraving is from the CPR publication *The New Highway to the Orient* of 1894. —WELLBURN COLLECTION, BCPM

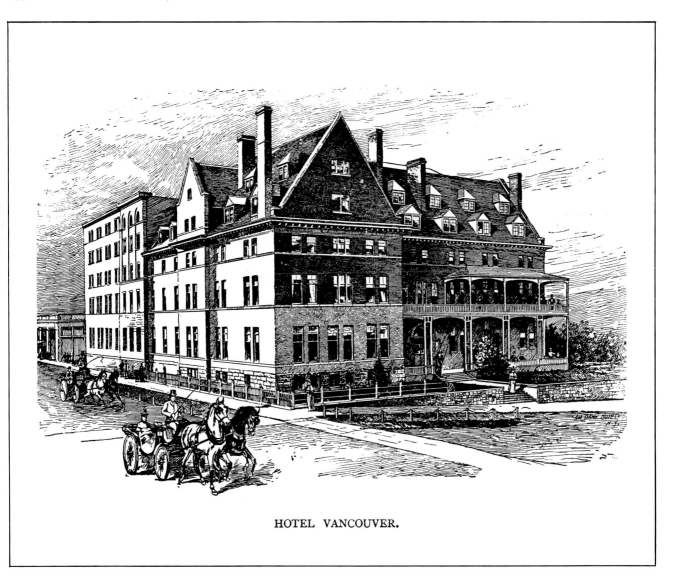

HOTEL VANCOUVER.

trans-Pacific service. It was a logical extension of the CPR's services to have a first class hotel at the railway's western terminus. The Hotel Vancouver was very different in design from the mountain resorts. Designed by Thomas Sorby, it was, unfortunately, a rather unattractive structure, with four stories, and faced with brick. Adjoining it was to be the city's new Opera house, also built by the CPR as part of its agreement for land grants within the city. Work on the Opera house was not rushed, and it opened in February 1891. While the hotel may have lacked some of the styling of the mountain resorts, it nonetheless provided excellent service to its patrons. It is interesting to note that revenues from the sale of lots in the Vancouver townsite provided the capital for the construction of the hotel, steamship wharfs and funds for the hotel at Banff. Like most of the major hotels, it soon required expansion and renovation. By the early 1900s, it was described as having been "entirely rebuilt" but the growth in business was so significant that a new structure to replace it was begun in 1913.

The hotel and resort system continued to be expanded and improved in British Columbia and throughout the CPR system. The hotels at Banff and Lake Louise were greatly expanded in the early 1900s, the depression of the 1890s retarding development that otherwise would likely have occurred sooner. Glacier House was enlarged by a new annex in 1889 and in 1904 another was added. Mount Stephen House was enlarged in 1901-02, and at Sicamous, on beautiful Shuswap Lake, a modest wooden-framed combination hotel and station was built in 1898 to serve as both a resort and a stopover point for passengers travelling to or from the Okanagan over the branch line that ran south from there to Vernon and Okanagan Landing. The Hotel Sicamous was located right on the lake shore and the company even operated a house boat and tug for those with means wishing privacy and a restful vacation or as a base for hunting and fishing parties. Other additions to the hotel system are noted later.

The 1890s were a tough and troubled decade for the CPR and most North American railroads. A long and devastating depression during the early 1890s had driven many American lines into bankruptcy. The CPR's financial picture was much better, owing in no small measure to the traffic to and from the Orient moving on the Empress liners. Still, traffic was down and there were severe financial complications involving CPR subsidiaries in the United States. In British Columbia there was major work ahead, upgrading the line, that could not be delayed. Much work was required to maintain and improve the right-of-way through the province and in 1894 a crisis situation was reached when the Fraser River flooded, disrupting traffic and causing extensive damage to the line, particularly in the lower Fraser Valley.

The Hotel Sicamous, on Shuswap Lake, was built in 1898 at the junction of the main line and the Shuswap & Okanagan which served the northern Okanagan Valley. The Hotel also included the station. For some years, the CPR operated a tug and houseboat on the lake. This photograph is from 1948. The structure was demolished in the mid-1960s.
—WILBUR C. WHITTAKER

Improvements and Expansion along the Main Line: the 1890s

44

The Fraser River flooded with devastating results in 1894 disrupting traffic for 41 days.
—G. W. EDWARDS, PABC, HP61412

When the CPR tried to reach a settlement over work required to upgrade the Onderdonk contracts, Van Horne took the commissioners on a tour to try to demonstrate the standards on the sections the CPR built itself. The following story, with some unquestionable exaggeration, was related in Walter Vaughan's biography of Van Horne:

He [Carey] increased the speed, letting the engine hum over the steel at a pace that delighted Van Horne. The cars rocked; the armchairs and loose furniture of the private car piled together like a ship's furniture in a hurricane. Men held to their seats with difficulty, and in one of the lighter cars not all were successful in doing that. 'Adirondack' Murray's dinner was spilled over him. The train raced through the lower canyon of the Kicking Horse. What recked the dizzy passengers that they were travelling a most interesting section of rockwork or, emerging from the canyon's gloom to the luminous valley of the Columbia, could see the radiant peaks of Sir Donald and Mount Stephen? In a stretch of fifty-one miles to Golden, made in an hour, the engine never stopped or slackened speed. As a breath-taking climax, the seventeen miles between Golden and Sir Donald [Donald] were made in fifteen minutes; and when Carey's engine stopped just beyond Sir Donald, Jimmy French, Van Horne's coloured porter, ran up to him. 'You tryin' to kill us?' he cried. 'All dose genmuns back theah are under the seats. Only the boss left,' he added proudly, 'sittin' up in his chair with his pipe.'

The flooding of the Fraser River in 1894 was the worst on record and, fortunately, was not repeated on such a scale for another 50 years. The damage was immense and extensive and caused extended delays in service over the CPR. The waters began rising to flood stage in the Fraser in May, following a winter of heavy snow falls and a cold spring. Sudden warm weather brought a rush of water down the Fraser, flooding an extensive area—at least 1,500 square miles—of the valley. The floods were so severe that service on the main line was disrupted for 41 days and the costs of repairs were estimated at $550,000. The railway was powerless to do much for the stranded farmers and it fell to the riverboats to rescue livestock, provide supplies, and distribute seed so that crops could be replanted. A sternwheeler docked within three blocks of the centre of Chilliwack during the height of the floods. There were to be other floods on the Fraser but it would not be until 1948 that they approached the seriousness of the 1894 season.

Improving the line through British Columbia was in part at least a legacy of the original construction. The wooden bridges deteriorated quickly and by the early 1890s, many were due for replacement. Other work, including building of retaining walls and better slide protection was also required. The CPR had never been happy with the standard of construction of the line on the Onderdonk contracts through the Fraser and Thompson canyons. Following the turning over of the trackage to the CPR by the Federal government, a long period of arbitration followed. The issue was, of course, highly political. Since the government had been responsible for the line built by Onderdonk, a high settlement would have been embarrassing to both Prime Minister Macdonald and J. H. Pope, his minister responsible for railways. Both men had strongly supported the CPR during the construction, and George Stephen, mindful of their help, was not anxious to push the case as hard as he might. Arbitration procedures were established and they eventually resulted in the CPR being awarded $579,225 in 1891, actually only a small fraction of the costs that the CPR had contended would be involved in improvements. Expert witnesses were called by both sides and the judgements were difficult. The Fraser Canyon sections had indeed been temporary but so too were many features of the CPR's own construction. Both the government and the CPR had been desperately short of money to finish the work; both took cost-cutting measures. It was most important at the time that the railway be completed and generate revenue to help pay its costs. Higher engineering standards would come later.

The actual reconstruction work on the line involved replacing most of the wooden trestles and retaining walls with steel and/or masonry structures. Such work was expensive, but it did have an enduring quality. The new bridges would last many years, being replaced only when traffic volumes and the weight of equipment required stronger structures.

Nearly 100 years later, many of the masonry works were still supporting the main line traffic of the CPR, with traffic volumes and train weights that Van Horne could only have dreamed of. Throughout the Fraser and Thompson canyons along the Onderdonk contract sections, many bridges were replaced. To the east, the loop bridges in the Selkirks were reconstructed and, in 1894, the spectacular wooden bridge over Stoney Creek was bypassed with a graceful steel arch. Similarly, the bridges over the Columbia were replaced with new structures as were the other major bridges in the Selkirks. This program took some years to complete and it was the turn of the century before some of the major projects were finished. Within its first 15 years of operations, the CPR right-of-way was taking on a permanence and quality that would see the company well equipped for the growth in traffic that the early 1900s would bring.

Two branch lines were constructed south from the main line in the 1890s. The first was built using the charter of the Shuswap & Okanagan Railway (S&O) and ran from Sicamous along the shore of Mara Lake and followed the Shuswap River through a developing farming region to the head of Okanagan Lake at Okanagan Landing near Vernon. The 51-mile (82-km) line opened in 1892 and provided a railhead for the rich agricultural lands throughout the Okanagan Valley. To provide a connecting service down the lake, a steamer was required. As a result, a shipyard was established at Okanagan Landing and work began on a sternwheeler with ample freight and passenger capacity. This was the steamer *Aberdeen*, completed in 1893. She was the beginning of the CPR fleet on Okanagan Lake which was expanded over the years to include, in addition to several small vessels, the sternwheelers *Okanagan* and *Sicamous* as well as several tugs and a fleet of barges.

By this combination of rail and steamer services, communities as far south as Penticton had a direct route for their produce to the CPR main line. Without this service, many highly productive agricultural areas could not have been developed.

The legal background to the S&O is complicated. In summary, it was incorporated by a group of B.C. entrepreneurs which included: J. A. Mara, who had extensive interests in interior steamboats; Frank S. Barnard, of the B.C. Express Company and other ventures; R. P. Rithet; James Reid of Quesnel; Thomas Earle; J. H. Turner; D. M. Eberts; F. G. Vernon; Moses Lumby; and E. B. Hannington. Originally, a provincial subsidy of $4,000 per mile (about $2,500 per km) was offered but this was cancelled following a Dominion government offer of $3,200 per mile (nearly $2,000 per km). Finally, an agreement was reached between the S&O, the CPR and the two levels of government whereby the S&O was to build the line and, on completion, lease it to the CPR which was to operate it. The CPR was to pay 40 percent of the gross earnings of the S&O as rental to operate the line and the

In the 1890s a major rebuilding program was carried out all along the main line to replace the original wooden structures with new ones of steel, cast iron and masonry. One such project was the replacement of the wooden truss span over the Salmon River (later renamed the Nahatlatch River), a tributary of the Fraser, 7.6 miles (12.2 km) north of North Bend.
—PABC, HP61348

The new structure over the Salmon River was a graceful silver steel arch span. In this picture from the early 1890s, 4-4-0 No. 374, the locomotive that pulled the first passenger train into Vancouver and which was later preserved in the city, leads a northbound freight over the bridge. —VPL, 423

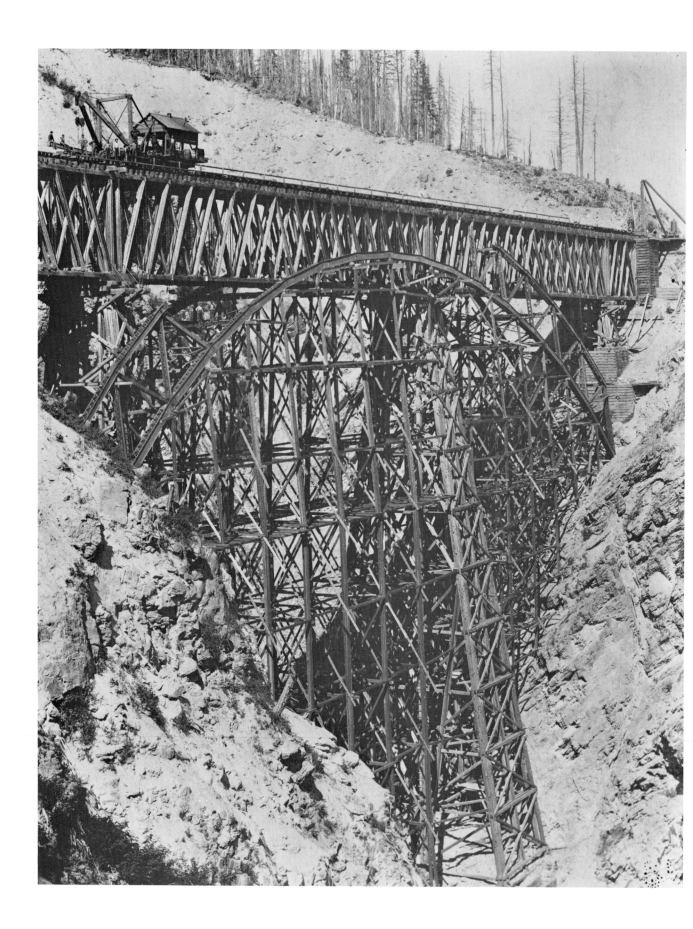

48

In 1893, the original wooden bridge over Stoney Creek was replaced with a steel arch span that was to become perhaps the most famous bridge on the entire CPR system. The new bridge was built around the original structure and there was minimal disruption of traffic as the work progressed. Here, the steel arch is taking shape, supported by a maze of falsework. —PABC, HP77633

The new Stoney Creek bridge became a feature of the line that was photographed frequently. This image of the bridge was captured soon after the reconstruction and shows a westbound passenger train well out onto the span. The burnt-over mountain sides are testimony to the fires that nearly destroyed several of the key bridges in the 1880s. —CPCA, 8018

Mountain Creek Bridge also required replacement. This work was completed in 1902. The process chosen was to use a hydraulic monitor and flume to wash gravel from surrounding deposits and the gravel was used to fill the major approach spans of trestle work. This reduced the length of the required new steel span considerably from 1,086 feet (331 m) to 585 feet (178 m). —PABC, HP77638

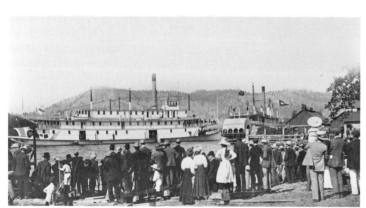

The branch line from Sicamous on the main line to Vernon and Okanagan Landing completed in 1892 gave rail access to many rich farming areas in the Okanagan Valley. Beginning in 1893, CPR steamers operated down Okanagan Lake as far south as Penticton. In this turn-of-the-century scene, the passenger train has arrived at the Vernon station. A much larger stone and brick station was built in 1912. In the scene at left, the CPR sternwheelers *Okanagan*, built in 1907, and the *Aberdeen* of 1893, are at Kelowna during the Regatta of 1907.
—PABC, HP85111; KELOWNA MUSEUM

A steam-powered track inspection car at Enderby in 1902 was ample justification for a photograph.
—VERNON BOARD OF MUSEUM & ARCHIVES

Vancouver's second station was an imposing structure which also housed company offices. The station was built in 1898, a time when the yards and facilities in the city also were being expanded. This photograph was taken in 1903 and shows a yard engine passing equipment being readied for an eastbound train.

—PABC, HP21064

Clean and polished was the order for the day for this special train, operated for Cornelius Vanderbilt, photographed at Kamloops in 1892 or 1893. The 591 was a class SR 4-6-0, built by CP's New Shops, Montreal, in 1892. It was typical of passenger power west of the mountains.

—TRUEMAN & CAPLE, VPL, 9560

Arrowhead, at the northern end of the Arrow Lakes, became an important terminal and transfer point between the railway and steamers operating down the Columbia River to the Kootenays. The branch line from Revelstoke was extended to this point in 1896. This photograph from about 1910 shows the train from Revelstoke being switched prior to the return run. The locomotive is No. 1250, a 2-6-0.
—W. GIBSON KENNEDY COLLECTION

The 1890s saw extensive reconstruction work all along the main line through British Columbia. Many of the original wooden bridges were replaced with masonry arches including the one at the "Jaws of Death" along the Thompson River. These stone bridges were amazingly well built, as this photograph from June 1983 attests. The train is the *Okanagan Express*, an excursion train featuring restored heavyweight equipment whose yearly trips, which began with this run, have proven very popular. —DAVID WILKIE

William C. Van Horne, shown in substantial profile, made frequent inspection trips over the railway. This one is from 1894.

—PABC, HP61336

S&O was to turn these over to the province. The province guaranteed the four percent interest on the bonds for the road. The bonds were not to exceed $1,250,000 or the cost of construction, which ever was less. If the earnings were insufficient to pay the interest, then the debt was to remain due from the S&O.

In the early years of operation, the line did not pay its way but, as settlement of the Okanagan expanded, so too did traffic and the line became an important extension of the CPR system in British Columbia.

The second branch line was built from Revelstoke towards the head of Upper Arrow Lake. The story of railroad development in the Kootenays is covered in Chapter Three. Suffice to say that the region was booming in the 1890s. Traffic to the area was handled largely by sternwheelers and the run up the Columbia River to Revelstoke was treacherous and uncertain. The branch line bypassed the worst sections of river navigation, facilitating traffic movements to and from the south. The first section was built in 1893 along the Columbia to Wigwam, a distance of 17 miles (27.5 km). The branch was finally extended to Arrowhead in 1896.

The 1899 Rogers Pass Slide and Changing Operations

The small station and yards of Rogers Pass, located less than two miles (3 km) east of the summit of the pass, served the helper crews working on the grades and also served as a brief water stop for the through trains. Facilities included a two-stall locomotive shed, water tower, station and section house. The site was located deep in the shadows of the surrounding peaks at the base of several slide paths. It proved to be a dangerous location indeed. At about 4:00 p.m. on Tuesday, January 31, 1899, a slide swept down on the tiny settlement of Rogers Pass.

Fortunately, a slide had come down earlier by 19 Shed and nearly everyone in Rogers Pass was out on the line clearing the snow. The slide came without warning and with frightening speed. Like an immense tidal wave of snow, it engulfed the yards, hitting the combined station-boarding house with devastating results. Those within heard the roar of the slide but it came with such speed that there was no escape. Inside were the day operator, William Cator, his wife, four-year-old son and three-year-old daughter, the night operator Frank Carson, a yard hostler named Vogel, a Chinese cook and a waitress, Annie Berger.

Next, in fact almost simultaneously, the slide demolished two shacks then overwhelmed several Chinese boarding cars. For the two men inside it was a terrifying moment. The cars were rolled over and over by the force of the snow and smashed into the locomotive shed. But, miraculously, the trapped men escaped with minor injuries. Inside the engine-house, James Ridley, a wiper, was not so lucky. The tender of No. 409 overturned and he was crushed to death.* Somehow, another worker named Barnes escaped without serious injury.

* A later report in the *Revelstoke Herald* (February 4, 1899) noted that Ridley was killed from a blow on the head in a small shack nearby.

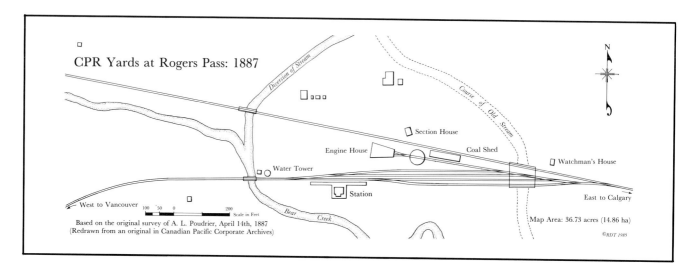

CPR Yards at Rogers Pass: 1887

Diversion of Stream

Course of Old Stream

N

Section House

Engine House

Coal Shed

Watchman's House

Water Tower

Station

West to Vancouver

100 50 0 200
Scale in Feet

East to Calgary

Bear Creek

Based on the original survey of A. L. Poudrier, April 14th, 1887
(Redrawn from an original in Canadian Pacific Corporate Archives)

Map Area: 36.73 acres (14.86 ha)

©*RDT 1985*

After the 1899 disaster, the yards and station facilities in Rogers Pass were relocated to a safer area about one mile (1.6 km) to the west. This photograph by R. H. Trueman shows the yards in September 1901. Behind the five-stall roundhouse and turntable is the coaling facility and in the centre are the six tracks of the stub-end yard. At right is the watertower and station with the main line. —CVA, 2-113

The station and small yards at Rogers Pass were the location of the disastrous slide of 1899. Snow slides came down with incredible speed and force and could demolish anything in their paths with the exception of the specially constructed snow sheds. The train in the distance is the *Atlantic Express* while the engine at right is a pusher. —PAC, C5303

As the snow settled, a quiet fell over the scene. The few survivors in the settlement immediately began to search through the remains of the snow covered buildings. After digging and pulling away the rubble, they found only Vogel and Annie Berger alive. Vogel was unhurt, but the young woman had two broken legs and other severe injuries. Cator, standing near the door when the slide hit, was carried away while Vogel dove under the table just in time. Carson, asleep upstairs, died in his bed. Mrs. Cator, rolling pin and pastry in hand, was found with the Chinese cook in the kitchen. The children, Charlie and Ethel, were not far away. Surprisingly, the family pets, a caged bird and two dogs, survived. In a moment, seven people had been killed. Another slide down the line took the life of a Swedish labourer, bringing the loss to eight.

There were a few consolations because it could have been worse. A special train carrying Superintendent Marpole and Assistant Superintendent Duchesnay, due in the yards at the time of the slide, had been delayed by troubles with the locomotive. Fortunately, with other slides in the pass, the *Atlantic Express* had been held at Glacier and the *Pacific Express* detained at Donald until the line was clear. Had one of these been in the yards at Rogers Pass at the time of the tragedy, the casualties would have been much higher.

It was clear that the site of the facilities was not a safe one and a relocation of the yard, station and locomotive facilities to a site about one mile (1.6 km) to the west was begun and in place later that year. The new site was still about one mile north (east by timetable direction) of the actual summit and, thankfully, a site safe from avalanches. In 1907-08, the yards were rebuilt and the line relocated over the summit between mileages 99.17 and 100.4. Opened for traffic in 1909, this change improved the efficiency and capacity of the yard by eliminating the deadend (stub) tracks, lengthening the sidings and making it a through yard. Several snow sheds were bypassed in the line relocation. The facilities at Rogers Pass remained a base for crews and snowfighting operations until the completion of the Connaught Tunnel in 1916.

Another major relocation of facilities that would have a permanent impact on the operations of the railway occurred in 1899. At that time, the divisional facilities at Donald, in the Columbia Valley to the east of the Selkirks, were moved to Revelstoke, a more central point for handling the traffic over the Mountain Section and west to Kamloops. The project involved a major expansion of facilities at Revelstoke and the relocation of many families from Donald. The CPR assisted with the move and provided new property in Revelstoke. The yards and shops at Field also were expanded and larger facilities were built at Laggan (later Lake Louise) to the east of the summit. With these changes, Donald faded in its importance to the railway although it survived as a logging and sawmilling community. The Mountain Section then included the entire route from Laggan to Revelstoke. Follow-

The railroad unions were an important side of the life of employees. Their role was a broad one including negotiations with the CPR but it also had many of the qualities of a fraternal order. Typical of the period, this ribbon from the Glacier Local of the Brotherhood of Railroad Trainmen belonged to Fred Johnson. The front was used on festive and union occasions while the reverse, black and edged in silver, was worn for funerals or other memorial services. In the dangerous and rugged mountains of British Columbia, the Memoriam side of the ribbon would have been worn all too often. —BCPM

ing the completion of the Spiral Tunnels a decade later, Laggan was phased out as a major facility. Field became the division point for the route through the mountains with the responsiblity for traffic and equipment to the east being handled from Calgary.

The 1890s also saw considerable development of Vancouver's terminal facilities including expansion of the yards, improvements to the docks and the construction of a new station in 1898. Vancouver was growing rapidly and its importance as a port increased dramatically. A further expansion in the Vancouver area just after the turn of the century was the construction of the Vancouver & Lulu Island Railway. This branch ran from English Bay to Steveston and was completed in 1902. In 1908-09 a further extension was made from Eburne Junction to New Westminster. The branch was controlled by the CPR by lease but was in turn leased to the British Columbia Electric Railway in 1907 which operated the line as part of its interurban system.

A significant change in company management occurred in June 1899, when Van Horne, by then Sir William, retired as president and took on the position of chairman. Van Horne remained an active and dynamic individual after his retirement from the presidency and went on to build railroads in Cuba but he left the future of the CPR to his successor Thomas George Shaughnessy (later Baron Shaughnessy). Van Horne died in 1915 at age 72. Shaughnessy was a most capable and far-sighted man who had been with the company since the trying years of construction. He was to see the CPR expand dramatically through southern British Columbia and on the Coast. His tenure as president lasted until 1918 when he became chairman, a position he held until his death in 1923.

Operations on the Field Hill

Any new system as large and complex as a railroad takes time to run smoothly and the new CPR no doubt had its share of difficulties. It simply took experience for the crews to work smoothly as teams and for the men to get to know their equipment. This knowledge had to come quickly in the mountains, though, or there would be mistakes and accidents. Rigid procedures were developed for operating over the entire line and these helped ensure the safety of passengers, freight and train crews. The steep grade over Kicking Horse Pass was a particular concern from a safety perspective. The ascent from Field, while dramatic, was not the problem that the descent from Hector was. It was easy to stop a train climbing the Field Hill; quite another matter to stop one coming down the 4.5 percent grade west of Hector at the summit of the Rockies. The distance to Field was only 7.12 miles (11.45 km) but passenger trains were required to run this distance in a *minimum* of 47 minutes, with speed limited most of the way to eight miles per hour (12.9 km per hour). For both passenger and freight trains, running times and tonnages were strictly controlled. As a further precaution on freights, tonnage ratings on the hill were reduced by one third during night operations.

In the event that a westbound train should lose its brakes and be unable to stop, safety switches were installed at three locations, each about one mile (1.6 km) apart on the steepest section of grade. These were normally set to divert descending trains off the main line onto short uphill spurs which would enable the engineer to bring a runaway train to a stop. Engine crews had to signal to the switch tender in advance by sounding four short whistle blasts indicating that their train was under control. The switch would then be thrown enabling the train to continue down the main line. If the switch tender realized, after throwing the switch for the main line, that the train was moving faster than the authorized speed, he would press a button in his shack. This would ring an electric gong in each of the other shacks and in the operator's office at Field, alerting all concerned that a train was running too fast. Switch tenders could then be sure that their switches were set for the runaway spurs. This procedure worked well and was a prudent necessity on such a steep grade. Crews who violated the procedures were subject to dismissal. The instructions for operating trains on the Field Hill were detailed and very explicit. Careful tests of brakes, sanders and all related equipment were required before trains could proceed down the grade.

Even when Field was reached, precautions were taken, by setting the east switch to divert any following train onto an adjacent siding. While most of the precautions were to prevent runaways of trains proceeding downgrade, the same basic problem also affected trains working up the hill. To ensure safety on eastbound freight trains, a pusher engine behind the last car was mandatory.

Controlling and monitoring the movement of trains over the Field Hill was a critical problem in the safe and efficient operation of the railroad. In an age before radios and electronics, manual or mechanical systems had to be devised that kept all involved aware of train movements that affected them. These included the operators and dispatchers, the switch tenders and the crews of any trains on the line. Careful attention to the operating systems using timetables, regulated train speeds, train orders and clearances, and operating rules was vital but it was considered insufficient for the special conditions of the Field Hill. Telegraphs helped to monitor train movements and the switch tenders, as well as operators, were required to keep careful records of trains as they passed along the line. As a further precaution, however, a special block was established between the west yard limit of Hector and the east yard limit of Field.

A simple, yet ingenious, system—the Electric Staff System—was used to regulate train movements up and down the Field Hill through this special block. The system involved two features called "absolute" and "permissive" systems.

Conductors and enginemen are both responsible for seeing that the Brake is in perfect working order, and properly connected through the whole train before starting from Hector. No train will leave Hector until the Conductor has ascertained that the nearest switch tender is on hand. No train or light engine will follow a passenger train, or section, carrying passengers out of Hector until such train has been reported as having arrived at Field and is protected there by having switch set. It is the duty of the Conductor of a train containing passengers to register immediately he arrives at Field, and of the Operator at Field to advise Hector accordingly. They must not risk safety of train in the interest of time, but must carry out these directions positively and carefully....

Remember that safety in handling trains down the grade is assured only by having them under complete control at the summit. Always bear in mind that brake resistance decreases as the speed of train increases, and therefore, the absolute necessity of having trains under control from the start.

Source: CPR Pacific Division Timetable No. 12, October 13, 1907.—BCPM

The climb to the summit of the Rockies through Kicking Horse Pass was a spectacular one. Richard H. Trueman recorded this scene of three engines working an eight car *Atlantic Express* upgrade to the summit in the late 1890s. The train, which included an open observation car, is just approaching the first safety switch while the pusher at the back is moving slowly onto the Howe Truss bridge spanning the Kicking Horse River. —REVELSTOKE MUSEUM

Field was the base for the pusher locomotives and crews. Locomotive 1603, a class M4a 2-8-0, built in November 1904 by Montreal Locomotive Works, was nearly new and obviously a source of considerable pride for the crews. Behind is No. 1081, a Baldwin-built 2-8-0 (class SE3 of 1899) and a third, unidentified 2-8-0 probably another M4a. This photo was taken in 1905 or 1906.
—R. H. TRUEMAN, REVELSTOKE MUSEUM

Locomotive 569, a class D9b compound of Schenectady manufacture, is under the firm control of its engineer as he eases a westbound down the Field Hill past the first safety switch in the Upper Kicking Horse Canyon. The photo was taken about 1907 and the days of the original grade over the Field Hill are numbered. Soon too, the 569 will be rebuilt with simple cylinders. It will remain in service until 1939.
—AUTHOR'S COLLECTION

It is nearly train time at Field as passengers and CPR personnel gather around the platform in front of Mount Stephen House and the station. Soon the 2-8-0, assisted by another pushing on the back of the train, will begin its labour of pulling the eastbound up the 4.5 percent grade of the Field Hill to the Great Divide. —PAC, C7805

60

The dining room at Field boasted "Meals At All Hours" and for the crews operating over the Field Hill or in from the west, it was a welcome sight indeed. —CPCA, A2321

Ice houses were essential structures at most major terminals for servicing refrigerator cars carrying perishables. In later years they also provided ice for the air conditioning in passenger cars. This is the ice house at Field about 1915. —CPCA, A2320

The former allowed only one train in the block while the latter permitted trains to follow at prescribed intervals. The absolute system governed westbound passenger trains and trains following westbound passenger trains while the permissive system could be used for other movements. The system relied on the crews passing steel staffs and rings to and from the operators. These gave authority to move a train over the special block and made sure that there could never be trains travelling in opposite directions, at the same time, over this section of line. Special electrical-mechanical devices were used, one at each end of the block. These devices, which held and dispensed the staffs, were electrically connected and synchronized so that a staff could only be taken from the device by the joint action of the operations at both ends of the block.

The absolute movements were directed by a steel rod six inches (15 cm) long, turned for about two thirds of its length into rings of varying dimensions to form a key. The permissive staff was a steel rod, equipped with 11 removable rings, any one of which served to authorize a train to pass through the block. Trains could not enter the block until a staff or ring had been given to the engineer or conductor by the operator on duty. When given a ring, the train crew had to stop and see the permissive staff to verify its location. The last train moving through the block in a given direction under the permissive system had to obtain the staff and the balance of the rings chained together. Once delivered to the operator at the other end of the block, movements could proceed in the opposite direction if needed.

If traffic was heavily in one direction and there was an accumulation of staffs at one end of the block, they could be transferred to the other end in the custody of a conductor who was required to sign a receipt and to carry a dated list specifying the number and class of staffs or rings transferred. At the other end of the block, he was required to turn them over to the operator and was then given a receipt. If the system became inoperative for some reason, train movements through the block were governed by conventional procedures based on the timetables, train orders and operating rules. All of these precautions added to the complexity of operating over this short but treacherous section of line, but they helped ensure the continued safe passage of trains over the Field Hill for the first quarter century of the CPR's history.

Inevitably, a section of railroad like the Field Hill left some unusual and almost legendary tales to tell. The following illustrate some of the dangers of operating on the Hill and tell something of the types of men who worked on the trains over the summit of the Rockies. Remember, however, that trains were operated over the Field Hill with remarkable safety for over 20 years.

In late January 1889, a 14-car loaded coal train ran away on the Field Hill with tragic consequences. Engine 314 was leading the train with Jack Spencer, engineer, and Charles

Fidler, fireman. Coming down the hill, the train gathered speed and by the time the second safety switch was cleared, it was out of control. The switchtender apparently thought he heard the engine whistle for the main line so threw the switch. With the train out of control, the crew jumped just before it derailed and one of the brakeman, a man named Phelan was killed and the fireman died shortly after from his injuries. Fortunately, the rest of the crew escaped unhurt. The locomotive was rebuilt and put back in service.

The notoriety of 314 was not over. On the night of July 30, 1894, locomotive 314 was pushing an eight car train up the Field Hill. When about two miles east of Field, the boiler of the locomotive blew up killing Engineer Barton Wheatley and Fireman Alfred Hunt. Fred Johnson, the conductor, recalled the accident for the Coroner's jury:

"I was sitting on top of the second car in front of the engine that exploded. I heard a report but did not pay much attention to it. I thought it was a rock slide. I saw the dust on the mountain and said to my brakeman Crump, who was sitting beside me, it is going to strike our car, and I prepared to save myself if the car went over. When the dust cleared I saw the boiler rolling down the hill and it struck the car I was on and knocked it over. I jumped as it went over. I went at once to recover the bodies. Wheatley's body was found between 25 and 50 yards from the explosion below the track and Hunt's body from 150 to 250 yards off in the same direction."

What led to the explosion was impossible to determine. The engine had been overhauled just a few days before and the engineer and fireman were both capable and experienced men. The remains of the locomotive were retrieved and it was rebuilt once again and returned to service on the Field Hill.

In January 1904, engineer John Ladner was easing locomotive 1077 and a 10-car coal train — the maximum tonnage permitted one engine westbound — down the hill. The first and second safety switches were cleared but by the time he was approaching the third, he was losing control. He used sand and a full brake application. Details from this point are unclear. The switchman was ready and the safety switch was kept in position to divert the train but he thought the train was whistling for the main line and began to throw the switch. Unfortunately, however, the locomotive hit the safety switch, jumped off the rails and continued down the track a short distance before careening toward the mountainside and crashing. The cars piled into the wrecked locomotive and were demolished. Both the engineer and Andrew Emslie, the fireman, were killed. Brakeman George Gove was seriously injured when he was thrown to the track. The conductor, riding the caboose, and the other crew members were not hurt. It took the work crews two days to recover the bodies of the engine crewmen.

The bodies of the two men were taken by train to Revelstoke and from there, a special train carried them to Kamloops for funeral services. Superintendent Thomas Kilpatrick issued passes to over 70 people from Revelstoke to travel to the

To Enginemen, Trainmen, Safety Switch Tenders and Operators at Hector and Field.

———

Regulations for Operating Passenger Trains on the Kicking Horse Grade.

———

Speed Limit and Time Allowance of Trains, Hector to Field.

STATIONS	DISTANCE Miles	SPEED mph	RUNNING TIME Minutes
HECTOR			
to			
Summit Board	0.46	5	5
to			
No. 1 Safety Switch	1.25	8	10
to			
No. 2 Safety Switch	0.94	8	7
to			
No. 3 Safety Switch	0.9	8	5
to			
Yoho	0.4	8	4
to			
Tunnel	0.77	8	6
to			
East Switch	2.4	15	10
FIELD			47 Mins.

* * *

Rules Governing the Maximum Tonnage, and Number of Cars to be Handled in any one Descending Train:

By Day—
-2 Engines 15 Loads or 25 Empties, 550 equiv. tons
-1 Engine 10 Loads or 20 Empties, 350 equiv. tons

By Night—
-2 Engines 10 Loads or 20 Empties, 400 equiv. tons
-1 Engine 7 Loads or 15 Empties, 250 equiv. tons

Source: CPR Pacific Division Timetable No. 12, October 13th, 1907. —BCPM

Running times for light engines and freight trains under seven cars was the same for passenger trains noted above. For freight trains over seven cars the maximum speed was reduced by two or three miles per hour and the running time increased to one hour.

funeral. At Kamloops businesses in town closed for two and one half hours for the services.

Again, it must be emphasized that the incidents described were atypical. The railway operated over the Field Hill for a quarter of a century with a remarkable safety record—a record that the crews could be proud of. It took courage and great attention to detail to ensure safe train operations in the mountains and the crews consistently exhibited these qualities.

When the 4.5 percent grade of the Field Hill was finally eliminated by the Spiral Tunnels in 1909 (described in the next chapter), it is doubtful if any of the operating crews felt the slightest pang of regret.

The dominant feature of the Field yards was its cut-stone roundhouse which was the base for servicing the pusher locomotives for the Field Hill. In this scene from about 1906, the shop crew poses outside the roundhouse with a then new M4e 2-8-0 No. 1644 drawn partly out of its stall. —CPCA, 2749

 **ENGINEMEN, TRAINMEN, OPERATORS, AND SWITCH TENDERS :**
Obey the Rules, be watchful, and run no risks.

The early 1900s brought extensive changes to the CPR in British Columbia. New, heavier locomotives were added, traffic grew and the system was expanded. The CPR experimented with the new Mallet (compound) articulated locomotive to increase its capacity in the mountains. The 1950, pictured above at Field, was the first. With an 0-6-6-0 (or 0-6 + 6-0) wheel arrangement it was a symbol of main line power. The 131-ton (133-tonne) locomotive was built at CP's Angus Shops in 1909. Five more were built (one with simple cylinders) but, while powerful, the locomotives were difficult to maintain and the design was not a success. —REVELSTOKE MUSEUM

CHAPTER 2   EXPANSION ON THE COAST; RECONSTRUCTION IN THE MOUNTAINS

The Princess Fleet and the Esquimalt & Nanaimo Railway

The coast of British Columbia was an area of increasing economic importance by the turn of the century, with mining, logging, sawmilling, and fish canning being most significant. Many small communities developed in connection with these industries and the growing local trade combined with the finished products for export meant an increasing demand for services. Just as the CPR had developed trans-Pacific shipping to bring more business to the railway, there was also a possibility of improving traffic volumes and earnings in general by moving into the coastal shipping business. In effect, coastal steamships were the maritime equivalents of branch lines.

From the early 1880s, steamship connections with the CPR had been provided principally by the Canadian Pacific Navigation Company (CPN), a shipping firm that was not affiliated with the CPR.

In January 1901, the CPR purchased control of the CPN and immediately began improving the fleet and expanding the services. This was the beginning of the CPR's famous fleet of Princess steamships.

Expansion on the Coast continued with a substantial move onto Vancouver Island. In 1905, the CPR purchased control of the Esquimalt & Nanaimo Railway, an independent line, completed in 1886, running along the southeast coast of the Island. The acquisition of the line was an important one since it included the valuable E&N Land Grant as well as the railway. The purchase price was $2,330,000, which included $1,080,000 for the railway itself, the balance paying for the nearly 1.5 million acres (0.6 million ha) of unsold Land Grant. The E&N was retained as a separate company, which was at first operated by the parent company and then leased, although the leasing arrangements were not formally completed until 1912.

The Vancouver Island line, at the time of the CPR take-over, was limited to its 77-mile (124-km) main line between Victoria and Wellington, just north of Nanaimo. The railway connected the coal mining districts of Wellington, Nanaimo, and Ladysmith with Victoria and the naval base of Esquimalt and was becoming increasing important in handling forest products. Passenger traffic was healthy and since the turn of the century, the railway had been operating profitably.

Completed in 1886, the E&N had been, in part, a settlement with Vancouver Island for the broken promise of making the Island the western terminus of the CPR. The federal government subsidized the line with a cash payment of $750,000 and a land grant comprising a strip 20 miles (32 km) wide running along the east coast of the Island.* In total, allowing for later adjustments, the E&N received approximately 1,900,000 acres (770 000 ha) of land by 1905. The construction of the railway was undertaken by Robert Dunsmuir, the Island's leading industrialist, his son James, and John Brydon, with considerable backing from Collis P. Huntington, Leland Stanford and Charles Crocker, the giants of the Central Pacific in California.

The line was difficult to construct; the section north of Victoria over the Malahat range being particularly rugged. Heavy rock work was encountered over much of the route. One tunnel was required and many wooden trestles were needed, including a massive structure at Niagara Canyon and another impressive bridge at Arbutus Creek. North of Shawnigan Lake, the work was much easier and the only major obstacles were rivers to be bridged. John A. Macdonald, who, after losing personally in the 1878 federal election in which his party regained control of the government, had won a seat in a by-election in Victoria, made his only visit to the Island and drove the last spike on the E&N at Cliffside, near Shawnigan Lake, on August 13, 1886.

The beautiful *Princess Victoria*, launched in 1902 and placed in service in 1903, set the standards for the CPR's new coast steamship services based in Victoria. Fast intercity vessels like the *Princess Victoria* and smaller coastal steamers provided an extensive and reliable service to cities and coastal settlements all along the B.C. Coast, to Seattle and other Washington ports and to southern Alaska. —CPCA

* The story of the Esquimalt & Nanaimo Railway Land Grant is complex. Lands along the east coast of Vancouver Island were reserved for railway purposes in 1874 but the delay in construction caused problems as settlers moved in and as unsuccessful attempts were made to arrange for the construction of a railway on the Island. The land was transferred to the Dominion government in 1884 (C.14, Statutes of B.C.) "for the purpose of constructing, and to aid in the construction of a Railway between Esquimalt and Nanaimo, and in trust to be appropriated as they may deem advisable..." The lands were transferred to the E&N Railway on April 21, 1887 following the completion of the line and its acceptance by the government. There were many disputes over title to property and related rights and these were resolved by the Vancouver Island Settler's Rights Act of 1904 (C.54, SBC). The settlement was in favour of the settlers so it was necessary to compensate the railway for acreage lost from the Land Grant (C.17, SBC 1910). This property (20,000 acres or 8094 ha) was located in several blocks in central Vancouver Island. Additionally, (86,346 acres or 34 944 ha) immediately north of the original grant was transferred to the E&N in 1905 as compensation for lands already alienated by British Columbia prior to the act of 1884. Finally, in 1925, under a provision of the 1910 act, foreshore and coal rights were transferred to the E&N in the Union Bay and Fanny Bay area.

An additional feature of the 1884 legislation was the transfer by British Columbia to the Dominion government a parcel of land in the Peace River district of 3.5 million acres (1.42 million ha). This transfer, which involved the agreement for railway land grants on the Mainland, was to provide for lands alienated prior to the establishment of the Railway Belt through the province.

North of Victoria the E&N Railway climbed over a rugged range of low mountains called the Malahat. This section was the most difficult for the contractors but presented later travellers with spectacular views. Here, a southbound passenger train eases down grade with a sweeping view of Finlayson Arm in the distance. The two-car train is powered by one of the line's four Schenectady-built 4-4-0s.
—GERALD E. WELLBURN COLLECTION

In its early years, the E&N was closely tied to the Dunsmuir coal mines. This train, powered by 4-4-0 No. 7, is one of the frequent miners' commuter trains operated between the town of Ladysmith and the important mines at Extension.
—AUTHOR'S COLLECTION

Shawnigan Lake was a popular destination for excursion trains on the E&N as well as an established summer resort. This photo shows the northbound passenger train stopped outside Koenig's Hotel in a summer view from 1900. The rear car in the train is the parlour car *Strathcona.* —PABC, HP82583

Chemainus developed as a logging and sawmilling centre on southern Vancouver Island and a major traffic source for the E&N. This is the interior of the station in the early 1900s. —PABC, HP62778

With one of the line's 4-6-0s on the front, an E&N freight works upgrade along Shawnigan Lake. —GERALD E. WELLBURN COLLECTION

E&N No. 10 was transferred to the Dunsmuir's Wellington Colliery Railway prior to the sale of the E&N to the CPR in 1905. No. 10 is ready to pull away from one of the mine tipples at Extension with a coal train destined for Ladysmith. —BCPM

The Strathcona Hotel was another major resort on Shawnigan Lake. —R. MAYNARD, PABC, HP49606

The E&N was extended north to Wellington, the site of the Dunsmuir family's mines, and also into Victoria. The arrival of the first train in Victoria on March 29, 1888 was a cause for great celebration and Robert Dunsmuir was the hero of the day. He died the next year and control of the E&N and the colliery interests was consolidated by his elder son James. James Dunsmuir, like his father, entered politics. He was Premier of British Columbia from 1900 to 1902, and served as Lieutenant-Governor from 1906 to 1909.

The E&N developed a healthy local trade as settlement spread along the east coast of Vancouver Island. The area was rich in timber and there were many localities suitable for agriculture. In addition, coal mines along the E&N at Nanaimo, Wellington, and Extension (near Ladysmith) had developed into significant industries. The major mines at Wellington, at the northern end of the E&N, Cumberland, about 50 miles (80 km) to the north, and at Ladysmith were owned by the Dunsmuir interests. The Ladysmith mines were directly tied to the E&N by a branch line and produced significant traffic for the railway. In 1901, construction began on a separate spur line between Extension and the shipping wharves at Ladysmith. This line was in operation by the time of the sale of the E&N to the CPR, saving Dunsmuir's Wellington Colliery the cost of routing all of the coal produced over the E&N.

Passenger traffic grew steadily on the E&N and there was good business in local freight. Perhaps what attracted the CPR most, however, was the potential for expansion. In the 10 years after the CPR acquired control of the E&N, the CPR expanded trackage on the Island to include a branch line to the eastern end of Cowichan Lake (1911), and an extension of the main line north from Wellington to Parksville and on to Courtenay by 1914. In addition, another branch was built west from Parksville to Port Alberni on the Island's west coast in 1911 and a short section of track was extended from the main line to Crofton. These new lines required a significant expansion in rolling stock, locomotives and facilities on the E&N. A new roundhouse was built at Victoria in 1913 and many other improvements were made. Bridges were filled or replaced and the general standards of the line were improved. A significant feature of the route that was replaced was the wooden trestle over Niagara Canyon near Goldstream. This structure was replaced with the iron and steel cantilever bridge originally built at Cisco on the main line in the Fraser Canyon in 1884. Heavier equipment on the main line required a more substantial structure so the bridge was dismantled, moved to Vancouver Island, and reassembled with a lengthened centre section on new masonry piers next to the old trestle. The relocated bridge was to serve the E&N well, remaining in use well past its one-hundredth anniversary.

The purchase of the E&N brought to the CPR an assortment of motive power and equipment. The locomotives are summarized in the accompanying table. Very rapidly, more

ESQUIMALT & NANAIMO RAILWAY
Ticket-Coupon 4
Good for One Trip for One Person between
VICTORIA & SHAWNIGAN LAKE
Not good if detached from portion bearing signature.   FORM 226

ESQUIMALT & NANAIMO RAILWAY
Ticket-Coupon 3
Good for One Trip for One Person between
VICTORIA & SHAWNIGAN LAKE
Not good if detached from portion bearing signature.   FORM 226

—GERALD E. WELLBURN COLLECTION

Esquimalt & Nanaimo Railway Steam Power to 1905

Road No.	Type	Builder/No.	Date	Dimensions† (inches)	Weight of engine (pounds)	Notes
1	4-4-0	Sch'y/1910	12/1884	17x24/63	82,000	1.
1	4-6-0	Bald./18546	1/1901	19x24/58	116,000	2.
2	4-4-0	Sch'y/1911	12/1884	17x24/63	82,000	3.
3	4-4-0	Sch'y/1913	1885	17x24/57	75,000	4.
4	4-4-0	Sch'y/2206	1886	17x24/57	82,000	5.
5	4-6-0	Sch'y/3067	1890	18x24/55	104,000	6.
6	4-6-0	Bald./15322	5/1897	19x24/58	116,000	7.
7	4-4-0	Bald./	12/1880	16x24/	64,800	8.
8	0-6-0T	Bald./4356	1878	9x16/39	32,000	9.
10	4-6-0	Bald./17370	1/1900	19x24/56	113,200	10.

† Cylinder bore x stroke/driving wheels - diameter

Notes:
1. (No. 1) Wrecked near Ladysmith September 18, 1900, and scrapped.
2. (2nd No. 1) To CPR and renumbered 228. Sc. 1928.
3. (No. 2) Sc. by 1911.
4. (No. 3) Sc. by 1911.
5. (No. 4) Sc. May 1913.
6. (No. 5) Named *McGinty*, at least unofficially; renumbered CPR 227 in 1913. Sc. February 1925.
7. (No. 6) Renumbered CPR 229 in 1912. Sc. Nov. 1928.
8. (No. 7) Acquired secondhand. Sc.
9. (No. 8) Originally built for South Wellington Colliery as *Premier*, 3' gauge; to Dunsmuir Diggle & Co., 1879; to Wellington Colliery Ry, 1883; widened to standard gauge and used on E&N as No. 8 although actual legal transfer to E&N may have been as late as 1905; to CPR and Sc. December 1912.

10. (No. 10) Wrecked near Ladysmith September 18, 1900, rebuilt; to Wellington Colliery Ry. as No. 10; to Canadian Collieries (Dunsmuir) Ltd., as No. 10; Sc, ca. 1938. Note: the status of No. 10 remains uncertain. It was purchased for the E&N (the Baldwin invoice survives) and lettered for the railway but its main role seems to have been handling the colliery trains from Extension to Ladysmith although it was used on the E&N main line as well. It may be that the Dunsmuir interests did not make too fine a distinction between Wellington Colliery and E&N property since colliery traffic was handled over the E&N routinely. There appear to have been significant transfers of equipment from the E&N to the Wellington Colliery prior to the sale of the E&N to the CPR. Perhaps this explains the status of No. 10; it was transferred to the Wellington Colliery within a year or two of its arrival on the Island. The timing could have coincided with the construction of the Wellington Colliery's own direct line, which eliminated use of E&N trackage, between Extension and Ladysmith. Apparently, there was no No. 9 on the E&N during the Dunsmuir era, although Wellington Colliery No. 9 operated on the E&N occasionally. The colliery engine No. 9 may have been carried on E&N books briefly which could account for the gap in the roster. In later years, under CPR control a 2-4-2T (MLW #50749) was operated as No. 9 on the E&N as the Victoria yard engine.

General Note Re: CPR Renumbering. While the E&N was acquired by the CPR in 1905, the formal leasing was not concluded until 1912. References to E&N locomotives only appear after October 1911 in CPR records.

General Note Re: Locomotive Statistics. Sources differ slightly on features such as driver diameter. For example, CPR folio sheets show No. 6 as having 50-inch driver centres and 5½-inch tires for a total diameter of 61 inches. The above are from Baldwin records and tires may have been changed.

Abbreviations: Bald. - Baldwin Locomotive Works; MLW - Montreal Locomotive Works; Sch'y. - Schenectady Locomotive Works; Sc. - scrapped.

equipment was moved over to the E&N. Some of it was new, such as several CPR D4g Ten-wheelers, but the majority of equipment assigned (either by lease, sale or loan) was older power from the main lines. Ten-wheelers and Consolidations dominated E&N operations until the retirement of steam power although a few yard engines were used on the Island line as well.

The E&N became very much a component of the Island's forest industry. Logging and sawmilling in the Cowichan Valley depended on the E&N for movement of both logs and finished lumber as did mills in other communities along the line. Shipments from Port Alberni to the east coast of the Island were particularly valuable. To save handling, rail car ferry terminals were operated at Ladysmith (in use before the CPR takeover) and at a point on Nanoose Bay, north of Nanaimo, called Jayem. From these two facilities barges carried rail cars to and from the Mainland. The tugs and barges were operated by the CPR's B.C. Coast Steamship Service. With the purchase and expansion of the Esquimalt & Nanaimo, the CPR had acquired an important property and at last brought the transcontinental railway to Vancouver Island. The later story of the E&N is developed in subsequent chapters of this book.

The CPR also extended its hotel system onto Vancouver Island. In Victoria, the Empress Hotel was completed in 1908 on the quiet and picturesque Inner Harbour of the province's capital. The hotel became a major feature of the city and a stopping point for the rich and famous. It served a very functional link in the CPR's system for people travelling on the company's coastal steamships which were based in Victoria and provided connecting services to Seattle, Vancouver and points all along the British Columbia and south Alaska coasts. The Empress, built to the designs of well-known local architect Francis M. Rattenbury, was an immediate success. It underwent enlargements in 1910 and 1911, and a new wing was added in 1929.

Improving the Main Line

Engineering solutions to the problems of locating the original main line had not always been successful. To overcome a short adverse grade west of Field over Muskeg Summit, a grade revision was undertaken between Field and Ottertail. Completed in 1902, this relocation of the main line produced a much more uniform profile in the climb up the Kicking Horse River to Field. Another problem of particular significance had arisen near Palliser in the Kicking Horse Canyon. There, to circumvent a large bend in the Kicking Horse River, a tunnel had been driven through an unstable clay bank. However, it caved in soon after service began and could not be successfully reopened. To avoid further delay, a diversion was built following the bank of the river on a 22-degree, 15-minute curve. Despite the fact that the tunnel was never put in service, it was called either Mud Tunnel, because of the nature of the material it was driven through, or Corry Brothers' Tunnel, for the contractors who tried to construct it.

The diversion was not a permanent solution because the curve was too sharp to permit unrestricted use of the main line. Sharp curvature on any line produces maintenance problems, speed restrictions and reductions in the tonnage capabilities of locomotives. To overcome the restrictive curve, a new 693.5-foot (211.8-metre) tunnel was driven through the shoulder of the mountain to the west of the old, unsuccessful bore. What made the tunnelling particularly difficult was the wet blue clay that comprised most of the material through which the tunnel was dug. The tunnelling was expensive and dangerous. First, two parallel headings were driven at the top of the sides of the tunnel and then another heading was cut through at the top, or crown, of the tunnel. These were expanded and timbered and then the lower materials could be removed as further timbering was carried out.

Because of the heavy pressure of the overlaying materials, a reinforced concrete lining had to be applied immediately following the excavation and timbering. The lining required was four feet thick at the base of the walls, tapering to three feet thick on the sides and two feet at the crown. The new tunnel not only eliminated the sharp curve in the main line but also reduced the length of track by 1,192 feet (363.3 m). Unfortunately, the tunnel, even with the full concrete lining, continued to cause maintenance problems and was the scene of a serious accident, described later. Finally, in 1953, the overburden was removed entirely, leaving the lining as a unique snow shed.

Another major engineering feature of the main line requiring work was the bridge over the Columbia River just west of Revelstoke. This 1,070-foot (326-m) wooden span was a critical link in the main line and a more permanent, steel structure was required to carry the increasing volumes of traffic and at the same time reduce maintenance costs. The bridge to be replaced (actually the second structure at this point because a temporary bridge was in place during the construction period) used Howe truss spans: three 150-foot (45.7-m) deck, one 150-foot through, and one 100-foot (30.5-m) and a further 120-foot (36.6-m) deck type. As well, 250 feet (76.2-m) of trestle approaches. The spans rested on rock-filled abutments. The through Howe span, put in place in the early 1890s, was designed to permit steamer navigation upstream from Revelstoke on the Columbia. The new steel bridge, fabricated by Canada Foundry of Toronto, incorporated four 150-foot (45.7-m) deck and one 150-foot through truss span and two 100-foot (30.5-m) and two 40-foot (12.2-m) deck plate girder spans. The new bridge was assembled in 1907 and remained in use until 1968.

Other examples of major works during this period include improvments to the terminal facilites at Vancouver. A new pier (Pier A) was built between Thurlow and Burrard streets

Bill Miner

Bill Miner gained fame as British Columbia's most celebrated train robber. Born in 1847 in Kentucky, he was convicted of his first robbery in 1866. He spent the next decades of his life in and out of San Quentin and other prisons. The story moves to British Columbia in September 1904, when he and two associates robbed a westbound passenger train near Mission in the Fraser Valley and escaped with about $7,000 in gold and cash. For a time, Miner apparently was living near Princeton. Then on May 8, 1906 Miner, William Dunn and Louis Colquhoun robbed *The Imperial Limited* at Ducks (Monte Creek) east of Kamloops and escaped with little loot. The gang was captured on the 14th as they made their way south. Tried later that month in Kamloops, Miner and Dunn were sentenced to life imprisonment while Colquhoun received 25 years. They were moved to the penitentiary at New Westminster by train. However, Miner escaped in August 1907, fleeing into the United States. Later he held up another train and apparently travelled to Europe. In 1911, he robbed yet another train, this time in Georgia, was captured and again sent to prison, only to escape. Recaptured, he again escaped from prison but was again recaptured and died in prison on September 2, 1913.

His story was told in the fictionalized film *The Grey Fox* which starred Richard Farnsworth.
—M. SPENCER PHOTO, VPL, 748

A westbound passenger train pauses at Kamloops in this scene from about 1910. Some stations such as Kamloops featured carefully-tended gardens and lawns for the enjoyment of passengers. —PABC, HP66197

Ten-wheeler 983 (class ST12) was a North British product of 1903. The compound engine is shown at Kamloops in the early 1900s. This machine is typical of the power used west of the Selkirks and was probably the type of locomotive involved in the robberies of Bill Miner. At right is fireman Jock Rutherford while in the centre is the engineer, probably Dan Murphy.
—REVELSTOKE MUSEUM

Increasingly heavy traffic over the main line forced the CPR to replace the original cantilever bridge over the Fraser at Cisco. The new bridge rested on the original masonry foundations and piers. The photo probably dates from World War I; the new Canadian Northern Pacific is visible above the CPR.
—BYRON HARMON, ACR, NA71-1623

73

adjoining the esplanade yard. Additionally, a new rail car transfer slip was built to permit more efficient handling of barges operating to the E&N Railway. By this time, too, the original bridge over the Fraser River at Cisco was no longer adequate for the heavy trains operating on the main line and it was replaced by an impressive new structure consisting of three steel through truss spans resting on the original masonry piers. The old cantilever bridge, was moved to Vancouver Island. The new bridge was operational by 1909.

From the beginning of operations over the CPR in British Columbia two major bottlenecks had existed to traffic. The first was the gruelling grade out of the Kicking Horse valley at Field towards the summit of the Rockies and the second was the snow-bound climb over Rogers Pass in the Selkirks. The Field Hill was given priority because of the need for expensive helpers over the 4.5 percent grade and the very real problem of safety for trains descending the Hill.

The solution to the grade problem of the Field Hill was found in the use of two spiral tunnels cut into the mountain sides of the steep-walled valley of the Kicking Horse River. Several tunnelling options were considered before the final plan was adopted. John E. Schwitzer, a gifted CPR engineer, is credited with developing the solution to the grade in the Kicking Horse Canyon. The design of the tunnels permitted a longer line and, consequently, a reduction of the excessive portions of the grade between Field and Hector. The upper spiral, Tunnel No. 1, was 3,255 feet (992 m) long making a turn of 234 degrees in the base of Cathedral Mountain. The curve was on a 573.7-foot (174.9-m) radius with a compensated grade (to allow for the curvature and wet rails) of 2.2 percent. The actual grade was 1.6 percent. The tracks climbed 48 feet (14.6 m) between portals. Tunnel No. 2, was located on the opposite side of the valley and cut into Mount Ogden on approximately the same radius over a curve of 232 degrees. At 2,921 feet (890 m), this tunnel resulted in an increase in track elevation of 45 feet (13.7 m).

Significant relocations were also required beyond the tunnels to rejoin the old main line. Towards Field, another tunnel of 170 feet (51.8 m) was required and two steel bridges were needed to cross the Kicking Horse River. Overall, the line was increased in length by 8.2 miles (13.2 km). The net result of the project was a criss-crossing of the valley three times instead of the original straight climb up from Field.

A contract was let in September 1907 to the Vancouver firm of Macdonnell, Gzowski and Co. and work began on the massive project. Construction of the new line took 20 months with the project being basically completed in July 1909. Even though steam equipment was used, about 1,000 men were employed to remove the 500,000 cubic yards (382 280 m³) of rock from the surface cuttings and 150,000 cubic yards (114684 m³) of rock — mostly crystallized, brittle limestone

Taming the Field Hill — the Spiral Tunnels

Work on the tunnels proceeded through the winters between 1907 and 1909 when they were completed. This is the lower portal of Tunnel No. 1, the upper spiral, with the upper portal visible to the right. The landscape is cold and desolate. —CVA

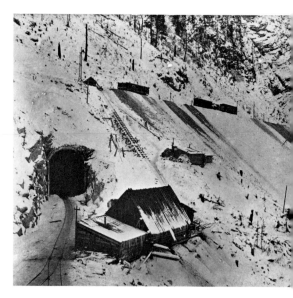

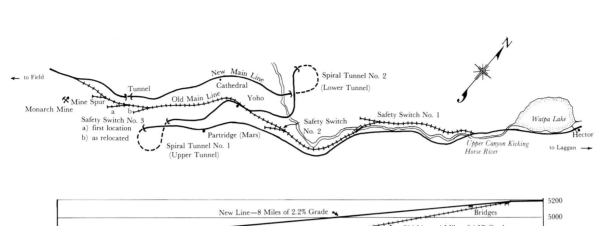

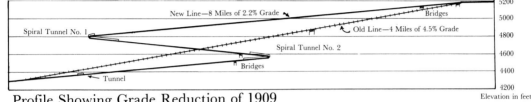

Profile Showing Grade Reduction of 1909

Elevation in feet

Spiral Tunnels & Field Hill Grade

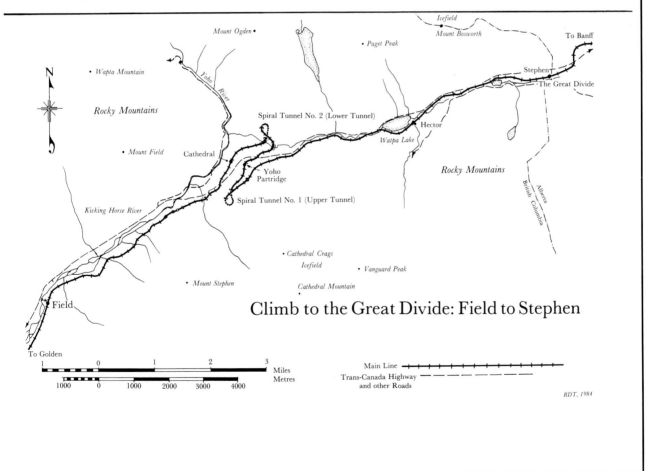

Climb to the Great Divide: Field to Stephen

Main Line
Trans-Canada Highway
and other Roads

Miles
Metres

RDT, 1984

—from the tunnels. Seventy-five carloads of dynamite or, in excess of 1,500,000 lbs (680 400 kg), were required for the blasting. The cost of the charges alone was over $250,000.

Camps were set up at each of the Spiral Tunnels. The equipment included steam plants to produce compressed air for drilling the tunnels and for powering the steam shovels used to muck out the blasted rock. Originally, it was planned to have labourers do the mucking out work but it was soon found that the use of the air-driven steam shovels was more efficient. Four of these machines were used, one working from each end of both tunnels.

As tunnelling progressed, problems were encountered with the drilling. The rock was so brittle and fractured that the drills jammed and slowed down the work considerably. It was found necessary to enlarge the bores to make room for timber lining over large sections of the tunnels. Initially about 25 percent of the tunnels was permanently timbered and it was eventually decided to enlarge the remaining lengths of the tunnels to permit future concrete lining.

The engineers did their jobs well for when the drilling crews met, working from each end of the tunnels, they were nearly exactly in line. To accomplish such precision, very careful calculations had to be made allowing for the grade and curvature of each tunnel. To test the accuracy of the design work, the engineers simulated the construction project by laying out the tunnel curves and other details on the prairie before beginning construction.

Completed and in use during the summer of 1909, the Spiral Tunnels were both a financial and engineering success. Moreover, they became one of the major attractions of the CPR main line — a curiosity and an engineering wonder. The cost was approximately $1,500,000 but the operational savings were significant. On the old line four 154-ton (156.5-tonne) 2-8-0 locomotives were required to move a 710-ton (720-tonne) train from Field to Hector. On the new line a single 2-8-0 could handle 980 tons (996 tonnes). Additionally, the terminal at Laggan could be removed and facilities consolidated at Field. Not only was the number of locomotives and crews reduced but the speed of trains over the line was increased from four or five to 25 miles per hour (6.5 to 40 km per hour). With increasing traffic, safety on the line was also significantly improved by the elimination of the hazardous descent into Field.

The construction of the Spiral Tunnels was a major engineering accomplishment and finally brought the Field to Stephen section of the main line up to acceptable standards of gradient. Special steam shovels, operating on compressed air were used in the tunnels for removing the rock. Note the drilling crew at the tunnel face and the air line leading to the shovel.
—AUTHOR'S COLLECTION

The CPR took a generally conservative approach to locomotive development during the steam era and its motive power reflected a steady improvement of proven designs such as Ten-wheelers and Consolidations. From the early 1900s into the 1920s, the emphasis shifted to larger and more powerful 4-6-2, 2-8-2, 2-10-0, and 2-10-2 types for main line services. Interesting exceptions to this process of development were the

Mallets for the Grades and New Rotaries

The spiral tunnels dramatically eased the grade down from Kicking Horse Pass but did nothing to detract from the scenic qualities of the ride for passengers. This photo from about 1925 shows the *Trans-Canada Ltd.* (Train No. 7), descending the grade between the tunnels. Above the train is the old grade, used as a highway, and above that are the tracks leading up to the summit from the supper spiral.
—C. R. LITTLEBURY, NORMAN GIDNEY COLLECTION

Tunnel No. 2, the lower spiral, has been the subject of numerous photographs and was featured in CPR advertising. Byron Harmon, the well-known Banff photographer, recorded an eastbound freight passing over the lower portal of the tunnel within a few years of the project's completion. —ACR, NA71-5442

Between Field and the lower spiral, two short tunnels and several slide sheds were required. This tunnel took the tracks through a spur of rock below the upper spiral.
—BYRON HARMON, ACR, NA71-5399

CPR's small group of Mallet articulated and one simple articulated 0-6-6-0 locomotives.

By 1909, even with the grade reductions in the Rocky Mountains, a move to larger locomotives for pusher service was considered desirable. The type of machine built was a variation of locomotives built for several major railroads (including the Baltimore & Ohio, Great Northern, Northern Pacific, and Denver, Northwestern & Pacific) in the United States facing heavy traffic over mountain grades. The design featured a large boiler mounted over an articulated frame with two independent sets of driving wheels each powered by a set of cylinders. The rear set of cylinders operated on high pressure and exhausted into a low pressure pair powering the forward drivers. The locomotives were called Mallets after the French engineer who developed the design.

The Mallet proved to be a dominant type of motive power in the United States and the designs were refined and enlarged to produce some of the finest steam power ever operated. On the CPR, however, the Mallet proved to be little more than a short-lived experiment. All of the CPR Mallets were 0-6-6-0s, with the cylinders placed in an unusual arrangement under the middle of the boiler, back to back. On other roads, the low pressure cylinders were mounted at the front of the locomotive immediately ahead of the drivers.

The first of the CPR machines, No. 1950, was built at the CPR's Angus Shops in 1909. An impressive machine, weighing 262,000 lbs (119 000 kg) in working order plus its tender, the machine was designed to deliver a tractive effort of 57,400 lbs (26 040 kg). The locomotive was considered an experiment and extensive tests were run on the machine both in eastern Canada and also between Field and Stephen. In 1910, after modifications to its cylinders and an attempt to reduce its weight somewhat, it was tested over the Selkirks. The results were impressive. The Mallet was able to handle 663 tons (674 tonnes) from Revelstoke to Golden and managed 724 tons (736 tonnes) from near Beavermouth to Rogers Pass. For comparison, a 2-8-0 was normally limited to about 424 tons (431 tonnes) over Rogers Pass.

The tests were sufficiently promising that, in 1911, the CPR took delivery from its own shops of another five 0-6-6-0s; four (Nos. 1951-54) were Mallets and the fifth, No. 1955, was a simple machine with all cylinders working on high pressure steam. These locomotives were placed in service in the mountains as pushers. They were renumbered in 1912 to the 5750-5755 series but, in the end they were not as successful as hoped. The Mallets were unusual in their maintenance requirements and their complicated machinery caused problems as they became older. They were all rebuilt to conventional 2-10-0s (Nos. 5750-5755) using the original boilers and other fittings, but the articulated running gear was scrapped.

The rotary snow plows that had been used during the first years of operation in the mountains had proven very effective in battling the seemingly endless snowfalls and slides but

The snow slides that challenged the rotary crews could be enormous. This one, along the Illecillewaet River, was 500 feet (150 m) long and 57 feet (17.4 m) high. Too deep for the rotary to clear completely, the snow had to be shovelled into the cut for the rotary to blow clear. —H. V. DAVIS COLLECTION, BCPM

The new rotary plows were impressive, rugged machines, built to tackle the worst snow slides of the Selkirks. The steel girder frame is clearly visible in this picture as are the reinforced blades and generally heavy construction. No. 400810 was photographed in Revelstoke in the early 1940s. In the later years of steam operations, normally two rotaries and three wing plows were assigned to Revelstoke. Additionally, rotaries were based at both Field and Beavermouth.
—JIM HOPE

At Yale, in the Fraser Canyon, one of the large rotaries and its crew pause between battling drifts from the record snows of 1949. —CPR

there were obstacles even they could not overcome. If large rocks or trees hit the rotary's cutting wheel, the knives could be badly damaged and the rotary put out of action. Repairs could be time-consuming and expensive as well as delaying the opening of the main line. It became clear, with experience, that improvements could be made in the design of the plows to overcome some of these problems.

In the spring of 1909, an order was placed for two massive new plows of much heavier construction that, it was hoped, would at least minimize the damage caused by slide debris. The new machines, built by the Montreal Locomotive Works, each weighed 260,000 pounds (117 936 kg) and included many improvements over the earlier machines. The main frame was of heavy steel construction, resembling a bridge girder, while the wheel was driven directly by the plow's engine. The cutting wheel was made of cast steel with heavy, reinforced cutting knives.

The new plows were a success and it was found that the heavier blades could cut through trees four inches (10 cm) in diameter without damage and, because the angle of the cutting wheels had been modified, they did not break when striking rock or other heavy obstructions. The new rotaries helped to improve the situation in the mountains and the older machines were upgraded to improve their efficiency. However, the danger and hard work of keeping the lines open remained as the winter of 1910 was to demonstrate so dramatically and tragically in Rogers Pass.

A westbound passenger train, led by 2-8-0 3811, pulls through Bear Creek station on the ascent of the Selkirks during bleak winter weather. The photograph was taken between 1913 and 1916.
—VPL, 9687

The winter of 1910 attacked the railroads of western North America with untempered vengeance. Heavy snows built up in the passes and the slide danger grew with each fresh fall. On February 28, in the Cascade Mountains in Washington, a sudden warming of the weather brought rains which, at 1:00 a.m. on March 1, triggered a massive slide. It was a devastating blow to the Great Northern. Two trains, stranded by other slides, taking refuge at the tiny station of Wellington, were swept down the mountain side. When the final toll was taken, 96 people had died.

As the Great Northern fought to clear its line and recover from the impact of the Wellington slide, CPR crews were out battling snow in Rogers Pass. Eighty-eight inches (2.24 m) of snow had fallen in just nine days. On March 4, a large slide swept down from the mountains and blocked the tracks. The location was about one and one half miles (2.5 km) west of Rogers Pass on a grade-reduction diversion opened in 1909. The old line, which ran through an extensive snow shed (17 Shed), was about 50-60 feet (15-18 m) to the west of the new line which was not covered by a shed. The slide came down from the west side of the pass, over the old snow shed and blocked the main line.

In response, a rotary plow train with locomotive 1751 was sent to open the blocked line. Hurriedly, a Japanese labour

Disaster in Rogers Pass

"Well, it must have happened pretty fast for the engine," LaChance recalled, "because after I got out I couldn't hear the engine. The engine should have been blowing a lot of steam, but there was no sound there. Everything was just dead." Cold, alone and badly injured, he could only wait. But fortunately, Johnny Anderson, the road foreman, had been down the tracks telephoning to report progress. "...I see a lantern, you know, a brakeman's lantern, coming up along there, right along the edge of the slide. By gosh, as soon as I seen that I hollered, and it stopped. I hollered again, and 'Who is that hollering?' he said. And by gosh, it was Johnny Anderson the road foreman. I said, 'It's Bill LaChance.' Oh, he come up and he says, 'Bill, where are they all?' I said, 'They're all gone. A man never got a breath of air after he got in and that snow hit them. There's nobody in sight and I've been here quite a little while.'"

For Johnny Anderson, whose brother Charlie was among the dead, the toll was too heavy. On March 14, he wrote to Allan Urquhart, extra gang foreman, in the Fraser Canyon:

I just took a notion to drop you a few lines this evening. No doubt you have seen in the daily papers about the terrible accident we had at Rogers Pass. I lost my Brother Charlie he was buried here in Revelstoke yesterday. I have resigned my position and have not worked since the accident happened as I certainly don't want another experience like it. It has completely unnerved me as far as bucking snow is concerned. We had a storm that lasted for 10 days and during that time we had over 8 feet of a snowfall besides slides. I was clearing a slide at the New Diversion opposite 17 Shed. I left for about ½ hour to go down to the Watchshed at 18 Shed and send a message to Revelstoke when I returned I found everything buried a slide about half a mile long had come down from the south side of the track. I found the Rotary pitched right on top of the shed. Everything was in darkness and the wind blowing hard and 58 men buried in the slide. I have been to one or two funerals every day this week and there is a large number of bodies left at the undertaking parlor. My relief has not come yet but I heard today that they sent for T. Nichols to come up and relieve me. Poor J. J. Fraser was with me and was caught. He came up from Field for a few days to help me out. There were also 3 Extra Gang Foreman, One Mason Foreman and one Section Foreman killed.

Well Allan you can imagine how bad I felt about losing all those men... and let me know how you like it and how soon you are ready for the Section Foreman as I intend to get a section from Billy.

Yours very truly,
J. Anderson.

gang was picked up and the men went to work clearing the debris from the path of the rotary. Trees, rock and other material had to be removed and, with blowing snow and high winds, the going was tough. As the men worked on into the cold darkness, near midnight, another slide came down from the other side of the valley. Unheard above the wind and the noise of the machinery, without warning, the slide swept down on the unsuspecting men from the east off the heavily treed face of Avalanche Mountain. In an instant, the crew was buried. Sixty-two men died. Only Bill LaChance, locomotive fireman, survived of the 63 men working in the cut.

Tumbled and thrown by the irresistible force of the snow, somehow, he came to the surface and though badly injured lived until help arrived.

Conductor R. J. Buckley was found alive but very badly injured and he died shortly afterwards. Fortunately, however, three others not in the direct slide path were spared. D. McRae, a bridge carpenter, heard timbers cracking, yelled a warning and was blown by the wind generated by the slide onto the top of 17 Shed, stunned but otherwise not seriously hurt. Two linemen, some distance from the slide path, also survived. As word went out of the disaster, rescue crews were assembled. In Revelstoke, a relief train was organized and sent out immediately. Firebells were rung through the town as a call went out for volunteers. "The response," noted the Revelstoke Mail-Herald, "was noble on the part of all who were called and in a short space of time a large number of men with shovels assembled at the depot with medical men, druggists and others when a train was quickly made up and despatched to the scene of the disaster." By noon of the next day, men had been brought in from as far away as Kamloops and over 500 were either at the site or on their way. Clearing the slide and removing the bodies — it soon became clear that there was little hope of finding anyone alive — was slow work because there was so much debris in the slide. It was impossible to use the rotary plows to clear the tracks because of the bodies.

The scene that greeted the relief crews was staggering. The rotary plow had been lifted up and dropped on the end of the snow shed while the tender was thrown onto the shed some distance away. The Mail-Herald reported that "the slide stretched for over 600 feet and in places was over 30 feet deep. Over 600 feet of the shed was torn away and added to the destruction, the massive timber being splintered to match wood." The men worked until 4:00 a.m. at the scene but by that time the storm was too severe and they went back to Glacier until daylight. They found the men buried in the snow and ice; some were crushed by the debris or the machines, others in standing positions where they were completely entombed by the snow. It was a scene that none was ever to forget.

As if the slides of March 4 had not been bad enough, the next morning another slide came down and blocked the line

Maintaining the line through Rogers Pass was a constant and dangerous battle. The noise and vibration from a heavily-working train could be sufficient to bring down a slide from the peaks above. This snow shed at Mile 88.26 has served its purpose, keeping the tracks clear. A photograph, taken immediately after this one, served as the basis for the cover and frontispiece illustration for this book.

—BYRON HARMON, ACR, NA71-1643

The disastrous slide of 1910 claimed 62 lives and left a nightmare task for the crews who had to reopen the line. Byron Harmon photographed the scene of the slide as men dug and probed through the snow. The rotary plow threw the snow clear of the tracks. In a situation such as this, the plow would be used to blow the snow clear of the scene as the men shovelled it into the cut. —H. V. DAVIS COLLECTION, BCPM

Operations over Rogers Pass

Winter in Rogers Pass. The heavy snows and the substantial construction of the snow sheds are clear in this photo from about 1910. —GLENBOW MUSEUM, NA1248-28

Some of the staff at Glacier House and probably the fireman or engineer pose on the pilot of one of the heavy 2-8-0s assigned to Mountain Section. —ACR, PA132-9

Glacier House and Glacier Station, about 1910, a quiet retreat in the mountains. A detailed map identifying the buildings is included on page 86. —PAC, C20495

A cold wind off the mountains whips the smoke and steam away from the two locomotives on the head end of this eastbound passenger train at Glacier. These photos can be viewed in three-dimension with the aid of a stereo viewer.

—BYRON HARMON, ACR, NA71-5815

An eastbound passenger train eases through the yards at Rogers Pass. The train is led by a D9 Ten-wheeler, fitted with a large snow plow, and a 3800 2-8-0. The rolling stock includes some of the new, all-steel passenger cars in the final years of operations over Rogers Pass. To theleft of the station is the boarding house. A plan of theseyards is shown on page 87.

—YOUNG & KENNEDY, REVELSTOKE MUSEUM

Rounding the Loops, an eastbound works upgrade through Cambie towards Glacier House.
—ACR, NA33-154

The Loops on the west side of Rogers Pass were a dramatic feature of the line. This Byron Harmon photo shows an eastbound freight working upgrade over the second crossing of Loop Brook just east, by timetable direction, of the location shown at right. Construction work in the distance and the 3800 on the train date the photo from the last few years of service of the old line over the pass.—ACR, NA71-1636

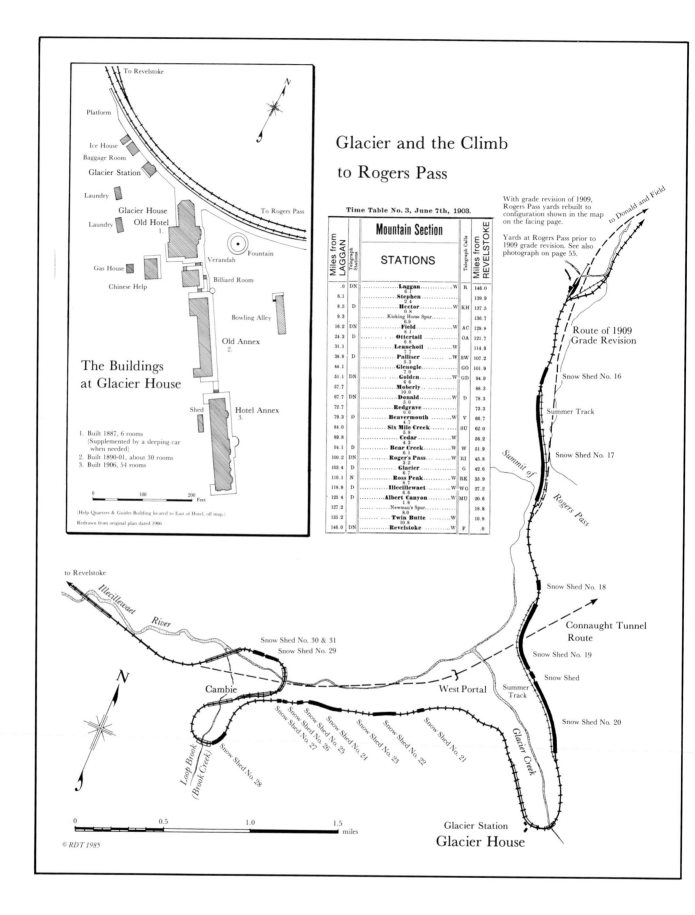

Glacier and the Climb to Rogers Pass

The Buildings at Glacier House

To Revelstoke
Platform
Ice House
Baggage Room
Glacier Station
Laundry
Glacier House
Old Hotel 1.
Laundry
Gas House
Chinese Help
Verandah
Fountain
Billiard Room
To Rogers Pass
Bowling Alley
Old Annex 2.
Shed
Hotel Annex 3.

1. Built 1887, 6 rooms (Supplemented by a sleeping car when needed)
2. Built 1890-01, about 30 rooms
3. Built 1906, 54 rooms

0   100   200 Feet

(Help Quarters & Guides Building located to East of Hotel, off map.)

Redrawn from original plan dated 1906

Time Table No. 3, June 7th, 1903.

Miles from LAGGAN	Telegraph Stations	STATIONS — Mountain Section	Telegraph Calls	Miles from REVELSTOKE
.0	DN	**Laggan** ...W	R	146.0
		6.1		
6.1		**Stephen** ...		139.9
		2.4		
8.5	D	**Hector** ...W	KH	137.5
		0.8		
9.3	.	Kicking Horse Spur...		136.7
		6.9		
16.2	DN	**Field** ...W	AC	128.8
		8.1		
24.3	D	**Ottertail** ...W	OA	121.7
		6.8		
31.1		**Leanchoil** ...W		114.9
		7.7		
38.8	D	**Palliser** ...W	SW	107.2
		5.3		
44.1		**Glenogle**...W	GO	101.9
		7.0		
51.1	DN	**Golden** ...W	GD	94.9
		6.6		
57.7		**Moberly**...		88.3
		10.0		
67.7	DN	**Donald** ...W	D	78.3
		5.0		
72.7		**Redgrave** ...		73.3
		6.6		
79.3	D	**Beavermouth** ...W	V	66.7
		4.7		
84.0		**Six Mile Creek** ...W	SU	62.0
		5.8		
89.8		**Cedar** ...W		56.2
		4.3		
94.1	D	**Bear Creek** ...W	W	51.9
		6.1		
100.2	DN	**Roger's Pass** ...W	RI	45.8
		3.2		
103.4	D	**Glacier** ...	G	42.6
		6.7		
110.1	N	**Ross Peak** ...W	RK	35.9
		8.7		
118.8	D	**Illecillewaet** ...W	WG	27.2
		6.6		
125.4	D	**Albert Canyon** ...W	MU	20.6
		1.8		
127.2		Newman's Spur...		18.8
		8.0		
135.2		**Twin Butte** ...W		10.8
		10.8		
146.0	DN	**Revelstoke** ...W	F	.0

With grade revision of 1909, Rogers Pass yards rebuilt to configuration shown in the map on the facing page.

Yards at Rogers Pass prior to 1909 grade revision. See also photograph on page 55.

to Donald and Field
Route of 1909 Grade Revision
Snow Shed No. 16
Summer Track
Snow Shed No. 17
Summit of Rogers Pass

to Revelstoke
Illecillewaet River
Snow Shed No. 30 & 31
Snow Shed No. 29
Cambie
Loop Brook (Brook Creek)
Snow Shed No. 28
Snow Shed No. 27
Snow Shed No. 26
Snow Shed No. 25
Snow Shed No. 24
Snow Shed No. 23
Snow Shed No. 22
Snow Shed No. 21
West Portal
Summer Track
Connaught Tunnel Route
Snow Shed No. 18
Snow Shed No. 19
Snow Shed
Snow Shed No. 20
Glacier Creek
Glacier Station
Glacier House

0   0.5   1.0   1.5 miles

© RDT 1985

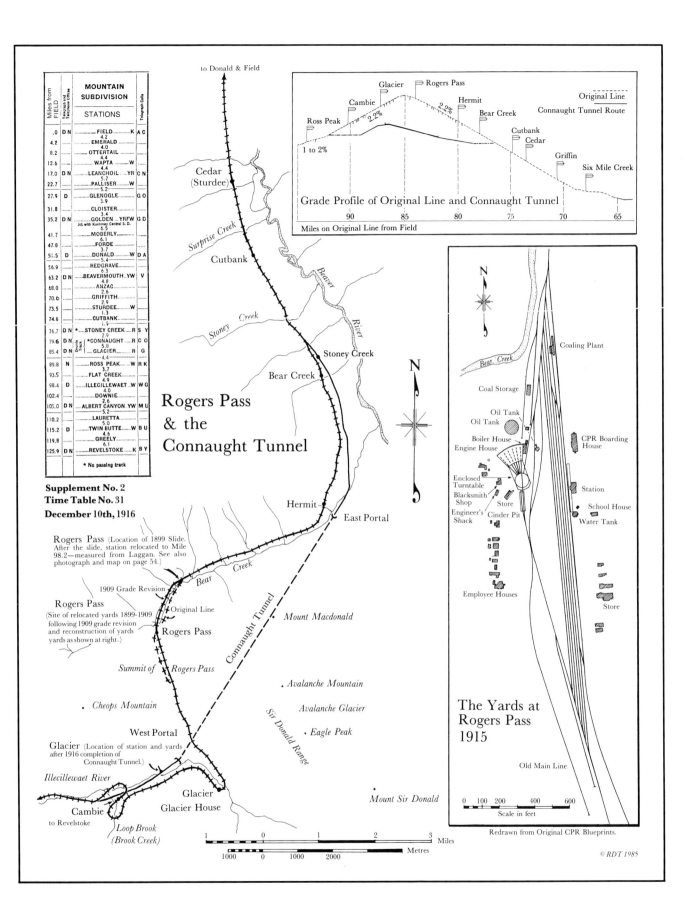

The Yards at
Rogers Pass
1915

Rogers Pass
& the
Connaught Tunnel

Supplement No. 2
Time Table No. 31
December 10th, 1916

Miles from FIELD	Telegraph and Telephone Office	MOUNTAIN SUBDIVISION STATIONS	Telegraph Calls	
.0	D N	FIELD	K	A C
4.2		EMERALD		
8.2		OTTERTAIL		
12.6		WAPTA	W	
17.0	D N	LEANCHOIL	YR	C N
22.7		PALLISER	W	
27.9	D	GLENOGLE		G O
31.8		CLOISTER		
35.2	D N	GOLDEN Jct. with Kootenay Central S.D.	YRFW	G D
41.7		MOBERLY		
47.8		FORDE		
51.5	D	DONALD	W	D A
56.9		REDGRAVE		
63.2	D N	BEAVERMOUTH	YW	V
68.0		ANZAC		
70.6		GRIFFITH		
73.5		STURDEE	W	
74.6		CUTBANK		
76.7	D N	*STONEY CREEK	R	S Y
79.6	D N	*CONNAUGHT	R	C O
85.4	D N	GLACIER	R	G
89.8	N	ROSS PEAK	W	R K
93.5		FLAT CREEK		
98.4	D	ILLECILLEWAET	W	W G
102.4		DOWNIE		
105.0	D N	ALBERT CANYON	YW	M U
110.2		LAURETTA		
115.2	D	TWIN BUTTE	W	W B
119.8		GREELY		
125.9	D N	REVELSTOKE	K	B Y

* No passing track

Grade Profile of Original Line and Connaught Tunnel

Miles on Original Line from Field

Original Line
Connaught Tunnel Route

Ross Peak
Cambie
Glacier
Rogers Pass
Hermit
Bear Creek
Cutbank
Cedar
Griffin
Six Mile Creek
1 to 2%
2.2%
2.2%

to Donald & Field
Cedar (Sturdee)
Surprise Creek
Cutbank
Beaver River
Stoney Creek
Bear Creek
Stoney Creek
Bear Creek
Hermit
East Portal

Rogers Pass (Location of 1899 Slide. After the slide, station relocated to Mile 98.2—measured from Laggan. See also photograph and map on page 54.)

1909 Grade Revision
Original Line
Rogers Pass

Rogers Pass
(Site of relocated yards 1899-1909 following 1909 grade revision and reconstruction of yards yards as shown at right.)

Bear Creek
Connaught Tunnel
Mount Macdonald

Summit of Rogers Pass
Cheops Mountain
Avalanche Mountain
Avalanche Glacier
Eagle Peak
Sir Donald Range

West Portal

Glacier (Location of station and yards after 1916 completion of Connaught Tunnel.)

Illecillewaet River
Glacier
Glacier House
Cambie
to Revelstoke
Loop Brook (Brook Creek)

Mount Sir Donald

N

Bear Creek
Coaling Plant
Coal Storage
Oil Tank
Oil Tank
Boiler House
Engine House
Enclosed Turntable
Blacksmith Shop
Engineer's Shack
Cinder Pit
Store
CPR Boarding House
Station
School House
Water Tank
Store
Employee Houses
Old Main Line

0 100 200 400 600
Scale in feet

Redrawn from Original CPR Blueprints.

Miles
1 0 1 2 3
1000 0 1000 2000
Metres

© RDT 1985

east of the pass at 14 Shed destroying a portion of the structure. Fortunately there were no injuries. Until the slides could be cleared, Rogers Pass was isolated from both directions. Cut off in the yards was Train 97, the *Pacific Express*, which had been waiting for the line to reopen to the west.

Bill LaChance was taken back to Revelstoke and recovered from his injuries and the crews reopened the tracks. Operations over the pass eventually returned to normal. For Revelstoke, the aftermath of the slide was prolonged. The week following the slide left the community stunned as each day brought more funerals. Two inquests into the tragedy followed. The first jury could not reach a unanimous verdict but the second concluded that the deaths were accidental and added a rider that the CPR should refrain from working its men in snow slides on stormy nights. Witnesses had testified that the men customarily went out as soon as slides were reported, to try to open the line as quickly as possible. No one had considered the location dangerous as no slides had ever been reported coming down at that location before. Until the disaster struck, it had been a tough but routine mission. On Sunday, March 20, 1910, a memorial service was held at the Revelstoke opera house. The public notice announcing the service, bordered in black, read "in honor of the memory of the men who were overwhelmed while on duty by the avalanche at Rogers' Pass, B. C. on the night of March 4th, 1910."

The slides of March 1910, were the worst to hit the Selkirks, at least in terms of lives lost. As the railroad officials looked back to other slides, including the one of the bleak winter of 1899 when the facilities at Rogers Pass had been swept away, to the thousands of hours of back-breaking work, to the delays and frustrations, they must have questioned the wisdom of fighting to keep the line open over the pass.

Piercing the Selkirks: the Connaught Tunnel

The horrible disaster of March 1910 added new urgency to solving the problem of winter conditions over the Selkirks. Unlike the Field Hill, the main line over Rogers Pass did not have excessive grades. Although the tracks were forced to loop and twist their way to the summit, the maximum grade was an acceptable, if steep, 2.2 percent. Snow sheds virtually covered the line through the mountains but even with this protection the railway was still vulnerable to closure in winter and spring. There were other strictly pragmatic considerations. Between 1910 and 1913 traffic was increasing so rapidly on the CPR that, if the rate of increase had continued, double tracking of much of the main line would have been required. Simply put, Rogers Pass was becoming an expensive and dangerous bottleneck on the CPR; it had to be eliminated.

The solution that emerged was the construction of what was then to be the longest railroad tunnel in North America. A double tracked, five-mile (8-km) long tunnel was to be cut under Mount Macdonald, eliminating entirely the loops west

Construction on the Connaught Tunnel began in 1913 from both directions. This is the western end with the camp established and the surface excavation work well advanced to the point of tunnelling. The opening at left is the main or centre heading, yet to be enlarged to the full size of the tunnel. The tunnel at right is the pioneer tunnel.

A. C. Dennis, one of the principal engineers involved with the project described the work at the western end of the tunnel in a paper before the American Society of Civil Engineers in 1917: "The west pioneer heading was started by an incline, 300 feet [91 m] long, from the rock outcrop, 700 feet [about 210 m] east of the west portal, about 150 feet [45 m] above the main heading level, and 50 feet [15 m] south of the main tunnel line. This location was selected in order to provide dumping ground, shorten the length of heading to be driven, avoid soft ground tunneling, and permit an earlier beginning than by waiting for the approach cut excavation.... The pioneer tunnel, in rock was 7 feet [2.1 m] high and 8 feet [2.4 m] wide."

—CPCA, 1138

of Glacier and the remainder of the original main line over the Selkirks. The planned tunnel was to reduce the elevation of the highest point on the line by 552 feet (167 m). It was to be a massive and costly project, but the results would greatly increase the capacity of the line to handle growing freight traffic while at the same time eliminating what was considered, from an operational standpoint, one of the most costly sections of rail line on the entire CPR system.

The project was put out for tender in April 1913 with a circular letter noting that, "the necessity for this tunnel is so great and the expenditure so large that it would be worth considerable money to this company to have the tunnel completed as soon as possible. Therefore, everything else being equal, the party who will guarantee completion in the shortest time will be the one who will receive the work..." The contract for the project was given to Foley Bros., Welch and Stewart on July 1, 1913, with completion scheduled for January 1, 1917. A. C. Dennis acted as superintendent for the contractors.

For the CPR, J. G. Sullivan, Chief Engineer of Western Lines, had overall responsibility, with F. F. Busteed as engineer in charge.

Because of the time pressure to complete the work, several methods were considered for carrying out the tunnelling. Finally, a system using smaller pioneer tunnels running parallel to the axis of the main shaft was adopted. These allowed work to progress at several points along the tunnel, rather than just at the two ends. The pioneer tunnels were, in effect, access routes to numerous points along the main tunnel. The scheme evolved from tunnelling methods used in Europe and was adapted by Sullivan, Dennis and their staffs to take into account the higher labour costs in North America and the conditions at Rogers Pass. A pioneer tunnel was dug from each end, offset from the center line of the main tunnel by 50 feet (15.25 m). The pioneer tunnel from the east portal was offset to the north of the main tunnel while the pioneer from the west portal was offset to the south. The use of pioneers meant that, as well as permitting work to proceed at several points, better ventilation could be provided, which improved the efficiency of blasting and mucking out. Moreover, the work of drilling, blasting and mucking out could be done from the access points to the pioneers without interfering with the work at other points.

The next problem that had to be tackled was ventilation for the tunnel if steam power was to be used on the trains. Initially, it was assumed that electric locomotives would be required for such a long tunnel. This was the solution used by the Great Northern in Washington and by other railroads in similar situations. However, it was concluded that to electrify just the section through the tunnel would increase the costs so substantially that the major cost savings from the whole project would have been sacrificed. A program to electrify longer sections of the main line was also considered but the costs were felt to be prohibitive even with projected increases in traffic. Instead, it was decided to install a diesel-powered ventilation plant using a new system of air nozzles that permitted a rapid replacement of air in the tunnel. Fresh air, in quantity, was required, not only for the crews and passengers but also for the efficient combustion of fuel in the locomotives. In general, oil — cleaner burning than coal — was used in the locomotives operating through the tunnel.

Before work could begin on the excavation and tunnelling, construction camps had to be built. Camp 1 was established at Glacier and included the headquarters facilities, while the second camp was situated on the west side of the pass near what was to become the west portal of the tunnel. The third camp was built at Bear Creek about six miles (9.7 km) to the east of Glacier. The camps provided modern accommodations for the workers and offices for the contractors and CPR staff working on the project. Power plants, machine shops and stores buildings were also required. The enormous snow falls of winter posed special problems even in the camp design. Covered, elevated walkways had to be built to connect the buildings and the structures themselves had to be built to withstand accumulations of up to 12 feet (almost 4 m) of snow. The total labour force required for the project was about 500 men.

At each end of the tunnel, a considerable amount of excavating had to be done and on the west end, a major diversion of the Illecillewaet River was required. The rerouting of the river, about 900 feet (275 m) from its original course, was to reduce the danger of flood damage to the right-of-way. The approaches to the tunnel were, in themselves, major projects. On the west, 1,700 feet (518 m) had to be excavated while on the east, 2,600 feet (790 m) had to be dug. Steam shovels and light railways were used to speed up this work.

Driving the tunnel was carried out from both ends simultaneously with the pioneer tunnels eventually allowing 12 intermediate headings to be worked. Steam shovels, operating on compressed air, were used in the tunnel to move the rock blasted out from the faces. The shovels were positioned on the centre line of the tunnel with standard gauge tracks laid on each side for dump cars to be moved in and out to remove the waste. This proved to be a very efficient system and the drilling crews pierced the last barrier separating the west and east bores on December 19, 1915. Much work remained to be done enlarging the tunnel and the drilling and blasting continued until July 6, 1916, in time for the Duke of Connaught, Governor General of Canada, accompanied by the Duchess and Princess Patricia, to be taken through the tunnel on July 18 with a party of dignitaries. On reaching the western portal, the Duke named the tunnel "The Selkirk" but it was later renamed in his honour. The tunnel was opened for regular traffic on December 9, 1916. The cost (including complete lining finished several years

Boring the Connaught Tunnel took these men and other crews months of drilling with compressed air equipment. Seepage in the tunnel could make the work cold and wet. It would be several decades before safety standards developed to include hardhats and steel-toed boots for workers in these conditions. —CPCA, 3672

90

Construction from the east side also made use of a pioneer tunnel. Here, a construction train in the cut leading to the East Portal is being loaded with rock and fill by a Marion shovel at right. The pioneer tunnel at this end of the project was started in September 1913 about 50 feet (15 m) north of the main tunnel, 700 feet (about 210 m) west of the east portal, and about 60 feet (18 m) above the main tunnel. A. C. Dennis described the method of operations: "This location was adopted in order to save 700 feet [about 210 m] of pioneer tunneling, to reduce the quantity of soft ground heading, to enable work on the heading to start sooner than that on the approach cut, and to get rid of the muck readily... The heading was run as nearly level as drainage would permit. The grade of the main heading reaching the grade of the pioneer at the third cross-cut, the two former crosscuts being driven to the dip, and material from the main heading being hoisted up the incline... The maximum monthly progress was 776 feet [237 m]. The daily average was 20 feet [6 m] for the entire drift in rock."—CPCA, 1124

later and the grade revision) was estimated to have been nearly $8.5 million.

The completed tunnel was 26,400 feet long — exactly five miles (8 km) — and pierced Mount Macdonald 5,690 feet (1734 m) below its summit. In cross section, the tunnel measured 24 feet (7.3 m) high and 29 feet (8.8 m) wide. The grade in the tunnel was only 0.98 percent although the ruling grade of the line remained unchanged at 2.2 percent (uncompensated). Approximately 1,100 feet (335 m) of tunnelling at each end had been through clay and boulders but the rest had been through the solid rock — mica schists and quartzite — of the heart of the Selkirks. Because of the softer materials near the portals, concrete lining was required immediately on the outer sections.

Just as the Spiral Tunnels had become a dramatic feature of the main line over the summit of the Rockies, so too did the Connaught Tunnel become a highlight of the Selkirk line. A tough, twisting 14.5 miles (23 km) of exposed mountain grade were eliminated and replaced with a superior line 4.42 miles (7.1 km) shorter and 552 feet (168 m) lower. In addition, the straight track of the tunnel and the new alignment replaced an equivalent of seven complete circles of winding line. Moreover, nearly 4.5 miles (7.25 km) of the snow sheds could be abandoned as could the yards and facilities at Rogers Pass.

The construction of the tunnel had certainly been timely. By the time it was opened, the world was deep in war and the CPR was short of labour and equipment. Based on the average traffic for 1912 and 1913, Chief Engineer J. G. Sullivan had projected that the tunnel would produce annual savings of over $170,600. However, traffic was growing rapidly and this indicated that by the time the tunnel was opened the amount saved was probably closer to $356,000 per year. The savings were of course very significant but the railway also benefited by having a more reliable and generally more efficient operation not nearly as subject to the unpredictable slides and snow falls of Rogers Pass.

With the completion of the Connaught Tunnel the old line over Rogers Pass could be removed for salvage. Because of heavy demands of the war for steel and equipment, dismantling the line took on some urgency. The decision to scrap the line was reached in late July 1917 and the work had to be completed before snow closed the pass. With the line partly dismantled and without the protection of the snowsheds, it might well have been uneconomical to continue with the work the following spring. Snow could be expected any time after the middle of October. Complicating the work was a labour shortage. Three hundred men were required for the work, but as higher wages were being paid for farm workers on the prairies, the labour force kept trickling away. At times no more than 100 were at work on the line. Nonetheless, the dismantling operations proceeded. Work began on the snow sheds from the summit downgrade in both directions. Donald, to the east, was a storage area for salvaged materials.

The diesel-powered ventilation fans, to clear the tunnel of smoke, were located at the West Portal. In this photo, taken over 20 years after the tunnel was completed, a T1b Selkirk emerges from the tunnel. Operation through the tunnel was left handed (the opposite of conventional CPR practice), to place the engineer in the centre of the tunnel rather than against the wall. In this way his visibility was not as likely to be obscured by smoke.
—NICHOLAS MORANT, CPCA, M2756

The opening of the tunnel in 1916 did not end the project. Only about 6,000 feet (1830 m) had been lined and it was decided soon after that, to avoid any chance of rock fall, the balance of the tunnel should be concrete lined. Work started in 1920 with the project completed in 1925. This scene, taken while the lining was in progress, shows several children, probably the families of some of the supervisory staff. The construction camp included homes, a school, bunkhouses, dining hall, recreation hall and other facilities. In the distance is an eastbound passenger train in the new Glacier yards.
—LEONARD FRANK, LANCE CAMP COLLECTION

Vancouver's New Station and Terminals

As the harvest season passed, so too did the labour shortage, and the work progressed more rapidly. On September 18, the old main line was broken at Rogers Pass and by the end of the month 11.5 miles (18.5 km) of track had been lifted and by the same time 16,000 feet (4877 m) of snow shed had been dismantled with most of the materials salvaged. As soon as track removal was completed on the western slope of the pass, the work shifted to the east and by October 15 a total of 25,000 feet (7620 m) of snow shed had been dismantled with 5,000 feet (1524 m) of this, not warranting salvage, being burned. Eighteen miles of track were salvaged as well as significant quantities of equipment. On October 18, just after the work camps were dismantled and most of the crews paid off, the first snows of the long winter fell on the pass. All that remained were the bridges, which were scheduled for removal the following year.

The original work had left the long centre section of the tunnel unlined and there were continuing problems of rock falls in the tunnel. To overcome this difficulty, more internal lining was required. This work was carried out during the winter of 1920-21. A construction camp was located at Glacier, the station at the west portal of the tunnel, and accommodations were provided for 200 men. Without interrupting traffic, the tunnel was lined with concrete in what was often a difficult operation. One of the main problems was the large amount of smoke in the tunnel particularly following the passage of heavily-loaded westbound trains.

Glacier House remained in operation as a summer resort, connected to the railway by road at the new station of Glacier just west of the Connaught Tunnel. However, the hotel complex was not to last long. The CPR increasingly focused its efforts on the major hotels at Lake Louise and Banff, where modern stone and concrete structures replaced the earlier hotels and the importance of Glacier House declined, its original function as a meal stop long since passed.* The summer of 1925 was the last season the hotel remained open for guests and it was dismantled in 1929. For Rogers Pass, a quiet descended that would remain virtually unbroken until the construction of the Trans-Canada Highway over the pass in the late 1950s.

The rapid growth of freight and passenger traffic over the CPR and the expansion of Vancouver and surrounding districts required the development of new terminal facilities by 1912. The existing station, an impressive building just 14 years old, was structurally sound, but it had become inade-

---

* Additions had been made to the hotels at both Lake Louise and Banff including more permanent, fire-resistant structures of reinforced concrete. In 1924 a wing of the hotel at Lake Louise burned and was replaced by a modern structure by the following year. Fire had also destroyed the north wing of the hotel at Banff and new facilities were completed there by 1928.

quate to handle the traffic. Moreover, two new Empress liners were under construction and scheduled to join the trans-Pacific service in 1913. New and improved facilities were needed to handle these fine ships. When the *Empress of Russia* and *Empress of Asia* did enter service in 1913, they set new standards of travel on the Pacific and helped assure the CPR's future as a major force in trans-Pacific shipping. Their passengers and cargoes added significantly to the business of the railway and contributed to Vancouver's continued rapid development.

The CPR retained Barrott, Blackader and Webster of Montreal to design the new station with Westinghouse, Church, Kerr and Co. of New York and Montreal acting as project engineers. The new station and office building was to be located just east of the existing structure, fronting on Cordova Street. The station was to service four passenger tracks and provision was made for expansion. Road viaducts were planned to extend both Granville and Burrard streets over the tracks to the steamship piers. The new steamship pier — Pier D — was to be located at the foot of Granville Street. This structure, completed in 1913, provided berthing for two large coastal steamers and rooms for baggage, freight handling, ticketing and passenger waiting areas. Initially, the pier measured 376 x 150 feet (115 x 46 m) but in 1918, it was expanded another 537 feet (164 m) in length to accommodate more and larger vessels. The design of all the facilities was intended to provide for quick and easy transfer between the company's rail and steamship operations. The new terminals were estimated to cost nearly $1,250,000. At the same time the nearby Hotel Vancouver was being modernized and enlarged at an additional cost of $2,000,000.

As design and construction progressed on the new terminal facilities on Burrard Inlet, work was also proceeding on new major freight yards about 18 miles (29 km) to the east of Vancouver at Coquitlam. Despite its ideal harbour front location, Vancouver had limited space for freight yards and moreover, property in Vancouver generally was too valuable to devote to additional yards when adjacent areas were available. Some expansion did occur at the False Creek (Drake Street) yards and the roundhouse there was increased by 12, 90-foot (27.5-m) stalls and a new turntable to service better the passenger locomotives and yard power running into Vancouver. The new yards at Coquitlam were designed to accommodate freight arriving from the East and to assemble traffic originating in the West. A double "hump" yard capable of handling 5,000 cars was built. The yards were divided into eight different units for handling the traffic. These were: receiving from the East, departure for the East, repair yards, eastbound classification yards, westbound classification yards, receiving from the the West, departure for the West, and holding yards. The locomotive facilities included a 12-stall roundhouse for servicing both main line power and switch engines. In the Fraser Valley, the main line

Vancouver boomed in the years before World War I and so too did the CPR. A new station, shown at right, was completed in 1914. The coastal and trans-Pacific steamship fleets were expanded greatly and a new pier was built. The three steamers in port are the *Princess Adelaide*, *Princess Patricia* and *Princess May*.
—LEONARD FRANK

As the city of Vancouver grew, so too did the communities in the Fraser Valley. Service to and from points in the valley was frequent with milk and other agricultural products being carried to Vancouver in an efficient and speedy manner. This photo is at Mission where a branch left the main line to cross the Fraser and connect with the Northern Pacific at Huntington/Sumas on the border with Washington. —PAC, C24465

The Vancouver Roundhouse

The shop crew outside the first CPR roundhouse in Vancouver. Near Pender and Carrall streets, it was used until the facilities were completed at False Creek. —CANADIAN PHOTO CO., CVA CANP38

The roundhouse at False Creek (Drake Street) was the focus of locomotive servicing in Vancouver. This partial panorama view of World War I vintage shows the roundhouse at right, the water tower and sand house in the centre and the long trestle leading to the coaling dock. Stores and passenger car servicing yards were located to the right, behind and west of the roundhouse. The CPR vacated this site in the early-1980s and the area was developed for Expo 86. The oldest section of the roundhouse was restored and used as a pavilion. —CVA PAN85A

There was a constant parade of steam power in and out of the Drake Street shops during busy times and the crews were kept busy servicing, fueling and watering the machines. Here, 3836, an N3a class 2-8-0 of 1912 vintage, is ready for another freight assignment in the mid-1920s. Passenger power, in the form of an immaculate G2r Pacific No. 2520 and a D9c Ten-wheeler, gleams in the low morning sun on the ready track in 1927. —KEN MERILEES

was double tracked between Port Coquitlam and Ruby Creek.

Vancouver's new station was completed in the summer of 1914 and the other facilities became operational in 1913-1914 as well. The completion of these projects plus the new Spiral Tunnels and the beginning of work on a tunnel through the Selkirks was timely, for the world was on the verge of a war that few could foresee as the most brutal the world had yet endured. Unintentionally perhaps, the CPR was in a good position to play a major part in the war ahead.

The impact of the war was felt in several ways. On the Coast, two new steamships being completed in Britain were chartered to the Admiralty and the trans-Pacific service was seriously disrupted by the *Empress of Russia*, *Empress of Asia* and *Empress of Japan* being used as armed merchant cruisers for varying periods in the first years of the war. The *Empress of India* was sold as a hospital ship and in the final months of the war, the *Russia* and *Asia* were used as troop ships. For the railway itself, major extensions of double tracking and other improvements in B.C. had to be deferred, except for the Connaught Tunnel project. In the early years of the war, traffic fell off significantly, but as the economy adjusted to wartime demands, traffic rose to pre-war levels. Many experienced men left the company to serve in the military and their skills were missed. At the same time, there was serious nationwide inflation; revenues, based largely on regulated freight rates, and wages for employees, did not keep up with costs. This serious problem for the CPR and its workers was eventually rectified, at least in part, by rate increases and higher wages at the end of the war and in the immediate post-war years.

The Hotel Vancouver was a showpiece of the city for many years. The original hotel was soon insufficient for the business and, through addition and much new construction, was replaced in 1915 by the structure shown above. It featured a roof garden and all of the expected amenities. —VPL, 6570

The Silk Trains

An important feature of CPR operations during this period and into the 1920s was the silk train. The Empress liners and other vessels brought extremely valuable cargoes of silk to Vancouver destined for brokerage houses or banks on the Eastern Seaboard of the United States. Competing with the CPR, other companies brought shipments into Seattle for movement over the Great Northern or other U.S. lines. Because the first train loads of the season received the best prices, and also because of the high value and perishable nature of the silk and consequent high insurance rates, every effort was made to hasten the shipments east. A single shipment could be worth well over $1,000,000.

Special trains — "Silkers" — were waiting at dockside when the Empresses arrived and the silk was loaded with dispatch. The CPR had a definite advantage over rival lines in the race to markets because the Empresses were the fastest ships on the Pacific and also travelled by a shorter "great circle" route across the North Pacific. The silk trains were given priority across the system and even special movements would have to take a siding to let the silker go racing by. The CPR was able

HOTEL SYSTEM

CANADIAN PACIFIC RAILWAY

Name of Hotel, Plan, Distance from Station and Transfer Charge	Altitude	Season	No. Rooms	Rate per Day	Single Meals		
St. Andrews, N.B.							
The Algonquin— 1 mile—25 cents.	150	June 20-Sept. 30	200	$5.00 up	B. $1.00	L. 1.25	D. 1.50
McAdam, N.B.							
McAdam Station Hotel— At Station.	A 445	All year	16	3.00 up	B. .50	L. .75	D. .75
Quebec, Que.							
Chateau Frontenac— 1 mile—50 cents.	300	All year	375	5.00 up	B. 1.00	L. 1.00	D. 1.50
Montreal, Que.							
Place Viger Hotel— At Place Viger Station. 1½ miles from Windsor Station—50 cents.	A 57 E	All year	125	3.50 up / 1.50 up	B. .75 / L. .75 / D. 1.00 / also a la carte		
Winnipeg, Man.							
The Royal Alexandra— At Station.	E 760	All year	475	2.00 up	a la carte		
Calgary, Alta.							
Palliser— At Station.	A 3425 E	All year	315	4.00 up / 2.00 up	B. 1.00 / L. 1.00 / D. 1.25 / also a la carte		
Banff, Alta.							
Banff Springs Hotel— 1½ miles—25 cents.	A 4625	May 15-Oct. 15	350	4.00 up	B. 1.00	L. 1.00	D. 1.50
Lake Louise, Alta							
Chateau Lake Louise— 2½ miles—50 cents Narrow Gauge Railway	A 5670	June 1-Oct. 15	365	5.00 up	B. 1.00	L. 1.00	D. 1.50
Field, B.C.							
Mt. Stephen House— At Station.	A 4066	All year	65	4.00 up	1.00		
Yoho Valley Camp							
Field—11 miles.		July 1-Sept. 15	15	4.00	1.00		
Emerald Lake (near Field), B.C.							
Emerald Lake Chalet— 7 miles—$1.00.	A 4066	June 15-Sept. 30	16	4.00 up	1.00		
Glacier, B.C.							
Glacier House— At Station.	A 4086	May 15-Oct. 15	90	4.00 up	1.00		
Balfour, B.C.							
Kootenay Lake Hotel— ¼ mile.	A 1700	June 15-Sept. 15	55	3.50 up	B. .75	L. .75	D. 1.00
Sicamous, B.C.							
Hotel Sicamous— At Station.	A 1146	All year	60	3.50 up	B. .75	L. .75	D. 1.00
Penticton, B.C.							
Hotel Incola— Near Steamer Wharf.	A ..	All year	62	3.00 up	.75		
Cameron Lake, B.C.							
Cameron Lake Chalet— Vancouver Island	A ..	May 1-Sept. 30	....	3.50	....		
Vancouver, B.C.							
Hotel Vancouver— ½ mile—25 cents.	E 100	All year	650	2.00 up	a la carte		
Victoria, B.C.							
Empress Hotel— 100 yards—25 cents.	E Sea Level	All year	320	2.00 up	a la carte		

A—American. E—European. Rates subject to alteration.

The CPR hotel system was outlined in the system timetable of October 1, 1916. —BCPM

to deliver cargoes in New York just 13 days after an Empress sailed from Yokohama. The competition found it very difficult to compete with that performance.

To illustrate one of the more famous examples of the priority given the silk trains, in 1919 the special train carrying Prince Albert, later King George VI, left Vancouver near midnight. Four hours later, the silk train departed. Near noon the next day, the passenger train was ordered into a siding to let the silk train pass by.

Gradually, however, the silk trains decreased in importance as the Japanese increasingly used their own ships to carry the silk, via the Panama Canal, directly to East Coast ports. The introduction of synthetics also reduced the demand for silk and despite reduced rates on the CPR route, the business all but disappeared by the mid-1930s.

Before proceeding with the story of operations on the main line it is first necessary to bring up to date the development of the CPR's routes through the Okanagan and the Kootenays.

A worried official paces up and down the tracks and the engine crew watches for their signal to move as last-minute details are completed prior to the departure of this silk train from Vancouver. The cargo could be worth a million dollars and no excuses will be acceptable for any delay to this train.
—LEONARD FRANK, LANCE CAMP COLLECTION

The arrival of the first train at Penticton over the Kettle Valley
Railway was cause for celebration. May 30, 1915 was a day to
be noted; the long-desired Coast-to-Kootenay railway was a
reality. Trains could now run all the way from Vancouver
through to the Okanagan, east to the Kootenays and on to
Alberta via the Crowsnest Pass. All that remained was the link
over the Coquihalla Pass. —STOCKS FAMILY COLLECTION, IPB

CHAPTER **3**   CANADIAN PACIFIC AND
                       GREAT NORTHERN: ACROSS
                       THE SOUTHERN BOUNDARY

Expansion into the Kootenays: 1891-98

With the completion of the main line through to the Pacific, and the development of facilities and equipment to ensure its year-round operation, the next problem to be faced was providing enough traffic for the line to pay its way and make a profit. In British Columbia, additional traffic came from several sources, including the trans-Pacific liners, but it was clear that a lucrative field for development lay in the area to the south of the main line—the Kootenay district. Early explorations in this region, north of the boundary with the United States, indicated great potential for mineral and timber developments and also some excellent areas for agriculture. However, for any of these visions to become reality, adequate and reliable transportation was a necessity.

In the late 1880s and early 1890s, the most direct routes to the Kootenays were either down the Columbia River from the main line of the CPR at Revelstoke or, by rail line and steamboat from Spokane (Spokane Falls), Washington or Bonners Ferry, Idaho. As the wealth of the area began to be realized, the pull from these two spheres increased. By the late 1880s, a small sternwheeler, the *Dispatch*, had been placed in service on the Columbia from Revelstoke and, in 1890, she was replaced by the much larger, more satisfactory steamer *Lytton*. Operated by an independent concern, the Columbia and Kootenay Steam Navigation Company (C&KSN), the *Lytton* was able to provide a reliable service between the CPR main line at Revelstoke and Northport, Washington with a frequency of one or two round trips a week during the navigation season. From Northport, the Spokane Falls & Northern connected through to Spokane and the main line of the Northern Pacific.

A particular barrier to funnelling north the traffic of the Kootenay Lake area was the unnavigable section of the Kootenay River between Kootenay Lake and the Columbia. To bypass the long series of rapids and falls, it was necessary to traverse a rough 30 miles (45 km) of wagon road and this was time consuming and costly. Moreover, since it was possible to operate steamers from Kootenay Lake upstream from the southern end of the Lake as far south as Bonners Ferry, Idaho, it made the route to the CPR unattractive. Traffic continued to move to the United States.

To overcome the obstacle of the Kootenay River, a short section of railroad was constructed in 1890-91. Chartered as the Columbia and Kootenay Railway and Navigation Company, or simply the Columbia and Kootenay, it was built between the steamer landing at Robson and Nelson, a distance of 27 miles (43.5 km). The provincial government provided a land grant of 10,240 acres, tax free for 10 years, per mile (2575 ha/km) of completed railway. The federal government provided a cash subsidy of $112,000.

The CPR acquired the charter in 1890 under a 999-year lease and built the line, providing in effect, a rail portage route. In this form, while the line was important to the development of traffic to and from the West Kootenays, it was, in itself, not very impressive. Van Horne is reported to have described it as a line "from nowhere to nowhere." Its real significance was that it represented the first move of the CPR into southeastern British Columbia and was the beginning of a process that would ultimately see a secondary route built from southern Alberta, through the Crowsnest Pass along the southern border of the province to Vancouver.

The construction of this short stretch of railroad greatly facilitated the movement of traffic to and from the region. "Traffic," noted the Nelson *Miner* on August 1, 1891, "is mainly merchandise for Nelson and Ainsworth and passengers." The paper also noted that "the track of the C&K is reported to be in good condition, now that the ballasting is underway. Several of the curves are pretty sharp, but until the traffic increases, fast trains will not be run. The operating headquarters are being removed from Sproat to Robson, 2¼ miles [3.6 km] up the Columbia. The yard at Nelson is being cleared of stumps, and the depot buildings have been painted." The CPR took over full control of the isolated railway in 1892.

The C&KSN increased its fleet significantly to meet the growing traffic from the region and added the steamer *Nelson* for service on Kootenay Lake. In addition, the company built a large steamer, the *Columbia*, and purchased yet another, the *Kootenai*, to augment the Revelstoke — Robson service. With these improvements, it was possible to move mail, passengers and freight on Canadian-owned vessels or rail lines from most of the important mining areas developing in the district.

The situation stabilized, but by the mid-1890s, the development of the West Kootenay district was accelerating. The Spokane Falls & Northern was extended north to the Canadian border and, under the charter of the Nelson & Fort Sheppard Railway, was built to the shore of Kootenay Lake and opened for traffic on December 19, 1893. This line was built by Daniel Chase Corbin, a Spokane entrepreneur and mining man, who also controlled the Spokane Falls & Northern. Corbin had experienced delays in construction so that by the fall of 1893, he was running out of time to complete his railroad within the deadline imposed by his charter.

Corbin's crews completed the line on time, but only just

The Miner, November 25, 1893:

. . . the first loco with the track laying machine and rail and tie cars came round the hill into view of Nelson early Sunday morning.

Every three of four minutes the loco's whistle tooting and the train's advance of 32 feet announced the laying of a set of rails. This was kept up all day Sunday. Nearly everyone who could manage it, went out on the grade to see the track-laying machine work. Those who have seen the machine work will doubtless wonder why it has been termed labor-saving.

It assuredly does prevent many from securing work on the road, but what of the men working on the machine. If you have ever seen a man work real hard you should compare him with any of those who work on the machine.

The remaining three miles which yet remain to be laid will be completed within the next few days. The materials trains can be heard coming and going at all hours of the night and the whistle is sweet music to the ears of Nelsonites.

Spokane Falls & Northern 4-4-0 No. 7, shown at Nelson, was typical of the power on the line before Great Northern locomotives became common on the routes into British Columbia.
—FRED JUKES, W. GIBSON KENNEDY COLLECTION

The Columbia & Kootenay Railway between Robson on the Columbia and Nelson on Kootenay Lake was the first CPR branch line to penetrate southeastern British Columbia. The line bypassed the unnavigable sections of the Kootenay River and connected with steamer services at both ends of its route. The falls and rapids of the Kootenay River were to be a valuable source of electric power for the mining industry in the region.
—PABC, HP82577

barely. It passed inspection and was opened to traffic with a twice-weekly winter schedule but ballasting and much track work remained to be done for the railroad to be in first-class condition. The N&FS received a land grant of 10,240 acres (4144 ha) per mile of line for a total grant of somewhat over 580,000 acres (about 235 000 ha). The actual size of the grant is in some doubt as other sources note the land grant as being as large as 614,400 acres (248 650 ha). *Poor's* reported that, for the year ending June 30, 1895, the line had carried 4,153 passengers and moved 6,310 tons (6411 tonnes) of freight. However, expenses of $27,740 exceeded operating revenues by $6,476. Fortunately, both traffic and earnings were to improve significantly and in 1898, for example, the road posted net earnings of $62,917. Two locomotives, three passenger cars and 21 freight cars comprised the road's equipment in 1895, but of these, one passenger car and all of the freight equipment was leased.

The 55-mile (88.5-km) route of the N&FS, more direct than the rail and steamer service offered by the CPR and the C&KSN, was a significant challenge to the CPR in the district. Fortunately for the CPR and unfortunately for the N&FS, the charter authorizing the construction of the Columbia and Kootenay gave the line exclusive rail access to Nelson. As a result, the N&FS had to content itself with building a station on the outskirts of the community beyond the city limits. The mountainous landscape of the area complicated the picture further and precluded the N&FS from developing extensive terminals near Nelson since the CPR controlled the most suitable lands as well. The C&KSN had no reservations about dealing with both the CPR and its competition, and so good steamer connections were available on the lake.

Throughout the early 1890s, prospectors scoured the mountains of the West Kootenays and slowly the mineral wealth — gold, silver, copper, zinc and lead — of the district became apparent.

Promising discoveries developed into lucrative mines at Nelson, Rossland and at several locations in the Slocan Lake district midway between the Columbia River and Kootenay Lake. The development of all of these discoveries depended directly on improvements in transportation facilities to make recovery of the ores financially practical. Those on either Kootenay Lake or the Columbia River had ready access to the new rail and steamer lines, but those in the Slocan were more isolated. Expansion of transportation facilities became almost unavoidable.

The next CPR expansion south into the Kootenays came in two sections. From Revelstoke in 1893, tracks were completed south for 17 miles (27.5 km) along the Columbia River to a point called Wigwam. This short branch, extended in 1896 to Arrowhead 10 miles (16 km) further south, bypassed some of the more difficult sections of river navigation on the Columbia and, as a result, improved the reliability and effectiveness of the steamers operating south on the Arrow Lakes — Columbia River route to the Kootenay mining districts. Also in 1893, a charter was granted to the Nakusp & Slocan Railway to build a line connecting the Arrow Lakes with the Slocan Valley to the southeast. This line was completed and in operation in 1895 and gave the CPR, which had acquired the charter on a lease, a direct rail link, via the steamer route on the Arrow Lakes, with the Slocan mines.

Rail access for the Slocan came next from the east under the 1892 charter of the Kaslo & Slocan Railway (K&S). Despite the somewhat half-hearted efforts of the CPR to control the traffic of the West Kootenays, much lucrative freight had continued to move south through Nelson over the N&FS to Spokane and, by steamer, south down the Kootenay River (spelled Kootenai in Idaho) to Bonners Ferry, Idaho. The construction of this new line gave American interests even better access to the mining traffic of the region. Although several prominent British Columbia businessmen, including John Hendry, were involved with the K&S, its financial backing came from the Great Northern.

The K&S was built as a three-foot (0.91 m) gauge line that for physical characteristics, at least, seemed more in character with those of the mining districts of Colorado than of British Columbia. It was a spectacular piece of mountain narrow gauge railroad with spidery bridges, and the track perched precariously for hundreds of feet along canyon walls. The line followed the Kaslo River inland from Kootenay Lake up a steep and rocky route into the mountains over a two-percent grade. Many bridges and trestles were required, and around Payne Bluff, the tracks seemed to grip the rock face by will power alone.

There were delays in beginning construction but, in 1895, the route was finally opened to traffic between Sandon, which had developed as the richest of the mining towns in the Slocan District, and Kaslo on Kootenay Lake. The company received a land grant from the province of 254,000 acres (102 780 ha). The main line from Kaslo to Sandon was 28.8 miles (46.4 km) long and was laid with 45 pound (18.6 kg/m) steel. In 1897, a three mile (4.5 km) branch line was built to the mining camp of Cody. Equipment consisted of several small wood-burning locomotives and about two dozen pieces of rolling stock. Because of the mountainous nature of the line and the heavy snowfalls that periodically closed the route, the K&S acquired a used rotary snow plow from the Rio Grande Southern in Colorado.

Competition between the two lines was fierce and led to one of the more amusing and bizarre incidents in the railroad history of southern British Columbia. In December 1895, a major dispute developed over terminal lands at Sandon. The CPR began building a station and yards on K&S property but the K&S gained an injunction to stop the work. Next, the CPR had the injunction overturned. However, the K&S had not given in and, after checking its legal position further,

One of the biggest mining developments in the Kootenays occurred in the Slocan district between the Columbia River and Kootenay Lake. Rich ore deposits led to the growth of many almost instant towns. The heart of the Slocan was Sandon, a frontier boom town if ever there was one. It became the focus for the development of both a CPR branch line and the narrow gauge Kaslo & Slocan. A CPR special is shown in the upper photo at Three Forks near Sandon. The locomotive is decorated for what appears to be Queen Victoria's Jubilee of 1897. The lower photo shows Sandon, during its heyday with a K&S train in the distance.

—MILTON PARENT COLLECTION; PAC, PA32203

proceeded to tear down the depot and remove the yard trackage while the CPR crews were away eating. "The spectacle," reported *The Kaslo Claim* on December 21, 1895, "of one railroad hitching to and dragging down with a locomotive the depot building of a rival road is an unusual one in any country, yet that is what the good people of Sandon witnessed last Tuesday afternoon...A large crowd gathered and cheered, all evidently in sympathy with the little road. No attempt was made to deter the men, but the C.P.R. officials made an effort to secure a warrant for the arrest of Supt. McGraw. Judge Sproat refused to issue a warrant, saying he thought the K&S people were right."

While the narrow gauge K&S was cheaper to build and to operate than the CPR's line into Sandon, the standard gauge CPR route offered significant advantages. Most importantly, the CPR could move loaded cars of ore and other freight directly onto barges for transport up and down the Arrow Lakes and connection with the main line. The narrow gauge cars from the K&S could not be operated over the standard gauge tracks to the south. All freight therefore had to be transferred by hand, costing time and money, at each end of the Kootenay Lake steamer route.

Steamer connections at Kaslo were provided by the C&KSN and a rival line, which, after some halting beginnings under other operators, became the International Navigation and Trading Company (IN&T) backed by the Great Northern. By 1896 there were several new, impressive steamers on Kootenay Lake including the C&KSN's fast and elegant *Kokanee*, and the IN&T's *Alberta* and *International*. Connecting the mining and agricultural communities on Kootenay Lake with Nelson and the railways, the steamers served as extensions of the branch line system that was gradually expanding into southeastern British Columbia. On the Columbia, other large and impressive vessels were added to the C&KSN fleet. However, since the C&KSN was an independent company, a critical link in the CPR's access to the district was not fully in its own control. This situation was rectified in 1896, when negotiations began between the CPR and the C&KSN for the purchase of the steamer fleet interests. The agreement was finalized late in 1896 and the purchase took effect in 1897. Expansion of the fleet followed quickly with the new stern-wheelers *Kootenay*, *Slocan* and *Rossland* being in service by the winter of 1897-98. The operations later were known as the British Columbia Lake and River Service.

With this purchase, the CPR was in a better position to control its own affairs in the area. At the same time, another branch line was built and opened for service in 1897. This one connected the southern end of Slocan Lake with the Columbia and Kootenay Railway at a point called Slocan Junction (later South Slocan), 12 miles (19 km) west of Nelson. There were important reasons for the construction of this branch. It provided direct rail access between Nelson, the major commercial centre in the area, and the growing Slocan Valley mining communities. *The Slocan City News* commented enthusiastically on May 29, 1897, shortly before the line was completed, "When the line from Slocan Crossing, 32 miles [51.5 km], is completed, travellers can leave Spokane in the morning and be in Slocan the same evening, a saving of a day and one half." But more importantly from the CPR's point of view, it provided a rail and steamer route between Nelson and Nakusp, via the Nakusp & Slocan Railway, that bypassed the narrows of the Columbia River between Upper and Lower Arrow Lakes. In the summer, the narrows were not a serious problem for navigation but during particularly low water periods and during the winter when ice would build up, steamer navigation could be brought to a halt. The resulting disruption of passenger, mail and freight services was a weak link in the CPR connections north with the main line at Revelstoke. While the new route via Slocan Lake could be blocked by ice, it was less subject to closure than the Columbia River and became the preferred routing during the winter months.

As the 1890s drew to a close, the pace of railroad development in the southern Interior of British Columbia accelerated. The next major focus of construction was Rossland, east of the Columbia River, and just north of the border with Washington. There, copper-silver-gold ores were first uncovered in 1890 on the eastern slopes of Red Mountain. As the prospects were explored and the extent of the deposits understood, development proceeded, with most of the capital coming from businessmen based in Spokane. Initially, the ores from the mines at Rossland were moved down to the Columbia by horseback or by horse and wagon, and then shipped south for smelting or, more directly, by wagon to Northport. Although growth of the mining industry in the region was slow during the early 1890s and was further dampened by the Depression of 1893, by 1895, claims were being staked at a furious rate. Rossland, at first a tent and shack town, then later a well-established city, was built among the mines. Clearly, however, if the potential of the deposits was to be realized, a more efficient system of transport — a railroad — was needed, as was a smelter.

Two developers and promoters, both Americans, became key figures in the construction of railroads to the Rossland mines at this time. One was Daniel Corbin of Spokane; the other was Frederick Augustus Heinze of Butte, Montana. Corbin had been interested in the Boundary district for some time and had built the Spokane Falls & Northern-Nelson & Fort Sheppard route between Spokane and Nelson. He was determined to build a connecting route between Northport on the SF&N and Rossland. This would provide a direct route for the rich ore to be moved south. His plans included a smelter at Northport. Because the route was an international one, two separate companies were established under different charters. The Washington section became the Columbia & Red Mountain Railway, while the British Columbia end was

The diminutive, narrow gauge Columbia & Western connected Trail on the Columbia with the rich mines of Rossland. The Le Roi Mine at Rossland developed from one of the most lucrative chalcopyrite (the copper also had traces of gold and silver) strikes in British Columbia. The Le Roi ultimately produced $30,000,000 before the Rossland mines closed in 1929. This photo captures the first train-load of ore from the Le Roi being readied for shipment. The small wooden hopper cars are lettered "CR&KR" presumably for the Columbia, Rossland & Kootenay or perhaps the Columbia River & Kootenay, neither of which was the real name of the railway. The Le Roi Mine is now part of the excellent Rossland Museum. —PAC, C7859

The steamer landing of Trail developed quickly into one of the most important cities in southeastern British Columbia. It served at first simply as the river port for the Rossland mines but, after a smelter was built on the bluffs above the townsite in 1895-96, Trail took on greater significance. This winter scene from the late 1890s shows the smelter in the distance with the city in the foreground. At the river's bank is the steamer *Lytton* with two barges. Note also the switchbacking narrow gauge tracks leading down to the landing. —COMINCO

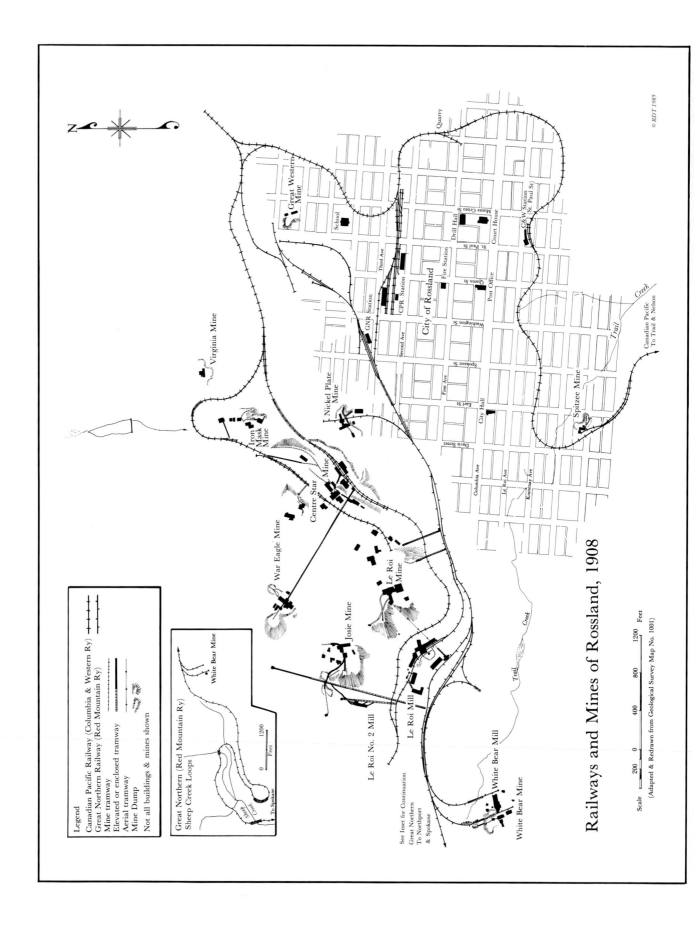

Railways and Mines of Rossland, 1908

(Adapted & Redrawn from Geological Survey Map No. 1001)

© RDT 1985

Legend
Canadian Pacific Railway (Columbia & Western Ry)
Great Northern Railway (Red Mountain Ry)
Mine tramway
Elevated or enclosed tramway
Aerial tramway
Mine Dump
Not all buildings & mines shown

Great Northern (Red Mountain Ry)
Sheep Creek Loops

Scale

| 200 | 0 | 400 | 800 | 1200 | Feet |

0   1200
Feet

White Bear Mine

To Spokane

Sheep Creek

Virginia Mine

Great Western Mine

School

Nickel Plate Mine

Iron Mask Mine

Centre Star Mine

War Eagle Mine

Josie Mine

Le Roi No. 2 Mill

See Inset for Continuation
Great Northern
To Northport
& Spokane

Le Roi Mill

White Bear Mill

White Bear Mine

Le Roi Mine

GNR Station

CPR Station

Fire Station

Third Ave

St. Paul St

Second Ave

Queen St

First Ave

Earl St

City Hall

Davis Street

Columbia Ave

Le Roi Ave

Kootenay Ave

Spokane Ave

Washington St

Post Office

Monte Cristo St

Court House

Drill Hall

City of Rossland

C&W Station
(St. Paul St)

Quarry

Spitzee Mine

Trail Creek

Canadian Pacific
To Trail & Nelson

Trail Creek

Sternwheelers were the key to early transportation south of the CPR main line and even the early railroads depended on them for supplies and critical connections to and from isolated areas. The Columbia & Western made use of the sternwheelers of the Columbia & Kootenay Steam Navigation Company to bring in all its materials, rolling stock and locomotives. Here, the *Trail* brings in a barge load of rolling stock (lettered CR&KRR) for the little narrow gauge line. The steamer also is pushing a barge of coal.
—PABC, HP1259

simply the Red Mountain Railway. Corbin was given a charter, but not a subsidy, by the British Columbia government over the opposition of the CPR and other Canadian interests, who argued that the line would take the profits south of the border.

Heinze, who owned a smelter in Butte, Montana, was brought to Trail in 1895 by Eugene S. Topping, one of the original owners of the first claim at Rossland, the owner of the Trail townsite and an enthusiastic promoter of Rossland-Trail. Young — just 25 — and energetic, Heinze quickly became a major figure in the district with expansive plans for development. A smelter site was laid out at Trail and Heinze proposed to build a refinery at Spokane to process the smelter matte.* Discussions were held with Corbin over use of his rail lines to take the matte to Spokane but Corbin's plans were not yet finalized. Heinze continued to implement his plans and obtained a contract to process ore from the rich and economically dominant Le Roi Mine. He was also given a government grant of timber for the smelter. With these in hand, he started construction on the smelter in late 1895. Still unable to reach an agreement with Corbin guaranteeing construction of the line to Spokane, Heinze cancelled his proposed refinery in Spokane and expanded his own railroad plans, no doubt hoping to gain a monopoly on the transport and smelting of Rossland ores. Initially, however, he had to build a line between the Le Roi Mine at Rossland and his smelter site on the Columbia River at Trail. Heinze was granted a provincial charter which provided a land grant of 11,200 acres per mile (about 2820 ha/km) of narrow gauge track constructed. Moreover, the charter gave Heinze permission to extend his line (standard gauge this time) all the way to Penticton and for that portion of his railroad he was offered 20,000 acres per mile (about 5030 ha/km).

Originally known as the Trail Creek Tramway, the 3-foot (0.91-m) gauge railway was opened as the Columbia & Western Railway in 1896. The little line was a primitive venture of light construction. The grade twisted and switch-backed its way up to Rossland over a 13.8-mile (22.2 km) route generally following the course of Trail Creek. The grade on tangents was 4 percent with curves compensated .04 percent per degree of curvature. There were 38 curves of 25 degrees and six of these turned 180 degrees or more. In addition, there were two switchbacks. Laid with extremely light rail of only 28 pounds per yard (13.9 kg per m) on six-foot (1.8-m) ties, the line was capable of handling only small,

* The process of converting ore to nearly pure metal is a complex one. The first stage, usually carried out near the mine site, is concentration, where the ore is crushed and rock removed. Chemical processes are also used to remove as much waste as possible in order to reduce transportation costs. Smelting further purifies the ore. Usually it is heated to high temperatures and, with the addition of limestone, more impurities are removed, producing the "matte." Refining, the final stage in purifying an ore, produces a nearly pure metal which can then be used in manufacturing.

low capacity rolling stock. Secondhand equipment was acquired from a variety of sources, including the Alberta Railway & Coal and the Utah & Northern. *Poor's Manual of Railroads* for 1897 (reflecting 1896 information) listed the following equipment on the line: 3 locomotives; 5 passenger cars; baggage and related, 2; freight, 40 and "others," 10 (for a total of 57 cars.)

Locomotives and rolling stock had to be delivered to Trail by steamer or barge and the routing was sometimes complicated. The Nelson *Miner* of November 28, 1896 noted that Thomas Brownlee, a C&W conductor, was in Nelson waiting to take two coaches to Robson so that they could be barged down to Trail. "The coaches will be transferred by barge from the N&FS road to the C&K and at Robson will again be loaded on barges and floated down to Trail.* One engine, six box cars and 14 flat cars were sent by boat from Northport to Trail but the coaches are too large to be loaded on the boat and as it is almost impossible to take a barge from Northport to Trail, the coaches had to be sent by way of Nelson."

While the little line may not have been particularly impressive, compared to the larger standard gauge railroads, it was given a warm welcome by the citizens of both Trail and Rossland. In service early in June 1896, it immediately became an important trade and travel route.

With the growing ore traffic and the boom in the district the company reported to *Poor's* that by December 1896, the profits of the line were $20,000 per month. The total investment was noted as being $250,000. While profits apparently were not sustained at that level, they remained significant and were reported for the fiscal year ending June 31, 1897 as $103,846 (net). These earnings were produced by moving 78,170 tons (79 420 tonnes) of freight which grossed $154,368. Passenger traffic grossed an additional $32,160.

Pleased with the success of his Rossland-Trail line, Heinze made grander plans that called for a standard gauge railway to connect Rossland-Trail with the Coast via Penticton under the Columbia & Western charter granted to him by the provincial government in 1896.† There were further difficulties with Dan Corbin over the initial routing, which crossed the line of the proposed Red Mountain Railway, and Heinze was forced to alter his plans somewhat. At the same time, however, his other business interests were in difficulty and Heinze found himself financially overextended. Just how serious Heinze was in his long range plans is open to question

---

* At this time there was no direct rail connection between the N&FS and the C&K at Nelson, nor was there a proper transfer slip at the N&FS terminal at Five Mile Point. The N&FS steamer dock comprised a single track built out into the lake so that, as the lake level rose and fell seasonally, passengers and freight could be transferred between the trains and the steamers. Moving the passenger cars onto barges would have been a difficult, but unavoidable, task.

† The charter provided for the construction of the C&W only as far west as Penticton.

Are You Going?
On Next Sunday's Excursion to Deer Park

The Rossland Coronet Band will give an excursion to Deer Park next Sunday and everyone in the district will be there with them. A special train on the C.& W. R. will leave Rossland at 7. am next Sunday, arriving at Trail at 7.45 where it will be met by the C.& K.S.N. Co's palatial steamer *Lytton* and the ride up the Columbia will begin at 8 o'clock sharp arriving at Deer Park at noon.

At Deer Park, the fun will properly commence. The bills announce that there will be a baseball game between Rossland and Trail teams for a purse of $150, foot-racing and out-of-door sports. Returning, the steamer will leave Deer Park at 6. pm and the down trip will be made in quick time.

The fare for the round trip will be $2 from Rossland and $1.50 from Trail. This is the cheapest rate ever known in Kootenay, and many will take advantage of the opportunity to visit the beautiful new townsite of Deer Park.

The Trail Creek News, June 12, 1896.

The narrow gauge Columbia & Western brought rail service to Rossland and greatly improved the economics of moving the rich ores for smelting. Its main limitation was the small capacity of its freight equipment. What it lacked in size, it more than made up in charm.
—COMINCO

The construction of the Red Mountain Railway and its connections through to Northport in Washington gave the Columbia & Western strong competition. The Red Mountain carried large quantities of valuable ore south for smelting since the interests controlling the Le Roi mine ultimately controlled the Northport smelter as well. This is an early view on the line to Rossland. —BURLINGTON NORTHERN

but he began construction on the first section of standard gauge line in 1897. Following the west bank of the Columbia, this line ran north from Trail to a point (later known as Robson West) just opposite Robson for a distance of 21.5 miles (34.6 km). Robson was the terminus of the CPR's Columbia & Kootenay and the principal landing for the steamboats operating north to connections with the CPR main line. Heinze had, in effect, tied his smelter and railways into the CPR system by the most direct route available and in 1898 he was negotiating the sale of his holdings and the C&W charter with the CPR. The standard gauge line was opened for traffic on October 27, 1897 with most equipment leased from the CPR.

The bargaining was tough with the CPR represented by Walter Aldridge, a capable mining engineer. From Heinze's initial offering at $2,000,000, a price of $600,000 was finally agreed to for the C&W itself, and about 270,000 acres (nearly 110 000 ha) of land (one half of its land grant) plus $200,000 for the smelter (actually the interests of the British Columbia Smelting and Refining Company). At the time, the CPR was not particularly interested in acquiring the smelter but in later years it was to prove a very worthwhile acquisition. The agreement was finalized on February 11, 1898, and the CPR found itself with a new branch line directly connected to one of the most lucrative mining areas in British Columbia, as well as a smelter and a key charter to extend its influence to the west. With its recently acquired steamer operations on the Columbia River and on Kootenay Lake, the CPR had vastly expanded its influence into the southernmost parts of the province.

Before proceeding with the story of CPR expansion along the southern boundary of British Columbia, we must return to Dan Corbin and his lines from the south. Corbin had not pushed construction of his route to Rossland but after unsuccessfully trying to have his charter amended to allow narrow gauge construction and other concessions, he forged ahead. Working under the supervision of Edward J. Roberts, Corbin's crews completed the line in December 1896, after working through the mountains in rough winter conditions. The railway was laid with 56-pound rail (27.8 km/m) and was dominated by curves for over half its route. The grade averaged 2.75 percent.

Initially, cars had to be ferried across the Columbia to Northport until a steel bridge could be completed. It was finished in October 1897. With the Columbia & Red Mountain finally joined to the Spokane Falls & Northern, the mines of Rossland had a direct connection with Spokane by the railroad and the economic link that already existed was greatly reinforced. While the rail link was proceeding, work also began on the smelter at Northport, financed largely by the interests controlling the Le Roi mine. At the same time, Heinze enlarged his facility at Trail. However, Corbin offered particularly attractive rates over his lines to the Northport smelter and when it was opened on January 1, 1898, it was in an advantageous position and drew off most of the ore from the American controlled mines at Rossland.

Spokane was the business centre for the mining and industrial development that was proceeding in the Rossland area at this time. With the completion of the railway and improving economic conditions generally, both Rossland and Spokane boomed. It was not just the ore traffic that resulted in this joint prosperity but the cumulative effect of all of the related requirements of mining, including coke, coal and limestone for smelting, materials for construction, machinery, food, clothing, household items, and a multitude of other products that went along with a rapidly expanding industry and population in the Rossland area. Production at the mines doubled and doubled again.

Production from the Rossland Mines 1894-99

	Tons of Ore (Tonnes)		Value
1894	1,856	(1684)	$75,510
1895	19,693	(17865)	702,359
1896	38,075	(34542)	1,243,360
1897	68,804	(62419)	2,097,280
1898	111,282	(100955)	2,470,811
1899	172,665	(156664)	3,229,086

Source: Report of the Minister of Mines (1895-1900).

The mines were producing a variety of ores yielding gold, silver and copper. In 1899, for example, the Rossland mines produced: 102,976 ounces (2919 kg) of gold valued at $2,127,482; 185,818 ounces (5268 kg) of silver valued at $105,173; and 5,693,889 pounds (2 582 748 kg) of copper worth just under $1,000,000. It was little wonder that the prosperity of the mining district seemed limitless.

The spirit of enthusiasm for the boom is captured in an editorial from *The Trail Creek News* of June 19, 1896:

Tonnage in Trail Creek

It is marvelous—the amount of tonnage arriving at Trail this spring, with three steamers running into Trail, yet the C. & K.S.N. Co. cannot keep the consignments of freight to Trail Creek cleaned up.

In two days of last week, the steamers of the C. & K.S.N. Co. landed in Trail 500 tons of coal, coke, lime rock and general merchandise. Every day sees the steamers of this company in Trail, loaded down to their full capacity. Yesterday the steamers "Nakusp", "Trail" and "Lytton", and the train of the Columbia & Western Railway were all in Trail at one time, and the aggregate number of passengers served by the three boats and the train was over 400, while the tonnage handled in that day amounted to over 250 tons. And this is a town not yet a year old, and the season has just begun.

Through the mid-1890s, control of the major mines at Rossland was largely in the hands of Americans, but by 1898,

The Great Northern acquired control of Dan Corbin's lines into British Columbia and became a major factor in railroad development across the southern districts of the province. The GN brought needed capital and new equipment to the lines. In this winter scene at Rossland No. 471 leads an ore train.
—W. GIBSON KENNEDY COLLECTION

The Red Mountain Railway climbed to Nelson from the west up through the valley of Sheep Creek by a series of spectacular loops. The line reached Rossland in December 1896.
—BURLINGTON NORTHERN

Rossland with its mines was a key centre of mining activity in the 1890s. Its appearance was typical of the towns that developed over and around a rich deposit of ore. A Red Mountain train is stopped at the station in the foreground.

The cars are lettered "Spokane Falls and Northern Railway" for Corbin's major line to the south. —W. GIBSON KENNEDY COLLECTION

Canadian and British capital began to take over, as the CPR purchase of Heinze's interests demonstrated.

The details of these developments go well beyond the story of the railroads in the region. In general terms, however, the influence of American business in the district had been greatly reduced by the early 1900s, but the rivalry for rail access to the southern districts of British Columbia continued. The story is complicated by politics, promises and many speculative ventures that led to railway charters. In 1897, a charter was granted by the British Columbia government giving authority for the Vancouver, Victoria & Eastern Railway & Navigation Company (VV&E) to build a Coast-to-Kootenay (Rossland) line that would provide a short, direct route from the West to the new mining districts.

Originally promoted by William Mackenzie and Donald Mann, in 1901 the charter of the VV&E came under the control of the Great Northern Railway. This left the whole of southern British Columbia from the Boundary district through to the Coast open to serious competition from the American transcontinental. Coupled with GN incursions to the east, it became clear that the CPR was not to have a monopoly along the Canadian-American border.

Previously, in 1898, after a complicated misunderstanding, the Spokane Falls & Northern also had been acquired by the Great Northern. As a result, the important routes to Nelson and Rossland came under the control of a major American line. Of particular importance, the line was controlled by James J. Hill, formerly with the CPR but in the 1890s, throwing all of his considerable energies into his own lines. His GN, completed to the Pacific Coast at Seattle in 1893, was coming into increasing competition with the CPR over traffic in the Mid-west as well as transcontinental business and it soon became clear that the Kootenays were to become another focus of rivalry between the two companies.

Great Northern interest in southern British Columbia was not limited just to the Nelson-Rossland area. In the late 1890s, it began what was to become a significant expansion into the Kootenays, the Boundary district, the Crowsnest Pass and the coast region. By World War I, the Great Northern, operating under a number of subsidiaries, had established a route that crisscrossed the British Coumbia border 12 times and formed what became known as the GN's third main line.

The beautiful sternwheeler *Kokanee* was one of the vessels in the fleet of the Columbia & Kootenay Steam Navigation Company that was acquired by the CPR in 1896-97. The sternwheelers provided important feeder services and links in the rail routes. To be its own master, the CPR needed to own these services in the Kootenays, particularly with its major plans for expansion. The *Kokanee* was built at Nelson in 1896 and is shown above on a beautifully calm afternoon nearing Kaslo. —PABC, HP1641

Through the Crowsnest Pass and West to Kootenay Lake Country

Crossing British Columbia as it did several hundred miles north of the American border, the CPR was at a decided disadvantage in reaching the developing mining, farming and lumbering areas in the Kootenays and Boundary district of the province. Over the years, pressure had increased for the construction of a Canadian route across the southern regions of the province. The CPR had taken slow steps in this direction with the construction of the railroads between

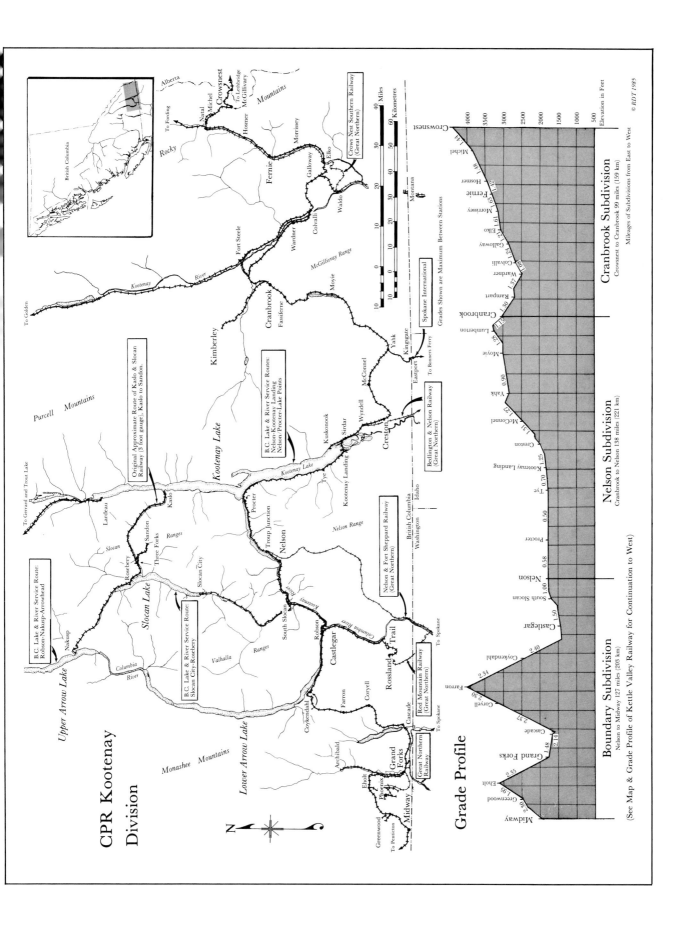

CPR Kootenay Division

B.C. Lake & River Service Route:
Robson-Nakusp-Arrowhead

B.C. Lake & River Service Route:
Slocan City-Rosebery

Original Approximate Route of Kaslo & Slocan
Railway (3 foot gauge), Kaslo to Sandon.

B.C. Lake & River Service Routes:
Nelson-Kootenay Landing
Nelson/Procter-Lake Points

Bedlington & Nelson Railway
(Great Northern)

Nelson & Fort Sheppard Railway
(Great Northern)

Red Mountain Railway
(Great Northern)

Great Northern
Railway

Crows Nest Southern Railway
(Great Northern)

Spokane International

Grades Shown are Maximum Between Stations

© RDT 1985

Grade Profile

Boundary Subdivision
Nelson to Midway 127 miles (205 km)

Nelson Subdivision
Cranbrook to Nelson 138 miles (221 km)

Cranbrook Subdivision
Crowsnest to Cranbrook 99 miles (159 km)

Mileages of Subdivisions from East to West

(See Map & Grade Profile of Kettle Valley Railway for Continuation to West)

Elevation in Feet

The opening of the CPR line through Crowsnest Pass in 1898 brought a major change to the traffic patterns of the area. An entirely new east-west connection was available. The line through the Rockies was much easier to construct than the original main line had been. The most interesting feature was the loops, shown here, west of the summit as the tracks descended the slopes to the Elk River. The train is a four-car, westbound passenger train that will run as far as Kootenay Landing. —GLENBOW MUSEUM, NA 3490.77

116

The *Rossland* was one of the first new steamers added to the CPR's fleet, later known as the British Columbia Lake & River Service. Built as an express passenger vessel for the Columbia River route, the *Rossland* could steam at over 20 miles (32 km) per hour. This photo shows her after being reconstructed in 1910. —PABC, HP738

Crossing the Columbia at Wardner required a major bridge composed of Howe truss spans. In this photograph, workmen are repairing the structure as a westbound train approaches the span. —BCPM

Robson and Nelson and the line connecting Nakusp with the Slocan district. However, it was not until 1896 that the company's *Annual Report* revealed the real extent of CPR plans. It was then that the company announced it had negotiated the purchase of the Columbia and Kootenay Steam Navigation Company fleet (the sale to take effect early in 1897) and more importantly its determination to expand westward from the prairies through the Crowsnest Pass.*

The *Annual Report* noted that:

Your Company will continue at a disadvantage in competing with the American lines (which have already reached Nelson, Rossland and other important centres in these districts) until it shall have direct railway connections of its own. Until then the greater part of the mining traffic will be beyond its reach, and will continue to be as at present, carried by the American lines southward.

Your Directors are strongly of the opinion that any delay in securing your interests in that direction will be extremely danger-ous, — that unless your Company occupies the ground others will, the demand for shipping and travelling facilities being most urgent. The Directors feel that they cannot too strongly urge the immediate construction of a line from Lethbridge to a connection with your Columbia & Kootenay Railway at Nelson, a distance of 325 miles, and anticipating your approval they have already taken steps towards commencement of the work on the opening of spring...

The interests of the country *are large* and so much concerned in this question that your Directors confidently expect reasonable assistance at the hands of the Dominion Government.

The CPR was not to be disappointed in its assistance from the federal government and the province had already com-mitted itself to the project through the charter of the British Columbia Southern Railway (BCS) which the CPR acquired. The federal subsidy was for $11,000 per mile, with the total not to exceed $3,630,000, while the province contributed (via the B.C. Southern charter agreement) a land grant totalling about 3,350,000 acres (1 356 000 ha) all of which was not taxable until leased or alienated. The final settlement from the federal government was, however, a complex one, known as the Crow's Nest Pass Agreement, which, while providing the cash subsidy for the line, imposed many restrictions on rates for a number of commodities, particularly grain, so important to the economy of the developing prairies. At the time, the new rate restrictions resulted in significant reduc-tions but still provided a profit margin for the CPR. The flaw in the legislation, from the CPR's point of view, if not anyone else's, was that no time frame was specified for the rates to remain in effect and it was interpreted that they should remain in effect forever. But later, as inflation and other cost factors increased, the "Crow Rates" were to be a growing point of contention between the CPR, the federal government and shippers. It would not be until the early 1980s that a new arrangement for freight rates and subsidies for western grain would be developed.

* In many early documents, the name of the pass is spelled Crow's Nest or Crows Nest.

117

Another party in the Crowsnest line agreements was the Kootenay Coal Company which owned large blocks of coal land in the pass. This company acquired all of the coal bearing lands in the BCS land grant except for a block of 3,840 acres (1554 ha) which the CPR was to retain and 50,000 acres (20 235 ha) transferred to the federal government. The CPR's coal lands were, in the words of the 1897 *Annual Report* "quite sufficient for the protection of the public as well as the Company, if need be, against unduly high prices."

The Crowsnest coal fields, situated on either side of the Crowsnest Pass were highly significant attraction of the route. The immense coal deposits, with aggregate thicknesses of 125 feet (38 m) or more, and readily mined, were to develop into one of the most important mining areas of the province. They would provide a readily available source of coal for the CPR as well as being a key component of industrial expansion. The already rapid industrial development of British Columbia provided a ready market for both coal and coke as did Canadian and American markets to the east and south.

The construction of the line west from Lethbridge through the Crowsnest Pass proceeded rapidly during 1897 and 1898. The grade, compared to the main line to the north, was much easier. East of the pass, in Alberta, the line climbed up an easy grade that averaged less than 0.4 percent. The maximum grade of 2.2 percent was a short section between Macleod and Sentinel. Overall, the construction, except for major bridges, was uncomplicated. West of the pass, the grades were steeper on average but still moderate. Descending from the pass to the west, the line averaged just under one percent with the maximum grade of 1.3 percent located between Mile 63.3 and Mile 65.5. To maintain the slow descent from the summit a large loop was required just west of the summit, in the Michel Creek Valley. McGillivray station, named after Donald McGillivray, one of the engineer-contractors working on the line, was situated on the loop. From there, the line descended towards the Kootenay River following Michel Creek and the Elk River. With the grade out of the mountains completed, construction through the Kootenay Valley was easier, but to avoid heavy mountain construction westwards, the tracks were taken north to Cranbrook and then southwest, past Moyie Lake to Yahk just a short distance north of the Idaho border. From there the tracks proceeded west through to Creston near the flat lands where the Kootenay River flows into Kootenay Lake. Just north of Creston, however, the tracks terminated at Kootenay Lake at a station called Kootenay Landing. The total distance from the summit of the pass to Kootenay Landing was nearly 182 miles (292 km). In British Columbia, divisional facilities for the operation of the line and maintenance of the equipment were established at Cranbrook and Crowsnest.

At Kootenay Landing, steamer docks and a railcar transfer slip were constructed forming a temporary terminal for the line. The tracks were not built through to Nelson because of

Kootenay Landing was the end of the line because railroad construction along Kootenay Lake would have been extremely expensive. Sternwheelers met the trains to carry passengers and mail to Nelson. The steamer shown is the *Moyie*, built in 1898, and in the background is a tug, the *Ymir*, and a barge used to move freight cars. —PABC, HP1624

The tug and barge service on Kootenay Lake was a major feature of CPR's rail operations in the Kootenays. In 1901, tracks were extended from Nelson east to Procter, reducing the length of the tug and barge service and freeing the operation from the problems of occasional ice on Kootenay Lake's West Arm. Here, a tug nears Procter with two transfer barges. The photo shows the CPR's Kootenay Lake Hotel in the distance. —COMINCO

the costs that would have been involved in blasting a right-of-way along the rugged, precipitous shoreline of Kootenay Lake to the mouth of its West Arm at Procter. The gap was originally 55 miles (88 km) long, but in 1900, the tracks were extended east from Nelson, 20.5 miles (33 km) to Procter. This short addition bypassed the West Arm of Kootenay Lake which, during bad winters, was particularly susceptible to ice accumulations sufficient to bring the railway barge services and passenger steamers to a halt.

Actual track construction was completed on October 7, 1898 and an inaugural excursion was operated on December 7, 1898 for city council representatives, members of the Chambers of Commerce and other dignitaries from Nelson and the other important communities of the West Kootenays. A new sternwheeler, the *Moyie*, just completed at the Nelson shipyard, was used on the excursion. With receptions and banquets held en route, the guests were treated to a firsthand look at the new line, and the new steamer. For the people in the once comparatively isolated communities of the region, the new rail line suggested permanence, prosperity, access to the world for their products and better mail, passenger and freight service from the rest of Canada.

Construction had been relatively easy, but there had been other serious problems. Labour conditions for the workers on the contracts had been appalling, sufficiently so that a commission was appointed by the federal government to review the situation. The reports revealed low wages, poor food and accommodations and many other problems with the subcontracts. The labourers had clearly been taken advantage of and there were ongoing problems of illegal liquor, gambling and prostitution.

Rebuilding and Extending the Columbia & Western

While work was progressing to a conclusion on the Crowsnest line, the CPR expansion into southern British Columbia also proceeded west of the Columbia River towards the Boundary district. The *Annual Report* for 1897 (prepared in 1898 after the negotiations with Heinze were finalized) noted:

... that the interests of your Company may be protected in Southern British Columbia, it is necessary to move on westward from the Columbia River at Robson, the western end of your line, so as to reach the Boundary Creek District — about 100 miles — during the present year... The opening of mines in the Boundary Creek district has been retarded by the lack of transportation facilities, but the mineral deposits have been proven to an extent sufficient to justify the belief that this is the richest district yet discovered in the Province.

West of the Columbia, the most immediate problem was rebuilding the narrow gauge line between Trail and Rossland and beginning the extension of the standard gauge section of the Columbia & Western from Robson westward towards Grand Forks and the Boundary district. The little narrow gauge line had operated at a profit during its brief, three-year career, and there had not been a single passenger or employee fatality, but it was totally inadequate for the anticipated growth in traffic in the district. Since the difference in gauge also made it necessary to reload any through freight, it was obvious that the line needed to be reconstructed to standard gauge. The only real complication in the work was that it had to be carried out without interrupting the flow of traffic to and from Rossland.

The work began in August, 1898 and required laying out and grading what amounted to a new railroad. The original line, with its light rail and low standard of construction, was suitable for widening and improving over only limited parts of the route. Grading and bridging work, under contract to Winters, Parsons & Boomer, was completed in the fall of 1898, but an early winter delayed completion of the conversion to standard gauge until the following spring. Grades on the line remained a problem and even after reconstruction, a 4.6 percent maximum grade remained. All of the 25 degree curves were removed, with the curvature reduced to 20 degrees, and the Tiger switchback, was relocated with a single loop at the upper switch and a complete spiral at the lower. Even this change did not eliminate all switchback operation and the trains still had to reverse directions twice on the climb up the Trail Creek Valley. On the curves, which were still tight by main line standards, the gauge was widened by one inch (2.54 cm) and the outer rail was superelevated (raised) one inch. These changes in track standards helped locomotives and cars ease through the tight curves. Many bridges were eliminated and the remaining structures were strengthened to take the heavier standard gauge traffic. A one half mile long spur was added to the Centre Star and War Eagle mines and a new terminal and passenger station was built at Rossland.

The next spring, tracklaying by the company's own crews began under the supervision of Superintendent F. P. Gutelius, who had also overseen the construction of the original line for Heinze. The line was laid with 60-pound (29.8 kg/m) steel, replacing the original 28-pound (13.9 kg/m) rail. Track work was carried out during the day while traffic was operated over the line at night. The crews worked quickly and were able to re-lay as much as 3,800 feet (1160 m) in a day. With the new track in place, a third rail was laid, temporarily spiked down and connected to the old line to permit traffic to continue moving at night.

On June 14, all of the standard gauge line was in place except for the switches which were still narrow gauge. On the 15th, Roadmaster Sullivan divided the crew of 100 men into six gangs and between 7:00 am and 1:00 pm, the standard gauge switches were installed. The narrow gauge equipment was stored in the smelter yard and at 1:00 that afternoon, the first passenger train from Smelter Junction left for Rossland where it arrived two hours later. The train was made up of a CPR 2-8-0, and two passenger cars. Speeds on the line were to

A loaded ore train stops for water on the rebuilt Columbia & Western connecting Rossland with Trail. The original narrow gauge line was insufficient for the volume of traffic to and from Rossland. Converting the line to standard gauge also eliminated the costly transfer of freight to and from the narrow gauge equipment.
—W. GIBSON KENNEDY COLLECTION

A major obstacle for the construction crews in building the Columbia & Western to the Boundary mines was the crossing of the Kettle River at Cascade east of Grand Forks. The curved trestle is shown under construction. The view is looking towards the west.—COMINCO

The reconstructed Columbia & Western still posed formidable operating problems for the CPR. The steep grades taxed the capacity of any locomotive and prompted the CPR to acquire its first Shay in 1901. Designed for mining and logging service, the locomotive could outpull any conventional engine on the grades. Two others were acquired and used on the Kootenay mining branches but the CPR preferred the flexibility of using its standard locomotives and did not order more Shays.
—COMINCO

be restricted for safety: passenger trains to 12 miles (19 km) per hour; freights to 8 miles (13 km) per hour. With the completion of the work, Rossland was provided with direct rail access, without break-in-bulk (reloading) of freight through to Nelson and, via the ferry service on Kootenay Lake, to the new line over the Crowsnest and on to the East.*

While the work of rebuilding the Rossland-Trail line was in progress, preparations were being made to extend the tracks to the west and the Boundary district. The contract for the line was awarded to the firm of Mann, Foley Bros., & Larson on June 4, 1898. Within days the work had begun and the labour force soon grew to 5,000 men surveying, clearing, grading, blasting and, eventually, laying track. Work on this line was heavy and the grades much tougher than on the new Crowsnest line to the east. From Robson West, just north of the present city of Castlegar, the tracks began a stiff climb above the west shoreline of Lower Arrow Lake. Swinging south, away from the lake, to follow the course of Dog Creek, the tracks climbed upward to the summit at Farron. The grade averaged 1.9 percent and at maximum reached 2.4 percent. West of the summit, all the way down to Cascade where the tracks crossed over the Kettle River on a magnificent wooden trestle, the grade was as steep as the eastern climb had been.

West of Cascade, the line followed an easy route through rolling valley lands, rich for agriculture, to Grand Forks. But from Grand Forks west, the route once again climbed steeply over the mountains to reach Greenwood, where mining development was proceeding rapidly, and Midway at the end of track 100 miles (160 km) west of Castlegar. To reach Greenwood, the route swung north permitting the tracks to cross the mountains through Eholt Pass. It was a steep climb; the grade averaged 1.83 percent and reached a maximum of 2.4 percent. To the west of the pass, the grades were almost as steep averaging 1.25 percent and reaching a 2.3 percent maximum descending grade between Greenwood and Midway.

The greatest obstacle on the entire route was Bulldog tunnel, approximately 25 miles (40 km) west of Castlegar, and just east of the summit. The bore was 2,991 feet (912 m) long, and took from late 1898 until mid-1900 to complete. As an interim measure, to permit operation of the line and to move construction materials west, a series of switchbacks was built—five on the west side and six on the east side of the mountain through which the tunnel was driven. The grade on the switchbacks was 4.0 percent, uncompensated on the curves, and the curves were 22 degrees. While most of the heavy rock work on the railroad was done by hand, an air compressor plant was ordered by McLean Bros., subcontractors for the tunnel work, and taken to the tunnel to facilitate

* Until March 1902, when the Columbia was bridged at Castlegar, cars were ferried across the river causing some delay in shipments.

The expansion of the Columbia & Western to the Boundary District brought the CPR to the mining centres of Grand Forks, Phoenix and Greenwood. The Granby smelter at Grand Forks was a major source of traffic. These two photos show CPR trains crossing over the Granby dam. Both photos are from about 1900 but the view below probably pre-dates the scene at left. Note that the deck truss span is enclosed at left. Both locomotives are 2-8-0s and the trains are composed mainly of wooden ore cars.
—PABC, HP44089; VPL 2372

Crossing the Columbia at Robson required this major structure completed in 1902. The span at right turned on the circular masonry column to permit steamer navigation regardless of the height of water under the bridge. The vessel behind the bridge is the *Lytton*, used during the construction of the bridge to ferry rail cars back and forth across the river. —CVA, CANP174

Eholt, at the summit of the grade between Grand Forks and Greenwood, was the junction point with the branch line leading to the mines at Phoenix to the south. The locomotive is the CPR's second Shay, No. 1902, which was used on the line. —PABC, HP51803

the work. Three weeks were required to make the steam plant and compressors operational but, once working, the system was able to supply air for seven drills at each end of the tunnel. Another machine McLean Bros. brought in to speed the work on their subcontracts was a steam powered scraper, reportedly the first of its kind manufactured and for which they received a patent. Operated by a single 35 hp. donkey boiler, the machine was capable of handling three cubic yards (2.3 m³) of gravel at a time.

Work on the tunnel was slow and expensive. McLean Bros. gave up the contract and it was taken over by O. Olson, who employed a gang of 120 men on the project. Elsewhere on the line, construction proceeded rapidly with the tracks reaching Cascade in August 1899. Through the mountains, the line was laid with 73-pound rail (36.2 kg/m), while to the west of Cascade, lighter steel was used.

Commenting on the line in September 1900, CPR president Shaughnessy noted that, "this road is by all means the most expensive the CPR has ever constructed. The country throughout the entire distance is exceedingly difficult, and the engineering difficulties very great. The entire route has cost the Company in the neighbourhood of $40,000 a mile, or a total expenditure of nearly $4,000,000 for 100 miles of line."

Meanwhile, contracts had been let for the construction of branch lines to reach the most important developing mining areas in the mountains west of Grand Forks. From Eholt, at the summit of the grade between Grand Forks and Midway, a branch line with several spurs was built south to the mines in the vicinity of Phoenix and from Greenwood, a six-mile (9.6-km) line was extended northwest to Deadwood Camp. These lines became important sources of traffic for the new route west of the Columbia.

The new mining branches required powerful locomotives, suited to the heavy grades both at Rossland and in the Grand Forks area. The solution for the mining trains came in the form of Shay locomotives. These were a type of locomotive developed for logging and mining railroads and built by the Lima Locomotive Works of Lima, Ohio. These were particularly powerful locomotives and able to pull exceptionally heavy loads on steep grades. However, they were handicapped by low speed.

For the CPR, Shays appeared to provide the answer to the problem of moving empty trains of ore cars between the smelter at Trail and the mines at Rossland. Similarly, they were to be useful on the grades at Phoenix and also on the Mother Lode branch line from Greenwood. The first of the locomotives, No. 111 (Lima No. 612, outshopped August 9, 1900), arrived in Rossland in May 1901, and was placed in service on the ore trains. For its time, this Shay was a large locomotive and weighed in at 112 tons (113.8 tonnes) in working order. At the time it was one of the largest Shays yet built and the most powerful locomotive in the CPR roster, exceeding in size the 2-8-0s built for the main line. By virtue of

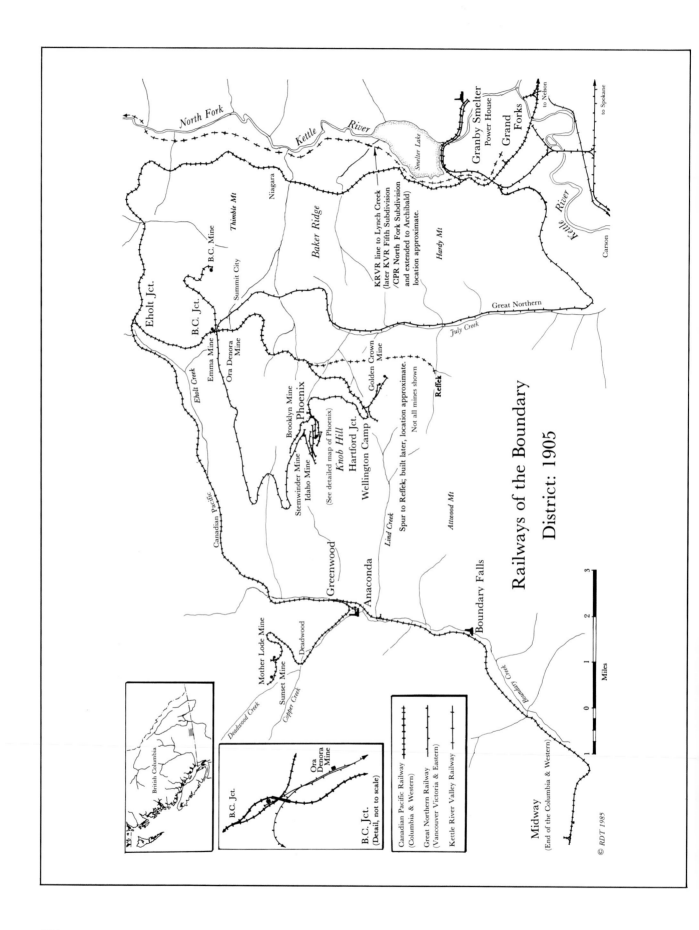

Railways of the Boundary District: 1905

North Fork

Kettle River

Smelter Lake

Granby Smelter
Power House
Grand Forks

to Nelson

to Spokane

Kettle River

Carson

Niagara

Thimble Mt

Baker Ridge

KRVR line to Lynch Creek
(later KVR Fifth Subdivision
/CPR North Fork Subdivision
and extended to Archibald)
location approximate.

Hardy Mt

B.C. Mine

Summit City

Eholt Jct.

B.C. Jct.

Emma Mine

Eholt Creek

Ora Denora Mine

Great Northern

July Creek

Brooklyn Mine

Phoenix

Golden Crown Mine

Reflex

Knob Hill

Hartford Jct.

(See detailed map of Phoenix)

Stemwinder Mine

Idaho Mine

Wellington Camp

Canadian Pacific

Lind Creek

Spur to Reflex; built later, location approximate.
Not all mines shown

Attwood Mt

Greenwood

Anaconda

Boundary Falls

Mother Lode Mine

Deadwood

Sunset Mine

Copper Creek

Deadwood Creek

Boundary Creek

British Columbia

B.C. Jct.

Ora Denora Mine

B.C. Jct.
(Detail, not to scale)

Canadian Pacific Railway
(Columbia & Western)

Great Northern Railway
(Vancouver Victoria & Eastern)

Kettle River Valley Railway

Midway
(End of the Columbia & Western)

3

2

1

0

Miles

© RDT 1985

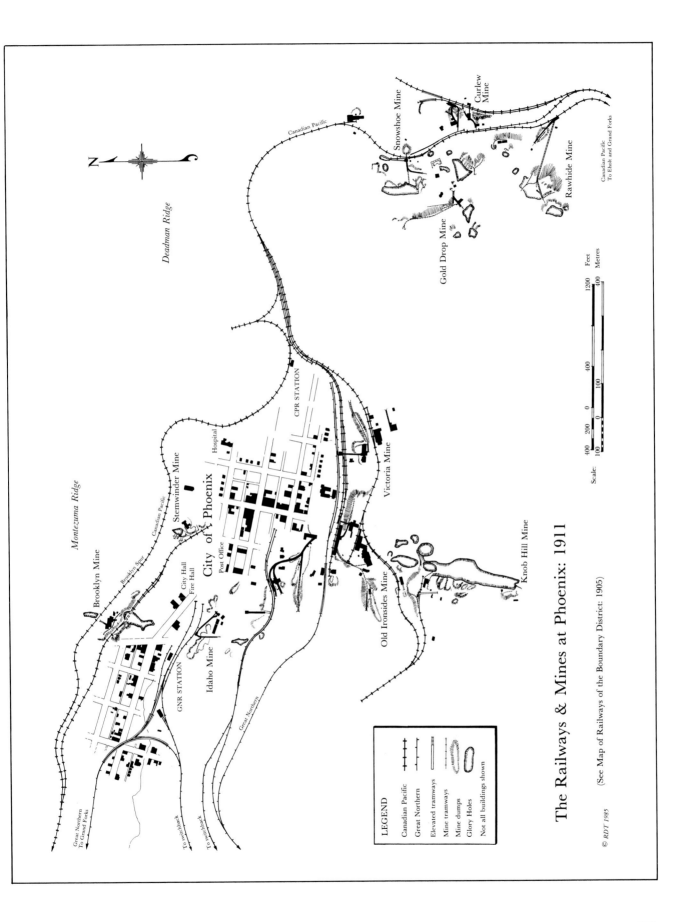

The Railways & Mines at Phoenix: 1911

(See Map of Railways of the Boundary District: 1905)

© RDT 1985

LEGEND

Canadian Pacific
Great Northern
Elevated tramways
Mine tramways
Mine dumps
Glory Holes
Not all buildings shown

Scale:

Feet
Metres

Montezuma Ridge

Deadman Ridge

Brooklyn Mine

Brooklyn Spur

Canadian Pacific

Sternwinder Mine

City Hall
Fire Hall

GNR STATION

Idaho Mine

Great Northern
To Grand Forks

To switchback

To switchback

Great Northern

City of Phoenix

Post Office

Hospital

CPR STATION

Canadian Pacific

Victoria Mine

Old Ironsides Mine

Knob Hill Mine

Snowshoe Mine

Gold Drop Mine

Curlew Mine

Rawhide Mine

Canadian Pacific
To Eholt and Grand Forks

The economic development of ores was closely tied to the availability of smelters, and the rich copper ores of the Boundary mines attracted enough investment to secure nearby smelters. Major plants were built at Greenwood (owned by the B.C. Copper Company and shown at left), Boundary Falls and at Grand Forks. —PABC, HP82575

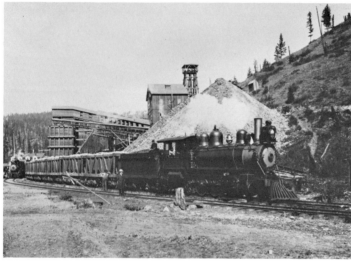

Ore trains are loaded at the Mother Lode Mine at the end of a short branch line running to the west of Greenwood. —NOTMAN PHOTO, VPL 1782

The mines of Phoenix spread across the mountains as rich deposits of ore were recovered. The town itself grew up between the mines and the rail lines. —W. J. CARPENTER, COMINCO

Phoenix

The town of Phoenix was once one of the busiest boom towns of southern British Columbia and was served by both Canadian Pacific and Great Northern branch lines. But the fortunes of any mining town are fickle. Eventually, the mines closed and both the CPR and GN abandoned their lines. However the mines did reopen and in the end the whole townsite of Phoenix disappeared as open pit mining worked through the remaining deposits. The town of Phoenix, itself a product of the mines, passed with them.

The GN's line to Phoenix from Grand Forks climbed steeply out of the rich, fertile valley of the Kettle River. Here, two GN locomotives labour mightily to drag an empty ore train up to the Phoenix mines. This grade, now long-abandoned, remains clearly visible west of Grand Forks. —PABC, HP44087

A mixed train at the CPR station at Phoenix.
—W. GIBSON KENNEDY COLLECTION

its design, the Shay could pull twice the loads uphill that one of the 2-8-0s could, but it was slower. The use of the first Shay at Rossland was of sufficient interest for it to be featured in *Scientific American* in August 1901.

Two other Shays (Lima Nos. 689 and 824) were ordered for this type of service. The second (CPR No. 112, later No. 1902) arrived in 1902 and the third (CPR No. 1903, later No. 5903) the following year. Despite their advantages on the steep grades, they were unusual locomotives requiring extra spare parts and when larger conventional locomotives became available, the Shays were no longer required. The last of the CPR's three Shays was scrapped in 1920.

*   *   *

In just ten years, the CPR had expanded its operations in British Columbia dramatically. A rail line had penetrated the southern parts of the province from the Crowsnest Pass in the Rockies to Midway, half way to the coast, and branch lines reached nearly all of the important mining districts. Another branch reached the head of Okanagan Lake, and CPR steamships operated on the Columbia River, and on Okanagan, Kootenay and Slocan lakes. But the expansion was not yet complete; the route through to the coast from Midway, across the Cascade Mountains and the other formidable ranges, remained to be built. However, despite almost continuous agitation from business interests and the public for the line to be built, it was 10 years before work began on the route. In the meantime the Great Northern had made significant advances into the region. Competition once again seems to have forced the CPR's hand in starting construction.

By the late 1890s, the Great Northern was exerting an increasing influence along the southern border of British Columbia. GN lines penetrated the Lower Mainland and would soon reach Vancouver, branch lines ran to both Rossland and Nelson and the GN controlled the Kaslo & Slocan and operated several large sternwheelers on Kootenay Lake under the title of the International Navigation and Trading Company (IN&T). The story of GN expansion is complex and involves a collage of Canadian and American charters.

In 1898, the GN began to consolidate its position in the Kootenay Lake region by forming the Kootenay Railway & Navigation Company (KR&N). This new company was incorporated in England with H. W. Forster, MP, chairman. The KR&N officially took over the operations of the K&S and the Kootenay Lake sternwheelers of the IN&T the following year. In addition, it built a branch line north from Bonners Ferry to Kuskonook on Kootenay Lake. This line, built under the charters of the Kootenai Valley Railway in Idaho and the Bedlington & Nelson in British Columbia, was intended to provide a connection between Bonners Ferry and

Great Northern steamers, operating under the Kootenay Railway & Navigation Company, ran between Nelson, Kaslo, Kuskonook and way points and competed directly with the CPR for traffic. Two of the vessels were the *International*, shown above right with an excursion crowd at Kaslo, and the beautiful *Kaslo*, the pride of the GN fleet, shown below, backing out into Kootenay Lake on a crisp winter day.
—PABC, HP1575, HP1547

The Great Northern Expands in Southern British Columbia

the GN's steamboats which in turn served the Kaslo & Slocan Railway and Nelson and the nearby mining districts. The line presented few construction problems and, to save duplicate construction, used CPR trackage between Wyndell and Sirdar Junction just south of Kootenay Lake. A terminal and steamer dock was built at Kuskonook and the line opened for service in 1900.

To complement the service, a new sternwheeler, the fast and elegant *Kaslo*, was built at the KR&N shipyard at Mirror Lake just south of Kaslo and placed in operation in 1900. Additionally, the KR&N constructed a smaller sternwheeler, the *Argenta*, to provide the steamer connection with another GN venture to the north. This route was to penetrate a developing mining district in the Lardo (or Lardeau)-Duncan district to the north of Kootenay Lake. Like so many others, it involved direct competition with the CPR and was the Great Northern's furthest northward penetration into British Columbia. It was also one of the shortest-lived. Grading began from Argenta on Kootenay Lake in 1899 on what was called the Kaslo & Lardo-Duncan Railway but in the same year the CPR, using the Arrowhead & Kootenay Railway charter (later the Kootenay & Arrowhead), also began work on its line. For a time work proceeded on both railways, but the GN was clearly overextended and the Lardeau mining boom quickly collapsed leaving little incentive to continue. As far as is known, no GN trains ever operated on the line and the Lardeau area was left to the CPR.

The CPR route initially was more logical than the GN's since, as its charter name suggested, it could have been built through to connect with the CPR's rail and steamer lines running to Arrowhead at the northern end of Upper Arrow Lake. However, the tracks never passed Gerrard, a small community at the southern end of Trout Lake, and to save construction costs, a rather primitive steamer service was provided on the lake to operate as far north as Trout Lake City. Initially, this service was operated using the small sternwheeler *Victoria* but she was soon replaced by the tug *Procter*, transferred from Kootenay Lake service. Significant traffic never materialized on the isolated line and what there was dwindled to a point where a rail car took over from mixed train service in 1928.

The Great Northern's next expansion into the Kootenays was to build into the important Crowsnest Pass coalfields. The Great Northern had acquired the Crows Nest Pass Coal Company and with it an important source of fuel for its locomotives and the industries it served. Moreover, in the Boundary district near Grand Forks, the GN bought into the Granby Consolidated Mining, Smelting & Power Company which operated the important smelter at Grand Forks which required large quantities of coal. It was a logical consolidation of mining, smelting and transport interests.

Construction began in 1901 and was completed between Swinton, near the Morrissey mines, and the GN main line the following year. By 1904, the tracks had been extended through to Fernie and four years later reached the mines at Michel. The Montana portion of the route was known as the Montana & Great Northern while the B.C. portion was built under the charter of the Crows Nest Southern.

To the west of Rossland, the next GN penetration of British Columbia was by way of a line connecting with the Spokane Falls & Northern at Marcus (near Kettle Falls). The right-of-way crossed the Columbia River and followed the Kettle River to a border crossing just south of Christina Lake. From there, the tracks turned due west to reach Grand Forks and the Granby Smelter. Completed in 1902, the route gave the GN access to the rich mining district of Phoenix. A branch line was constructed from Grand Forks to the Phoenix mines and opened to traffic, after considerable delays caused by legal actions and opposition from the CPR, in 1905. The completion of the line decisively broke the CPR's monopoly on the Phoenix mines' traffic with the GN being able to divert two thirds of the traffic and at the same time reduce freight rates.

Whereas the CPR line swung north to Eholt to pass around the mountains west of Grand Forks, the GN turned south to once again follow the Kettle River into Washington before returning north into B.C. From Curlew, Washington, 12 miles (19 km) south of Grand Forks, a line extended south to the mining town of Republic while the route through to the west — sometimes called the GN's third main line — swung north again recrossing the border near Midway, 15 miles (24 km) distant. Once again, the tracks skirted the border, passing through Myncaster and Bridesville before re-entering Washington just north of Molson. Continuing on to the west, the line reached Oroville in 1907. Later, in 1914, connections were made to the south with the GN main line at Wenatchee providing a north-south route through Washington's northern Okanogan Valley and a much more direct access for through traffic.

West of Oroville, the GN line again crossed into British Columbia, following the Similkameen River through the developing agricultural communities of Cawston and Keremeos and on through the Okanagan Range to the mining centres of Hedley and Princeton. The line was completed through to Princeton in 1909 and work proceeded to extend the railroad on to the west. With this pace of construction, the Great Northern was keeping several steps ahead of the Canadian Pacific in reaching the increasingly important agricultural and mining districts between the end of CPR track at Midway and the main line following the Fraser River to the west. In the Fraser Valley, Great Northern lines were also being extended slowly, lessening the distance between the branch lines in the Boundary and Similkameen districts and the Coast.

Despite the rapid expansion of GN lines, there were some setbacks. The Slocan mining boom and with it the K&S had

A Great Northern freight steams across the Elk River at Fernie about 1910. The expansion of the GN into the Crowsnest Pass proved a lucrative move but as the demand for coal fell the traffic declined leaving the GN little business on its line. Fernie, like many mining towns had its share of tragedy. Explosions, and other disasters had a heavy toll and the town was destroyed by fire in 1908. Ten people died and if it hadn't been for the heroic efforts of GN and CPR train crews many more would have died.
—CHARLES E. TURNER, AUTHOR'S COLLECTION

After the abandonment of the K&S, the CPR took over the line and rebuilt it to standard gauge. This gave the CPR a route between Kaslo, Slocan Lake and Nakusp. Service was maintained to Kaslo by both sternwheelers and tugs and barges. In this photo from the 1940s, the *Moyie* has brought in a barge to Kaslo and the cars are being switched off the barge by the train crew. When it became uneconomic to maintain crews on the isolated line, the entire train, including locomotive and caboose, was moved by barge. —E. RON MATTHEWS

faded. Traffic declined and a slide blocked the branch to Cody in 1909. The next summer, a bad forest fire did extensive damage to the line and it was closed. The GN sold the little railway to a group of local citizens in 1911 who reopened part of the route but in 1912, it was transferred to the provincial government. The line was turned over to the CPR who rebuilt it to standard gauge and connected it to the Nakusp and Slocan branch to the west. The Bedlington & Nelson was not a success either. The line to Kuskonook saw little traffic after 1904 and it was abandoned in 1913. The trackage south to the border followed in 1916.

The Kettle Valley Railway, CPR's Last Gap to the Coast

Despite its early commitment to build west from Midway, the CPR was slow to act. Poor economic conditions in British Columbia during the 1890s and the heavy costs involved delayed construction. Politically there was mounting pressure for a Canadian-controlled route that would provide ready access and communications between the widely separated population centres of the southern regions of the province.

Desirable as the Coast to Kootenay line was, building a railroad between Midway and the main line of the CPR near the Coast was not to be an easy or straightforward task. The country was rugged, mountainous, and, particularly in the Cascades, subject to heavy snows. The mountain ranges were massive and generally ran in a north-south direction, providing no easy routes for construction of an east-west rail line. While the distance separating Midway and Hope at the head of the Fraser Valley was only about 125 miles (200 km), by the time the last rails were laid on the twisting, curving, climbing route that the intervening geography and reasonable economy dictated, the length of the route was nearly 300 miles (480 km), most of it up and down and almost none of it straight.

This final major expansion of CPR routes through southern British Columbia was done under the authority of the charter of the Kettle Valley Railway Company and, unlike most other charter names, this one became well known and endured as a part of the CPR's story just as the Esquimalt & Nanaimo was to survive on Vancouver Island. The CPR acquired the charter on a 999 year lease in 1913 but the line was legally maintained as a separate corporate identity until 1956, when the name was finally changed to the CPR and the company absorbed. As an operating section of the CPR, the KVR remained a separate entity for many years with the crews having independent seniority from other CPR operations in the province until the end of 1930. Then, on January 1, 1931, the KVR became the Kettle Valley Division of the CPR and the operations of the KVR were fully integrated into the other divisions of the Canadian Pacific in B.C.

Before the story of the KVR's construction is recounted, it is first necessary to understand the development of other lines that became part of, or at least formed part of the background

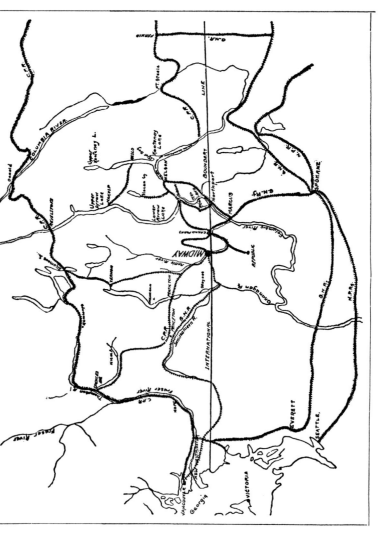

Until the Kettle Valley Railway was built through to the Coast, Midway was the end of CPR trackage west of Nelson. Lumber and agriculture became the main basis of the town and it was also a CPR crew change point between the Carmi and Boundary subdivisions. When the tracks were removed between Penticton and Midway in 1979-80, Midway once again became the end of operational trackage west of Nelson. The last steam power to run into Midway was former CPR 2-8-0 3716 running on the British Columbia Provincial Museum's Museum Train. Near midnight, 3716 steams quietly outside the station in August 1978. —ROBERT D. TURNER, BCPM

Midway, like so many other small towns along the CPR, provided a great opportunity for land speculation. Newspapers in the towns ran frequent ads promoting their communities as great centres of growth. Few ever came true. This pretentious ad was from *The Dispatch* of 1902.

to, the Kettle Valley system. These include the Kettle River Valley Railway, which was a Canadian company not to be confused with the charter applied for by Daniel Corbin, the Midway & Vernon Railway, and the Nicola, Kamloops & Similkameen Coal & Railway Company.

Unlike so many other lines that were chartered by promoters and speculators, the Kettle River Valley Railway actually began construction and operated trains over its own lines. It was supported by the citizens of Grand Forks and headed by Tracy Holland, a businessman originally from Ontario. His scheme was to build a railway connecting the mining district of Republic in Washington to the new smelter at Grand Forks. Holland and his associates received a provincial charter in 1900, but to operate into the United States, a federal charter also was required. The railway was incorporated by the federal government in 1901 and given authority to build a line from Cascade City on the B.C.-Washington border to Carson City with a 50-mile (80-km) branch from the vicinity of Grand Forks up the Kettle River Valley, and another via Greenwood to Midway. A charter (the Republic & Kettle River Railway — R&KR) was obtained from the State of Washington for the construction of a line from Cascade City to Republic and from there, via the Sanpoil River Valley to Spokane. Like so many early railroad charters, these were vastly more ambitious than the construction that followed. However, in 1902, the KRVR was able to open trackage between Grand Forks and the border (3.91 miles/6.29 km) and from there, another 30 miles (48 km) south to Republic.

From the beginning, the KRVR was in direct competition with the mighty Great Northern for the traffic between Republic and the Grand Forks smelter. There were protracted arguments over rights-of-way, delaying tactics to force the GN into expropriation procedures, and the KRVR even secured an injunction to stop the GN from crossing its tracks near Grand Forks. The GN used similar tactics and had obtained an injunction to stop the R&KR from building a trestle over its right-of-way near Curlew. Unenforceable because it was granted by a Canadian court, the injunction prompted a confrontation between the two companies. GN crews were dispatched on a quiet Sunday in early January 1902 to dismantle the trestle but a few stalwart construction workers from the R&KR called in reinforcements and finally posted an armed guard at the site. Holland's little rail line beat the Great Northern into Republic but the battle was not over. Injunctions and legal battles followed.

The GN needed access to the smelter — access blocked by a KRVR injunction. The GN went to the Railway Committee of the House of Commons in Ottawa and was granted permission to cross the KRVR to complete its access to the smelter. This did not nullify a court injunction that Holland had obtained, but the GN put in its crossing during the night of Sunday, November 9, 1902. Next morning, the KRVR responded by parking one of its locomotives, a box car and a flat car squarely across the diamond crossing, blocking the GN tracks. A tense day followed as GN construction workers were forced to unload rail and other materials needed for track construction and carry them around the obstruction. However, late in the day, a telegram was received from Vancouver stating that all litigation had been dropped and the KRVR train was removed from the crossing. Literally and figuratively, the KRVR had backed off and the GN had its line to the smelter.

The settlement was based on a trade off of interests. The agreement allowed the KRVR to maintain a level crossing with the GN at Pelham Flats, four miles (6.5 km) south of Curlew, and in return, the KRVR withdrew all injunction suits against the GN.

The KRVR was in no way able to compete with the GN, which quickly took most of the traffic from the Republic mines. Unfortunately, traffic statistics for the line are incomplete as reported in *Poor's Manual of Railroads*, apparently reflecting only traffic within Canada, but they give a clear picture of a railroad in trouble. In the year ending June 30, 1902, the KRVR carried only 1,447 passengers for earnings of just $230. Freight, noted at 33,810 tons (34 350 tonnes), produced only $5,131 in revenue. Other earnings brought an additional $35.00 but operating expenses exceeded revenues by $331. This trend continued with little sign of the railroad ever being able to repay its investments. Not long after the GN gained control of the traffic to the smelter, Holland resigned from the management of the company. However, the KRVR did see potential to the north if a line could be built to another developing mining area known as Franklin Camp. Hopefully, tracks could eventually be laid all the way through to Vernon. A federal subsidy of $3,200 per mile (or about $2,000 per km) was granted in 1903 and construction progressed slowly, finally ending in 1907 at Lynch Creek, just 15 track miles (24 km) to the north of Grand Forks.

By 1907, conditions for the KRVR were terrible. Copper prices were down, and traffic had all but disappeared between Grand Forks and Republic, forcing suspension of service south of Grand Forks. Freight had fallen off to only 11,434 tons (11 617 tonnes). Passengers had grown to 5031 but the passenger volume yielded only $278 in revenue, bringing the yearly loss to $1,047. By the end of the 1909 fiscal year, traffic had all but disappeared. Tonnage had dropped to just 2,355 tons (2393 tonnes) or 29,198 ton miles earning just $1,549. Passenger volumes declined towards oblivion, with only 144 being reported carried, producing earnings of only $82. The deficit for the year was $1,113. In the meantime, the trackage in Washington had been renamed the Spokane & British Columbia and both ends of the line were being operated under the title of the Kettle Valley Lines. Its modest equipment roster included just three locomotives, five box cars, 13 flat cars and 10 other pieces of rolling stock.

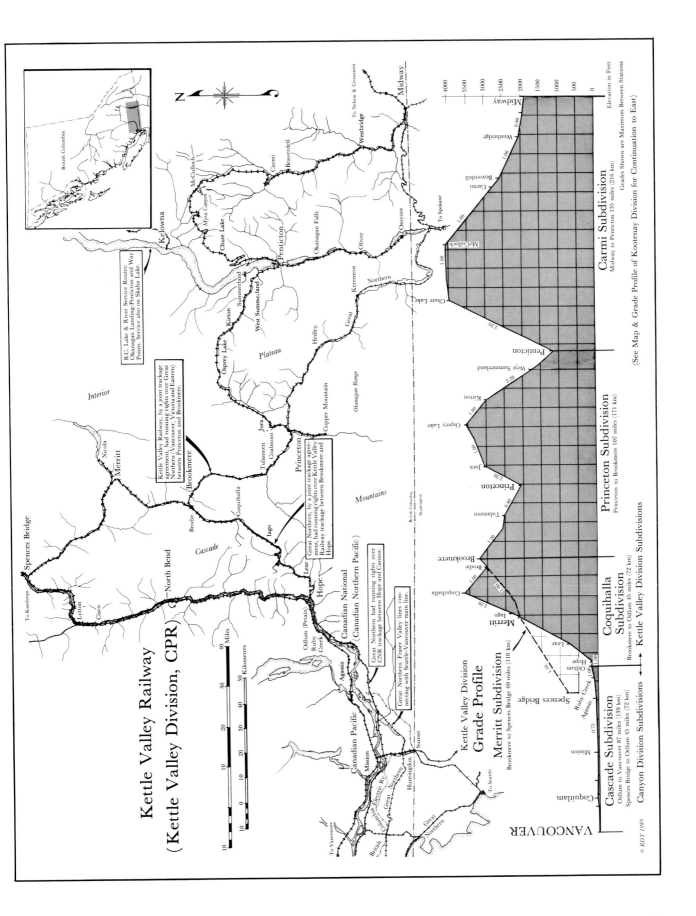

Kettle Valley Railway
(Kettle Valley Division, CPR)

Kettle Valley Railway, by a joint trackage agreement, had running rights over Great Northern (Vancouver, Victoria and Eastern) between Princeton and Brookmere.

B.C. Lake & River Service Routes: Okanagan Landing-Penticton and Way Points. Service also on Skaha Lake.

Great Northern, by a joint trackage agreement, had running rights over Kettle Valley Railway trackage between Brookmere and Hope.

Great Northern had running rights over CNR trackage between Hope and Cannor.

Great Northern Fraser Valley lines connecting with Seattle-Vancouver main line.

Canadian Pacific
Canadian National (Canadian Northern Pacific)

Miles
Kilometres

Kettle Valley Division
Grade Profile

Elevation in Feet
Grades Shown are Maximum Between Stations

(See Map & Grade Profile of Kootenay Division for Continuation to East)

Carmi Subdivision
Midway to Penticton 135 miles (216 km)

Princeton Subdivision
Princeton to Brookmere 107 miles (171 km)

Coquihalla Subdivision
Brookmere to Odlum 45 miles (72 km)

Merritt Subdivision
Brookmere to Spences Bridge 69 miles (110 km)

Cascade Subdivision
Odlum to Vancouver 87 miles (139 km)
Spences Bridge to Odlum 45 miles (72 km)

Kettle Valley Division Subdivisions
Canyon Division Subdivisions

© RDT 1985

135

However, before the next stage in the Kettle Valley Lines' troubled history is proceeded with, the other two railroads that ultimately contributed to the CPR's southern route need to be outlined.

The next of the three lines, even less successful than the KRVR, was the Midway & Vernon. Backed and promoted by businessmen from Greenwood, the Midway & Vernon Railway was chartered by the B.C. Legislature in 1901. Powers were granted for the construction of a line from Midway, west to Rock Creek and from there, northwesterly to the west fork of the Kettle River which was to be followed over to the Okanagan and eventually to Vernon. A cash subsidy of $4,000 per mile (about $2,486 per km) was offered by the government. The route would have provided a direct connection between the CPR's Shuswap & Okanagan at Vernon and the Columbia & Western at Midway. Capital was fixed at $2,000,000 and authority was given by the Provincial Legislature for bonds to be issued to a value of $35,000 per mile (or approximately $21,000 per km).

Initially, the promoters were unable to attract capital despite an improved subsidy offered by the provincial legislature in 1902. Work was required to begin by January 1, 1904. To keep the project and the hope of the subsidy alive, construction had to begin and the Midway & Vernon did so in the most minimal way possible. An engineer was hired to begin laying out the right-of-way near Vernon and before long a force of two men were at work grading the line near Kalamalka Lake. Financing obstacles persisted for another year and it was not until the summer of 1905, with some backing from New York, that McLean Bros., contractors, were hired to begin work grading the line westward from Midway. But once again, only slight progress was made. A large work force completed grading as far as Rock Creek but by autumn, work had stopped and the eastern interests failed to come through with the promised capital. No further work was done and the graded right-of-way remained unused until the CPR finally began work in 1910 building to the west from Midway.

The third of the three lines that contributed to the route of the Kettle Valley was the Nicola, Kamloops & Similkameen Coal & Railway Company. This line, whose charter was originally granted in 1891, and extended in 1903, was leased by the CPR in 1905 following major labour disputes in the Vancouver Island coal mines which supplied the CPR with coal for its western lines. The CPR was anxious to have alternate supplies of coal. Important coal deposits had been discovered in the vicinity of Merritt approximately 40 miles (65 km) southeast of Spences Bridge on the CPR main line and these were the immediate goal of the CPR. Construction began quickly and the line was opened to traffic between Spences Bridge and Nicola, near Nicola Lake east of Merritt, in 1907.

While the incentive for building the line had been the coal

With the construction of the CPR's Nicola, Kamloops & Similkameen Coal & Railway Company between Spences Bridge and Merritt, the little town along the Thompson River took on new importance as a junction point. This is Spences Bridge's station in the early 1900s. —AUTHOR'S COLLECTION

The line between Merritt and Spences Bridge followed the Nicola River for most of its route on an easy grade. This photo from 1978 shows a wayfreight, then operating five days a week, rolling through the valley lands and crossing the Nicola River. —ROBERT D. TURNER

in the Merritt-Nicola vicinity, the line was also the first step, from the west, in the construction of a route between the main line and Midway. In the *Annual Report* for the fiscal year ending June 30, 1905, the announcement of the lease was made along with the statement that "it is intended that this line shall be gradually extended through the Similkameen Valley, and, eventually, to a connection with your Columbia and Western section at Midway." The *Report* also noted that, in another move to gain greater independence over its coal supplies, development work on a coal mine at Bankhead, on company lands near Banff, was nearing completion and promised "not only to safeguard your fuel supply in that district but to be a source of considerable profit." For a few years, however, no work was done beyond either Merritt or Nicola on the promised extension through to Midway. But for residents of the district, the line was still important as mining, forestry and agriculture developed as regional industries. Important companies operating near Merritt over the years were the Nicola Valley Pine Mills and the Middlesboro Collieries. Once work began on the KVR, Merritt would become an important point for construction crews to begin building to the southeast.

The Coast to Kootenay Railway Becomes a Reality

The troubled Kettle Valley Lines had received most of its financial backing from a firm known as the Trusts & Guarantee Company. To determine the fate of its investments, the company sent James Warren to Grand Forks to assess its prospects. Warren recognized quickly that as an independent concern, the railway was doomed, but he saw promise in the value of its charter as a means for completing the promised CPR Coast to Kootenay route. As a consequence Warren met with Thomas Shaughnessy in 1908 and an agreement evolved which led to the CPR leasing the Kettle Valley Railway (as the line had been renamed) and beginning construction through to the Coast via the Coquihalla Pass in the Cascade Range. The agreement also involved the provincial government which was led by Premier Richard McBride, who had based much of his government's programs on railway expansion in British Columbia. McBride agreed to provide a subsidy for the construction of the KVR, and with the agreement in hand as part of an expansive railway policy, called a provincial election. McBride was returned to office in an overwhelming victory that gave a clear indication of popular support for the rapid expansion of the province's rail lines including the KVR, the fledgling, provincially-backed Pacific Great Eastern and the developing Canadian Northern transcontinental.

For its part, the province agreed to provide a subsidy of $5,000 per mile (about $3,100 per km) for the route between Penticton and a junction with the Nicola, Kamloops & Similkameen Railway, near Merritt. The section between Midway and Penticton was to be built without subsidy although it was granted a free right-of-way through crown land. In addition, public lands were made available for necessary timber, stone and gravel. Similar provisions were made for the projected line between Grand Forks and Franklin Camp. In addition, the two unsubsidized sections were to be free of taxation for 10 years following the completion of the line to Nicola and Merritt. Later, the province granted $200,000 for the construction of a bridge across the Fraser near Hope that was to provide both a road and rail crossing of the river and agreed to subsidize the route over the Coquihalla Pass at a rate of $10,000 per mile (about $6,200 per km). The KVR also was to take over the assets of the Midway & Vernon Railway including the graded right-of-way west from Midway. The agreements between the KVR and the British Columbia government required the company to build 25 miles (40 km) of line in 1910, 50 miles (80 km) in 1911 and a further 50 in 1912 with the remainder of the route being completed by 1914, four years after the signing of the agreements. The Coquihalla section was required to be finished in 1915, although this last date was later extended.

The financial arrangements between the KVR and the Midway & Vernon were settled by arbitration. The last major legal barrier to construction was to have the federal charter for the KVR modified to allow for the construction of the line through to Hope via the Coquihalla Pass and this was accomplished in March 1910. The required provincial legislation also was enacted that year. Warren continued in charge of the KVR and was given a high degree of freedom by the CPR. Andrew McCulloch, a talented and experienced engineer, was in charge of the whole construction project and the KVR and the CPR were fortunate in having a man of his abilities available for the task.

The actual construction of the KVR was a major undertaking that took from 1910 to 1916 to complete. The route finally adopted from Midway through to the Coast was a spectacular, fascinating and rugged one. The survey work was gruelling and demanding, and laying out the line took many months in the field before the whole route could be mapped out in detail. Fortunately, many surveys had been carried out across the southern Interior over the years, so there was at least a good basis for route selection but problem areas, like the Coquihalla Pass, still had to be resolved.

From Midway, the line was pushed westwards towards the Okanagan Valley, following the course of the Kettle and Westkettle rivers northwards until it swung west into the mountains separating the Kettle drainage from the Okanagan Valley. Unlike the Cascades, Selkirks or Rockies, the ranges between Midway and the Cascades were not sharply peaked or scenically spectacular. Instead, they were lower and rounded but deeply cut by rivers. For the surveyors and contractors, they were a formidable barrier. From the Westkettle River, the tracks climbed to the Hydraulic Lakes and Hydraulic Summit (elevation 4,165 feet, or 1270 m) and from

The structure over the West Fork of Canyon Creek typified many of the major wooden trestles required on the Kettle Valley.
—STOCKS PHOTO, BCPM

there, the route, which was later called the Carmi Subdivision, twisted and turned over an amazing series of bridges and tunnels through the isolated and beautiful Myra Canyon. From the summit the long descent into the Okanagan Valley necessitated a steady, uninterrupted 2.2 percent grade all the way into Penticton. The glaciated western face of the mountain ridge gave no easy route for the railway and from the ridge top, overlooking the farms of Naramata and vistas of Okanagan Lake, the line made two long sweeping switchbacks down the steep slopes of the valley sides. At the end of the upper switchback, the engineers were forced to route the line through a curved, horseshoe-shaped tunnel over 1,600 feet (485 m) long that turned the line back on itself in order to maintain the grade as it descended to Penticton.

From Penticton west, there was no respite. The grade began immediately on leaving the flat valley bottom and climbed steadily up through the dry benches and hillsides to Trout Creek, just south of Summerland. Over this stretch to the summit, the grade averaged 1.4 percent and reached a maximum of 2.2 percent. The crossing of Trout Creek represented the greatest obstacle on the line and required a major steel bridge with long timber trestle approaches. The grade followed Trout Creek into the mountains to a high, forested summit marked by several small lakes — Osprey, Link, and Chain — before dropping down towards Princeton following the course of Hayes Creek. Again, the maximum grade was 2.2 percent and to maintain even that steep grade, a series of loops had to be engineered to take the line the final miles down into Princeton. These loops, between the stations of Belfort and Jura, became one of the more famous features of the line. The original surveys for the route west of the summit took the line north of Princeton but, with the developing coal mining in the Princeton-Coalmont area, a major revision was incorporated into the plans before actual construction began on this section. This relocation of the KVR main line route to Princeton brought the KVR in direct contact with the Great Northern's VV&E as we shall soon see.

The generally north-south line between Merritt and Princeton, which, as will be explained later, incorporated trackage built by both the KVR and VV&E, penetrated the canyon of the Tulameen River and the beautiful aspen parklands and forested uplands east of the Cascade Mountains. From Princeton, the line ran northwest and then north, following Otter Creek through to its headwaters and reaching the summit of the grade at Brookmere at an elevation of 3,157 feet (962.3 m). Just a few miles past Brookmere, at a point called Brodie, the line diverged. Continuing on to the north, the tracks extended on to Merritt down the course of the Coldwater River, while the other line penetrated the Cascades to the southwest via the spectacular and daunting Coquihalla Pass, through to Hope on the Fraser River. The line crossed the Fraser and joined the main line at Petain (later renamed Odlum).

From Brookmere to the summit at Coquihalla, the engineers were able to maintain a modest maximum grade of 1.0 percent but from the summit (elevation 3,346 feet, or 1020 m) to Petain (elevation 182 feet, or 55.5 m), it was only with great difficulty that a line with a 2.2 percent maximum grade could be found. Overall, the average grade was 1.83 percent. In 36.3 miles (58.5 km) from Coquihalla to Hope, the line dropped 3,464 feet (1056 m). In order to keep to these limits, and to penetrate the rugged canyon of the Coquihalla, numerous bridges, tunnels and snow sheds were required. The Coquihalla route was daunting not only from an engineering point of view but also because of the weather. Its western faces received the full force of winter snowfalls just as the western flank of the Selkirks did along the main line to the north. Snowfalls at Coquihalla summit averaged over 450 inches (about 11.5 m) a year and some years, the fall exceeded 600 inches (15.25 m). The record winter of 1945-46 saw 642 inches (16.3 m) fall on the pass. The net result was a section of railroad that was not only tough to build and to maintain, but particularly difficult, dangerous and costly to operate. To the railroaders, the Coquihalla became something of a legend — a section of line the oldtimers never ceased to recall with amazement, humour and often sadness, since nearly all had lost friends or acquaintances to accidents in the Coquihalla.

The Coquihalla Pass route required many enormous bridges. This one, at Bridal Veil Falls (later Fallslake Creek), was one of the most spectacular. This photo shows the bridge after the line was abandoned. —PIERRE MORIN

All the way across from Midway to Hope it had been a major battle for the surveyors to keep the line within reasonable limits for grades and curvature. Even so, the route was circuitous and at times tortuous. Tunnels and bridges, both expensive and time-consuming components of construction, were required in abundance. The track was seldom, if ever, straight for more than a few hundred feet. But the line was feasible and it was built.

Work began at Midway, Merritt and soon after, at Penticton. The first construction was south from Merritt following the Coldwater River. The contractors were Macdonnell, Gzowski & Co., who were given the job of building the first 29.5 miles (47.5 km). Construction proceeded on schedule and by the summer of 1913, Andrew McCulloch was able to report that 3,000 men were employed in construction and that two steam shovels were also in use on the line.

Slowly and surely, the VV&E was closing the gap between the GN subsidiaries in the Fraser Valley and its lines connecting through to Spokane. A problem was a route through the mountains east of Hope. One possibility involved an eight-mile (13-km) tunnel. But the cost of such an undertaking would have been prohibitive. A more practical surface route still meant 92 miles (150 km) of track to connect Hope and Princeton, with grades of 2.5 percent on the western climb to the summit. The GN was unhappy with both options, and in 1910 undertook further surveys. In charge of the construction

Completing the Kettle Valley and Construction through the Coquihalla Pass

It was the Great Northern's VV&E that first reached Princeton and penetrated the canyon of the Tulameen River to the west. Later, the trackage was part of the agreement with the CPR for operations between Princeton and, via the Coquihalla Pass, Hope. Operating over what was once part of the Great Northern, just west of Princeton, a CPR freight, photographed in July 1981, winds along the Tulameen River heading for the main line at Spences Bridge.
—ROBERT D. TURNER

and the survey work was the VV&E's chief engineer J. H. Kennedy.

While work on the surveys through the Hope Mountains proceeded, grading progressed during the summer of 1910 in a northwesterly direction on the first 16 miles (26 km) of line from Princeton up the Tulameen River towards the coast. A. Guthrie & Co. were the contractors. This section required heavy work since the canyon of the Tulameen upstream from Princeton was deep and rugged. To maintain an acceptable gradient from Princeton, a major tunnel — 1,063 feet (324 m) long — was required just west of town and from there a great deal of rock work and blasting was needed to grade the line. In 1911, the tracks were laid over this new route as far as Coalmont where coal deposits were being brought into production. At the same time, Chief Engineer Kennedy was able to report that the latest surveys carried out through the Hope Mountains by W. W. Auburn and M. A. Butler had reduced the gradient of the projected line to 2.2 percent but at the cost of 15 tunnels including one over 1,000 feet (305 m) in length. The route was to cross the mountains through the Coquihalla Pass. Both the KVR and the VV&E had focused down onto the Coquihalla Pass as the key passage between their connections from the West and their lines through to the Boundary district, the southern Interior and, for the VV&E, Spokane.

It made little sense for two lines to be built through the Coquihalla, if in fact there was even room through the narrow canyon to build two railroads. But initially, neither company was willing to give up what might have proven to be advantageous to the other. Arguments were presented in Ottawa before the Board of Railway Commissioners but without resolution. Complicating the picture was an agreement reached between the VV&E and the new Canadian Northern Pacific (CNP), a transcontinental line owned by Mackenzie and Mann building towards the Coast. It permitted VV&E trains to use its line down the Fraser Valley from Hope. The agreement saved the VV&E building 37 miles (60 km) of parallel track between Hope and Sumas Landing (later renamed Cannor) on the Fraser. Running rights over this route cost the VV&E $50,000 per year in payment to the Canadian Northern. Coincidentally, the GN made available to the CNP running rights into Vancouver thus saving the new Canadian line great expense in building from Port Kells on the Fraser River to New Westminster and Vancouver.

Finally a compromise over the Coquihalla was worked out in principle by mid-November 1912, and the details were finalized by April of 1913. In July an additional agreement cleared the way for the KVR's connections through the Princeton area. The two lines were to exchange running rights over their trackage through the disputed sections between Princeton and Hope. VV&E trackage was to be used by both lines between Princeton and Coldwater Junction while KVR trackage was to be used through the Coquihalla

Pass to Hope. In this way, both the KVR and the VV&E completed their through routes between the Coast and the Kootenays. The agreement required the VV&E to pay the KVR $150,000 for the running rights through the Coquihalla, while the KVR payed the VV&E $60,000 for operation over the line from Princeton to Coldwater Junction. Additional charges were levied based on the frequency of train service.

The construction of the VV&E line from Coalmont to Coldwater Junction was completed in 1914. The junction point became the division point of Brookmere and a small railroad community grew up there.

Meanwhile, Kettle Valley construction was underway on the gaps in the line between Midway and Penticton and between Penticton and Princeton. The trackage linking Midway and Penticton was delayed by the heavy construction and numerous bridges required between Carmi and Penticton. It was not until October 2, 1914 that the work was completed and the line ready for traffic from Midway through to Penticton. This route, described earlier, was particularly rugged with the section through the scenically spectacular Myra Canyon being notable for its succession of bridges and tunnels. In the 5.8 miles (9.3 km) between the stations of Myra and Ruth, there were 18 trestles and bridges and two tunnels. The bridges and trestles totalled nearly 4,750 feet (1450 m) in length, and although three of the largest wooden trestles were rebuilt in later years with steel, this difficult section of line was a constant maintenance problem and expense.

West of Penticton, the KVR had built as far as Osprey Lake by 1913, but the route beyond there had not been completed because grade revisions, which ultimately took the tracks to Princeton, were considered. This route was completed in 1915 making connection with the VV&E and bringing the joint trackage agreements into effect.

Finally, with the completion of the KVR to Princeton and its connection with VV&E trackage to Brookmere, the KVR had a through route between Midway and the Coast, albeit via Merritt and Spences Bridge. Only the Cascade Mountains, via the Coquihalla, remained to be crossed but the Coquihalla was probably the greatest challenge of all. The combination of topography and climate made construction both expensive and difficult. Grading work started from both ends of the line — Hope and a point on the line later named Brodie Junction — in 1913 and work progressed through 1914 and 1915 until stopped by winter weather just short of completion. All that remained were a few miles of track laying and the completion of the trestle over Ladner Creek. The western end of the line (38 miles or about 61 km) was built by MacArthur Bros. who, very soon after receiving the contract, had as many as 1,600 men at work. The eastern section was contracted to Twohy Bros. and they began building west from Brodie with a substantial workforce.

Some of the bridges were spectacular. The frame trestle

Penticton, at the southern end of Okanagan Lake, became a busy focus for construction on the Kettle Valley. Equipment was brought on barges from Okanagan Landing and crews began building east towards Midway and west towards Princeton. In 1915, at the time this photograph was taken in the Penticton roundhouse, the tracks had been completed from Midway through to Spences Bridge.
—VERNON BOARD OF MUSEUM AND ARCHIVES

Construction camps were built as needed and remains survived long after they were closed down. This abandoned rock oven, photographed in 1981, was used by crews building the line east of Penticton in 1913 and 1914.
—ROBERT D. TURNER

West of Penticton, the line had to be built through the rugged, rolling mountains of the Okanagan Highlands. From near Summerland the tracks followed the course of Trout Creek into the mountains. At Winslow, a siding near the major bridge spanning Trout Creek, a Marion Model 20 steam shovel was used to load ballast and fill. Tracks reached this point in 1912. —PABC, HP52475

East of Penticton, a construction crew works its way upgrade in 1914. Ahead of the train, men are laying ties and rail while behind, men are lining up the rails and completing the spiking. So far, only about every fourth or fifth tie has been spiked. —PABC, HP52461

Construction through the Coquihalla presented the engineers and crews with problems similar to those faced during the building of the line over the Selkirks a generation earlier. The line had to be protected from snow slides and extensive snow sheds were required. This is Shed 4 as it appeared in September 1915. Note the construction camp in the distance.
—W. GIBSON KENNEDY COLLECTION

The daunting Coquihalla route in winter, showing Sheds 1-4, in 1915.
—W. GIBSON KENNEDY COLLECTION

Work on Slide Creek Bridge was nearly done by November 1915 when this photo was taken. Note the timber from the falsework under the steel bridge.—W. GIBSON KENNEDY COLLECTION

constructed over Cultus Creek, the largest on the line, was 630 feet (192 m) long and required 750,000 board feet (5,800 m³) of timber to construct. Another over Bridal Veil Falls (the waterway was later renamed Fallslake Creek), and one that survived long after the rails through the Coquihalla had been removed, was over 400 feet (122 m) long and 120 feet (37 m) tall. This impressive structure required a central truss span over 100 feet (30 m) long to pass over the waterway. In total 43 bridges, 13 tunnels and 16 snow sheds were required.*
Undoubtedly the most famous of these features were the so called "Quintette Tunnels" deep in the steep walled, heavily forested, Coquihalla Canyon between Othello and Hope. Through this section of its canyon, the Coquihalla River rushes through a narrow, precipitous gorge and makes a sharp "S" shaped bend. The Quintette Tunnels were Andrew McCulloch's solution to the problem of bringing the railway through this gorge.

Earlier surveys had not produced a satisfactory answer to the route through this canyon. One proposal by the VV&E was for a mile-long tunnel. McCulloch decided to investigate for himself and began a survey of the 11 miles (18 km) east of Hope. Just examining the canyon was difficult, but it did not stop McCulloch. He had himself and his workers lowered in baskets by rope down into the canyon to survey possible routes. McCulloch found the answer to the Coquihalla dilemma by building the Quintette Tunnels on a perfectly straight alignment. As an unintended sidelight, the alignment of the tunnels provided a spectacular view down the tracks as the tunnels disappeared into the distance, succeeding ones visible through the portals of the next. Actually, there were only four tunnels, but one of them—Tunnel 12—had an opening on one side that gave the appearance of a fifth†
tunnel. Like all stations and major features on the line, the tunnels were numbered from east to west along the route from Brookmere to Odlum. To add to the scenic nature of this section of the line, crossings of the Coquihalla River were required between Tunnels 11 and 12 and between 12 and 13.

Work for the construction crews through the Coquihalla was difficult in the extreme. Temporary, makeshift bridges had to be built across the Coquihalla River through the canyon so that supplies and materials could be taken to work sites along the route. Often, the men had to work from precariously perched scaffolding, or ropes and ladders suspended along the cliff faces. Snow sheds were required to protect sections of right-of-way endangered by slides; work on

* Summaries from later years, presumably after some structures had been eliminated, combined, or removed, noted 48 bridges and trestles, 11 tunnels and five snow sheds on the line.

† The tunnels were located at miles 49.50 (Tunnel 10, 556 ft.—169.5 m), 49.55 (Tunnel 11, 100 ft.—30.5 m), 49.65 (Tunnel 12, 405 ft.—123.5 m), and 49.80 (Tunnel 13, 246 ft.—75 m). The two bridges over the Coquihalla River were at miles 49.6 (75 ft.—23 m) and 49.7 (174 ft.—53 m).

146

So difficult was access to the Coquihalla Canyon that crews had to use makeshift ladders down the cliff faces to work.

—W. GIBSON KENNEDY COLLECTION

The spectacular Quintette Tunnels along the Coquihalla River, just east of Hope, provided the solution, engineered by Andrew McCulloch, to the routing of the Kettle Valley Railway in the final miles of the descent of Coquihalla Pass.

—CPCA 7865

these was completed after the line was opened to traffic. The bridge over the Fraser River at Hope was a major construction project in itself. Armstrong, Morrison & Co. of Vancouver received the contract for the footings and foundation work, while the Canadian Bridge Co. did the steel work for the bridge. The structure, with an overall length of 955 feet (291 m), consisted of four steel spans, each 238 feet (72.5 m) long, which were supported by three concrete piers and two concrete abutments. The bridge was double decked, with the railway occupying the lower deck while a two-lane highway used the upper deck.

The winter of 1915-1916 was a particularly bad one, with heavy accumulations of snow across British Columbia. The snows were late leaving the passes, but by July 1916 the work was done and the Kettle Valley Railway's line and with it, the Vancouver, Victoria & Eastern's, had been completed through to the Coast. The long-desired Coast to Kootenay railway was a reality and, moreover, there were two through railway routes.

The opening of the Coast to Kootenay railway was significant and had lasting effects on the future development of southern British Columbia. Overshadowing the accomplishment, however, was the fact that Canada was entering its third year of fighting in World War I and the dreams of many who had hoped to see the southern districts of British Columbia prosper were destroyed by the war and the great changes it would bring to the province both economically and socially.

There were other changes as well. J. J. Hill, the tough, driving "Empire Builder" of the Great Northern, died on May 29, 1916, and with him passed the period of great competition between the GN and the CPR. While the GN's third main line was a reality its value was questionable for the Great Northern system. There was limited through traffic between Vancouver and Spokane; most could be handled more efficiently over the GN's main line route over Stevens Pass between Seattle, Everett and Spokane. With good connections between Vancouver and the GN main line, just 122 miles (196 km) to the south, the main line route was preferable to the twisting, contorted VV&E-W&GN line across the southern Interior of B.C. and northern Washington. Politics and nationalism had their effect too.

An early result of all these and other factors was the abandonment of plans to operate through trains over the VV&E and a slow curtailment of service on some of the GN's B.C. branch lines. Like the Kaslo & Slocan, they had ceased to be profitable and were either cancelled or were retained with reduced levels of service. After an inaugural train over the Coquihalla route in 1916, the GN made no effort to utilize the line and relegated the remainder of its third main line to branches. So in the end, the CPR had won *defacto* control of the Coast to Kootenay rail traffic and, moreover, the GN had helped to pay for its rival's final section of line. James J. Hill would not have been amused.

147

MacArthur Bros. won the contract for building the western end of the Coquihalla line. This was their Camp No. 5 in March 1914.
—W. GIBSON KENNEDY COLLECTION

The completion of the Coquihalla line made direct through service from the Coast to the Kootenays a reality. But for the operating crews, the battle had just begun. This scene of a freight at Romeo is characteristic of the cold, miserable winters that typified the Coquihalla as long as the trains ran through the pass.
—AUTHOR'S COLLECTION

At Penticton, the engine crew pose proudly beside their gleaming D9c 4-6-0 No. 572 soon after through service began on the Kettle Valley line. The Penticton station is behind the train.
—STOCKS FAMILY COLLECTION, IPB

Two major connecting lines were constructed in the early 1900s that added to the importance of the Kettle Valley-Crowsnest route through southern British Columbia. The first was the Kootenay Central Railway built between the main line at Golden and the Crowsnest route near Cranbrook. The actual junction point was called Colvalli, about 30 miles east of Cranbrook. Originally chartered in 1901, the Kootenay Central was projected to extend south into the United States but the line was never built south of Cranbrook. It was a logical north-south route from the main line south to the Crowsnest district and it was formally leased by the CPR for 999 years on January 1, 1911. From Colvalli to Golden it was 166.5 miles (268 km) by train and it was a long, lonely route. The entire line was within the confines of the beautiful, but sparsely settled Rocky Mountain Trench. The route was as nearly flat as a railroad could be with little difference in elevation over the entire distance. The divide between the Kootenay River flowing to the south and the Columbia flowing to the north was at Canal Flats.

Traffic on the line was in keeping with the development of the region and was never more than a few trains — usually mixed — each week throughout the steam era on the CPR. The line was a useful diversion route if traffic needed to be rerouted from either the main line or the Crowsnest Pass route but for the first 60 years of its existence, it remained little travelled and little known. In later years the Kootenay Central was to develop into one of the busiest sections of the entire CPR system, but that was far in the future. The major attraction on the line for passengers was Radium Hot Springs and other hot springs located north of Lake Windermere. The present station of Radium (previously named Park Gate) served as an entrance to Kootenay National Park on the western slope of the Rockies. This National Park, established in 1920, shared its northern boundaries with Yoho and Banff National Parks and while not as well known as the other Rocky Mountain parks was certainly as beautiful.

The other connecting route established by the CPR in the years preceding World War I was the Spokane International. This line connected the Crowsnest Pass line at Yahk via a short CPR branch to the international border at Kingsgate, B.C.-Eastport, Idaho, with Spokane, and was to prove a most valuable link in the system. The story of the Spokane International involves that veteran Spokane railroad builder and industrialist Daniel Chase Corbin, who had been instrumental in building the Spokane Falls & Northern and its affiliated lines to Nelson and Rossland in the 1890s. This time, Corbin worked with the CPR in establishing yet another connection between the Kootenays and Spokane.

Corbin negotiated an agreement with the CPR in which the Canadian railway payed one-eighth of the construction costs of the SI and received an option on 52 percent of the stock at a price to be settled by January 1917. These arrangements were in place in January 1905.

A north-south connection between the Crowsnest route and the main line was provided by the construction of the Kootenay Central through the Rocky Mountain Trench. The line saw little traffic throughout the steam era but blossomed with the redevelopment of coal mining in the Crowsnest in the early 1970s. This is the single combine for passengers, the caboose and a business car on the mixed train at Lake Windermere on July 29, 1947.
—WILBUR C. WHITTAKER

The Spokane International was an important gateway between the Southern Interior of British Columbia and Idaho and Washington. SI trains connected with the CPR at Yahk, as shown here in June 1939.—W. GIBSON KENNEDY

The construction of the Spokane International gave the CPR access to Spokane and, with its Soo Line connections in the midwest, provided a route between Chicago, Spokane and Portland. First class train service—the *Soo-Pacific Train De Luxe*—was established but World War I brought the service to an end. This is the westbound express at Crowsnest.
—GERALD E. WELLBURN COLLECTION

The special equipment built for the Soo-Pacific trains was used on other trains as CPR-Soo line trains continued to be scheduled through to the Pacific but over the main line. Cyril Littlebury photographed the Soo Line's *Yahk* at Field in the 1920s, probably operating on the *Soo-Pacific Express*. The observation cars were named for points along or near the route (for example, the CPR's *Spokane*). Each featured four compartments, a drawing room, a buffet and an observation room with adjoining open platform.
—LANCE CAMP COLLECTION

The railroad was to be built by Corbin who in exchange, received $30,000 in capital stock and an additional $30,000 in bonds at par value per mile of line. For completing the line he therefore acquired all of the SI's capital stock and bonds. Funding came from Corbin with security provided in part by the CPR. Construction of the SI proceeded rapidly with few major obstacles over its 140.8-mile (226.6-km) main line between East Spokane and Eastport, Idaho. Work was finished by November 1, 1906 and the line opened for traffic soon after.

The opening of the SI created a number of possibilities for both the CPR and Dan Corbin. Direct access was now provided to Spokane and hence connections with the Union Pacific (actually UP's leased Oregon Railroad & Navigation Co., later, the Oregon-Washington Railroad & Navigation Co.), the Northern Pacific, the Great Northern, the Spokane, Portland & Seattle (SP&S) and, later, the Milwaukee Road (Chicago, Milwaukee, St. Paul & Pacific). The most interesting feature of these connections was the possibility the UP afforded for a through route from the U.S. Mid-west to the Pacific Coast. Running via the CPR-controlled Soo Line from Chicago through Milwaukee and Minneapolis to the CPR at North Portal, Assiniboia (which in 1905 became part of the province of Saskatchewan), trains could then operate over the Crowsnest route to the SI interchange and from there to Spokane and on to Portland over the UP. Service between St. Paul and the Pacific Coast, via Crowsnest, was initiated in 1907 as the *Soo-Pacific Train De Luxe*. Soo Line and Canadian Pacific passenger cars, built by Barney & Smith, were even specially lettered "Soo-Spokane Line" for this service. This routing of traffic between the Pacific Coast and the Mid-west was in direct competition with the Great Northern. Unfortunately, the train only operated until the beginning of World War I in 1914. However, passenger connections were maintained between the CPR and the SI at Yahk through the steam era, with SI trains operating over the CP for 10 miles (16 km) between Kingsgate and Yahk. This service was discontinued in the early 1950s.

CP had some significant advantages in rate-setting abilities over the GN because of increasing restrictions from the American Interstate Commerce Commission. The eastern end of the route over the Soo Line also connected with the CPR main line making it possible for the CPR to run through passenger service between Vancouver and Chicago, again competing with the American transcontinentals. This connection had started as early as 1900 when cars from Chicago were added to *The Imperial Limited* at Regina. Later trains providing service through to the Pacific Coast from Chicago and the twin cities included the *Soo-Pacific Express* (which operated west of Moose Jaw in connection with *The Imperial*), *The Mountanieer* (inaugurated in 1923 as a summer only service), and the *Soo-Dominion* (usually running west of Moose Jaw in connection with *The Dominion*).

The SI was an important connecting route for the CPR, as well as a local road that contributed to the development of the communities it served. As business increased in the 1950s, larger yards were required to service the interchange between the two railroads and these were built at Kingsgate-Eastport on the border. After this, SI trains no longer ran through to Yahk.

The CPR exercised its option to purchase the SI in 1916 but later a half interest in the line was acquired by the Union Pacific. During the Depression years, the SI came under great financial pressure and went into receivership, being reorganized in 1941 as the Spokane International Railroad. In 1958, through an exchange of stock with the CPR, control of the SI passed completely to the Union Pacific and the line became the Spokane Sub-Division of the UP's Oregon Division. The route continues to be an important one and "run-through" freights are operated, using a mixture of CPR and UP power.

For Dan Corbin, the SI provided a direct connection through to the Crowsnest Pass where, through the encouragement of E. J. Roberts, he established the Corbin Coal & Coke Company, Ltd. to develop a major coal seam near McGillivray Loop on the CPR's Crowsnest line. A railway line was laid out to reach the coal seams.

This new railway, the Eastern British Columbia (EBC), was the last that Dan Corbin was involved with. Through an agreement with Shaughnessy, the securities of the SI were increased by $420,000 to pay for the cost of the line which in turn was organized as a subsidiary of the Corbin Coal & Coke Company on whose board of directors sat the directors of the SI.

The mines worked by Corbin Coke* & Coal were modern and impressive, tapping coal seams to over 250 feet (75 m) in thickness.†

The coal produced was in demand and was shipped via the EBC-CPR-SI route to Spokane, thus creating traffic for the SI and the CPR. While coal from the seam was also shipped to the CPR's smelter at Trail, most was shipped into Washington. In 1910, the first full year of production, nearly 125,000 tons (127 000 tonnes) were sold, 92 percent for export to the United States. Sales continued at high levels until 1913 when the underground fire forced the permanent closure of the No. 1 Mine. The Depression years of the 1930s forced the closure of many coal mines throughout British Columbia. Finally, in 1935, the Corbin workings were closed. The railway was removed in 1939, and in 1942, the company was dissolved, with much of the surviving equipment scrapped.

---

* Coke is produced by roasting coal in a coke oven. The process drives off gases through a process of destructive distillation. The resulting coke is used as a fuel in smelting.

† The thickness of the coal varied throughout the seams and between the deposits of coal there were often bands of shale. For example, at the No. 6 Mine, the total thickness of the seam was 436 feet (133 m) but this included many bands of shale so that the actual net thickness of coal was 278 feet (85 m).

Corbin, in the heart of the Crowsnest Pass, became an important mining community with its own railroad—the Eastern British Columbia— linking the mines to the CPR.
—ART TONDINI COLLECTION

An unusual feature of the operations at Corbin was the Roberts Mine which was an open pit using steam shovels to excavate and load the coal. Most mines in the Crowsnest in the early days were underground. Corbin Coke & Coal used two Shay locomotives, the No. 6 shown, and No. 5 (ex CPR No. 1903), and one Climax to move the loaded cars down to the Eastern British Columbia. No. 6 ended its days in logging service on Vancouver Island.
—ART TONDINI COLLECTION

The crew poses with EBC No. 2, one of two 2-8-0s built for the line in 1908 by Montreal Locomotive Works. —ART TONDINI COLLECTION

153

154

Michel was typical of the towns that owed their existence to the coal mines of the Crowsnest. The neatly laid out buildings are still new in this photograph but smoke and fumes from the mines and coke ovens will soon defy all attempts to retain the smart appearance of the structures.
—PABC, HP37286

The collieries at Hosmer in the Crowsnest Pass were developed and brought into production in 1910 by the CPR on its own coal lands but the operation was short-lived. The facilities were closed in 1914. —PAC, C43472

The mines at Coal Creek, south of Fernie and owned by the Crows Nest Pass Coal Company, were one of the major producers in the district. The mines were served by the Morrissey, Fernie & Michel Railway. This is the major tipple at Coal Creek but also evident in the photo are enormous quantities of pit props and three miners' coaches used on the frequent trains to and from Fernie. —PAC, PA17481

The Eastern British Columbia was not the only mining railroad developed to tap the Crowsnest Pass coal fields, nor was it the first. The other, the Morrissey, Fernie & Michel (MF&M), also had a direct connection with the story of the CPR and GNR, and operated from Fernie to the mines situated in the Coal Creek valley and from Michel to the Carbonado Colliery.

The Crowsnest Pass area developed quickly following the completion of the CPR through to Kootenay Lake in 1898. The arrival of the Great Northern in 1904 only hastened the growth in the area. The development of the two mining railroads — the Eastern British Columbia and the Morrissey, Fernie & Michel — were an expression of the scale of the operations on the western slope of the Rockies. Mining towns grew up quickly near the major collieries. Fernie was the largest in the district. Hosmer, at the CPR's own colliery, Michel and Natal east of Fernie, and Corbin near the summit of the pass were also principal communities. There were other mining towns to the east in Alberta including Coleman, Blairmore and Hillcrest, but they are beyond the limits of this account.

The MF&M was a subsidiary of the Crow's Nest Pass Coal Company which, in turn, was controlled by the Great Northern. Incorporated in 1903, it was intended to be a connecting road from the mines to the Great Northern's Crows Nest Southern. Coal from the mines — high quality bituminous and anthracite well suited for steam plants and coke production — could then be moved south, over GN lines to the Great Northern's main line at Rexford, Montana.

Until 1908, the only coal producer of consequence in the Crowsnest Pass area was the Crow's Nest Pass Coal Co., with mines at Coal Creek, Michel and Carbonado, but late in that year, the Corbin mines came into production and so did the CPR's mines at Hosmer. The coal produced at these mines became a significant source of traffic for both the CPR and the GN as most of the coal and coke was for sale to industrial centres beyond the vicinity of the Crowsnest.

In 1910, the collieries in the Crowsnest were producing nearly 1.1 million tons (1.12 tonnes) of coal and coke for sale and nearly all of this moved out over either the CPR or the GN. Over 80 percent of the coal from the field was sold for export to markets in the United States whereas over 95 percent of the coke production went to Canadian industry. However, much of the coke, destined for the smelters in the Boundary district was routed over the GN. For the Great Northern, the route was nearly all downgrade into Montana and the line featured long coal trains headed by a variety of power including the GN's big (for the time) L class 2-6-6-2s. This was one of the few regions in Canada that saw the use of Mallet locomotives although they also operated over GN lines to Vancouver.

The mines in the Crowsnest were not all long-lived. The CPR's own operation at Hosmer, only brought to full pro-

155

duction by 1910, was closed in 1914 with the beginning of World War I. As noted, the Corbin mines closed during the Depression years and the Carbonado Colliery, near Michel, was closed by 1920. The major Coal Creek and Michel operations of the Crow's Nest Pass Coal Company remained in production much longer. Coal Creek, and with it the Morrissey, Fernie & Michel Railway, was closed in 1957, while Michel continued in operation through the 1960s. By that time, coal, the dirty, unwanted fuel of the post-World War II era, had regained a place as an important energy source in the markets of the world and the Crowsnest field was redeveloped as a supplier of coal for export to Japan.

After the Boom Years:
The Great Northern Lines

After the collapse of the ambitious plans for a third GN main line across southern British Columbia, the system gradually declined except for the main line route between Vancouver and Seattle. In the Kootenay and Boundary districts the GN branch lines were largely dependent on the major industries in the region: logging, sawmilling, mining and smelting, and agriculture. The line to Fernie and Michel, the Crows Nest Southern, remained in operation into the Depression years but the steadily shrinking market for coal and the closure of all but the Trail smelter in the region left the line with little traffic. Trackage between Fernie and Michel was abandoned in 1926 and the following year, GN began operating over CPR trackage between Elko and Fernie. As a further economy measure, a gas car was brought in to handle the passenger service on the line, which since the early 1920s had been scheduled as a mixed train. With little possibility of improvements, the line to Elko was abandoned in 1937.

Service on the other lines followed a similar pattern of declining traffic and trackage abandonments. The line to Nelson proved more resilient and remains in service as a Burlington Northern branch line. Passenger service in the 1920s ran daily except Sundays but was operated with a gas car after 1928. In the 1930s, the service was down to a mixed, although it still connected through to Spokane after an all day trip. The war brought the end of the dwindling passenger service; it was discontinued in 1941.

To the west, service was abandoned into Rossland and Phoenix by the early 1920s. In the 1980s, the line to Grand Forks and Republic remains in service with a low volume of freight being handled. The twisting route from Midway west through Myncaster and Bridesville to Molson and Oroville was abandoned in the early 1930s but the route from Oroville to Keremeos continued in service much longer. The mines at Hedley remained in production until 1955. At that time, service was discontinued beyond Keremeos. Operations into Princeton were suspended in 1931 and the trackage removed a few years later. The last remaining section of the route into B.C. was closed following floods on the Similkameen River in 1972 which washed out a bridge.

Motive power on the Morrissey, Fernie & Michel included five 2-8-0s. No. 505, shown here, and 504 were the last ones acquired and came from Baldwin in 1913. They were withdrawn from service when the line was dieselized in 1947. The line also operated a gas car built in 1913 but it was sold to the Pacific Great Eastern as their No. 105 in 1920.
—DOUG RICHTER COLLECTION

Coal was loaded from the tipple at Coal Creek into box cars using a special rocking loader. It enabled the coal to be poured into the ends of the cars so that more could be carried.
—SPAULDING PHOTO, BCPM

Of the once busy and ambitious route, now little remains. Two quiet, lightly-trafficked branch lines are all that survive of the Great Northern in British Columbia aside from the Vancouver to Seattle corridor.

The Imperial Limited was the Canadian Pacific's premier
passenger train of the 1920s and Field was a centre of steam
power in the mountains. It is May 25, 1925 and 2-8-2 No. 5068
pulls past the ice house and water tower with 10 cars on the run
to Revelstoke. The P1b 2-8-2 (built in 1913 then rebuilt and
renumbered in 1927 to No. 5168) was typical of heavy
passenger power over the Selkirks during this period. Steam
railroading was never better.
—CYRIL LITTLEBURY, LANCE CAMP COLLECTION

CHAPTER 4

THE MODERN STEAM ERA ON THE CPR: 1920-1950

CHAPTER 4

Improvements in the 1920s and early 1930s

By the early 1920s, the labour shortages and the supply and operational problems of the war years had passed. The CPR had promised its employees who volunteered for military service a position of equal value to the one they left and credit for six months' pay. System-wide, over 11,600 employees joined the armed forces and of these, 1,100 died and another 2,088 were wounded. By mid-1920, the CPR had re-employed over 7,000 of its former employees and added an additional 11,300 returning soldiers to its work force. CPR employees had served with great distinction. Many had taken with them skilled trades and organizational abilities that proved highly valuable in the military. Over five percent of CPR employees received special decorations. The return of these men was a welcome relief to the strained resources of the system. The company had not been just patriotic in promising its employees jobs on their discharge; it had been pragmatic as well. A highly-skilled labour force was far more difficult to replace than machinery.

A significant development for CPR management at this time was the retirement of Thomas Shaughnessy as president and the promotion of Edward Wentworth Beatty (later Sir Edward) to take his place in 1918. Beatty's background was in law and he was a capable and dedicated leader for the CPR. He saw the railway through the expansive years of the 1920s and the Depression of the 1930s with energy and skill. Under his direction, the railway, steamship and hotel operations reached their pre-World War II peak. In 1924, he also took on the position of chairman. With his health failing, he stepped down from the president's position in 1942 but remained chairman until his death in 1943. The position of president passed to D'Alton C. Coleman who for many years had been vice-president for western lines. Coleman served as president until 1947.

Following World War I, the CPR was able to continue improving its railway system in British Columbia. The era of extensive branch line construction had passed and only two significant expansions of CPR rail service occurred in the province. However, improvements were made in the terminals, facilities, locomotives and rolling stock. On the Coast,

On May 24, 1925, the day before the photo on the opposite page was taken, a light snow dusted the mountains and clouds hung below the ridge tops. Cyril Littlebury photographed the Coast Freight at Cathedral on the Field Hill. The train is waiting for No. 4 to pass before proceeding downgrade to Field. The engineer is E. C. Graham and his engine is 5030, a P1b class 2-8-2. —LANCE CAMP COLLECTION

The climb out of the Kicking Horse Valley to the summit of the Rockies blended spectacular scenery and some of the CPR's finest steam power. The combination was an irresistible subject for Cyril Littlebury, a dedicated railroad and steamship photographer, who produced what is probably the finest series of photos of the main line of the CPR in British Columbia during the 1920s and early 1930s. In this dramatic photo, Littlebury captured S2a 2-10-2 No. 5806 assisting D9c 4-6-0 No. 594 up the Field Hill above the upper Spiral Tunnel on May 25, 1925. The train is No. 4, the *Toronto Express*. —LANCE CAMP COLLECTION

the steamship fleet was significantly expanded and new Empress liners were added to the trans-Pacific fleet.

The first extension of rail service was in the Okanagan. An agreement was reached with Canadian National to permit CPR freight trains to operate over new CN trackage between Vernon and Kelowna. Previously, CP freight had to be moved by barge from Okanagan Landing to Kelowna. This new arrangement, which took effect in 1925, gave CP direct rail access to all of the major centres in the Okanagan Valley. However, it was not until 1935 that CPR rail passenger service was extended to Kelowna over this route. The delay in passenger service gave a reprieve to the CPR's passenger sternwheelers — the *Sicamous* and the *Okanagan* — operating on Okanagan Lake. Another addition to CPR services in the Okanagan was a short branch line built from Penticton south to Skaha (Dog) Lake. A barge service was operated the length of the lake, connecting to a further section of trackage running as far south as Haynes, 16 miles (26 km) south of Okanagan Falls. This line, opened in 1923, was built to serve the developing agricultural areas of the southernmost section of the Okanagan Valley, the driest part of British Columbia.

The second extension of the system began late in the 1920s — the completion of trackage along the shore of Kootenay Lake between Kootenay Landing and Procter. This gap of just 34 miles (55 km) had been a major obstacle since the completion of the line through the Crowsnest Pass in 1898 but the heavy cost of construction along the mountainous lakeshore had deterred the CPR from completing the route. Instead, the sternwheelers, tugs and barges of the B.C. Lake and River Service had bridged the gap in the rail line. However, by the late 1920s, traffic had increased substantially, the Trail smelter was increasing production and developing fertilizer byproducts (from chemicals recovered from air pollution control measures), and a general upgrading of the entire Crowsnest-Kettle Valley was underway.

Work began on the project in mid-1929 with Dutton and Grant of Winnipeg the major contractor. The work was heavy and a great deal of blasting was required to prepare the grade. Compounding the problems, forest fires in late August burned out several of the construction camps although, fortunately, all of the men escaped. In all, five rock tunnels, totalling 2,139 feet (652 m) in length, and numerous bridges were required. Many of the bridges were ones originally used on the main line but removed when heavier structures were required. The line's ruling grade was only 0.4 percent and maximum curvature was 12 degrees. Tracks were laid with 85- and 100-lb steel (38.5 and 45.4 kg/m). Construction crews continued at work on the line through 1930 and it was opened for traffic on January 1, 1931. With the line in full operation, it was possible for the CPR to retire most of its steamers on Kootenay Lake. Only the sternwheeler *Moyie* and the tug *Granthall* were retained for the service to Kaslo, Lardeau and other points along the northern shores of the lake.

Decapods like 5779 were the heaviest type of power working west of Field during the 1920s. The big R3c 2-10-0, with its snow plow pilot, was photographed at Field on May 24, 1924 by Cyril Littlebury. —LANCE CAMP COLLECTION

An immaculate 5174, fresh from a major rebuilding with a new boiler and cylinders, is ready for passenger duties out of Field on June 16, 1927.
—CYRIL LITTLEBURY, LANCE CAMP COLLECTION

The Rockies in the 1920s

Pusher, No. 5803, running light, eases past the tiny station at Yoho in the rain on June 6, 1925.
—CYRIL LITTLEBURY, LANCE CAMP COLLECTION

Snow in the Mountains. Two almost new 2-10-2s, the largest CPR steam power of the day, work up to the summit past Cathedral Mountain and Mount Stephen on April 17, 1920. —W. HENDRY, LANCE CAMP COLLECTION

The Imperial Limited, behind G2 4-6-2s 2520 and 2614, eases into Vancouver station and the end of its journey across the country in 1928.
—CYRIL LITTLEBURY, LANCE CAMP COLLECTION

Around Vancouver Station

DURING THE GREAT DAYS OF THE *LIMITEDS*

Train No. 4, the *Toronto Express*, is ready to leave Vancouver on July 24, 1924. The wipers at the Drake Street yards have done their jobs well; 2654 is spotless.
—CYRIL LITTLEBURY, LANCE CAMP COLLECTION

Not all was glamour. Ten-wheeler 578 was on a westbound transfer freight nearing the Vancouver waterfront yards. The brakeman riding the pilot was taking his position rather casually. The engine, with its smoke deflector, also worked on the Kettle Valley.
—CYRIL LITTLEBURY, LANCE CAMP COLLECTION

In a power shortage, a 3600 2-8-0 could be assigned to the passenger trains. The 3681, with its wooden pilot, trimmed number board, and well-polished appearance, is certainly up to the task of pulling this passenger train in the 1920s. The station is on the left and Pier B-C is in the centre distance. To the right is Pier D with, just visible, the funnels of the liner *Niagara*, from the service to New Zealand and Australia.
—CYRIL LITTLEBURY, LANCE CAMP COLLECTION

Snow and fog combine to make a cold, grey day on the Vancouver waterfront as an eastbound freight works past the Alberta Wheat Pool elevator. Grain became an increasingly important export through Vancouver during the 1920s as facilities and markets were developed. The traffic added greatly to tonnage on the railway and eventually became one of the major cargoes shipped from Vancouver.
—JAMES CROOKALL, CVA, 260

From 1887 until July 1932, CPR trains and transfer movements had to cross through busy sections of Vancouver to reach the False Creek yards. Here, a switcher stops streetcars and traffic at Hastings and Carrall streets in June 1932 just before the opening of the tunnel under Vancouver. —N. D. B. PHILLIPS, CVA, CANP51

The tunnel under Vancouver was 4,600 feet (1402 m) long and 22.5 feet (6.85 m) high. Its width varied from 16-19 feet (4.9-5.8 m), depending on the curvature, and overall the gradient was very slight. Ventilation fans were installed at the western portal. Cyril Littlebury photographed 4-6-2 No. 2702 coming out of the tunnel from the Drake Street yards probably in 1932. The engine was to be coupled onto an eastbound passenger train at the station.
—LANCE CAMP COLLECTION

The G4a 2700s replaced lighter Pacifics on the major main line passenger trains west of Revelstoke by the 1930s and remained in service until the retirement of steam power. This photo, taken on July 4, 1953, shows an aging 2705 arriving at the Vancouver station. —KEN MERILEES

Improvements on the main line included the concrete lining of the Connaught Tunnel, noted in Chapter II, and the strengthening or replacement of many bridges. The older structures were felt to be inadequate to handle the heavier equipment and trains anticipated in the next few years. In 1928 and 1929, extensive work was required on the bridges between Field and Revelstoke and eventually west to Taft. This program included replacing many structures and strengthening others notably the arch bridge over Stoney Creek and the steel viaduct over Mountain Creek. On the Thompson Subdivision, many improvements were made, including a new bridge in 1929 over the Nicola River just east of Spences Bridge and the replacement of the graceful steel arch over the Salmon River by a truss span. Improvements were also made to signalling and communications. By the fall of 1926, automatic electric block signals had been installed all the way between Field and Revelstoke. Later, they were extended all along the main line. This signalling system provided a safer, more efficient method of controlling train movements over the main line than the existing manually controlled blocks.

A major improvement on the Kettle Valley was the reconstruction of the bridge over Trout Creek near Summerland. The work involved replacing the long trestle approaches to the bridge with fill and six steel deck plate girder spans. Originally, the east approach required 270 feet (82 m) of trestle while the west needed 475 feet (145 m). Fill replaced all but 60 feet (18 m) of the eastern approach with the steel work completing the span up to the original steel centre section across the chasm.

On the E&N on Vancouver Island, a major program of bridge reconstruction and filling also was undertaken. Particularly notable was the replacement of bridges over the Trent and Big Qualicum rivers. Another interesting bridge project was the modification of the long bridge over the Fraser River at Mission to carry motor vehicles as well as rail traffic. An agreement was reached with the British Columbia government, who paid the CPR an annual rental of $7,500 and one-third of the repairs and operating expenses of the bridge. This arrangement permitted the government to discontinue operation of a ferry across the river.

Prompting most of the improvements to the bridges and roadbed on the main line during the late 1920s was the development of heavier, more powerful locomotives and a need for greater flexibility in the assignment of existing large locomotives. The last new heavy power introduced for mountain operation had been the 2-10-2s of the 5800 series built in 1919 and 1920. During the 1920s, many other locomotives had been added to the roster, including 2-8-2s and 4-6-2s, but heavier machines were clearly needed to increase the capacity and speed of passenger and freight movements through the mountains. Not only was there more traffic to be moved, but the rolling stock being used was itself heavier as steel cars

The murder of Doukhobor leader Peter Verigin on October 29, 1924 brought great sadness and confusion to his community. An explosion ripped apart the coach he was riding, killing Verigin and eight others, less than one mile west of Farron. The photograph shows the arrival of the train carrying his remains at Brilliant, the agricultural community he established.
—THOMAS GUSHUL, VPL, 179

Improvements to many sections of the Kettle Valley were carried out during the 1920s. Here a wooden trestle near Carmi is being filled. An elderly 2-8-0 is providing the power for the train and for the Lidgerwood winch just ahead of the locomotive. A ballast plow, at the far end of the train, was connected by cable to the Lidgerwood. Once at the dump site, the plow was pulled the length of the train unloading the fill.
—CVA, 300

Handsome 2300 G3d 4-6-2s worked into Field from the East. With large (75-inch/190 cm) drivers, they were not well suited for mountain service but since pushers were required in any case, they were not seriously handicapped.
—VPL, 31388

169

replaced predominantly wooden ones. Two particularly significant new locomotive designs were developed in the late-1920s and were placed in service during 1929. These were the 4-6-4, 2800 series, class H1 Hudsons, and the 2-10-4, 5900 series, class T1 Selkirks. Initially, the use of the 2800s was confined to other parts of Canada and it was not until 1940, with the construction of the five H1e Hudsons (described later), that this type was assigned to operate regularly in B.C. However, the 5900s were designed for mountain service from the beginning and they were used extensively in the Rockies and Selkirks between Field and Revelstoke. They were also used on the Field Hill and west of Revelstoke as far as Taft, a distance of 24 miles (38.7 km). Technical details of the locomotives accompany the illustrations.

The Selkirks proved to be an entirely successful design of locomotive well suited to both freight, passenger and pusher services in very tough conditions. They were reliable, durable machines and with only minor mechanical developments and cosmetic changes to produce a streamlined appearance, were reordered in the late 1930s and again in the late 1940s. The introduction of the Selkirks was not the only significant change in equipment on the CPR in British Columbia during this period. There were steady increases in the numbers and size of freight cars to keep pace with the growth in traffic, but of more interest to the public at least, were the changes and improvements to passenger rolling stock.

Prior to World War I, the CPR ceased acquiring wooden passenger rolling stock and switched to all-steel cars. However, the war made the extensive acquisition of new rolling stock impossible and it was not until the 1920s that large orders were placed. However, with the growth in traffic in the 1920s, much of the new equipment was required simply to provide for the increased volumes of business and wooden equipment remained in service, particularly in secondary services, until the end of the steam era.

Before the War, the premier train across Canada had been *The Imperial Limited*, which operated a daily service with a running time of about 100 hours. As noted earlier, a through service also was provided between St. Paul and the Coast. Initially this was by a connection with *The Imperial Limited* but later, it operated as a separate train called the *Soo Pacific Train De Luxe* and similar names. After the War, new expanded services were required and on June 1, 1919, the *Trans-Canada Limited* was introduced (as Trains 7 and 8 between Montreal and Vancouver and as Trains 9 and 10 for the Toronto-Sudbury sections). This luxury train carried first-class passengers only and operated on a year-round schedule. *The Imperial Limited* continued to operate in addition to the new trains. In 1923, the summer season *Mountaineer* was introduced between Chicago and Vancouver (Trains 13 and 14). These trains received a steady flow of new equipment during the 1920s and, in 1929, a re-equipped *Trans-Canada Limited* was inaugurated. Each set of equipment cost over

By the late 1920s, heavier passenger trains and growing freight tonnage prompted a major reconstruction of the main line between Field and Revelstoke to permit the use of heavier locomotives. Until that time, the S2a 2-10-2s had not operated west of Field and with new, larger power on order, in the form of the T1a Selkirk type 2-10-4s, bridges and turntables had to be strengthened or replaced. Stoney Creek Bridge was one. After reconstruction, with a second arch on each side, the bridge was ready to take the CPR's heaviest power. As a dramatic test, four locomotives, an R3 2-10-0, an S2 2-10-2, a T1 2-10-4 and another R3 2-10-0, were moved onto the bridge.
—H. V. DAVIS COLLECTION, BCPM

The new 2-10-4s were massive engines, measuring nearly 100 feet (30.5 m) long and weighing, with tender, 750,000 lbs. (340 tonnes) when fully loaded. With a tractive effort of 77,200 lbs. (35 tonnes) plus an additional 12,000 lbs. (5.4 tonnes) if equipped with a booster, they were the most powerful locomotives on the CPR system. All were oil fired. Westbound between Beavermouth and Glacier over the steepest grade, they were rated at 1050 tons (1066 tonnes), twice the tonnage rating of an N2b 2-8-0 and 350 tons (356 tonnes) more than an R3 2-10-0. At Field, above right, 5916 and 5902 pause, side by side, on August 13, 1939, a decade after entering service. In 1930, a new 5902, with what is obviously a well-used snow plow pilot, was photographed with some of the men who would come to know these machines well, on the turntable at Revelstoke.
—RAILWAY NEGATIVE EXCHANGE;
W. HENDRY, LANCE CAMP COLLECTION

$1,000,000. The orders for new equipment in the 1928-29 fiscal year were impressive. The company ordered 169 passenger cars that year, including 29 eight-section sleepers, two single room sleepers, 15 observation cars, 11 buffet parlours, 15 dining cars, two cafe parlours, and 15 first-class coaches. Freight car orders totalled over 8,800 and in addition, 408 service cars were purchased or built in company shops.

In a move to develop further its tourist facilities in Victoria, an impressive wing was added to the Empress Hotel and the CPR built a glass-enclosed swimming pool and conservatory behind the Empress Hotel. The new facility, named the Crystal Gardens, was opened to the public in 1925 and became a feature attraction and recreational facility in the city.* These improvements to the hotel system complemented the developments to the B.C. Coast Steamship Service which was expanded throughout the 1920s.

The coastal steamers not only acted as effective feeders to the railway, but they were important in their own right for tourism and traffic.

The trans-Pacific shipping services were improved significantly during the 1920's. The old *Empress of Japan* and *Monteagle* were retired, being replaced by the much larger and faster *Empress of Canada* and *Empress of Australia*. The last liner added to the fleet was the magnificent *Empress of Japan* of 1930. Expanding its operations even further, the CPR purchased a half interest in the liners *Niagara* and *Aorangi* and formed, with the Union Steam Ship Company of New Zealand, the Canadian Australian Line in 1931.

The Vancouver terminals became a particular focus of attention and development during the 1920s. New facilities were required for the steamships as well as for the railway. A major new pier complex (Pier B-C) was developed on Burrard Inlet to serve the Empress liners and other deep-sea vessels. This impressive structure was located between the existing Pier D, to the east, and Pier A, to the west. Preliminary work began in 1921-22 when dredging and filling started but it was not until July 4, 1927 that the pier was officially opened. The coastal liner *Princess Louise* was the first vessel to dock at the new facility.

A major problem in Vancouver had been the line connecting the shops and yards on the north shore of False Creek with the Burrard Inlet yards. The tracks ran through a heavily developed section of the city and required seven level road crossings in a distance of 1,600 feet (490 m). In addition, there were two crossings of B.C. Electric Railway tracks. Since all

Selkirk No. 8000, shown here at Field, was a unique locomotive on the CPR. Completed in May 1931, then tested in the East, it was placed in service that fall between Field and Revelstoke. The locomotive was a joint project of the CPR, the American Locomotive Company and the Elesco Feedwater Heater Company. Externally, it resembled the 5900s, but there were many fundamental differences. Instead of using a conventional boiler, the steam generating system was comprised of a low pressure boiler operating at 250 psi (1725 kPa), a high pressure boiler working at 850 psi (5860 kPa) and a special firebox unit designed for a pressure of up to 1,700 psi (11 700 kPa). The last was a closed circuit system using distilled water which, through a system of heat transfer coils, extended into the high pressure boiler. The low pressure boiler acted as a feedwater heater and purifier for the high pressure boiler.

The engine was a three-cylinder compound and there were many other features distinguishing the 8000 including its oil burners, firebox and combustion chamber design and the metals used in its construction.

In use, the 8000 produced a saving of about 15 percent in fuel consumption when operating in the Selkirks and it was less prone to slipping than were the conventional 5900s. However, in pool service, the crews found the machine difficult to adjust to. Maintenance was high and it was withdrawn in 1933 for modifications. Returned briefly to service in 1935-36, it was then retired and scrapped in 1940. —BCPM

---

* The Crystal Garden (often called the Crystal Gardens) was built following an agreement, which included tax concessions, with the City of Victoria. The CPR agreed to build and operate the facility for 20 years. The agreement was renewable for another 20 years. In 1964, the building passed to the city and in 1971 was closed when a new public swimming facility was opened. For several years, the fate of the structure was uncertain but a determined effort led to its restoration and reconstruction as a conservatory and tea room which was opened in 1980.

Some Hazards

SNOW & SNOW SLIDES
IN THE MOUNTAINS

Rotary 400807, one of the earliest CPR machines (formerly Rotary C), is in action at Revelstoke to clear the yards after a heavy snowfall. —H. V. DAVIS COLLECTION, BCPM

The crew of 2706 on an eastbound passenger train has to dig out at North Bend after hitting drifted snow in the Fraser Canyon on December 27, 1939. —LANCE CAMP COLLECTION

There is heavy, blowing snow as this crew at Revelstoke, second photo on right, prepares one of the big rotaries for action in January 1926.
—CPCA, 17768

In January 1935, slides at Three Valley, west of Revelstoke, closed the line and buried part of train No. 4 and another locomotive 14 miles (22.5 km) west of Revelstoke. Fortunately, no one was injured and after hours of cold, tough work, the line was reopened. The rotary at right was sent out to clear the line and is working west along Summit Lake in Eagle Pass.
—H. V. DAVIS COLLECTION, BCPM

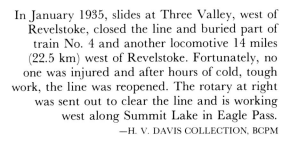

Some Disasters

WRECKS, WASHOUTS, SLIDES AND FLOODS

Problems were not confined to the main line. This washout, just east of Penticton, wrecked the locomotive and mail car of the *Kootenay Express.*—STOCKS FAMILY COLLECTION, 1PB

A snapshot recorded the disaster that overtook a crew working on a derailment east of Revelstoke in 1936. The tender, being towed away, broke free and, unheard above the storm, crashed into the unsuspecting crew; 16 men died that March 2nd.

On September 5, 1931, with heavy rain and warm weather melting the glaciers, the Illecillewaet River flooded and overflowed its channel filling the mouth of the Connaught Tunnel with 10-12,000 cubic yards (75-9100 m³) of rock, mud and debris. The only option was to dig it out; the work took until September 10.

On July 11, 1928, the boiler of pusher 5775 exploded near Glacier killing three railwaymen. The boiler flew five car lengths down the track, demolishing two cars in the train. "Not for many years," commented *The Revelstoke Review*, "has Revelstoke experienced such a sense of sorrow as [from the deaths] of Maurice Roger, Matthew Stanbury and William M. 'Billy' Clay."
—THREE PHOTOS, H. V. DAVIS COLLECTION, BCPM

January 1929 was a bleak month for Revelstoke. Two men died in a head-on collision near Lauretta on the 27th, and the next day, locomotive 5767, running back light to Beavermouth with 5779, fell through the eastern approach span of Surprise Creek Bridge. Engineer Bert Woodland and Jeffrey H. Griffith, the fireman, were found dead in the wreck. It took until February 17 to reopen the line.

—H. V. DAVIS COLLECTION, BCPM

CPR traffic between the two sections of its Vancouver terminals crossed through this section of the city, the problems with vehicular traffic, growing steadily in the city during the 1920s, can be well imagined. To overcome the problem, a tunnel was designed to pass under the city. The plans called for a single track tunnel beginning at the yards near Pier A at the end of Thurlow Street and then, swinging east, it was to pass under downtown running beneath Dunsmuir Steet to emerge at False Creek near the Georgia Street viaduct. Notably, 43 percent of the tunnel was curved. A contract was let to the Northern Construction Company and J. W. Stewart, Ltd. for the work, which was estimated to cost $1,500,000. The tunnelling was carried out completely from the east portal and was completed in 1932. The tunnel remained in use until the CPR phased out its False Creek yards in the early 1980s prior to the construction of the facilities for *Expo 86* which opened in Vancouver in 1986.

The operation of the main line, even after more than 35 years of service, was a constant challenge. There was always the unexpected. Slides, floods, accidents and fires could always occur without warning, killing, destroying months of work and valuable structures, or simply disrupting traffic. Most of the time, however, the railway operated without major difficulty. The crews were experienced and well trained, and the railway's physical plant was well maintained and improved over the years. The continuing investments in facilities and motive power refined and improved the CPR's operations through British Columbia. It was an efficient, safe and effective railroad system.

Winter conditions were particularly trying and sometimes caused major delays. Accidents, sometimes tragic, could also close the line. In October 1921, for example, a double-headed, 31-car eastbound freight crashed into a wall of fallen rock in Palliser Tunnel. By the time the final toll was in, seven men had died. On January 28, 1929, pusher engine 5767 fell through the approach span of Surprise Creek Bridge killing the crew. A new span was under construction but it took until February 17, 1929 to reopen the main line. During the closure, traffic was diverted over the Kettle Valley-Crowsnest route or over the Canadian National. There were other accidents and closures of the main line and other routes, particularly the Coquihalla. Some are illustrated here. They portray some of the hazards and frustrations that were, and are, part of railroading in the mountains of British Columbia.

Wrecks, washouts, slides and floods were not everyday occurrences on the main line but they did come with sufficient frequency to plague the crews and test the nerves of the most experienced men and their families at home. They were hazards of the trade.

The Depression Years

The prosperity and growth of the 1920s ended with devastating impact with the collapse of the stock market in late 1929.

Despite everyone's hopes, there was no quick recovery; conditions only got worse. Prices fell and unemployment grew. Mills could not sell lumber, prices and demands for metals fell* and farmers could not sell their produce. When markets could be found, the prices often did not cover the costs of production and transport. Then, on the prairies, the droughts struck the grain belts of Alberta and southern Saskatchewan. The focus of most people's activities shifted to one of simple survival and maintaining hope, if hope were possible, for the future.

The CPR and its thousands of employees shared the onslaught of the Depression with the country as a whole. Traffic and revenues declined, trains were reduced in frequency or eliminated altogether, and for many railroaders, there was little work. With trains operating less frequently, less maintenance work was required and shop and track forces were severely cut back. By 1933, the major shops were working only about half time. In 1933, wages were cut 10 percent and since 1928, the number of employees had dropped by one third to just under 50,000, nation-wide. For the railroaders with seniority who still had work, the wage cut was counteracted by the general decline in prices. But the problem for many was that their hours of work had fallen too. For men with lower seniority, on the spare board for example, who in the 1920s would have held regular runs and hence have had steady income, there was often little or no work. Seasonal or part-time work, if it could be found, helped carry many through the Depression. An engineer or machinist might work in a garage or drive a truck — any job that was available. Many of these employees, laid off with the Depression and the curtailment of services, never returned to the CPR.

For stockholders, the return on investment was cut as revenues fell. Common stock dividends were cut in half to five percent in 1931 but after that, for 10 years, no dividends were paid. In 1933, there was no dividend for preferred shares either. By 1933, CPR revenues had fallen to below one half the level of 1928 and through the mid to late 1930s, revenues from rail operations did not meet fixed costs; only supplemental revenues from hotels, steamships and other sources saved the situation.

Passenger operations during the Depression years were significantly reduced as the following comparison between 1928 and 1932 summer schedules for the transcontinental passenger trains illustrates.

* Fortunately for the CPR, the operations of the Trail smelter owned by its subsidiary, Consolidated Mining & Smelting Co., continued to be profitable and added significantly to company revenues during the Depression years. Because of its continued operations, it also generated significant freight traffic on the railway and as a result also helped maintain employment for the crews and businesses in the surrounding communities.

The drumhead signs from the CPR's finest trains of the late 1920s. —CPCA

East of Revelstoke, the trains stopped to let passengers have a brief stretch and view of Albert Canyon of the Illecillewaet River.
—CPCA, 17722

176

The magnificent fully re-equipped *Trans-Canada Limited* of 1929 was the Canadian Pacific's last great extravagant investment in passenger equipment before the onset of the Depression. Features of the train included a solarium lounge car, carefully finished dining car, a variety of sleeping car accommodations (there were no coaches in the train), bathrooms, ladies' smoking rooms and card rooms. Each of the 12 train sets required for the service was reported to have cost one million dollars.

The Depression brought an end to the *Trans-Canada Limited* and its fine rolling stock was assigned to other trains.

Fortunately, in the 1970s and 80s, through the determined work of the Cranbrook Railway Museum, under its director Gary Anderson, the *Trans-Canada* was reassembled from an assortment of original cars long since relegated to work train service. From under countless layers of paint emerged the elegance of the original wooden panelling and the possibility of restoration. After thousands of hours of work, the train was ready, although not fully restored, for display at Vancouver's *Expo 86*, and permanent preservation at Cranbrook.

Behind a graceful G2, No. 2520, the No. 7 nears the end of its long journey from Montreal as it rolls along the shore of Burrard Inlet, past rows of empty grain cars at the Alberta Wheat Pool, and on to the Vancouver station. It is an overcast Sunday, July 20, 1930.
—CYRIL LITTLEBURY, NORMAN GIDNEY COLLECTION

Transcontinental Services 1928 (all daily)

Soo-Pacific Express (Nos. 5 and 6) (operating between Vancouver and Chicago)
Trans-Canada Limited (Nos. 9-7 and 8-10)
The Imperial (Nos. 1 and 2)
Vancouver Express (No 3) and *Toronto Express* (No. 4)
The Mountaineer (Nos. 13 and 14) (operating between Vancouver and Chicago)

Transcontinental Services 1932 (all daily)

The Dominion (Nos. 5-3 and 4-6)
The Imperial (Nos. 1 and 2)
Soo-Dominion (Nos. 3-13-3 and 4-14-4) (operating between Vancouver and Chicago but combined with *The Dominion* between Moose Jaw, Banff and Vancouver)

This was a significant reduction in scheduled trains and at peak times, the name trains could be operated in several sections which the comparison above does not show. Passenger service on the southern Kettle Valley-Crowsnest route remained on a daily basis but with the improvement of through service along Kootenay Lake. However, service on some of the branch lines was curtailed. For example the twice weekly mixed between Cranbrook and Golden was reduced to weekly service. On the Esquimalt & Nanaimo, the Parksville-Port Alberni line's service was cut back to a daily return service. In the West Kootenays, the Nelson-Slocan City-Rosebery and Kaslo-Sandon-Nakusp services were reduced from three times a week to two. Additionally, while a daily train service was maintained between Robson West and Rossland, an additional daily run between Nelson and Rossland (Nos. 701 and 702) was dropped. Freight services fell during these years to a significant degree, as reflected in traffic statistics. In 1928, system wide, 42,977,000 tons (43 665 000 tonnes) had been moved but by 1932 the volume had shrunk to 22,613,000 tons (22 975 000 tonnes) — little more than half. Passenger volumes were hurt equally badly. In 1928, 14,751,000 revenue passengers were carried. Four years later, the total was only 7,916,000. Both freight and passenger traffic were to fall still further in 1933 before beginning a gradual recovery. It would take until the War years of 1942-43 to regain the pre-Depression volumes.

The Depression saw the closure of the CPR's Hotel Vancouver. However, the circumstances were not entirely negative as the CPR entered into an agreement with the CNR for the joint operation of the new CNR hotel being built in the city. It was obvious to both companies that neither hotel could operate economically in the Depression years so the old hotel was closed and later demolished. The new hotel took on the name Hotel Vancouver and was opened in 1939.

Fortunately, however, by the late 1930s, conditions were improving and traffic was definitely recovering. Some new rolling stock and locomotives had been added during the

For the trans-Canada tour of King George VI and Queen Elizabeth in 1939, the CPR brought out its finest. A special train of CPR and CNR equipment was headed by regally-decorated Hudson 2850. A flawless run led to the class being called Royal Hudsons. The 2851 was a spare. Everywhere, the crowds turned out. —L. S. MORRISON

Streamlining

In 1938, the CPR took delivery of its second order of Selkirks, the T1b class (Nos. 5920-5929). No. 5926 is shown on June 26, 1949 westbound on *The Dominion*, descending the Field Hill in the rain. —DONALD DUKE

Top left
Near Vancouver's Pier B-C, the CPR displayed its Depression-era speedster, the streamlined 4-4-4 type 3001 and train on September 16, 1936. This equipment was designed for intercity services. —KEN MERILEES

Bottom left
Resplendent in royal blue and stainless steel, 2850 rests in Vancouver. After visiting Vancouver Island, the Royal Party returned east on the CNR. —NORMAN GIDNEY

Depression years and towards the end of the decade orders grew. Older equipment had been sidelined and scrapped and new machinery was needed. Newer, modern power including 10 more Selkirks for service in B.C. and Hudsons for use on other parts of the system were ordered. These also reduced maintenance requirements and crew costs, which for the operating employees was not particularly welcome. The Selkirks were numbered 5920-5929 and were class T1b. Unlike their predecessors, these machines were streamlined following the pattern established for 4-4-4 and 4-6-4 locomotives also acquired by the company.

The War Years

In 1939, with the threat of war growing, King George VI and Queen Elizabeth visited Canada. This was the first time a reigning monarch had toured the country and the celebrations were extensive. From the point of view of the CPR the tour demanded elaborate preparations. For the tour, a specially decorated train was assembled to carry the royal party westbound across Canada. The CNR handled the train for the return journey to the East. The CPR assigned one of its new 4-6-4s to the train (No. 2850) and, for the occasion, this locomotive was specially painted and crowns were added to the running boards. The locomotive performed flawlessly across the country and after it was returned to regular service, the crowns were retained on it. The other streamlined Hudsons (Nos. 2820-2859) were fitted with crowns and the locomotives were thereafter known as Royal Hudsons.

In September 1939, World War II began and the despair of the Depression gave place to the demands and horrors of war. British Columbia was far from the fronts but the impact of the war was still very real. The social and economic changes were dramatic as the war effort increased and many men and women joined the armed forces or became directly involved in war production or industrial expansion. For the CPR, the overall impact of the war was staggering. While much of the wartime story cannot be covered here, some aspects are particularly significant to the history of the CPR's operations in British Columbia. For the railway there was steady growth of freight traffic. Gasoline rationing and shortages of automobiles brought traffic back to the railways. A scarcity of shipping diverted lumber and other important freight over the rails from the Pacific coast to the East. Between 1938 and the peak of wartime traffic in 1944, traffic across the CPR system, measured in ton miles, more than doubled. This was accomplished with the addition of limited numbers of new locomotives (mostly 2-8-2s and 4-6-2s) and cars. In addition, passenger volumes increased dramatically with troop movements and the return of automobile travellers to the trains. Revenues rose with the increasing traffic so that the war contributed to a healthier economic picture for the CPR and its shareholders.

CPR motive power had been well maintained through the

Traffic on the old Shuswap & Okanagan, sometimes called the "Sleepy-Oh", changed dramatically in character with the growing war effort. Long troop trains became common running between Vernon and the main line. This 12-car train, behind 2-10-0 5773, was running northbound, one mile east of Armstrong on October 22, 1944. — JIM HOPE

Wartime labour shortages brought many women to work in occupations that traditionally had been considered men's positions. These women worked at the E&N's shops in Victoria cleaning locomotives and rolling stock. The young woman near the smokebox of the old freight hog is holding her fingers up in the familiar "V" for victory. She and her companions were "doing their bit" for the war effort. —CPCA, 3489

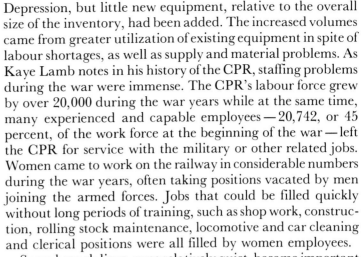

Depression, but little new equipment, relative to the overall size of the inventory, had been added. The increased volumes came from greater utilization of existing equipment in spite of labour shortages, as well as supply and material problems. As Kaye Lamb notes in his history of the CPR, staffing problems during the war were immense. The CPR's labour force grew by over 20,000 during the war years while at the same time, many experienced and capable employees — 20,742, or 45 percent, of the work force at the beginning of the war — left the CPR for service with the military or other related jobs. Women came to work on the railway in considerable numbers during the war years, often taking positions vacated by men joining the armed forces. Jobs that could be filled quickly without long periods of training, such as shop work, construction, rolling stock maintenance, locomotive and car cleaning and clerical positions were all filled by women employees.

Some branch lines, once relatively quiet, became important to the war effort. The trackage of both CP and CN into the Okanagan is one example because important military training camps were located at Vernon. Troop traffic on the branch was heavy and, when coupled with the seasonal fruit and produce rushes, conditions became particularly hectic and a real challenge for the operating crews. Traffic to and from the Trail smelter and the Sullivan Mine at Kimberley became extremely important to the war effort as did coal from the mines in the Crowsnest. Lumber and logs on the Esquimalt & Nanaimo were other important war-related products that took on new significance. The war years also saw a minor extension of trackage in the Okanagan when, in 1944, the Osoyoos Subdivision was extended south from Haynes, south of Oliver, to the town of Osoyoos, just north of the Washington border. This new trackage facilitated the movement of fruit and agricultural products from the southern-most end of the Okanagan Valley. Interestingly, it would prove to be one of the shortest-lived sections of CPR line in British Columbia. Trackage was abandoned between Okanagan Falls and Osoyoos in 1979 with the virtual disappearance of fruit traffic on the line due to competition from trucking.

The war years finally brought to the CPR in British Columbia a group of specially built Royal Hudsons for permanent assignment to passenger trains west of Revelstoke. These were all oil-burning machines, numbered 2860-2864 and classed as H1e, but they were essentially unchanged from the earlier subclasses of this highly successful design. In service in British Columbia, the new Hudsons were an immediate success and aided in moving the heavy wartime passenger trains. East of Revelstoke, through to Field, the trains normally were handled by Selkirks. Other wartime additions to the available motive power in B.C. were semi-streamlined versions of the very successful, pre-war designed, G3 Pacifics and P2 Mikados which were built in considerable numbers during and after the war. Freight and passenger road diesels,

Fortunately, some new equipment was available to help pull the growing traffic of the war years. Five new Royal Hudsons (2860-2864) were assigned to passenger trains between Vancouver and Revelstoke. No. 2863 was photographed at North Bend on August 11, 1940 beside elderly 2-8-0 No. 3613. With 12 cars to pull, it was the Hudson's first run out of Vancouver; the engineer was Trenholm Fee and the fireman Albert Martin. —ERIC A. GRUBB

New Pacifics such as G3g 2382, built in March 1942, eased the strain on older power. The locomotive was photographed at Sicamous on August 6, 1953. —JIM HOPE

In the spring of 1948, the Fraser River flooded, the worst innundation since the disastrous flood of 1894. High water overflowed the tracks, stranding farms and settlements. This scene was typical; a section crew watches helplessly as flood waters pour over the tracks. —CPR

The winter of 1949 brought heavy snows to the Fraser Canyon, blocking the line with repeated slides. The rotaries were called out to assist. So bad were conditions that on the CNR helicopters had to be used to take supplies into a stranded passenger train. —CPR

P2k class No. 5469, built in 1948, was typical of the 2-8-2s that joined the CPR roster during World War II and in the late 1940s. The 12 P2ks, all built in 1948, differed only slightly in details of appliances from the war-built locomotives. Here, 5469 is leading T1b 5926 eastbound out of Revelstoke in the early 1950s. The firemen on both locomotives are sanding out the flues, creating the black smoke, probably at the urging of the photographer.
—ALBERT H. PAULL, LANCE CAMP COLLECTION

were not to make their appearance on the CPR until the late 1940s.

CPR shipping services on the Pacific Coast were also affected by the war. The coastal liners *Princess Marguerite* and *Princess Kathleen* were both requisitioned for service in the Mediterranean where, in 1942, the *Marguerite* was torpedoed and sunk. Older vessels had to fill in on the important Triangle Route. The ocean steamships on the Pacific were completely disrupted by the war. All four of the Pacific Empresses were requisitioned for troop ship service. The *Empress of Japan* and *Empress of Canada* were withdrawn from passenger service in 1939 while the *Empress of Russia* and *Empress of Asia* were retained on the trans-Pacific run until November 1940, and January 1941, respectively. Service on the Canadian Australasian Line was also suspended after Japan entered the war. The *Niagara* was an early war casualty, when she struck a mine off New Zealand in 1940. The *Aorangi*, requisitioned early in the war, survived to re-establish the service in the late 1940s.

The war devastated the trans-Pacific fleet. Only the *Empress of Japan*, renamed *Empress of Scotland* after Pearl Harbor, survived and she never returned to trans-Pacific service. The Atlantic fleet had suffered equally heavy casualties and the *Scotland* was needed on the North Atlantic routes. For the CPR, the post-war service across the Pacific was to be the domain of its developing airline.

Management changes in the post-war years saw the retirement of D. C. Coleman in 1947 and his replacement by William M. Neal, another experienced railroader, as president and chairman. He was followed in 1948 by G. A. Walker as chairman (who served until 1955 when the duties were assumed by Mather) and William A. Mather as president. This period was to see many important and sweeping changes in the character of the railway as will be developed in the next chapter.

*   *   *

The following sections describe the operations of the railway during the height of the steam era in the decades before dieselization. There were many changes in operating procedures over the years including assignments of crews and types of locomotives; rare or unusual movements took place. These sections cannot describe in detail all aspects of steam era operations. Instead, they are intended to provide some examples and an overall survey.

The operation of a railroad is a complicated process of balancing economy and service. At the same time it requires constant movements of crews and equipment over the line as traffic conditions dictate. Traffic is often uneven and the dispatcher may find that he has crews and equipment in the wrong places. Fortunately, experience and planning can

Wartime tonnage is wheeled along by 2-10-0 5762 beside the South Thompson River east of Kamloops. This was one of the few places in British Columbia where locomotives could attain high speeds. The R3s were not designed for speed but the Hudsons were. Wally Huffman recalled firing on the 2800s as they routinely hit 60 miles (96 km) per hour along these straight, well-maintained tracks. —FRANK CLAPP

D4g 444 was branch line power at Revelstoke in 1944. —FRANK CLAPP

Operations in the Mountains During the Steam Era

Notch Hill, between Salmon Arm and Sicamous, was a base for pusher locomotives. Westbound, the pushers worked from Tappan (11.2 miles; 18.0 km) to the summit, while eastbound, they were added to the trains at Chase. The R3 2-10-0s were used extensively in pusher and general freight service. These R3d class, Nos. 5781 and 5785, are waiting for the next assignment at Notch Hill in July 1941.
—JIM HOPE

The S2a class 2-10-2s were the other major type of locomotive assigned to pusher, or helper, services. At first they operated east of Field, but with the rebuilding of the line west to Revelstoke and beyond, they operated over Notch Hill and even into Kamloops. No. 5806 is assisting a Selkirk on the Mountain Subdivision.
—CHARLES M. NELLES

185

usually overcome these problems. A significant factor in the routine operation of a system is the type and nature of the locomotives available on the line. Speed and, most significantly, tonnage ratings are critically important. To make the system work efficiently in mountainous country different types of equipment were required to keep the trains moving with as little interruption as possible.

Mountain grades greatly reduce the tonnage capacity of a locomotive and affect its speed as well. On severe grades, extra locomotives are often required both for their pulling power and braking capacity. Braking the heavily loaded trains on the long descending grades was as critical an operation as lifting the tonnage over the mountains. Crews regularly tested the air brakes on the trains and before a long descent was begun the brakes were applied and inspected. They were then released and re-examined and the retainers set (to maintain constant brake shoe pressure), and finally the train was ready to begin moving downgrade. On long grades, stops were required for brake inspections and to allow the wheels and brake shoes to cool off. With care and attention to detail, it was a safe, reliable procedure. For the CPR in British Columbia, the constant up and down nature of the line and the heavy traffic required a complex assignment of locomotives and equipment.

The largest and most powerful locomotives available to the CPR during this period were the 2-10-4 Selkirks. These machines, first introduced in 1929, were designed for heavy freight and passenger service in the mountains. Highly successful, the first 20 of 1929 were supplemented by another 10 in 1938 which arrived just in time for the tremendous rush of wartime traffic. Previously, the largest power had been the 5800 series Sante Fe 2-10-2s, which, with their low drivers and good boiler capacity were well suited to pusher and freight service. Similarly useful were the 2-10-0, class R3 Decapods of the 5700 series, built between 1917 and 1919. The R3s were used extensively in a variety of services from pushers and main line freight engines to heavy switchers in the yards at Field and Revelstoke. For the balance of its main line freight power, the CPR drew on its large fleet of 2-8-2s, 2-8-0s and to a lesser extent 4-6-2s. The 2-8-2s were versatile and useful locomotives, built between 1912 and 1948, spanning what might be called the modern steam era. These were employed in all aspects of freight and passenger service. The older 2-8-0s were used extensively in B.C., particularly on the Kettle Valley lines as will be described later. In the early years, they were the largest freight and helper power available and were used on the toughest sections of the main line. However, as larger machines became available they were relegated to the less mountainous sections of the main line, such as the Fraser and Thompson canyons, and to the secondary routes.

Passenger locomotives for main line service were more limited in the number of types. After the replacement of the

Winter in the Selkirks. Three 2-10-4s, one on the front, one two-thirds of the way back in the train and a third just ahead of the caboose, begin the climb out of Beavermouth, along the Beaver River towards the Connaught Tunnel under Rogers Pass. —CHARLES M. NELLES

The climb over the Field Hill could require three engines for a heavy eastbound such as this 14-car train of heavyweight cars. Two 2-10-2s were used to help the G4a 4-6-2 road engine. —ERIC A. GRUBB

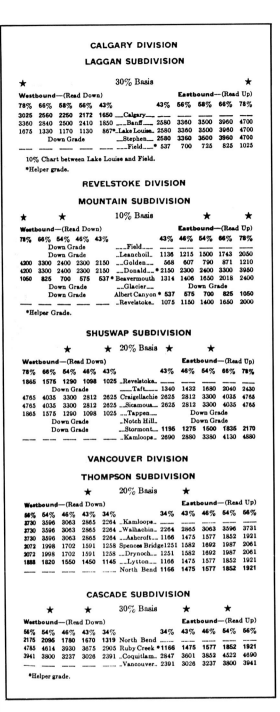

CALGARY DIVISION
LAGGAN SUBDIVISION

★   30% Basis   ★

Westbound—(Read Down)						Eastbound—(Read Up)				
78%	66%	58%	56%	43%		43%	56%	58%	66%	78%
3025	2560	2250	2172	1650	Calgary					
3360	2840	2500	2410	1850	Banff	2580	3360	3500	3960	4700
1675	1330	1170	1130	867	*Lake Louise	2580	3360	3500	3960	4700
Down Grade					Stephen	2580	3360	3500	3960	4700
					Field	* 537	700	725	825	1025

10% Chart between Lake Louise and Field.
*Helper grade.

REVELSTOKE DIVISION
MOUNTAIN SUBDIVISION

★   ★   10% Basis   ★   ★

Westbound—(Read Down)						Eastbound—(Read Up)				
78%	66%	54%	46%	43%		43%	46%	54%	66%	78%
Down Grade					Field					
Down Grade					Leanchoil	1136	1215	1500	1743	2050
4200	3300	2400	2300	2150	Golden	568	607	790	871	1210
4200	3300	2400	2300	2150	Donald	* 2150	2300	2400	3300	3950
1050	825	700	575	537	* Beavermouth	1314	1406	1650	2018	2400
Down Grade					Glacier			Down Grade		
Down Grade					Albert Canyon	* 537	575	700	825	1050
					Revelstoke	1075	1150	1400	1650	2000

*Helper Grade.

SHUSWAP SUBDIVISION

★   ★ 20% Basis ★   ★

Westbound—(Read Down)						Eastbound—(Read Up)				
78%	66%	54%	46%	43%		43%	46%	54%	66%	78%
1865	1575	1290	1098	1025	Revelstoke					
Down Grade					Taft	1340	1432	1680	2040	2430
4765	4035	3300	2812	2625	Craigellachie	2625	2812	3300	4035	4765
4765	4035	3300	2812	2625	Sicamous	2625	2812	3300	4035	4765
1865	1575	1290	1098	1025	Tappen			Down Grade		
Down Grade					Notch Hill			Down Grade		
Down Grade					Stormont	1195	1275	1500	1835	2170
					Kamloops	2690	2880	3380	4130	4880

VANCOUVER DIVISION
THOMPSON SUBDIVISION

★   20% Basis   ★

Westbound—(Read Down)						Eastbound—(Read Up)				
56%	54%	46%	43%	34%		34%	43%	46%	54%	56%
3730	3596	3063	2865	2264	Kamloops					
3730	3596	3063	2865	2264	Walhachin	2264	2865	3063	3596	3731
3730	3596	3063	2865	2264	Ashcroft	1166	1475	1577	1852	1921
2072	1998	1702	1591	1258	Spences Bridge	1251	1582	1692	1987	2061
2072	1998	1702	1591	1258	Drynoch	1251	1582	1692	1987	2061
1888	1820	1550	1450	1145	Lytton	1166	1475	1577	1852	1921
					North Bend	1166	1475	1577	1852	1921

CASCADE SUBDIVISION

★   ★ 30% Basis ★   ★

Westbound—(Read Down)						Eastbound—(Read Up)				
56%	54%	46%	43%	34%		34%	43%	46%	54%	56%
2175	2095	1780	1670	1319	North Bend					
4785	4614	3930	3875	2905	Ruby Creek	* 1166	1475	1577	1852	1921
3941	3800	3237	3026	2391	Coquitlam	2847	3601	3852	4522	4690
					Vancouver	2391	3026	3237	3800	3941

*Helper grade.

Tables of tonnage ratings for different classes of steam power on the main line subdivisions. Examples of the tonnage rating for different classes include: a T1 Selkirk was rated at 78 percent (meaning its tractive effort was nearly 78,000 lbs.), a S2a 2-10-2 at 66 percent, a P2 2-8-2 at 56-58 percent, an R3 2-10-0 at 54 percent, and an N2 2-8-0 at 43 percent. The tables reveal the effect of grades on haulage capacity. —WALTER PAFFARD COLLECTION

early 4-4-0s in the late 1800s, Ten-wheelers were commonly used. These were not large locomotives and they did, of course, require helpers on the mountain sections. Pleasingly designed D9s were used on the transcontinental passenger trains into the 1930s. The Ten-wheelers were operated extensively in later years in branch line services. During the 1920s, Pacifics from the G2 (2500 and 2600 series) were used in passenger service out of Vancouver. The G2s, with 69- or 70-inch (1.78 m) drivers were well-suited for the rolling main line west of the Selkirks. The route between Field and Revelstoke was the province of P1 class 2-8-2s during this time. The P1s were assigned to passenger services in the mountains until they were relieved by the first Selkirks delivered in 1929. Pacifics of the early G3 classes (2300s), with 75-inch (1.9 m) drivers operated in to Field from Calgary but were not normally operated to the west during the 1920s and 30s. Their large drivers were not a handicap climbing east out of Field because they required pushers in any case. However, in the 1940s, and until the end of steam, the later semi-streamlined versions of the G3s were used west of Revelstoke in passenger service. Locomotives particularly associated with passenger operations between Vancouver and Revelstoke and on the Field Hill in the 1930s and later were the handsome G4a 4-6-2s, built between 1919 and 1921. These locomotives were used on the passenger trains until the end of steam operations in British Columbia. They operated on all sections of the main line except from Revelstoke to Field where lower drivered power was more suited. This was the section where the T1 Selkirks were used extensively on both passenger and freight operations, performing the same role that the 2-8-2s had in the 1920s. The dual service Selkirks were the most powerful passenger locomotives available and they were employed on the trains east of Revelstoke. The famous Royal Hudson 4-6-4s were not used in great numbers in British Columbia. Only five (2860-2864) saw regular service and these were the last Hudsons built for the CPR. They were built in 1940 and were used west of Revelstoke on the main line. They were an ideal complement to the Selkirks, operating on the heavy wartime and post-war passenger trains. More details of these various locomotives are presented with the accompanying illustrations.

The worst sections of the main line, in terms of grades, in British Columbia were between the summit of the Rockies and Revelstoke over the Laggan and Mountain subdivisions. During the steam era, extra locomotives were required routinely at several locations. Helper crews were based at Field, Golden, Beavermouth, Revelstoke, and to the west at Notch Hill.

There were many variations in operations but the following section gives general characteristics and some examples of procedures. Approaching the Great Divide from the east, the regular passenger trains were handled by a G4, 2700 series Pacific in the 1930s and in later years by a Selkirk. One of

2700 could power a train from Calgary to Lake Louise, but from that point to the summit at Stephen, a helper was required. Eastbound, the 2700s required two helpers climbing the Field Hill. Adding to the loss of hauling capacity due to the steep grade was the problem of greasy rails in the Spiral Tunnels. Condensation from fuel gases settled on the rails and caused the locomotives to slip and lose some of their pulling power. This problem affected freight operations as well. Freight over this section of the line was assigned to P2 class, 5300 (and later, 5400) 2-8-2s and S2, 5800 2-10-2s for pushers. Later, T1, 5900 2-10-4s were used on the Field Hill as well.

With its heaviest tonnage moving westbound, the greatest problem for the CPR was the climb over the Selkirks since this section combined both steep ascending and descending grades. Pushers were stationed at Beavermouth to assist heavy westbound trains. Since the tonnage capacity of one of the 2-10-4s over the Selkirks was 1,050 tons (1066 tonnes), trains were normally made up in units based on the capacity of one locomotive with pushers added as required. As many as four locomotives were required on some westbound trains. The road engine was at the head of the train and then two helpers were cut into the middle of the train while the forth engine ran just ahead of the caboose. This permitted an even distribution of the train weight among the locomotives: the lead engine pulling its full tonnage rating, the second engine pushing, the third engine pulling and the fourth pushing. Eastbound trains, which were often made up of empty grain cars, were usually longer than westbounds for the same tonnage. Normally, only one pusher was required for these movements. This pusher was added at either Revelstoke or Albert Canyon and ran to the summit at Glacier. For passenger trains travelling westbound over the Selkirk Mountains, one helper was usually required from Beavermouth to Glacier.

A dispatcher had to take care not to have a buildup of power coming in from one direction at a terminal. Such a situation could leave him with insufficient crews and locomotives at key locations to handle the traffic on the line. This could be a particular problem with westbound traffic because it required more locomotives than did eastbound tonnage. Crews could build up at Revelstoke when they were needed to the east. To overcome this problem, it was sometimes necessary to run pushers and extra locomotives back over the line without tonnage. This was an essential, if sometimes inefficient, part of keeping trains moving through the mountains.

West of Revelstoke, over the Shuswap Subdivision to Kamloops, grades requiring helpers or pushers were encountered over Eagle Pass just west of the Columbia River, and over Notch Hill, between Tappan and Chase. Taft, to the west of Eagle Pass, was the turn around point for helpers operating out of Revelstoke and it was also the farthest west point the Selkirks were permitted to operate due to weight

Selkirk 5903 roars by a freight waiting "in the hole" for clear track ahead. Melting snow holds promise of spring but with it, there is the constant danger of slides and washouts.
—CHARLES M. NELLES

A young fireman leans from the cab of his Selkirk at Revelstoke in September 1952. With sufficient experience and seniority a fireman would advance to an engineer beginning on the spare board until he had enough seniority to bid on a regular run. —RAILWAY NEGATIVE EXCHANGE

Operations were complicated by the need to keep traffic moving with as little delay as possible. In this scene, two freights, having waited while a passenger train cleared the main line, are ready to continue. The engineer of the Selkirk at right now has a clear track ahead and the switches are lined up for him to proceed onto the main line. Although the trains are stopped, the scene is far from quiet; there is a constant thumping of air pumps, a whine of turbogenerators, the roar of escaping steam from the pop valves and the rush of air and exhaust through the stacks. The smell of hot oil and steam permeates the air, broken by the fresh, cool breeze off the mountains. Within a few minutes, the first freight will proceed and then the train at left, with pusher (5901), will resume its run. —CHARLES M. NELLES

restrictions on bridges. Notch Hill crews ran between Chase, 14 miles (22.5 km) to the west, and Tappen, 10 miles (16 km) to the east. Class R3, 5700 2-10-0s were normally operated on freights and as helpers over this section of the main line in the pre-War period although 2-10-2s also were used later. Passenger power was provided by the reliable G4 Pacifics and these engines ran between Vancouver and Revelstoke without change. It was on this section of line that the Royal Hudsons (2860-2864) were used after 1940.

The line presented few operational problems between Kamloops and Savona on the Thompson Subdivision. From there, however, for many years freight trains often had to be doubled over the hill between Savona and Walhachin, a distance of seven miles (11.25 km). Grade revisions in the 1930s eliminated this problem and enabled one 3600 or 3700 series N2 2-8-0 locomotive (typical power for the 1920s and '30s) to handle a 2,865-ton (2910-tonne) train to Spences Bridge. West of Spences Bridge, the rolling grades along the Thompson and Fraser rivers reduced tonnage ratings on these locomotives to 1,450 tons (1473 tonnes). P2s, often used in the 1940s and '50s, operating west of Kamloops could handle correspondingly heavier trains. For westbound trains, that could be handled by one locomotive into Spences Bridge, it was necessary to add a second engine from Spences Bridge all the way to Ruby Creek in the Fraser Valley. Eastbound freight movements also required two locomotives through the canyon country.

Extra tonnage that had to be left behind by the through trains was moved by P2 2-8-2s, stationed at North Bend, the beginning of the Cascade Subdivision.

The operation of trains during the steam era was efficient for the time but it was costly and meant a great deal of lost time switching equipment and required the use of many crews and locomotives. Such a situation was an invitation for new technology and the dieselization of the main line in the 1950s, described in the next chapter, initially permitted the elimination of all helper assignments and most equipment changes. The change was dramatic, altering the entire operating pattern of the railway and having a significant impact on the lives of the crews.

In the years after World War II, traffic over the main line through the mountains was heavy. Normally, there were three scheduled passenger trains operating in each direction on a daily basis. In the summer, an additional train operated and when traffic was particularly heavy extra sections might be required. Freight traffic added three scheduled trains a day in each direction as well as extras, way freights and work trains. Westbound trains were normally the heaviest, averaging about 2275 tons (2310 tonnes) while eastbounds, often returning empty rolling stock, were lighter, averaging about 1830 tons (1860 tonnes).

The demanding conditions on the main line of the Mountain and Laggan subdivisions required modern and efficient

Winter out of Revelstoke. Two Selkirks begin the climb up the Illecillewaet Valley to Rogers Pass with a long freight. —LANCE CAMP COLLECTION

NOTES FOR TABLE AT RIGHT

+ Capacity of CPR locomotives was rated in percentages reflecting tractive effort. In this case a 54% engine had a tractive effort of 54,000 lbs. See tables of tonnage ratings for these two subdivisions.

* Coal burning locomotives; all others were oil fired.

This is a representative assignment at the time studies were carried out for the dieselization of the two subdivisions.

Passenger locomotives operated between Calgary and Revelstoke. For work train and snow clearing service on the Laggan Subdivision, locomotives were taken from the pool as required.

Assignment of Steam Locomotives, ca. *1950*

LAGGAN SUBDIVISION

Type of Service	Numbers	Class	Capacity+
Passenger	5926, 5928,	T1	78%
	5933, 5934,		
	5935		
Through Freight	5925, 5927	T1	78%
	5427*, 5428	P2	58%
	5430*, 5431		
	5432*, 5433		
	5436*, 5438		
	5439*, 5441*		
	5442*, 5443*		
	5444*		
Pusher (Field)	5430*, 5352*	P2	56%
	5391*		
	5803, 5809	S2	66%
	5810, 5811		
	5812, 5813		
Wayfreight	1242*	G5	34%
Switchers:			
Exshaw-			
Canmore	1276*	G5	34%
Banff	3619	N2	43%
Spare for Repair	5363*	P2	58%
	5364*		
	5440*		
	5929	T1	78%

MOUNTAIN SUBDIVISION

Passenger	5923, 5930	T1	78%
	5931, 5932		
Through Freight	5902, 5903	T1	78%
	5905, 5908		
	5912, 5913		
	5914, 5917		
	5922		
Pushers:			
Beavermouth	5805, 5806	S2	66%
	5808		
	5906	T1	78%
Golden	5756, 5757	R3	54%
	5760, 5773		
Revelstoke	5901, 5907	T1	78%
	5915, 5918		
	5924		
Switchers:			
Revelstoke	5761, 5781	R3	54%
Field	5762	R3	54%
Work	5775, 5777	R3	54%
Spare for Repair	5904, 5910	T1	78%
	5916, 5920		
	5921		

power. In the years just prior to dieselization, typically 36 locomotives were assigned to each subdivision for main line and yard service and additional power operated into Revelstoke from the west. T1 Selkirks were the assigned passenger engines while other T1s handled the through freights on the Mountain Subdivision and T1s and P2s worked freight on the Laggan Subdivision. T1, P2, S2 and R3 locomotives were all used as pushers.

Major servicing facilities were operated at the division points of Field, Revelstoke, Kamloops, North Bend and Coquitlam through British Columbia on the CPR main line. It was at these points as well that train crews were based. Smaller facilities were located at the helper stations, branch line junctions and at other crew change points. The line east of Field was administered from Calgary as part of the Calgary Division and dispatching was handled from there. Revelstoke dispatchers controlled operations between Field and Kamloops (Revelstoke Division), while North Bend dispatched trains between Kamloops and the Coast (Canyon Division). The Pacific Region, including the entire main line west of Field, was under the supervision of the region headquarters in Vancouver.

Over the years, the administrative and operational division structure of the railway changed. In the early years, taking 1903 as an example, the entire route west of Laggan (Lake Louise) was called the Pacific Division with three Districts. No. 1 included the main line west to Kamloops (but not Kamloops itself) and the branches to Okanagan Landing and Arrowhead. District No. 2 included the remainder of the main line and branches to New Westminster, Huntingdon Junction at the United States border, and to Steveston. District No. 3 encompassed all of the lines in the Kootenays centering on Nelson. The extensive water routes on the lakes were also administered out of Nelson. The main line was divided into sections while the other lines (with the exception of the Lardo, Nakusp & Slocan, and Boundary sections) were normally termed branches.

Trackage from Kootenay Landing east over the Crowsnest Pass was part of the Western Division as was the main line east of Laggan. In earlier years, the Western Division's control reached as far west as Donald but this presumably changed after facilities were removed from Donald and moved to Field and Revelstoke in 1899. After the completion of the Spiral Tunnels, Field became the eastern end of the Pacific Division (later called the Pacific Region). During World War I, the term "division" was applied to smaller areas, for example between Field and Kamloops (the Revelstoke Division) and "subdivision" was used for sections over which crews would operate before crew changes, for example the Mountain Subdivision from Field to Revelstoke. Then the larger administrative areas became districts and, later, regions. At that time, the trackage between Kootenay Landing and Crowsnest became part of the new British Columbia District.

Steam returned to the Field Hill on July 8, 1986 when G5 Pacific 1201 from the National Museum of Science and Technology ran, unassisted by diesels, from Field to Calgary after a visit to *Steam Expo* in Vancouver and ceremonies at Port Moody marking the centennial of through train service on the CPR.
—ROBERT D. TURNER

Along the Main Line to the Great Divide

Beginning at the Vancouver Terminals, this series of photos follows the main line to the Grat Divide. There is a mixture of freight and passenger trains from a variety of time periods during CPR's years of steam operation.

The Vancouver Terminals

THE END AND ALSO THE BEGINNING

Cyril Littlebury photographed the engineer of
yard engine 6802 pausing to share his lunch
with some of Vancouver's ever-present seagulls.
—LANCE CAMP COLLECTION

Vancouver seldom experiences much snow, but
when it does come it can be wet and heavy.
This 1930s winter scene of a transfer freight from
Coquitlam to Vancouver was taken along
Burrard Inlet.
—CYRIL LITTLEBURY, LANCE CAMP COLLECTION

A terminal would be incomplete without its yard engines. No. 6939, rebuilt from a 1908-vintage 2-8-0 in the 1920s, was still hard at work in the Drake Street Yards in 1949. —W. GIBSON KENNEDY

Grain movements to Vancouver grew in importance during the 1920s and 30s. It is Tuesday, September 4, 1938 and M4f 2-8-0 3455 and R3c 2-10-0 5772 head a westbound grain train from Coquitlam to the terminals along Burrard Inlet. —NORMAN GIDNEY

The major yards and shops at Coquitlam were a centre of CPR operations during the steam era. Five locomotives, including two G4a 4-6-2s, are outside the roundhouse on July 27, 1947. No. 2711 was unusual in being fitted with "elephant ear" smoke deflectors. —NORMAN GIDNEY

It was just a routine water stop at Coquitlam for the crew of 4-6-0 No. 573 on September 9, 1953 until the standpipe stuck. Then the flood began. Getting soaked was unavoidable, but eventually they did stop the water. —ALBERT FARROW

The crew of a local freight switches cars outside the New Westminster station. Steam power was nearing its end in this view from the early 1950s. —NORMAN GIDNEY

196

Vancouver. It was either the end or the beginning of the 2,886-mile (4644-km) journey on the main line between the Pacific terminus and Montreal. Train No. 2, headed by a well-polished 4-6-2 No. 2388, was ready to leave the Vancouver station on June 30, 1952.
—JOHN C. ILLMAN

Vancouver to Kamloops

Yale. Heavy snows have blanketed the Fraser Canyon in this scene from 1949. The plow train, with a 5300 2-8-2 for power, worked down from North Bend, clearing drifts and slides. —CPR

Extra 3650 West takes the passing siding at Spuzzum in the Fraser Canyon on April 5, 1930. It will meet another train working east to North Bend. The headend brakeman is riding the pilot through the station and will throw the switch for his train once the main line is clear. The 3600s were typical freight power in the Canyon during the 1930s. —ALBERT H. PAULL

At North Bend, the engine crews changed, locomotives took on water if needed and the engines were given an inspection. It is June 30, 1952 and Train No. 2 will soon be on its way; 10 minutes was a typical stop at North Bend.
—JOHN C. ILLMAN

Racing through the farm lands of the Fraser Valley on Train No. 2, with nine cars, 2700 is on familiar rails. It is May 20, 1947 and the aging Pacific will take the train through to Revelstoke. Once into the Fraser Canyon, the work will really begin.
—ANDRE MORIN

Deep in the Fraser Canyon, an N2b 2-8-0, No. 3623, pulls through Kanaka between North Bend and Lytton. During the steam era, passing sidings like Kanaka were usually the site of a small station and section house and many also had a water tower. —ALBERT H. PAULL, PABC, CP670

A coincidence of topography and engineering brought both the CPR and the CNR to this point on the Fraser River, known as Cisco, where each crossed to the opposite side of the canyon. A CP freight train, hauled by a P2 2-8-2, is shown on the impressive span just as the locomotive clears the eastern abutments of the bridge. The CPR passing siding of Cisco is 1.5 miles (2.4 km) east of the bridge. —NICHOLAS MORANT, CPCA, M4611

East of Lytton, the CPR follows the dry banks of the Thompson River canyon through to Savona on Kamloops Lake. Albert Paull photographed this P2 westbound along the Thompson during the 1930s. Automobile travel across British Columbia during this era was still very much an adventure. P2s, like 5345, typically were assigned to through freights between Kamloops and North Bend. —PABC, CP965

Under heavily overcast skies, CPR Train No. 2 heading east, meets No. 1, westbound, at Basque along the Thompson on June 30, 1952. On No. 1 is 2387 while 2388 is powering No. 2. Basque was the point where both the CPR and the CNR shared the same side of the river and where construction of an interchange track was possible. The CNR's main line is at left.
—JOHN C. ILLMAN

200

Top left
A nearly new Royal Hudson 2860 pauses at Kamloops for a crew change in October 1941.
—JIM HOPE

Kamloops to Revelstoke

Sicamous was the point where passengers travelling to or from the Okanagan changed trains. Here No. 8, with 2864 and 2382, waits at the station on July 1, 1952. —JOHN C. ILLMAN

Southbound passenger train No. 708 from Sicamous to Vernon rolls through Armstrong in July 1942 behind D9c 585. —JIM HOPE

Lower left
Chase was where extra power was added to eastbound trains for the climb over Notch Hill. In this Cyril Littlebury photo from the 1930s, an elderly 2-8-0 has just coupled onto the G4 road engine on this train. —LANCE CAMP COLLECTION

Heavy power in the form of P2 5469 and R3 5787 was assigned to Train 954, an eastbound freight, rolling into Sicamous in July 1949.
—ANDRE MORIN

201

Selkirk 5914 and a Royal Hudson wheel an eastbound passenger train along Clanwilliam Lake, at the summit of Eagle Pass, towards Revelstoke. The 2-10-4s were only allowed as far as Taft, 15.5 miles (25 km) to the west.
—ALBERT H. PAULL, PABC, CP1195

Working west out of Revelstoke on July 12, 1952, 2-8-2 No. 5463 needs the assistance of a 2-10-2 to the summit of Eagle Pass but the helper will run at least as far west as Taft. There it will turn and work an eastbound over the grade. —WILBUR C. WHITTAKER

The Columbia River was in full flood on July 1, 1948 as Hudson 2861 led Pacific 2701 across the bridge into Revelstoke. The consist is heavy, with extra baggage, mail and express cars.
—WILBUR C. WHITTAKER

A clear winter day finds 5786 on a freight east of the Columbia
nearing Revelstoke. —ALBERT H. PAULL, LANCE CAMP COLLECTION

Albert Paull, a dedicated photographer, captured this exceptional portrait of CPR steampower at its finest. Selkirk 5909 and a Royal Hudson blast into Revelstoke with a heavy eastbound passenger train during the summer of 1944.
—LANCE CAMP COLLECTION

The yards at Revelstoke have been a major centre of railroad activity since the late 1890s. This 1920s view shows the roundhouse and backshops in the middle of the photo with the Revelstoke Hotel at left and the station in the foreground. —REVELSTOKE MUSEUM

Revelstoke

The Revelstoke station, photographed in 1951, housed dispatching offices and other divisional administration facilities. It was replaced in 1978.
—WILBUR C. WHITTAKER

Switching at Revelstoke was performed by 2-10-0s like No. 5778, photographed hard at work on July 1, 1952. —JOHN C. ILLMAN

WEST OF REVELSTOKE
Heading west, 5786 assists Royal Hudson
2860 out of the Revelstoke yards in 1944.
The aging 2-10-0 will run with the Hudson as
far as Taft, where it will wait for an
eastbound to help over Eagle Pass.
—ALBERT H. PAULL, LANCE CAMP COLLECTION

In the 18-stall Revelstoke roundhouse, crews
serviced power operating both east and west on
the main line and also to the south over the
Arrow Lake Subdivision. Sunlight penetrates the
gloom of the roundhouse on August 31, 1942
and reflects off the cleaned and polished surfaces
of Selkirk 5922 and Royal Hudson 2860.
—L. S. MORRISON

SOUTH OF REVELSTOKE
To the south ran the branch line to Arrowhead. From there,
sternwheelers connected with Nakusp and Robson. Once this
branch and the steamers were critical to the CPR's services to
the Kootenays. By July 1951, when this photo of D10g 918
pulling out of Revelstoke was taken, the service had dwindled to
minor importance. In 1954 the *Minto*, the last steamer on the
route, was retired.—WILBUR C. WHITTAKER

EAST OF REVELSTOKE
Beginning the battle over the Selkirks, 5921
leads an earlier T1a 2-10-4 out of Revelstoke in
another view from 1944. The 2-10-4s, named for
the mountains they challenged, were assigned to
both freight and passenger services.
—ALBERT H. PAULL, LANCE CAMP COLLECTION

207

In another of Albert Paull's striking photographs, two T1bs, led by 5920, head east just out of Revelstoke under towering columns of steamy exhaust. —LANCE CAMP COLLECTION

Revelstoke to Field

At Albert Canyon, 21 miles (34 km) east of Revelstoke, the operator holds up orders for the engineer of 5901 on June 22, 1941.
—A. R. JOHNSON, JIM HOPE COLLECTION

Slogging up to the Connaught Tunnel, 5120 leads another locomotive, a second 2-8-2, and a long passenger train towards the summit of the line over the Selkirks. Mount Sir Donald is in the distance. Bryon Harmon photographed this scene from the 1920s when the 2-8-2s were still assigned to passenger trains in the Selkirks.
—ACR, NA71-1610

The *Trans-Canada Limited*, behind Selkirk 5905, rolls into the approach cut of the Connaught Tunnel in this photograph from 1929 or 1930.
—CPCA, 21341

Stoney Creek, probably the most famous railroad bridge in Canada, was dusted in snow as T1b 5920 led Royal Hudson 2863 westbound in 1951 with the special train carrying Princess Elizabeth and the Duke of Edinburgh to Vancouver. —NICHOLAS MORANT, CPCA, 201

In the shadow of Mount Macdonald, a 2-10-0 drifts downgrade out of the east portal of the Connaught Tunnel leaving the barrier of the Selkirks behind. —BYRON HARMON, ACR, NA71-1581

Beavermouth was the base for pushers working heavy westbound trains over the Selkirks. This photo is from September 1952 and the days of steam are ending.
—RAILWAY NEGATIVE EXCHANGE

East of Golden the climb up the Kicking Horse began and helpers were required as far as Leanchoil. This view from the cab shows R3 5775 leading a 2-10-4 on an eastbound *Dominion* in August 1939.
—ERIC A. GRUBB, RAILWAY NEGATIVE EXCHANGE

The Kicking Horse Canyon provided a spectacularly scenic approach to the Rockies as this Byron Harmon photograph suggests. This train, composed mostly of tank cars, is heading east behind a 2-10-0. —ACR, NA71-5412

Two R3 pushers, 5762 and 5759 wait at Golden for the next assignment. —GLENBOW MUSEUM, NA3630-1

In from Calgary, the westbound *Dominion*, behind T1c 5934, waits outside the small station at Field in September 1952.
—RAILWAY NEGATIVE EXCHANGE

Field

Blasting into Field from the west, 5911 leads a long freight from Vancouver in September 1937.
—RAILWAY NEGATIVE EXCHANGE

Mist and cloud hang low over the mountains as the crew of Work Extra 5785 switches on the wye at Field on the morning of July 2, 1952.
—JOHN C. ILLMAN

The biggest and the last. T1c 5935, shown at Field on June 7, 1952, was the last steam locomotive built for the CPR, being delivered in 1949. By the mid-1950s diesels had come to the mountains and this engine was transferred to the prairies. —AUTHOR'S COLLECTION

Field to the Great Divide

There is an impatience in the air: passengers boarding the train, crew members making last minute checks and receiving orders, hammering air pumps, blowing off steam and, behind it all, the constant flow of the Kicking Horse River. CPR Train No. 8, the eastbound *Dominion*, is waiting for the arrival of No. 7, its westbound counterpart. Heavy summertime traffic on June 27, 1949 requires two S2 2-10-2s (5803 and 5812) to assist 5934, the road engine, over the Great Divide. —DONALD DUKE

213

With the main line clear ahead, an eastbound begins the climb out of Field that will take the train over the summit of the Rockies and into Alberta. Twelve or 13 cars are behind the road engine, a Pacific, and the 5803. The 2-10-2 will run as far as Stephen or perhaps Lake Louise before relinquishing the train to the Pacific for the downgrade run to Calgary. —VPL, 31386

The ascent from Field along the face of Mount Stephen and past Cathedral Crags took passengers through some of the most breathtaking scenery accessible to rail travellers anywhere in the world. As usual, a 2-10-2 is assisting the 2-10-4 on this eastbound.
—NICHOLAS MORANT, CPCA, 2200

The Dominion, with triple-headed power (5813, 5812, and 5923), giving a spectacular display, crosses over the Kicking Horse River nearing Yoho just before entering the lower Spiral Tunnel on June 26, 1949. —DONALD DUKE

Working heavily, 5810 and 5930 pull the first section of No. 8 through the lower Spiral Tunnel and over its west portal. This fine portrait of CPR steam in its final years in the mountains was recorded on June 26, 1949. —DONALD DUKE

Clear of the lower Spiral Tunnel, the engineers on 5813, 5812 and 5923 opened the throttles wide. The ground shook with their passing and the echoes lingered for long minutes through the mountains. This was the first section of the eastbound *Dominion*, on June 26, 1949, while 5934, easing downgrade, had charge of the westbound No. 3. —BOTH DONALD DUKE

216

Nearing the Great Divide, T1b Selkirk 5923, heads the eastbound No. 2 upgrade near Hector on September 4, 1950.

—ERIC A. GRUBB

Descending the Field Hill through Yoho, a 5900 rolls downgrade with No. 3, the westbound *Dominion*. Travellers can enjoy the beautiful late summer weather from the open observation car on this September 4, 1950.—BOTH ERIC A. GRUBB

Elderly P2 5378 leads a newer 5427 upgrade between the Spiral Tunnels on Second No. 8, *The Soo-Dominion*, while below another P2, 5323, assists Selkirk 5924 through Yoho in September 1950.—BOTH ERIC A. GRUBB

The Rockies in late summer form an incomparable background for the westbound *Dominion* as it rolls smoothly through Leanchoil west of Field. For the passengers the beauty of the Lower Kicking Horse Canyon lies ahead and then the climb over the Selkirks. It is September 3, 1950 and the locomotive heading the long train is the 5930. —ERIC A. GRUBB

Farther to the west, Royal Hudson 2860 pauses at Sicamous on a wet August 30, 1951. The rigours of the run through from Vancouver are showing in the appearance of the locomotive. But Revelstoke is just 45 miles (72 km) to the east and there a Selkirk will take over. With luck, the Hudson will have a good cleaning before returning on a westbound to Vancouver. —MAURICE CHANDLER

The E&N was a unique part of the CPR's British Columbia operations both because of its history as an independent railway and also because of its isolated nature and the scale of its operations.

After the major expansions following its acquisition by the CPR in 1905, the E&N settled into a pattern of operations that remained little changed, except for the modernization of equipment and the gradual cutback of passenger services, for the rest of the steam era on the railway. In 1925 the line was extended to Great Central Lake to serve a major mill built there to process the valuable stands of timber in the area. This line, known as the Great Central Subdivision, ran from Solly Junction, 3.2 miles (5.1 km) north (east by timetable direction) of Port Alberni to Great Central, a distance of just 10.2 miles (16.4 km). While other construction was contemplated, including lines to the west coast north of Port Alberni, none of these schemes was ever implemented.

Motive power on the E&N during the 1920s and '30s consisted of a variety of types of smaller locomotives — Ten-wheelers and Consolidations. The Ten-wheelers included the group of D4g 4-6-0s noted earlier, several D5a class machines of the 490 series, and three 240 series class C3a locomotives. Consolidations were in two major series, the 3100s and the later and slightly heavier 3200s, the latter much preferred by the engine crews. The 3100s were used through the 1920s but, by the late 1920s, they were supplemented and ultimately replaced by the 3200s. All of this power, with the exception of the D4g's, was old before it reached the E&N, but the maintenance crews did their jobs well and the old freight "hogs" were kept in remarkably good condition. An important feature of steam locomotives on the E&N after the CPR assumed control was that, almost without exception, they were oil fired. Despite readily available coal from the Island mines, oil was used because it was cleaner burning and less likely to cause forest fires from sparks.

Yard work was performed by a variety of locomotives including two 2-4-2s (originally Nos. 1997 and 1998 but after 1913, Nos. 6004 and 6005) built by the Montreal Locomotive Works in 1910-11 and 0-6-0 switchers. An unusual engine used briefly in yard service on the E&N in the early years of CPR control was No. 1999, an 0-4-2T later used as a switcher at the Weston Shops in Winnipeg. The light yard engines were required in Victoria due to the weight restrictions on the Johnson Street Bridge over which the E&N tracks crossed from the yard in Victoria West to downtown Victoria. When a new, more substantial bridge was built in the early 1920s, heavier locomotives could be operated into Victoria. In the early 1940s, new power, in the form of 30-year-old D10g 4-6-0s, was assigned to the Island and most of the older locomotives were replaced.

A typical day in the mid-1920s on the E&N saw a surprising amount of activity for a railroad of this size. Two passenger trains — one in the morning and the other in the afternoon —

normally powered by D4g Ten-wheelers, operated each way between Victoria and Wellington seven days a week providing Island residents with an excellent service for both travel and mail delivery, since the trains carried Railway Post Office, or RPO, cars. Connecting service was also provided north of Wellington to Courtenay on a daily except Sunday basis and from Parksville to Port Alberni three times a week. In addition, until April 26, 1926, a Wednesday and Saturday mixed operated between Duncan and Lake Cowichan as train Numbers 9 (westbound) and 10 (eastbound).

On Wednesday, September 15, 1925, for example, in addition to the passenger trains between Victoria and Wellington (using D4g's 460, 462, 464 and 465), the dispatcher's train sheet showed a variety of movements that typified E&N operations during this period. There were southbound and northbound scheduled way freights (Trains 24 and 25) operated on the Victoria Subdivision between Victoria and Wellington, one with Ten-wheeler 498 and the other with 2-8-0 No. 3180. In addition, there were four extras, in each direction, operating over the Lake Cowichan Subdivision. These trains were mostly carrying logs from the Cowichan Valley and the crews were based in Duncan. Two of these trains, carrying logs from the Elco operations at Cowichan, ran over the E&N's main line between Hayward Junction and Osborne Bay Junction. From there, they operated over a 2.5-mile (4.1-km) long branch to Crofton where logs the were dumped. A third, with logs from the Victoria Lumber & Manufacturing Company's Camp 10 operations, ran to the mill at Chemainus. Locomotives 3131, 3133 and 3186 were used on these particular extras and trains of 24 loads of logs were typical. A fourth eastbound extra handled logs from Charter Siding, 5.9 miles (9.5 km) east of Lake Cowichan, while the fourth westbound was a wayfreight, handling traffic to the mills in the district.

Because the run from Lake Cowichan to Crofton, via Hayward Junction, where the Lake Cowichan Subdivision joined the main line, was only 26.1 miles (42.0 km), a crew could make two trips a day over the line if traffic warranted. In fact, in terms of the number of trains operated, the Lake Cowichan Subdivision often saw heavier traffic than either of the lines north of Wellington to Port Alberni or to Courtenay.

Another crew, using Ten-wheeler 242, ran a wayfreight between Wellington and Duncan and return. Yard crews operated at Victoria and another crew with 0-6-0 6062 switched at Ladysmith. In mid-afternoon this crew then ran light to Wellington, dropped off their locomotive for repairs and returned to Ladysmith with 4-6-0 No. 228, one of the Dunsmuir-era survivors, for the next day's yard shift. North of Wellington, 4-6-0 No. 241 handled the wayfreight between Wellington and Courtenay and return. On the Port Alberni Subdivision, Ten-wheeler 495 took eastbound Train No. 8 from Port Alberni to Parksville Junction and returned as an extra with freight. A turn was also run to Great Central from Solly Junction, 3.2 miles (5.1 km) east of Port Alberni. The

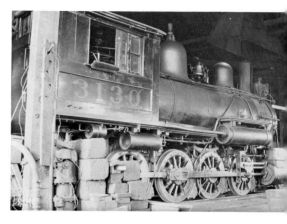

Typical of freight power on the E&N during the 1920s, a veteran L3a 2-8-0 3130 rests inside the engine house at Wellington between runs. Engines 3130, 3131 and 3132 were officially transferred to the E&N. These and other 3100s often worked log trains from the Cowichan Valley. —ALBERT H. PAULL, PABC, EN55

The E&N was crossed by a number of mining and logging railroads running from the interior of Vancouver Island to the Coast. The main line of Canadian Collieries (Dunsmuir) Ltd. crossed the E&N at Royston, south of Courtenay. This southbound was photographed on September 2, 1937. Either Harry Austin or Chris Wensley was the engineer. —DAVE WILKIE

Nearing Duncan, the mixed train from Lake Cowichan ambles along southbound on the E&N main line behind 3281, one of many 1900 vintage 2-8-0s of the M1 and M2 classes to work on Vancouver Island.
—ALBERT H. PAULL, LANCE CAMP COLLECTION

After the CPR takeover of the E&N, most of the locomotives transferred to the line were older machines. Significant exceptions were six D4g 4-6-0s built in 1912 and assigned to the E&N. Initially numbered 2460-2465 and later 460-465, typically they were used on the passenger trains as shown at right when, in October 1939, 463 was on No. 1 at Nanaimo. Of these engines, 460-463 were officially transferred to the E&N and operated on the line longer than the others. During the 1930s they were lettered for the E&N and had their road numbers shortened to 60-63, as in the photo at right of No. 63 about to leave Victoria.—PHILIP C. JOHNSON; DAVE WILKIE

same engine operated the next day in reverse, taking a freight through from Port Alberni to Parksville and returning with the westbound passenger train (No. 7).* The day's operations concluded with a crew handling a total of 90 loads of gravel from the pit just north of the Big Qualicum River for filling between Qualicum and Dashwood.

Traffic on the E&N was dominated by lumber and logs from the Island's rich forests. The southeast coast of Vancouver Island, the adjoining valleys and the Port Alberni-Great Central areas held some of the finest timber stands in Canada and the products of these forests gave the E&N a solid base of revenue, subject of course, to the vagaries of the lumber markets. The other dominant source of traffic was the Island's coal mines, centred at Nanaimo, Ladysmith (Extension), South Wellington and Cumberland. But after 1931, when the Extension mines closed, the market for coal fell off rapidly as oil became the preferred fuel. To illustrate the importance of these lumber and coal products to the E&N, during the 10 years between 1937 and 1946, of revenue cars loaded, 74 percent were forest products, 20 percent were coal while only six percent were general merchandise and other products.

The breakdown of this traffic provides some interesting insights into the character of the CPR's Vancouver Island line. The averages noted are for the 10-year period between 1937 and 1946. Coal traffic averaged over 6,766 cars per year and of this only 353 were shipped off the Island. For lumber, the average was over 11,000 carloads a year with nearly 9,000 destined for off-Island points. Log traffic, which averaged nearly 12,400 cars, was entirely local in origin and destination although the logs themselves were often towed to mainland mills or loaded on ships for export. Other forest products, such as shingles, averaged 2,100 carloads annually, with about one third shipped to the mainland. The war years brought interesting changes to the usual pattern of some of these commodities, particularly finished lumber. Wartime demands and restrictions on local consumption meant that local shipments fell dramatically from a pre-war average of 4,000-4,500 carloads to a 1943 low of only 570. On the other hand, export (from the Island) jumped from pre-war averages of 3,000-4,000 to over 15,600 in 1942. These were significant volumes of traffic and indicate the important role played by the E&N in the Island's forest industry.

The Princess ships of the British Columbia Coast Steamship Service of the CPR provided the passenger connections between Vancouver Island and the mainland of British Columbia, but it fell to tugs and barges to provide the E&N with its vital link for moving carload shipments of freight to

* It appears that at this time, Trains Nos. 7 and 8 were operating every other day over the Port Alberni Subdivision although in earlier years, and also later, the service was daily except Sundays. For a time in the late 1920s, two trains a day were scheduled over the line.

The E&N's major shops were moved to Victoria West (called Russells by the CPR) from Wellington after the CPR purchased the line. The roundhouse, completed in 1913, and the adjacent yards became a busy centre of activity. D4g 447, on what appears to be a work extra, is shown on the main line in the late 1940s, about to leave for points north. —MAURICE CHANDLER

Cordwood, trimmings from the sawmills, was an important domestic fuel on Vancouver Island and the E&N brought trainloads into Victoria. Flatcars, specially equipped with sides and ends, were used. The 3206, a 2-8-0, is shown in Victoria West crossing Esquimalt Road and the trackage of the B.C. Electric Railway with at least two carloads of cordwood on September 7, 1940. —NORMAN GIDNEY

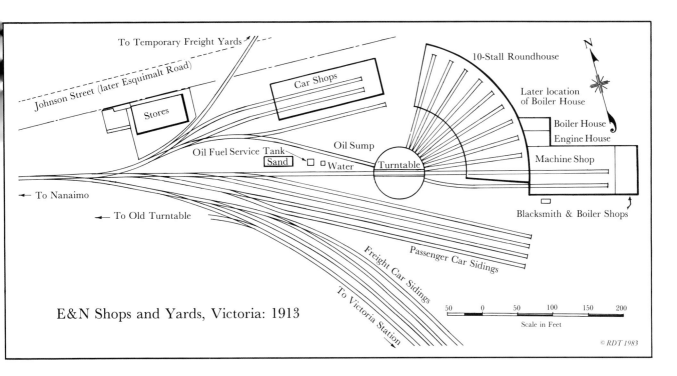

E&N Shops and Yards, Victoria: 1913

© RDT 1983

In the early 1940s, D10g 4-6-0s were transferred to the E&N and replaced most other locomotives in main line service. Sunlight catches the side of 922 in Victoria on November 1, 1947.
—MAURICE CHANDLER

Lower right
0-6-0 6151, the Victoria yard engine, switches two of the E&N's elderly wooden passenger cars near the shops on March 14, 1947. —MAURICE CHANDLER

Three D10g's, 918, 906, and 911, outside the roundhouse. After about 1911, all E&N steam locomotives, with only a few exceptions, were oil-fired to reduce the danger of forest fires.
—MAURICE CHANDLER

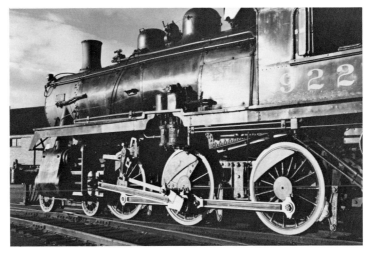

225

and from the Island. The tugs and barges (also operated by the BC Coast Steamship Service) ran from the transfer facilities at the CPR yards on Vancouver's waterfront to Jayem on Nanoose Bay, approximately 12 miles (20 km) north of Nanaimo, and to Ladysmith. To handle this traffic, the E&N stationed a locomotive and crew at Ladysmith and another at Wellington. Of the two facilities, the one at Ladysmith tended to be the busier. During the late 1930s and through the mid-'40s traffic averaged about 80 barges per month or approximately 1,000 movements a year.* While this may seem modest, cumulatively, at a capacity of 14 cars per barge, it could equal as many as 14,000 carloads a year being moved from the Island and some of this traffic, particularly the dominant lumber, shingles, poles and other forest products, was destined for distant points in North America. Additionally, inbound traffic contributed to revenue for the E&N although most cars being moved on the barges to the Island were empties returning for loading.

Passenger operations on the E&N had always been important to the railway but had never been very extensive. Because all points along the line were within a few hours of each other, the E&N was spared the expense of operating dining and sleeping cars. The scenery justified, as noted in earlier sections, the use of observation or parlour cars but coaches, baggage and express cars were more typical of the E&N. By the late 1930s, the passenger service had declined to a daily except Sunday train each way between Courtenay and Victoria with a connecting service between Parksville and Port Alberni. The second Victoria-Wellington train had been dropped in the early 1930s. Excursions, particularly from Victoria, were popular to Shawnigan Lake and other scenic points on holidays or summer weekends.

The assignment of locomotives on the E&N during its last years of steam operation provides further insights into the operations of the Island lines of the CPR. From the late 1930s through the early post-war years, the E&N operated an average of 22 serviceable locomotives to handle the variety of yard, freight and passenger assignments required. In March 1947, for example, 20 locomotives were on hand, of which 19 were serviceable. These comprised two U3c 0-6-0 switchers assigned to Victoria, three D4g Ten-wheelers and 15 D10g Ten-wheelers. Seven of the D10g's were based in Victoria: two for passenger service, two for freights between Victoria and Wellington, one for work trains, one as a spare for boiler washouts, and one for the night turn to Ladysmith to handle cars from the barges. At Duncan, one D10g and one D4g were based for log train service from Lake Cowichan, while at Ladysmith another D10g was stationed to switch the barges.

---

* The annual total for 1938, still reflecting the poor economy of the Depression was 493 barge movements (an average of 1.3 per day) while the wartime peak was reached in 1942 with 1,455 barges handled, or 4.0 per day.

Railcars were moved to and from the E&N by transfer barges pulled by tugs. The service was operated by the CPR's British Columbia Coast Steamship Service. In this photo from the late 1920s, the tug *Dola*, with a transfer barge in tow, is entering Vancouver Harbour.
—ALBERT H. PAULL, AUTHOR'S COLLECTION

Northbound over the Malahat, D10 923 pulls a holiday crowd on July 1, 1947. The train is about to enter the only tunnel on the E&N.
—MAURICE CHANDLER

The circus moved by train even to Vancouver Island. It was an exciting July 17, 1946 in Victoria West when the E&N's 915 arrived in town with Clyde Beatty's Trained Wild Animal Railroad Circus. Included in the featured attractions were elephants, a midway, and trapeze, tightrope, and wild animal acts.
—MAURICE CHANDLER

At Parksville, connections were made between the passenger service on the Victoria-Courtenay main line and the line to Port Alberni. August 14, 1947 found the crew of 926 switching. At this time a mail and a mail-express car ran through from Victoria to Courtenay and one coach, used to shuttle between Courtenay and Parksville, was run north of Parksville. The rest of the cars from Victoria ran through to Alberni.
—WILBUR C. WHITTAKER

Four more D10g's were based at the Wellington terminal: one for coal train service, one for Wellington-Port Alberni freight, one for Wellington-Courtenay freight and one to handle the traffic from the Jayem barge slip. Finally, at Port Alberni, a D10g was assigned to the passenger run to Parksville while another acted as pusher for the steep climb out of the Alberni Valley to Locharkaig at Mile 21.1 (34 km to the east). Switching at Port Alberni was carried out by a D4g. A third D4g was out of service in Victoria. It is interesting to note that Wellington, once the northern end of the railway, remained the terminal point for crews operating from Victoria and also for the crews operating on the extensions of the line to Port Alberni and to Courtenay.

The Esquimalt & Nanaimo, small and remote from the main line and major operations of the CPR, with its limited stable of steam power, was in the late 1940s to become the focus of a major technological change on the railway. It was to be the first division of the CPR to be fully dieselized and was to serve as a testing area for the new generation of locomotives that would eventually completely revolutionize the operations of the entire CPR system.

Steam Era Operations on the Kettle Valley-Kootenay Route

The southern route through British Columbia, comprising the Kettle Valley Division between Hope and Midway and the amalgamation of the branch lines to the east through the Crowsnest Pass that formed the Kootenay Division, differed significantly from the main line in the nature of the terrain it traversed and in the volume of traffic. The route was curving and twisting, and constantly up and down. Passenger traffic was much more limited and the service was slower. Freight related mostly to the industries in the southern Interior rather than the through traffic destined for Vancouver or the East that characterized the main line. The branch lines of the southern Interior often provided critical access to markets for mills, mines and farms and the passenger and mail services were vital social and business routes for communities that might have few other transportation options.

Steam power on these two divisions during the late steam era was dominated by mid-size freight engines that were used as required for general road service, helpers and, if needed, switching and passenger service. Consolidations of the reliable and tough N2 class were most common and they operated from one end of the route to the other. At the time the divisions were dieselized in the early 1950s, the N2s comprised 51 of a total of 92 locomotives in use. The next most common types of locomotives were the P1 2-8-2s. These locomotives were used in both freight and passenger service. In the early 1950s, 16 were in operation and, of these, six were considered passenger power. Other steam locomotives assigned to the southern divisions included smaller M4 2-8-0s that were used on some of the Kootenay branch lines and also as yard power, several of the ubiquitous D10 4-6-0s, five of the

The climb over the Malahat between Victoria and Shawnigan Lake provided a spectacular setting for the E&N and, with the major bridges at Niagara and Arbutus, was a prime location for photographs. John Newman recorded these striking scenes of E&N steam power in the years just prior to dieselization. At left, 909 on No. 1 with six cars just fills the steel bridge over Arbutus Creek while above, on January 5, 1946, 3266, an old freight hog due for retirement that September, thunders across the bridge.
—BOTH JOHN NEWMAN

229

big R3 2-10-0s and seven heavy yard engines of the V4 (6900 series) and V5 (6600 series) classes. In earlier years, more light power was in evidence with Ten-wheelers (both D9s and D10s), some 2-6-0s, older 3100 and 3200 Consolidations and also 3400 series 2-8-0s in use. As newer and larger machines were provided for the main line, heavier but older machines were assigned to the secondary routes like the Kettle Valley and Kootenay lines. The Kootenay Division, with its heavy traffic to and from Trail and greater number of branch lines, required more than twice the number of locomotives and crews assigned to the Kettle Valley Division.

The mountainous nature of the route complicated the operations significantly. It meant that helpers were required for passenger and freight trains over all the major summits between Hope and Crowsnest unless trains were running with very little tonnage. Helpers were needed over the Coquihalla Pass, for trains working in both directions out of Princeton and similarly for trains climbing out of the Okanagan Valley from Penticton, heavy trains climbing to Eholt required assistance, and over the rugged Farron Hill helpers and doubling were the rule. East of Nelson, helpers could be required between Wyndell and Goatfell for eastbound trains while westbounds needed assistance from Cranbrook to Fassiferne and trains could be doubled between Curzon and Goatfell. Westbounds might also need helpers from Wardner to Cranbrook. The Crowsnest itself was less of a problem; assistance was required only for particularly heavy trains. Helper services complicated the operations of the railroad significantly and added greatly to the costs. Many extra crews, equipment and facilities were required and a great deal of time was lost.

Winter added significantly to the difficulties of steam operations through the southern Interior. The snows of Coquihalla Pass became legendary — 500 to 600 inches (12-15 m) annually — and the pass was frequently closed for varying periods during the winter months while the plow crews tried to clear the line. When the Coquihalla was closed, traffic was rerouted north from Brodie (just west of Brookmere) to Merritt and from there to Spences Bridge and the main line. Ultimately, the utility of this alternate route, despite its being longer, and the costs of maintaining and keeping open the Coquihalla, led to the Coquihalla's abandonment. To the east, conditions were generally dryer through the Similkameen and Okanagan valleys. Further east, over Farron Hill, snow once again became a serious winter problem. In the Crowsnest, although the snowfall was not as great, the winters were also hard and long, adding to the toil of the railroaders.

For the train crews, duty on this line meant long hours of hard, unrelenting work. The locomotives assigned to the route were all hand-fired coal burners. It was not until the late 1940s, when working in conjunction with an oil company, that the CPR began to convert steam power on the Kettle Valley and Kootenay divisions to oil fuel. This conversion

The Kettle Valley and Kootenay divisions were home to a variety of steam power although nearly all was of 4-6-0, 2-8-0 or 2-8-2 types. D9c 569, in its early days main line passenger power, was on work train service at Grand Forks on May 21, 1951. —PHILIP R. HASTINGS

Snow was a dominant influence on operations on both divisions of the route across southern British Columbia. Coquihalla Pass and Farron Hill could be scenes of constant battles with slides and drifts. In this cold vignette, the crews of two snow-clearing trains, one with a rotary plow and the other with a wedge plow, stop for a break and a chance to plan strategy. The location is uncertain but it may be near Coryell on the west side of Farron Hill. —PABC, HP25716

A meet in Coquihalla Pass. No. 11 behind
engine 5224, is "in the hole" for No. 12 at
Romeo in the heart of the Cascade Mountains
on July 4, 1952. —JOHN C. ILLMAN

Brookmere, an isolated little town which owed
its life to the CPR, was the base for pushers
working westbound tonnage over Coquihalla
Pass. Three 2-8-0s, Nos. 3747, 3742 and 3647,
wait in the Brookmere yards, ready for the
next run. —JOHN C. ILLMAN

Just south of Summerland, the Kettle Valley's tracks crossed Trout Creek. The combination of the grade leading out of the Okanagan Valley and the impressive structure made it an interesting location for photography. The structure is nearly 240 feet (73 m) above the creek bed and over 600 feet (180 m) long. In the photo above looking south, 2-10-0 5758 leads 2-8-0 3627, 19 cars and two cabooses on a westbound over the bridge. The photo at left, looking north, shows the same train.

—NICHOLAS MORANT, CPCA, M4199, M4200

The Kettle Valley route featured many significant bridges including this impressive wooden trestle near Lorna. This photo shows work well advanced on a replacement steel bridge in 1936. —STOCKS FAMILY COLLECTION, IPB

After helping a freight out of Penticton, 5758 ran back downgrade and had just passed over Trout Creek when this photograph was taken in 1947. —W. GIBSON KENNEDY

produced substantial savings for the company — easier maintenance, reduced summer fire hazard and relief for locomotive firemen.

The snows, steep grades and rugged topography of the route made it more than just a challenge and hard work. It could be dangerous. For passengers, the safety record, through the care and attention of the crews, was exemplary. If there was danger of snow slides or other obstructions, the tracks were patrolled ahead of the passenger trains. If necessary, snow plows would precede the passenger trains. However, the work train crews and freight crews were more on their own.

So up and down was the route across southern British Columbia that there really was nowhere, except on the branch line to Osoyoos and along the shore of Kootenay Lake between Nelson and Creston, where the tracks were even close to being level for any significant distance. And similarly, there was nowhere of any significance where the tracks were not constantly twisting and turning. The major servicing points on the route, east of the Vancouver-Coquitlam area, were at Brookmere, Penticton, Grand Forks, Nelson, Cranbrook and Crowsnest. It was at these points that the operating and maintenance crews boarded or made their homes depending on their assignments, seniority and preferences.

Enginehouses, turntables, and related facilities for handling the steam power were located at these locations with Nelson and Cranbrook being the most significant. These larger centres were, in no small measure, railroad towns, and small communities like Brookmere depended almost entirely on the CPR for their existence. At the eastern end of the route, in Alberta, major shops were operated at both Lethbridge and Medicine Hat. There were other minor servicing points and turning facilities on some of the branch lines as well as the essential and frequent water stops every 10 to 15 miles (15-25 km) along the route depending on the grades, working conditions and tender capacities.

Passenger service across the CPR's second main line through British Columbia was complicated by the rugged country dominating the southern boundary of the province and the differing needs of the many small and varied communities served by the trains. On most branch lines, at least once weekly service was normally provided as late as the 1950s, because the area was late in receiving modern highways.

The system timetable issued on June 24, 1928, for example, shows a comprehensive passenger service system offered in the busy years before the Depression. The backbone of the service was provided by daily Trains Nos. 67 (westbound) and 68 (eastbound) operating between Medicine Hat and Kootenay Landing, with steamer connections through to Nelson. From Nelson, through to the Coast, the trains operate as Nos. 11 and 12. A connecting twice-weekly service was provided over the lonely miles between Cranbrook and Golden via Lake Windermere, two return trains each day except Sunday operated between Cranbrook and Kimberley,

233

and connections via the Spokane International were made at Yahk with the trains running through to Spokane.

To the west, Nelson was the hub for branch lines and steamer services in the West Kootenays. A daily service was operated from Nelson to Rossland (Trains 701 and 702) and a second train, connecting with Nos. 11 and 12, operated between Castlegar and Rossland daily except Sundays. Service was also provided to the Slocan Valley from Nelson, three days a week. From Slocan City, CPR steamers (and railway car barges for freight) operated to Rosebery, where connections were made through to Nakusp and also to Kaslo. Steamer service also connected Nelson (and Procter where a car ferry transfer facility was located) with isolated branch lines along Kootenay Lake running from Kaslo through to Nakusp and also from Lardeau to Gerrard.* On the latter, a Saturday-only service was provided which in later years was operated by a motor car very reminiscent of the famous "Galloping Geese" homemade railcars of the Rio Grande Southern in Colorado.

West of Nelson, Trains 861 and 862 ran daily except Sunday between Castlegar and Grand Forks on a schedule slower than the through trains to and from the Coast. In addition, a Tuesdays-only train operated on the branch from Grand Forks to Archibald, a distance of 19.9 miles (32 km). At Robson West, near Castlegar, trains connected three times a week with CPR steamers operating on the Arrow Lakes as far north as Arrowhead. From Arrowhead, a connecting train ran to Revelstoke and the main line.

In the Okanagan, passenger steamers of the British Columbia Lake & River Service connected with the trains at Penticton and ran to Kelowna and all other major points along the lake before connecting with rail service at Okanagan Landing. From there, via Vernon, a direct service was available to Sicamous on the main line. Additionally, on the branch line between Penticton and Haynes in the southern Okanagan, once a week service was offered. Aside from connections between Brookmere, via Merritt, to the main line at Spences Bridge, this was the extent of CPR passenger services south of the main line on the Kettle Valley and other lines through to the Crowsnest. Passenger service did not always reflect the general level of activity on all of the branches and some areas, such as the lines from Princeton to Copper Mountain or Castlegar to Trail, generated significant volumes of freight even if passenger service was not offered or was relatively modest.

The mountainous nature of southeastern British Columbia, and the scattered population, contributed to a slow development of highways and most of the passenger services offered in the 1920s survived, albeit often reduced in frequency, into the

* See the earlier discussion of the CPR's acquisition of the Kaslo & Slocan Railway which ran from Kaslo west to Sandon.

The Granby Consolidated Mining & Smelting Company's mine at Copper Mountain, south of Princeton, was an important source of traffic for the Kettle Valley Division. On the busy 13.6-mile (22-km) long line ore had to be moved to the concentrator at Allenby 6.0 miles (9.6 km) out of Princeton, supplies to the mine and concentrator, and the concentrates out to Princeton. After the mine's closure in 1957, the trackage was removed. —PABC, HP60663

Top right
Steamer service continued on the Arrow Lakes, Slocan Lake and Kootenay Lake into the 1950s serving isolated communities. One stop on Kootenay Lake served by the *Moyie* was Lardeau. The trackage beyond Lardeau to Gerrard saw little traffic and in place of a regular train, a rail car rebuilt from an automobile, provided a mixed train service from the late-1920s until 1942 when the line was abandoned. In this photo M600, a rebuilt Ford AA, 1.5 ton truck, was on the line. Earlier, a Model T was used. —MILTON PARENT COLLECTION

By the early 1950s, service on some of the branch lines often was only a once-a-week mixed train. Such was the case on the line to Nakusp via Slocan Lake. Shortly after 7:00 a.m. on June 21, 1951, on its Monday-only run, Train M841 with 2-8-0 3480, rolls along the quiet reservoir backwater west of Nelson on its way to South Slocan. There it will take the branch line to Slocan City before being loaded on the barge for the trip to Rosebery. At Rosebery, the train will return to dry land and run on to Nakusp.
—PHILIP R. HASTINGS

The Nelson Yards

Nelson was the major centre of operations for steam power in the West Kootenays. Crews based there worked on the main line, both east and west, and also on the branch lines to Trail, the Slocan Valley and to other points.

Four locomotives are outside the shops by the coaling tower in this scene from August 22, 1948. The power included 2-8-0s 3458 and 3456, 2-8-2 5207 and 2-8-0 3677. At right is a baggage car with special rooftop ventilators.—JIM HOPE

P1n class 2-8-2s, like 5210 shown at Nelson on May 24, 1948, were rebuilt from N2 2-8-0s between 1946 and 1949. No. 5210 (originally 3652) was rebuilt in April 1947. It sports an impressive snow plow that undoubtedly had its share of use during the previous winter.
—JIM HOPE

During the late 1940s and early 1950s, normally five yard shifts were run each day to keep traffic in the busy terminal moving. On June 21, 1951, one of the yard crews was hard at work with M4g 2-8-0 3487.—PHILIP R. HASTINGS

The lineup of power at Nelson could be impressive as shown in this morning scene from June 21, 1951. Included are N2a 3677, assigned to an eastbound extra, P1n 5261 and R3b 5758.—PHILIP R. HASTINGS

early 1950s. Full passenger trains were reduced to mixeds and service dropped from daily except Sundays to two or three times a week. Actual abandonments of passenger service and trackage was quite limited during the steam era. The isolated Lardeau branch was abandoned by the CPR in 1942 and the right-of-way used for a road. Only a small yard and the car ferry slip was left operational at Lardeau. Steamers, running from Procter, continued to serve the area until passenger service was discontinued in 1958 but freight continued to be barged to Lardeau until 1977. In the Grand Forks area, the North Fork Subdivision running to Archibald was abandoned in 1935, except for some trackage near Grand Forks. Previous abandonments in the area, as noted earlier, included the trackage to Phoenix in 1921 and the Mother Lode Subdivision from Greenwood in 1919.

Through passenger service over the southern boundary route across British Columbia remained an important alternative to the main line throughout the steam era on the CPR. The operation of the trains was far from a straight run through from Vancouver to Lethbridge and involved many changes to the consists of the trains to reflect the differing requirements of the service across the province. The following summary provides an insight into the passenger service in the years immediately before dieselization.

Daily service was provided both eastbound and westbound over the route between Medicine Hat, Alberta, and Vancouver following completion of the Kettle Valley Railway in 1916. The equipment operated varied over the years as the population of southern British Columbia grew and economic conditions changed. Mail and express were important to the maintenance of these services and the passenger trains frequently carried several headend cars for this business as well as express refrigerator cars and passenger service box cars.

Typically, based on the 1951 summer scheduling, eastbound No. 12 left Vancouver in late afternoon (5:35 p.m.), was in Grand Forks by noon the next day, and in Cranbrook about 11:15 p.m. Crowsnest was reached by 3:25 a.m. (losing an hour with the time change to Mountain Time), and Medicine Hat at 11:45 the same morning. Westbound, No. 11 ran on a similar schedule, leaving Medicine Hat at 6:10 p.m., arriving at Crowsnest at 3:00 a.m. (and then gaining one hour with the change to Pacific Time), stopping at Nelson over noon and travelling on to the Okanagan to reach Penticton at 12:45 a.m. The run through to Vancouver took until 11:50 that morning. Trains averaged 10 cars, or between 550 and 600 tons (558-610 tonnes).

Helper locomotives were required on these trains at many points all across the route once the mountains were reached. Eastbound, No. 12 needed assistance with consists of over 6 cars between Hope and Brookmere, Princeton and Jura, Penticton and Chute Lake, Midway and Eholt (when nine cars or more were being moved), Cascade and Farron and between Sirdar and Yahk (again, only for nine cars or more).

The *Kootenay Express* (Train No. 11) nears the end of its journey at Vancouver on August 3, 1934. At that time, the 959-mile (1543-km) run from Medicine Hat, Alberta, to Vancouver took just over 42 hours on the westbound trip for an average speed of about 23 miles (37 km) per hour. —CYRIL LITTLEBURY, LANCE CAMP COLLECTION

Both the *Kettle Valley Express* and the *Kootenay Express* operated with many changes of equipment en route. Here a pusher is on the back end assisting P1n 5264 with the heavy tonnage. —CPR

The *Kettle Valley Express* and the *Kootenay Express*

The *Kootenay Express*, behind G2d Pacific 2575, stopped at Cranbrook on July 3, 1952. The engine is receiving some adjustments while baggage, express and mail are being transferred. —JOHN C. ILLMAN

At Fernie, G5b 1205, less than one year old, is in charge of an impressive 10-car *Kettle Valley Express* in May 1946.—WILBUR C. WHITTAKER

The expresses met at Morrissey west of Fernie and just 44 miles (71 km) from the summit of the Rockies at Crowsnest on July 3, 1952. Both trains were pulled by G2s Pacifics: No. 11 (westbound) by 2575 and No. 12 (eastbound) by 2572. —JOHN C. ILLMAN

The massive CPR-owned Consolidated Mining & Smelting Company smelter at Trail and the Sullivan Mine at Kimberley have dominated traffic on the Kootenay Division since the early 1900s. This view of the Trail smelter shows the extent of the facility as well as the large rail yards. Nearby is an extensive fertilizer plant, installed in the late 1920s. During the steam era traffic might warrant four trains a day to Trail. —COMINCO

In 1936 Rossland-Trail passenger service was dropped. In 1940, when this photo was taken, a daily service ran from Nelson to Trail and return. The train, with D10 954 and a business car, is climbing from Trail towards the smelter. In the distance is 2-8-0 3606. In 1949, the passenger service south from Castlegar was discontinued. —W. GIBSON KENNEDY

240

Between Trail and Castlegar, trains frequently had to double over the 3.6 percent grade between Genelle and Poupore. N2b's 3623 and 3606 are shown working empty hopper and ore cars up the grade towards Castlegar on September 8, 1940. —W. GIBSON KENNEDY

The yards at the Trail smelter (Tadanac) required powerful switchers. Locomotives of a variety of types were used including M4a 2-8-0s, 6900 series 0-8-0s and large, modern V5a 0-8-0s such as 6605 built in 1931 and photographed in August 1949. —RAILWAY NEGATIVE EXCHANGE

Further east, through the Crowsnest, helpers were not normally required.

Westbound, No. 11 might first need a helper climbing the eastern slope of the Rockies between Pincher and Frank but only if the train was 13 or more cars in length. The same limits applied for the first 5.4 miles (8.7 km) out of Cranbrook to Fassiferne. Further west, between Labarthe (32.4 miles or 52 km west of Nelson) and Farron (i.e., the ascent of Farron Hill), a train of seven or more cars required assistance. Grand Forks to Eholt required two engines on six-car trains as did the climb west from Penticton to Kirton, a distance of 25.5 miles (41 km). Westbound passenger trains did not normally require assistance over the Coquihalla although winter conditions could make extra power essential on almost any part of the route.

There were frequent changes in the consists of Trains 11 and 12; cars were picked up and set off over the entire route. Particularly notable was the operation of the dining car only between Coalmont and Vancouver and the cafe-parlour car only between Penticton and Macleod (Fort Macleod), Alberta. Sleeping cars, too, were dropped off and picked up en route as required. Westbound, sleepers were picked up at Lethbridge and Macleod with one being set off at Nelson, while eastbound, one sleeper was set off at Penticton but another was picked up at Nelson. Westbound trains also set off sleepers at both Macleod and Lethbridge.

While passenger service over the Kettle Valley and Kootenay divisions was significant, and to the public, a highly visible part of the CPR's operations in southern British Columbia, freight was the most important in terms of revenue and formed the backbone of the system. During the steam era, the CPR was still the major carrier of freight through southern B.C. since the highways were still not well suited to long distance freight haulage. Freight trains served industries and communities throughout the region, handling incoming merchandise, and moving the products of the local mines, mills and farms for both processing and shipment to markets.

Freight operations on the Kettle Valley and Kootenay divisions were quite variable across the southern route. Through freights and wayfreights were operated on the main line subdivisions and some of the branches contributed further heavy traffic. In general, the busiest sections of the route were east from Nelson over the Nelson, Cranbrook and Crowsnest subdivisions (i.e., from Nelson east through the Crowsnest Pass into Alberta). This pattern of traffic remained unchanged in later years and led to the eventual cutbacks of service that, in the 1970s, severed the route between Penticton and Midway once through traffic had been diverted to the main line. To illustrate the different levels of through freight traffic, in 1950 the subdivisions east of Nelson averaged four to five daily through freights, both east- and westbound, while to the west the frequency was less than two trains in each direction a day. The frequency of train service was

With a background of the Rockies and the Crowsnest Pass, a westbound freight pulls out of the small community of Elko. The station, section house and water tower are in the distance and the track leading off to the right is to a hand-operated "Armstrong" turntable. —MICHAEL WOODHEAD

The Sullivan Mine at Kimberley became by far the most significant ore-producing mine in the East Kootenays. Its ore and concentrates have moved over the CPR to Trail for smelting since the early 1900s. —KIMBERLEY MUSEUM

reflected in the ton/mile statistics for the different sections of the line. For example, over the Coquihalla, through freight amounted to 28,208 m ton/miles westbound in 1950, while over the Nelson Subdivision, the figure was 353,447 m ton/miles.

Wayfreight operations on the main line contributed significant tonnages as well, the volumes varying directly with the amount of industry located along the route. Branch line volumes, particularly on the Copper Mountain, Rossland, Kimberley, and Osoyoos subdivisions were important to the railway and contributed long-haul tonnage as well. The first three noted were significant because of the tonnage related to the mining production from Copper Mountain near Princeton and from the Sullivan Mine at Kimberley and the smelter at Trail. The Osoyoos Subdivision was dominated by perishable fruit traffic from the southern Okanagan. It was highly seasonal with peak volumes; increased train operations were necessary during the harvest months of summer and early fall.

*   *   *

Built 30 years after the completion of the main line, the Kettle Valley route across the southern Interior never developed to the degree its early backers had hoped. Industry in the region grew, but the mining booms of the late 1890s and early 1900s faded. Aside from the major producers of coal in the Crowsnest, copper (when prices were high) near Princeton, ores from the Sullivan Mine at Kimberley with the associated smelter at Trail, and some scattered economically significant mines in the Kootenays, the region's economy was based on forestry and agriculture. These provided a sound basis for traffic for the Kettle Valley and Kootenay divisions but the route was so tortuous and indirect, compared to the improved and upgraded main line, that the role of the southern divisions was always a secondary one.

The very qualities that gave the Kettle Valley-Kootenay route its fascinating character — the rugged and beautiful country, the small towns and scattered industries, seasonal traffic, aging steam power, and the need for frequent helper services — made it an ideal early candidate for dieselization as the CPR began the immense conversion to more modern and efficient power.

Work on the CPR's Kettle Valley and Kootenay divisions was hard and tough, especially during winter, but the men accepted the labour and the hazards as part of the job. The crew posed on 3606 at Coykendahl, an isolated siding, water stop and train order office, on Farron Hill.
—L. S. MORRISON

Farron Hill in the summer was less formidable but instead of snow, the crews had to be careful of fires starting in the dry forests. N2b 2-8-0 3695 was the helper for 2-8-2 5250 on the eastbound *Kettle Valley Express* climbing Farron Hill on June 10, 1951. —PHILIP R. HASTINGS

Dieselization of the CPR brought sweeping and fundamental changes to the railway and its employees. In the post-war years, the economics of converting to diesel power could not be denied and, beginning in 1949, the switch to diesels for main line work began. The Esquimalt & Nanaimo on Vancouver Island was the first section of the CPR to be fully dieselized. It was an ideal testing ground. Baldwin roadswitchers completely replaced steam on the E&N in 1949 and handled all passenger, freight and switching duties. This photo shows Baldwin 8006, northbound on the Malahat, crossing Arbutus Creek with a typical freight consist on February 25, 1949. —JOHN NEWMAN

244

CHAPTER 5

DIESELIZATION AND THE TRANSFORMATION OF THE RAILWAY

Dieselization

The dieselization of the railroads of North America brought about a virtual revolution in economics and operating practices unparalleled in their history. In a period of just 15 years, from the end of World War II until the late 1950s, virtually every railroad systematically replaced its complete locomotive fleet, re-trained engineers and maintenance personnel, built new facilities, and modified operating schedules and procedures. The immediate impact on the railroad industry was as great as the change in technology and many long-established communities — helper stations, engine change points and servicing facilities — were made redundant. The advantage to the railroads was, quite simply, economic. Diesels (or more correctly, diesel-electrics) were significantly more fuel efficient, flexible and required smaller crews and much less maintenance and servicing. Depending on the circumstances, including the age of existing steam power, the railroads could save 25 percent or more of their operating costs each year. But these savings did more than help the dividend picture for stockholders. They also gave the railroads an opportunity to modernize after the wearing high-volume years of World War II when maintenance could not always equal the demands of service and, prior to the war, the lean Depression years of deferred upkeep and little new equipment. Even if diesels had not been available, replacements for this obsolete power would have been required. Moreover, the improved economics of dieselization made it possible for the railroads to better compete against the inroads of trucking which, with the expansion of highway systems, was able to attract an increasingly significant share of intercity freight.

For the CPR, dieselization began slowly; the company approached the new motive power with a cautious skepticism. Beginning in 1943, diesel switchers were purchased for yard work but main line diesels were not to be ordered for some time and then only in limited quantities. Steam locomotives based on the proven pre-war designs were built after the War. Pacifics, Mikados and Selkirks were all outshopped to meet the requirements for more power. The company was short of capital after the war because freight revenues had not kept pace with cost increases and despite a prosperous economy, the CPR's financial position was not what it should have been. Dieselization program was expensive. Moreover, management was somewhat conservative. However, there were individuals in the company committed to the idea of dieselization, notably Norris R. ("Buck") Crump, an experienced railroader and native of Revelstoke, whose father, T. R. Crump, had been superintendent of the Kettle Valley Division in British Columbia.

While dieselization was proceeding rapidly in the United States and gaining support during the mid-1940s, Norris Crump rose to senior management of the CPR. In 1949, he became a director and vice-president and from that point on, a rapid modernization of the rail system was only a matter of time. This capable and energetic man went on to become president (1955-1964) and chairman (1961-1972) of the company. He had a great influence on the company in many areas of its operations and saw the railway through a period of enormous change and development.

The year 1949 also marked the introduction of road diesels to the CPR and the delivery of the CPR's last new steam locomotives. The area chosen for the CPR's first significant venture into road dieselization was its Esquimalt & Nanaimo subsidiary on Vancouver Island.

The E&N on Vancouver Island was an ideal testing ground for the CPR's first attempt to dieselize an entire operating division. Compared to other parts of the system, the E&N was small and all steam power on the line could be replaced with a limited number of diesels. Moreover, because of the scale of the operation, modifications to shop facilities and crew retraining also were minimized as a result. Additionally, the service conditions on the Island were tough and varied. On the line from Victoria to Courtenay, the climb over the Malahat, north of Victoria, was steep and twisting while other parts of the route presented relatively easy grades. Between Parksville and Port Alberni, there were severe grades on both sides of the climb to the summit at Locharkaig. The maximum grade on the line was a 2.6 percent (compensated) climb just east of the summit. On the Lake Cowichan Subdivision, grades also exceeded 2.0 percent. Services ranged from the daily passenger trains to freight and heavy drags of log trains from Cowichan Lake. And while the E&N was not subjected to extremes of winter weather, conditions could be trying enough.

At the time dieselization was considered, 20 steam locomotives (19 operational and one out of service) were being used on the Island. Studies of the Island's traffic and of the performance of the steam power in use in 1947 indicated that 13 roadswitchers of 1,000 hp could cover all of the assignments on the Island. The replacement of the steam locomotives by diesels was, in general terms, on a one-for-one basis because a D10 was approximately equivalent in capacity to one diesel

Yard diesels were the first to appear on the CPR in British Columbia. One of the first was 7054, an Alco S-2, delivered in October 1947 and photographed, with a proud crew in Vancouver, one month later. No. 7053, an identical engine, ran tests on the E&N in November 1947.
—RAILWAY NEGATIVE EXCHANGE

Diesels for the Esquimalt & Nanaimo

Baldwins 8002 and 8004 were at Courtenay in the late 1940s handling a freight and the daily passenger train. The first five Baldwins were equipped with steam generators for passenger service. —TED ROBSON

On October 8, 1965, Baldwins 7075 and 8011 were rolling northbound on E&N No. 51 through Westholme north of Duncan. —JOHN C. ILLMAN

unit. The reduction in the number of units came largely from the increased availability and flexibility that the diesels offered. Consequently, crew time and labour costs were not decreased as much as when other divisions were dieselized.

The projected savings from dieselization were significant. Fuel costs alone were estimated to decrease by 75 percent, from nearly $240,000 to $60,000 per year and locomotive repairs were projected to decrease by two-thirds, from $60,000 to $20,000 per year. Additional savings were to come from somewhat decreased costs for crews, and lower expenses for engine houses, water supply and fuel handling. Overall, it was felt that the investment in dieselization could be recouped from the savings in operating costs, allowing for interest, in under seven years.

The studies recommended Montreal Locomotive Works RS-1 model diesels, and tests were also carried out on the E&N in November 1947 using an S-2 switcher (No. 7053). However, by the time orders were placed, neither MLW or General Motors could deliver the units without a lengthy delay. The Canadian Locomotive Company had made arrangements with Baldwin for the construction of 24 units, so the order went to CLC for the 13 roadswitchers, as well as 11 yard diesels. The Baldwins were built in the United States; CLC did not set up production for this type of diesel in Canada and these were the only Baldwin diesels acquired by the CPR. Initially, three of the switchers were used for Winnipeg yard service while the others went to Vancouver. However, eventually all of the CPR's Baldwins were concentrated in and around the Vancouver terminals and on Vancouver Island. The yard units also were assigned to the Island, some being used in road service as well. One of the unplanned outcomes of the project was that the E&N emerged with a unique group of diesels that came to be associated with the railway. Some of the roadswitchers did get transferred to the Vancouver-Coquitlam area for yard work, but their real home was Vancouver Island and they served there into the 1970s.

The diesels arrived on the E&N early in 1949, and by the summer, steam had been totally replaced. For the E&N, which seldom saw much in the way of new equipment, the sudden transformation to diesel power was a real bonus. Most E&N steam power was transferred to mainland operations for a few more years of service. It had been well maintained and even when 40 years old, the Ten-wheelers and Consolidations of the E&N were kept in spotless condition.

The Baldwin roadswitchers were numbered 8000-8012 and were the builder's model DRS4-4-1000s, while the complementary order of switchers were numbers 7065-7075, model DS4-4-1000. The first five roadswitchers were equipped with steam generators for heating the passenger trains. After the passenger service was taken over by an RDC, or *Dayliner*, in 1955, the steam generators were removed. The dieselization of the E&N was entirely successful and gave the CPR good

Baldwin yard diesels were assigned to Vancouver terminals and also worked on the E&N in both switching and road service. In this photo from 1969, 7074, then assigned to Victoria, switches cars through street trackage near the station. The yards north of the station were developed in 1908-1909. —ROBERT D. TURNER

In 1955 new yards were opened at Nanaimo. They included a new ferry slip which handled the E&N's rail car traffic to and from the mainland. Barges and the ferry *Princess of Vancouver*, built in 1955, provided the service. In this photo Baldwin 8001 is switching the self-propelled barge *Doris Yorke* in 1969. —ROBERT D. TURNER

The Victoria Shops

The Russells roundhouse in Victoria West was where the Baldwins were serviced and maintained on Vancouver Island. These photos show 8010 being serviced and 8004 on the turntable in the spring of 1969. Photographed in the distance through the roundhouse doors on March 18, 1975 was 8001, its stack capped after being withdrawn from service.
—ALL ROBERT D. TURNER

reason for carrying on with the dieselization program on larger, more significant divisions.

Operationally, the Baldwins were well suited to service on Vancouver Island. The only feature they lacked that would have been desirable was dynamic braking. This system would have lessened forest fire dangers during the summer season by reducing conventional brake applications which could produce sparks from hot brakeshoes. Initially, none of the diesels was fitted for multiple unit operation, but between 1961 and 1966 all of the roadswitchers were modified with the necessary equipment. This facilitated handling heavier trains; in the later years of their service as many as four roadswitchers were required on trains on the Port Alberni Subdivision and over the Malahat. Log trains on the Cowichan Lake branch normally required two units while some trains, operating on the flatter sections of the line, or with light tonnage, could manage with one unit.

The E&N Baldwin roadswitchers operated long after many diesels of similar vintage were retired. Six were badly damaged in accidents during 1973 and the rest, except for the 8000, were retired and scrapped in 1975.* In their last years of service, the roadswitchers had been partially replaced by GMD GP7R or GP9R roadswitchers and it was these General Motors units, particularly the GP9Rs, that ultimately replaced the Baldwins on Vancouver Island.

By the early 1970s, the yard diesels were replaced on the Island with MLW switchers which, in turn, were replaced by the early 1980s by GMD units. The Baldwin yard diesels lasted longer than the roadswitchers. However, most were sold or scrapped by the late 1970s. Surprisingly, 7070 and 7072 remained in service into the early 1980s, and returned to Vancouver Island, switching the railway car barges at Nanaimo. Finally, they were retired in 1982 ending the Baldwin diesel era on the E&N and the CPR.

The CPR did not turn immediately to other parts of British Columbia for dieselization. Next came the line from Montreal to Wells River, Vermont, which connected through, via the Boston & Maine, to Boston. After this program, the Schreiber Division, through the rugged Canadian Shield north of Lake Superior and Lake Huron, was dieselized. This section on the CPR main line was rugged and a real test for the diesels under demanding conditions of grades and weather. With this background, the CPR was ready to tackle dieselization of the main line through the mountains between Revelstoke and Calgary.

* The 8000 was used as part of a display train which toured many CP Rail terminals in British Columbia in 1986 marking the centennial of the completion of the railway. Unfortunately, the 8000 was not displayed on Vancouver Island where it had spent most of its working days.

Typically, during the 1960s, two Baldwins were assigned to freights to and from Victoria but as many as four might be required. In this photo, 8009 and another unit roll downgrade north of Malahat Summit. Tonnage on the busy line to Port Alberni often required four units. In the 1960s, multiple unit controls were applied to all the roadswitchers. The yard diesels were fitted with these controls as well, some as early as 1958. —ROBERT D. TURNER

Diesels for the Revelstoke to Calgary Main Line

Diesels were taking over increasingly from steam on the main line between Revelstoke and Calgary during 1952 and within a short time would replace steam entirely in the mountains. FP7A 4058 (later renumbered 1416) was less than eight months old when photographed in September 1952 from the caboose of a train waiting for it to pass just east of the Connaught Tunnel. —RAILWAY NEGATIVE EXCHANGE

At that time steam power operating on from Revelstoke to Field and east over the Great Divide comprised a reasonably uniform roster of heavy locomotives including most of the CPR's Selkirks, and solid ranks of the S2 2-10-2s, R3 2-10-0s, and P2 2-8-2s. Additionally, there were a few smaller locomotives for branch line or way freight service. Other steam power operating in from the west included the five Royal Hudsons, G4 Pacifics, and, for freight service, S2, R3 and P2s. In addition, the Selkirks based at Revelstoke also operated west as pushers as far as Taft. While all of this equipment had been well maintained, most had reached at least 20 years of age. New power even to meet increasing traffic and replace the older locomotives was certainly needed. As the change-over from steam proceeded, it altered forever the character of operations in the mountains and made possible the transition of the CPR's mountain operations into one of the most modern railroad systems in North America.

In operational terms, the main line between Revelstoke and Calgary was divided into the Mountain Subdivision, from Field to Revelstoke (125.7 miles, 202.3 km), and the Laggan Subdivision from Calgary to Field (136.6 miles, or 219.8 km).* The main advantage to be realized from the dieselization of these subdivisions was the elimination of the frequent and expensive helper operations and the overall economies that the retirement of steam would bring.

Significantly, these subdivisions had some of the CPR's newest and finest steam power including the last steam locomotives delivered to the CPR — Selkirks 5931-5935, built in 1949. The mighty Selkirks, built especially for the mountain grades of this section of the main line, were to be banished to the prairies.

To transform a route as significant as this one was not a simple task. New facilities had to be built for fueling and maintenance, equipment ordered, tested and made operational and crews trained. Despite the complexity of the transformation of the railway from steam to diesel, the conversion proceeded smoothly and the crews adapted quickly to the new power.

The orders for new equipment went to both General Motors and Montreal Locomotive Works but the wisdom of making the equipment roster more uniform was seen and the MLW units, except for yard diesels, were assigned to the Schreiber Division in exchange for more GM diesels. General Motors standard FP7 and later FP9 road units and GP7 and GP9 roadswitchers, all equipped with dynamic brakes, were to dominate the mountains for the next two decades. Other units did make an appearance for testing and for transfers.

Crew training began by sending experienced road foremen of engines to the Schreiber Division to be trained on diesels so

Main line road diesels came from the three major locomotive manufacturers in Canada. General Motors is represented by FP7A 4030 (built in September 1950) in passenger service on the Field Hill, while Montreal Locomotive Works (Alco) FA-2 4091 (built in October 1953) is typical of their cab units.
—RAILWAY NEGATIVE EXCHANGE; L. S. MORRISON

Canadian Locomotive Works (Fairbanks-Morse) CPA16-4 4054 (built in August 1952), shown roaring along the Illecillewaet River in 1954, was CLC's answer to the competition.
—RAILWAY NEGATIVE EXCHANGE

---

* Of this distance, 0.3 miles (0.5 km), from Mile 136.3 to Field, appears in the Pacific Region timecard.

In the early 1950s, the CPR acquired mostly streamlined cab units for road service but by the mid-1950s orders went increasingly for road-switchers, particularly the GP9R. They were used extensively on the main line in freight service through British Columbia. After more powerful units came in the 1970s, the Geeps still had years of work ahead in branch line and yard service. In this photograph from March 1964, five units, led by GP9R 8639, are pulling into Field from the east.
—RAILWAY NEGATIVE EXCHANGE

Yard diesels like SW9 7403 took over from older steam power. The engine was brand new when photographed at Revelstoke in 1953.
—MAURICE CHANDLER

that they, in turn, could supervise the training of engineers in their own division. Similarly, maintenance personnel were sent east for training. On the road, each engineer was required to operate for 1,000 miles (1600 km) under the supervision of a road foreman before being considered qualified to operate diesels. Since the average run between turnaround points was 125 miles (200 km), four trips, out and back, were usually required to gain the required mileage and training. Initially, the problem in the training program was not availability of crews and supervisors but of diesel units since it was impractical to hold crews over to wait for diesels to come in. As more units arrived and crews were trained, the program accelerated.

In service, the diesels fulfilled their promise by eliminating helpers, decreasing shop time and improving the efficiency of the entire operation. The dynamic brakes, in themselves, resulted in considerable savings. Theoretically, the dynamics could take the same tonnage downgrade that the units were able to pull up the same grade, provided that they operated within a restricted speed range of about 18-25 miles (30-40 km) per hour. When this could be accomplished, there was theoretically no need for the use of train brakes on the long mountain grades.* This reduced brakeshoe wear and overheating of wheels. The latter was significant because it led to "shelled-out" wheels, cracked wheels and broken flanges and other defects that were not only costly but also very dangerous. The Mechanical Department estimated that savings could be as high as $100,000 in this area alone, and in actual operation, the estimate proved conservative.

Initially, on heavy freight assignments, the diesels were run in four-unit consists† (operated by one engine crew) which, over the Selkirk Mountains, meant that approximately 3,200 tons (3251 tonnes) could be handled. This compared to the 1,050 tonnage limit of a single T1 class 2-10-4 locomotive on similar grades. Consequently, one set of diesels was able to replace at least three steam locomotives on a given train which also meant that helpers and their crews were not needed. On the Mountain Subdivision during steam operations, helper crews were stationed at Revelstoke, Beavermouth and Golden. For the Laggan Subdivision, they were based at Field and Lake Louise. With the complete implementation of dieselization, the need for most of these helpers was eliminated, along with the delays and expenses they required.

---

* The use of air brakes at frequent intervals was specifically recommended during periods of snow or blowing snow in order to keep the brake shoes clear of snow. If the brakes were not used frequently, there could be a build up of snow between the brake shoes and the wheels which could greatly increase stopping distances during a normal or emergency brake application with possible tragic consequences.

† The term "consist" is used to describe several diesel locomotives running together with multiple unit controls. This system enabled the engineer to operate several locomotives from the controls of the leading unit. Consist is also used in a railroad context to refer to the cars in a train.

Three F units lead a long grain train down the Field Hill toward the lower Spiral Tunnel in September 1952. —RAILWAY NEGATIVE EXCHANGE

Diesel power also was applied to some of the rotary snow plows. The steam boilers and engines were removed and electric motors were installed to drive the cutting wheel and other machinery. Power was supplied from an F7 B unit. Other diesels were used to push the plow. No. 400802 (originally Rotary D) was rebuilt in 1952 and was a successful conversion. Only two more rotaries, 400810 and 400811, were rebuilt. These were the two large rotaries built in 1911, but the plows were retired after the winter of 1954-55. Afterwards, locomotive plows, wedge plows and bulldozers were used. —CPR

By the summer of 1952, FP7s were making an increasingly important presence on the main line. On July 1, 1952, No. 4061 delivered in March 1952 and 4040, in service in October 1951, were in the Field yards ready for the next assignment. —JOHN C. ILLMAN

Later, as traffic increased and as unit train operations began, helpers based at Beavermouth (later Rogers)* were reinstated over Rogers Pass.

Following the dieselization of the main line between Calgary and Revelstoke, attention shifted to improving the operations of the Kettle Valley and Kootenay divisions to the south. Like the main line, these routes were rugged, demanding sections of railroad and well-suited to producing maximum economies from being dieselized. Moreover, the southern Interior of British Columbia was growing at a rapid rate and by the 1950s, the existing railway system was considered inadequate to meet the growth in the region. The dominant industry in the area was the CPR-owned Consolidated Mining and Smelter Company (Cominco) based at Trail and Kimberley. At Trail, the company's major smelter and nearby fertilizer plants were located and at Kimberley was the Sullivan Mine which produced ore for the smelter. Moreover, there was an expansion of the forest industry throughout southern British Columbia.

Studies completed in January 1952 showed that dieselization would not only increase the effectiveness and capacity of the two divisions but also result in considerable savings. The studies indicated that 73 diesel units could replace 92 steam locomotives while improving service. The principle applied was that train tonnages would be based on what a given unit, or combination of units, could haul from Nelson to Ruby Creek or over the Crowsnest Pass, without requiring extra assistance. Consequently, all helpers could be eliminated and no trains would normally need to double (be taken in two sections) over the hills.

The overall capital expenditure for the program was estimated at $17,383,529, but the net savings each year were over $2,525,000 which meant a return on investment of 15 percent; the savings would repay the capital costs in just over seven years. In operating expenses, fuel costs alone were estimated to drop by 56 percent (a saving of nearly $1,400,000) and an overall annual saving of 43 percent was projected. Since the CPR had the resources to fund the conversion to diesels, it was clear that the program made real economic sense. It would have taken very attractive investments elsewhere to have diverted the capital away.

Orders were placed with all three major diesel locomotive builders in Canada for the needed units and beginning early in 1953 they began to displace steam power. Initially the diesels worked freight and yard assignments but by mid-1953

Diesels for the Kettle Valley and Kootenay Divisions

A major new servicing facility for diesels was built at Nelson in 1953. The upper photo illustrates the completed shops with an FA-2 and FB-2 being fuelled while the lower photo shows the buildings under construction with GP7R 8419 receiving some attention. —CPR

* Beavermouth was flooded by Kinbasket Lake, the reservoir created behind the Mica Dam. In 1974, an 8.3-mile (13.4-km) diversion was built to reroute the tracks and the facilities for helper crews were relocated to Rogers.

Canadian Locomotive Company (Fairbanks-Morse) diesels took over on both the *Kettle Valley Express* (shown east of Princeton in April 1955 as No. 68) and the *Kootenay Express* (pictured at Moyie on August 8, 1957 and then running as No. 67).
—RAILWAY NEGATIVE EXCHANGE; JOHN C. ILLMAN

Nearing the end of their service on the Kootenay Division, CLC roadswitchers and C-Liners were still working out of Nelson in the early 1970s. In the photograph above, 4105, a model CPA16-4 passenger unit, has come into Nelson from Cranbrook in September 1974 less than a year before being retired. At right, just a few days earlier, two roadswitchers (model H16-44) lead the 4105 eastbound out of the Grand Forks yards at 7:30 a.m. The crew started the day early at Midway and worked east to Nelson. —BOTH ROBERT D. TURNER

CLC power dominated the Kettle Valley and Kootenay divisions for two decades. At left, three C-Liners labour with a long freight climbing the Coquihalla Pass.
—NICHOLAS MORANT, CPCA, M5987

259

CLC-FM Train Masters of 2400 horsepower (model H24-66) were assigned to heavy switching at Trail and on the steep grade to the fertilizer plant at Warfield. The last few in service were used at Trail. No. 8900 is pictured at Warfield on August 9, 1965. All were retired by the mid-1970s. —JIM HOPE

The Crowsnest Pass was a region of contrasts. In the photo at right above, the *Kettle Valley Express* rolls east on the Alberta side of the pass through Rocky Mountain scenery worthy of the national parks. The lower photo shows the yards at Michel with a roadswitcher moving long cuts of hopper cars beneath the smoke and steam from the tipple and coke ovens.
—BOTH NICHOLAS MORANT, CPCA, M6013, M7395

The CLC units required large quantities of cooling water and the crew of this westbound freight had to top off the tanks at Farron before continuing on to Grand Forks and Midway on August 20, 1974. —MICHAEL WILKIE

they were also assigned to the through passenger trains. By the end of the year the conversion was nearly complete. A mix of locomotives from the different builders was ordered for the program but the advisability of standardizing power was soon appreciated as it was for the main line operations and locomotives were reassigned leaving Canadian Locomotive Company (Fairbanks-Morse) units as the most common types of road locomotives on the Kettle Valley and Kootenay divisions while MLW switchers were assigned to the yards.

The types of units most commonly associated with the region included streamlined cab units of CLC model CPA16-4 (A units) and CPB16-4 (B units) for passenger service and similar units, (CFA16-4 and CFB16-4) for freight. Road-switchers of model H16-44 were used extensively on freights and some of the large "Train Master" diesels (Nos. 8900-8921), model H24-66, also were assigned to operations in the Kootenays, particularly around Trail, Warfield and the smelter yards at Cominco. At Nelson, new diesel shops were constructed to service the units operating on the two divisions. The Nelson shops became the maintenance centre for CLC power on the CPR in British Columbia.

The overall effect of dieselization on these two divisions of the CPR went well beyond the savings realized by the company. Much of the established pattern of operations and the nature of facilities and crew assignments was changed. Some more notable effects of the retirement of steam power included the elimination of Grand Forks as a crew change terminal, the phasing out of facilities at Brookmere, and the elimination of coaling structures across the divisions. Most watertowers were made redundant and soon disappeared along with the other steam-related structures.* As on other divisions, diesels meant profound changes for the train crews and other employees: elimination of jobs for some, retraining or reassignment for new and different operations for others. Change had its price and did not always come easily.

With the completion of the Kettle Valley-Kootenay dieselization program all that remained in steam in British Columbia was the main line between Revelstoke and Vancouver and a few areas such as the Windermere Subdivision. The main line passenger trains, including the new *Canadian* (described in a later section), featured diesel power by the mid-1950s and the remaining steam locomotives in British Columbia were retired soon after. The last stronghold of CPR

---

* Due to the need for helpers and the slow speed over the route between Nelson and Midway, train crews had been switched at Grand Forks. Crews operated between Nelson and Grand Forks, and between Grand Forks and Midway. Diesel operation made it feasible to run through between Nelson and Midway in one operating shift. An interesting change in operating procedures occurred in the 1980s when, with declining traffic west of Grand Forks, crews once again began using Grand Forks as a turnaround point and overnight stop. From there, twice-weekly "turns" operate to Midway.

Most Kettle Valley Division and Kootenay Division steam power was oil-fired at the time of dieselization. The conversions were carried out in 1949 and 1950 but coaling facilities were still maintained.

steam west of the Rockies was around the Vancouver terminals but during 1957 these engines too were retired. In just nine years, all CPR operations in British Columbia had been fully converted to diesel power.

In British Columbia, new equipment began to appear on the major CPR trains in the late 1940s, but a complete re-equipping of the transcontinental passenger trains did not occur until the mid-1950s. Although the CPR added over 500 new cars across its system by the end of 1954, the trains often still reflected a mixture of equipment. The new equipment was well-built, smooth riding and comfortable with modern, clean-lined interiors but it still did not have the striking exterior appearance and revolutionary quality that had characterized the new streamliners introduced on so many of the lines in the United States. In 1953 the CPR placed an order with the Budd Company for the construction of 173 stainless steel, streamlined cars to equip fully a new transcontinental passenger train and partially re-equip the existing *Dominion* and *Atlantic Limited*.

The train, to be called *The Canadian*, was to feature dome cars and a variety of attractive and comfortable accommodations ranging from coach seating and roomettes to more traditional berths and bedrooms. The designs for the cars were based on equipment operating on several railroads in the United States. In exterior appearance, the train was to resemble the renowned *California Zephyr* operating between Chicago and San Francisco over the Burlington, Rio Grande and Western Pacific lines. Many modifications were made for winter operating conditions on the CPR cars and the interior designs were all custom tailored for the new service. The trains were to be equipped with new rolling stock except for some tourist-sleeper cars rebuilt from existing cars but sheathed in stainless steel to conform to the general appearance of the new Budd cars.

There were seven types of new cars in the trains and they were ordered in differing quantities to reflect the consist of *The Canadian*. Eighteen each of baggage-dormitory, dome coach-buffets, diners, and dome observations were built along with 30 coaches and 71 sleeping cars of two different styles — the *Manor* and *Chateau* series. In addition to the new equipment, 22 older "G" series tourist sleepers were modified with stainless-steel sheathing and renamed into the "U" series (with names such as *Urquhart*, *Ulysses*, or *Uganda*) for service with the *Canadian*.

The new equipment order, which cost approximately $40,000,000, provided enough rolling stock for 15 train sets. *The Canadian* itself required seven of these sets of equipment to maintain the normal schedule. The extra cars were available for peak season travel, upgrading the consists for *The Dominion* and other trains. Extra equipment was also required because, east of Sudbury to Toronto and Montreal, the train was

The Canadian *and Passenger Services on the E&N and Kettle Valley*

Canadian Pacific's new streamlined *Canadian* was the company's last major attempt to retain its rail passenger business. The train was equipped with the finest available rolling stock and schedules were upgraded. In this photo from August 15, 1957, the eastbound *Canadian* was making a brief station stop at Golden before a daylight run through the Rockies.
—JOHN C. ILLMAN

The matched A-B-A units of *The Canadian* were photographed on the middle of the sweeping arch of Stoney Creek Bridge in this CPR publicity photo from the mid-1950s. Over the years, scheduling varied but it tended to emphasize daylight service through the Rockies. The trip through the Selkirks and the Fraser Canyon often was in darkness.

—NICHOLAS MORANT, CPCA, M6748

Nicholas Morant produced a series of photographs of *The Canadian* that featured the beautiful *Park* cars. This one highlighted the train crossing Mountain Creek in the Selkirks with the surrounding mountainsides in late Fall colours. —CPCA, M6614

divided into two sections requiring, in total, an extra baggage-dormitory car, diner, *Skyline* dome coach, and observation car. As first introduced, the regular 14-car consist for *The Canadian*, operating west of Sudbury, included the following:

1 Baggage-dormitory car
1 First Class Coach
1 *Skyline* Dome Buffet Coach
3 Tourist Sleepers
1 Diner
4 *Manor* Series Sleepers
2 *Chateau* Series Sleepers
1 *Park* Dome Lounge Sleeper

The usual motive power for the trains was an A-B-A set of General Motors FP7A and F7B units. Both the A and B units were fitted with steam generators for train heating.

The equipment for the new trains was sturdily built and durable as well as being attractively styled and elegant. Disc brakes, full mechanical air conditioning, public address systems, anti-wheelslide devices, tightlock couplers and sound proofing were some mechanical features of the cars.

Canadian Pacific billed *The Canadian* as the longest dome ride in the world at 2,881 miles (4636 km). The schedule was significantly improved over the running time of *The Dominion*. The scheduled transcontinental time had been 87 hours, 10 minutes, westbound; this was reduced to 71 hours, 10 minutes. Eastbound the time was improved by 12 hours, 30 minutes to 70 hours, 20 minutes.

The new *Canadian* was a dramatic success but, like nearly all North American passenger trains of the post-war years, its days of glory were limited. The new equipment slowed, but could not stop, the steady decline of passenger revenues as travellers increasingly chose to fly or drive.

Passenger service upgrading was also essential on many CPR branch lines during the 1950s. Many trains, including the E&N service on Vancouver Island and the *Kettle Valley Express* and *Kootenay Express*, were still using old, obsolete equipment although some new cars were finding their way onto the trains through southern British Columbia. No major changes were undertaken to the passenger service over the Kootenay and Kettle Valley divisions other than a gradual improvement in the equipment. However, the passenger rolling stock on the E&N, some of which dated to the turn of the century, was overdue for replacement. The short distance of the run between Victoria and Courtenay, just 140 miles (225 km), made the route ideal for the new Budd-built Rail Diesel Cars, or RDCs. These were self-propelled stainless steel cars that were built in several configurations ranging from full baggage to full coach. They were fitted with two diesel engines and modern, comfortable, air conditioned interiors. On the CPR, the RDC's were called *Dayliners* and one car was introduced to the E&N in 1955, replacing the picturesque, but expensive and obsolete wooden equipment

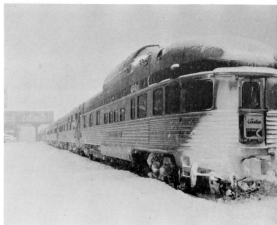

The Canadian's rolling stock was cleaned and washed at the end of the line. In this photo from February 1970, by which time the train was redecorated in CP Rail colours, a *Skyline* dome car was being pulled through the car washer at the Drake Street yards in Vancouver. Winter weather tested the best equipment. A snow-covered *Canadian* arrived in Vancouver on January 14, 1971 in a landscape looking more like the prairies than the Pacific Coast.
After VIA took over, passenger services out of Vancouver were concentrated at the CN station. The CPR station was restored and converted into a major transit centre.
—BOTH ROBERT D. TURNER

The Fraser and Thompson canyons rivalled the better-publicized Rockies for scenic beauty. Scheduling often took the passenger trains through the canyons after dark. Fortunately, there were exceptions, and delays or long summer days could give travellers an unexpected view of the Fraser, as on June 30, 1976. Timeless, the grandeur remained little changed. "We have been running along the Fraser River for the last 100 miles [160 km]," noted William Thompson, a traveller in 1891, "and the height of the mountains is something awful and grand."
—ROBERT D. TURNER

on the daily except Sunday trains between Victoria and Courtenay.

The *Dayliner* was an immediate success. Instead of two trains, each requiring a separate 1000 hp Baldwin diesel and four cars, one RDC handled the entire service with faster times en route. The one-way time on the northbound run (E&N Train No. 1) was reduced from 6 hours, 50 minutes to just 4 hours, 15 minutes with the RDC. Significantly, one RDC could make a return trip between Victoria and Courtenay in little more time than the standard passenger trains had covered the one-way distance. The improvement in running time and level of service made the RDC much more competitive with buses and road travel on Vancouver Island during a period when the roads on the Island were being steadily upgraded. Railway Post Office (RPO) service on the E&N had been discontinued and express and baggage service were not offered so in these terms the RDC marked a reduction in service, but for reliability, speed and comfort, not to mention economy, the *Dayliner* was a great improvement. In financial terms, there were obvious advantages for the CPR. First, maintenance requirements were significantly reduced with the retirement of the old equipment. Even car cleaning was greatly reduced. Second, locomotives were released for more profitable freight service and crew size was reduced from an engineer, fireman, conductor, two trainmen (one acting as baggageman), one express baggageman, and two RPO clerks on each standard train to just an engineer and conductor on a *Dayliner*. In later years, when a second *Dayliner* was added to the train, an assistant conductor also was required.

Soon after the *Dayliner* service was started on the E&N, the only other CPR passenger service on Vancouver Island, a mixed train between Port Alberni and Parksville, was discontinued. For reasons that were political, historical and, arguably practical, the E&N *Dayliner* was to survive all other CPR branch line passenger services in British Columbia and be included in VIA Rail Canada in the late 1970s.

Changes in passenger service were no less dramatic in the 1950s and early 1960s on the Kettle Valley route through southern British Columbia. In the post-war years, the road system of the province was systematically improved and automobile ownership increased significantly. One of the critical gaps in the highway network was completed late in 1949 when a road was opened between Hope and Princeton, providing for the first time a reasonably direct route from the Coast to the southern Interior. During the 1950s and 1960s work on upgrading and completing the road system was a major priority of the provincial government. The southern trans-provincial route — Highway No. 3 — in general terms paralleling the route of the CPR between Hope and the Crowsnest Pass, was finally completed to high speed standards in the early 1960s after years of construction and it opened the whole of the southern B.C. to fast road travel.

More than any other single factor, this road made the passenger trains, and indeed much of the freight service, on the Kettle Valley and Kootenay divisions redundant. To illustrate the impact of the road system on the CPR, in 1948, the average ridership between Odlum (Hope) and Penticton on eastbound trains had been 115 passengers. By the mid-1950s, it averaged only about 30 passengers per trip despite a healthy economy and growing population. Westbound, the traffic was slightly lower.

Important economies and improvements in service were realized with the use of diesel locomotives on the standard passenger trains. But even these savings were insufficient to save full service between the Coast and the Crowsnest or to attract passengers back to the trains. Trains 11 and 12 even provided a daylight service over the scenic Coquihalla and Trains 45 and 46 gave a second train a day over the route in each direction. The last two trains were not dieselized because their future was uncertain. They were dependent on fruit and other high value head-end business for much of their revenue and with steadily declining traffic, they were discontinued in September 1954. The traffic simply was not there.

In 1957, the CPR announced its plans to replace the existing equipment with RDCs and to put revised schedules into effect in October. In the meantime, tenders were called for trucking the mail between Medicine Hat, Alberta, and Nelson (effective October 1, 1957) and also between Nelson and Vancouver (effective November 1, 1957). The removal of the mail contracts from the trains meant that the frequency of service could be adjusted to reflect the low traffic volumes instead of just running the trains to meet the deadlines for mail delivery. Six RDCs were expected to replace the conventional trains and at the same time reduce travel time by 10 or 11 hours. On October 27, 1957, the trains (Nos. 45 and 46) began operating on the new schedule using abbreviated conventional trains of a passenger diesel, baggage car and coach until the RDCs could be delivered early in 1958. Trains 11 and 12 disappeared from the timetables at this time. At the same time the Spences Bridge-Merritt-Brookmere mixed train service was ended. Ridership was so low that the cancellation of the service was virtually unnoticed.

Social problems, resulting in terrorist bombings, emerged at this time and hastened the withdrawal of CPR services. The Sons of Freedom, a radical sect of the Doukhobor community, began a bombing campaign in the West Kootenays. On December 17, 1957, a bomb destroyed a section of CPR track, and took out three power poles and a link in a natural gas pipeline. Later, bombs were found in theatres in Nelson, Castlegar and Trail and on January 22nd, a bomb was found at West Summerland. These incidents were followed by an announcement that passenger service would be restricted to daylight operation through the area and, at the same time, the service between Penticton and Nelson would be reduced to twice weekly. The reductions had the support

Esquimalt & Nanaimo Train No. 1 (RDC 9199) crosses the Tsable River near the northern end of its run from Victoria to Courtenay on October 8, 1971. The line north of Parksville was closed between 1975 and 1977 when the timber trestle approaches to this span and the large bridge over French Creek both needed replacement. The CPR sought permission to abandon the line but it was not granted. —ROBERT D. TURNER

RDC 9064 eases across the Cowichan River on an intricate cast iron and steel bridge. The iron castings for the structure were produced by the Phoenix Iron Company of Philadelphia. —ROBERT D. TURNER

In September 1963, when this photograph was taken at Crowsnest, passenger service across southern British Columbia was nearing its end. Here, No. 45 and No. 46, the westbound and eastbound *Dayliners* met and a few passengers boarded the trains.—ANDRE MORIN

of federal Minister of Transport George Hees, because of the danger to the passenger trains. For a time, track patrols were sent out ahead of all passenger trains operating in either direction between Penticton and Faulder (6.0 miles-9.7 km to the west of West Summerland). The CPR was justified in being cautious because a bomb blast on a CPR passenger train near Grand Forks had killed Doukhobor leader Peter Vasilevich Verigin on October 29, 1924.

The net effect of the service changes was that when the *Dayliners* were introduced in March 1958, through service between the Coast and the Kootenays was but a memory. An overnight stop was required for eastbound passengers wanting to continue beyond Penticton although a close connection was available for westbound passengers. East of Nelson, conventional equipment remained in use pending the arrival of more *Dayliners* to complete the transition later in the year.

The cuts in passenger service were not popular and caused some controversy at the time, but when the bombing danger had passed, the service was not increased. Regardless of the bombings, it seems, the cuts would have been inevitable.

In the West Kootenays other passenger and freight services had been eliminated as well. These included the retirement of the last sternwheelers operated by the CPR.* The *Minto* was withdrawn from service on the Arrow Lakes in 1954 and the *Moyie* followed in 1957, to be preserved at Kaslo. The tug *Granthall* continued to operate on Kootenay Lake until 1958 when the barge service to Kaslo and Lardeau was taken over by a charter operator. Similarly, the *Rosebery*, last CPR vessel on Slocan Lake was retired in favour of a chartered diesel tug in 1956. The Kootenay area branch lines also lost passenger service during the 1950s although many had already been reduced to once a week mixed trains. Cuts in passenger service during this period reflected the continent-wide trends in passenger travel preferences. In its *Annual Report* for 1955, the CPR noted that in five years, system-wide, 119 trains had been discontinued and another 45 had been reduced in frequency. The decrease amounted to 2.4 million train miles per year. In 1955 alone, 39 CPR passenger services had been discontinued.

The End of the Coquihalla Line and Kettle Valley Cutbacks

While passenger services were being curtailed on the Kettle Valley route, the basic rail network of the southern Interior of British Columbia had not been affected. However, traffic patterns were changing. The improved road systems, more modern trucks, and mechanically refrigerated trailers all cut into freight traffic, particularly low-volume, high-value merchandise and perishables. Another significant loss in traffic came at the end of April 1957, with the closure of the Granby

* For a detailed treatment of the CPR's British Columbia Lake and River Service see *Sternwheelers and Steam Tugs* (Sono Nis Press, 1984).

The Canadian, the CPR's last and most famous trans-continental passenger train, roars out of the Connaught Tunnel in September 1964. This was the streamliner at its best: perfectly matched A-B-A diesels, the unbroken lines of the gleaming stainless steel cars, and the spectacular backdrop of the Selkirk Mountains.
—DAVE WILKIE

At right *The Dominion* accelerates westbound out of Revelstoke on a beautiful afternoon in July 1962. —BILL TURNER

Nearing Field, the westbound *Canadian*, with 4 diesels and 20 cars, eases downgrade past Cathedral Crags and through a short tunnel in the face of Mount Stephen in August 1969. The train is decorated in CP Rail colours, the final scheme applied to the train before it was taken over by VIA. —DAVE WILKIE

High over Niagara Canyon, southbound E&N *Dayliner* 9103 nears the end of its run from Courtenay to Victoria on June 19, 1976. —ROBERT D. TURNER

VIA's *Canadian*, with its 30-year-old equipment including former CPR and CNR rolling stock and locomotives, winds down the Field Hill through Yoho in August 1985. —ROBERT D. TURNER

269

Consolidated Mining and Smelting Company mine at Copper Mountain south of Princeton. This mine had accounted for 7,965 carloads of freight in its last year of operation which, out of a total of 20,417 cars, represented over one third of the division's originating traffic. Increases in forest products, particularly wood chips for use in pulp mills, and some additional mining traffic helped to counter the losses in freight traffic. There was still strength in the Kettle Valley Division but there was also weakness. The strength lay in the industrially-based traffic which certainly justified continued rail service. The weakness lay in the long and expensive-to-maintain sections of the line that generated little or no direct traffic: the Coquihalla and Carmi subdivisions.

The Coquihalla Subdivision, with its 38-foot (11.6-m) average snowfall, was the last section of the Kettle Valley Railway to be completed; now it was to be the first section of significance to be abandoned. The closure came unexpectedly on November 23, 1959 following a series of devastating washouts. Repair crews were called out but it soon became clear that at least a temporary closure was needed. The worst washout, near Lear, was over 100 feet (30 m) deep and would have required at least 100,000 yards (76 455 m³) of fill. Others that also severed the line would have required nearly equal amounts of work. At the end of November, CP announced that the line would not be reopened until spring and that all traffic would be diverted via Merritt and Spences Bridge.

With the line closed for the winter, it was possible to assess the damage more carefully and at the same time contemplate the future of the route. Always trouble-plagued, it had been described as the being the costliest section of railroad to operate on the continent. Repairs to the Coquihalla were never completed and in 1961 the CPR sought permission from the Board of Transport Commissioners to abandon the route altogether. Approval, following hearings, came in July and work began almost immediately to dismantle the tracks. Repairs had been estimated at nearly $310,000 and net salvage was determined to be $563,000. While the CPR had invested far more than this in upgrading the route in recent years, the decision was based on broader economic concerns by the railway. In future, the Kettle Valley and Kootenay divisions were to be more branch lines and much less a second main line across the province. They were, in effect, reverting to their original roles relative to the main line through British Columbia. Traffic destined for the Coast from the East Kootenays was to be routed via Cranbrook north to the main line at Golden. The distance was greater, but the main line was a higher standard railroad and the concentration of traffic would result in considerable economies particularly when the annual savings from closing the Coquihalla were considered. The Lake Windermere Subdivision (later re-named the Windermere Subdivision), which ran from Golden south to Covalli near Cranbrook, provided essentially flat running along the Rocky Mountain Trench. The greater

The *Dayliner* service across southern British Columbia was a relaxing way to travel and the scenery was beautiful but few people used the trains. Travel by car on the new highways was more convenient or attractive to most people. RDC-2 No. 9107 was assigned to Train No. 45 on August 3, 1961, photographed at Grand Forks as three passengers wait to board, and later at Midway. —PHILIP C. JOHNSON

An eastbound *Dayliner* rolls through Othello with a background of the forested mountains of the Coquihalla Pass in September 1959.
—ANDRE MORIN

Passenger service from Yahk to Spokane over the Spokane International lasted until the mid-1950s although only as a mixed train. This train was westbound from Kingsgate on July 22, 1954 when photographed near Sandpoint, Idaho. SI Alco RS-1s Nos. 201, 211, and 208 are pulling the train. —PHILIP C. JOHNSON

distance was in large measure compensated for by easier grades and less severe winter conditions.

The closure and abandonment of the Coquihalla did not mean the end of direct rail connections between Princeton, the Okanagan and the Coast; the route between Brodie, Merritt and Spences Bridge was still in service. The diversion of traffic did not have a significant effect on freight service, but it did lengthen the passenger run and contributed to further losses in ridership. Even before the closure of the Coquihalla, patronage had been depressingly low — averaging less than 30 passengers per trip between Penticton and the Coast. After the closure it averaged less than 10. The CPR estimated that at least 40 passengers were required to recover basic costs on the western end of the service.

It came as no real surprise when the CPR sought permission to abandon passenger service on the Kettle Valley-Crowsnest route in June 1962. With costs exceeding revenues by a nearly seven times (revenues were $86,100 vs. costs of $596,000), the application was granted to discontinue trains No. 45 and 46 in January 1964, despite protests from local communities and chambers of commerce. The last runs of the *Dayliners* after just six years of service were marked by little fanfare except by members of the Okanagan Historical Society who rode the last eastbound out of Penticton as far as Rock Creek on January 17, 1964. There were 92 passengers on the two RDCs (Nos. 9100 and 9022) and a crew of three: Engineer Dave McAstocker, Conductor Wilf Marquis and Baggageman Fred Smith. The train ran through to Nelson, ending passenger service over the entire route between Vancouver and Medicine Hat. RDC No. 9100 had made the run in from Spences Bridge to Penticton earlier in the day, ending service from the West.

Passenger service was but a memory on the Kettle Valley and Kootenay divisions, and the route faded from public notice. Freight was still handled in considerable quantities but with through traffic being diverted to the main line, business over the Carmi Subdivision between Penticton and Midway was very low. The route was very expensive to maintain and there was insufficient traffic to justify keeping the line open. Service was suspended in 1973 although trains still ran west from Midway as far as Beaverdell. Finally, in 1978 the subdivision was approved for abandonment and the tracks were removed over the next two years. There had been some hope by Okanagan area residents that portions of the line could be developed for a tourist railroad but they were unable to secure sufficient financial backing. In the southern Okanagan, the trackage south of Okanagan Falls, except for a spur to the Weyerhaeuser mill, was removed in 1979. The fruit traffic which had sustained the line was all being moved by truck. Traffic on both the Kettle Valley and Kootenay divisions was badly hit by the recession, competition from trucking and the decline in the forest industry during the 1980s. Fortunately, however, the reductions in business were insufficient to see any further cutbacks of operational trackage.

The process of modernizing and increasing the efficiency of the CPR in the West continued after the completion of the dieselization programs. There were many factors contributing to the necessity for these changes including increasing costs of labour and materials plus very significant competition from trucks and, potentially, from pipelines. Throughout North America, the railroad industry was suffering a continuing and serious loss of intercity, high value freight. Increasingly, the railroads were left with the low value, high volume, bulk commodities such as grain, coal, sulphur, potash and lumber to move over long distances. The railways responded with the development of trucking subsidiaries and "piggy-back" services but the result was still a significant shift of traffic away from the rail lines.

Passenger traffic had virtually left the railroads in favour of private automobiles, buses and the airlines. Similarly, the important mail contracts, which had maintained Railway Post Office services and helped to support many passenger train operations, were lost to air and truck services. By the late 1960s, the CPR was left with only two passenger trains in British Columbia. These were *The Canadian* and the solitary *Dayliner* operating on Vancouver Island. The passenger service, once paramount to the railway, was now a costly necessity and, from an operational point of view, an encumbrance to the efficient movement of freight. On the Coast, the passenger steamships of the B.C. Coast Service faded from the scene in the 1950s and early 1960s as government owned automobile ferries took over the most important surviving routes.

By the mid 1960s, the decline in passenger travel had reached such proportions, and costs risen so much, that the CPR was granted permission to discontinue *The Dominion* in 1966 although it continued to operate in the summer of 1967 as the *Expo Limited* to help accommodate the heavy travel to the world's fair at Montreal. In the next few years, conditions only worsened for the passenger trains as losses continued to mount.

In 1970, CP applied for permission to discontinue *The Canadian* and thus end transcontinental passenger service, although its real aim was to seek a federal subsidy for the service. With a Canadian Transport Commission ruling to continue the train as an essential service, CPR was entitled to a subsidy of 80 percent of the operating deficit. Since CNR also applied for similar support for its *Super Continental*, it was clear that the future of passenger trains, particularly the transcontinentals, in Canada would rest increasingly with the federal government. The process would take some years to complete, but the end result was the formation in 1977 of VIA Rail Canada which was given the responsibility to operate nearly all passenger train service in Canada. (Notable excep-

The Evolving Railway, VIA and Unit Trains

The twisted mass of Mount Stephen looms above this freight led by three new SD40s. These locomotives, first ordered by the CPR in 1966, and particularly the later improved SD40-2s, would become the standard locomotive on the CPR during the 1970s.
—NICHOLAS MORANT, CPCA, M8363

Both Canadian Pacific and Canadian National began an extensive modernization of their locomotive fleets in the late 1960s. Older, first generation diesels soon gave way to the new power which on both lines was usually represented by General Motors SD40s and SD40-2s. New SD40s are in charge of heavy tonnage on both banks of the Thompson River east of Lytton in this scene from September 1967. —ROBERT D. TURNER

tions in British Columbia were the passenger services on the White Pass & Yukon Route and the British Columbia Railway which were not included in VIA.) VIA took over both *The Canadian* and the E&N *Dayliner* services and has continued to operate both through the 1980s.

It was a time of deep and fundamental changes, some of which were painful and unpopular, some of which were dramatic and far-reaching. As it had in the past, the CPR was able to draw on a number of particularly able, pragmatic and farsighted individuals for its management during this period of extensive changes. Norris R. Crump served as president of the company until 1964, when his place was taken by Robert A. Emerson. Unfortunately, however, Emerson died in 1966. In 1972 Ian D. Sinclair took over from Crump as chairman and Frederick S. Burbidge became president. Burbidge, following Sinclair, served as chairman from 1981-1985. Under these and present senior executives William Stinson, Robert Campbell and R. S. Allison, Canadian Pacific Ltd. and CP Rail have remained committed to long-term development of the system.

Physically, the CPR was going through other transitions in the 1960s. Dispatching was modernized with centralized traffic control eliminating the need for many small stations. Locomotives were changing too. The original diesels in main line service were being supplemented with and eventually would be replaced by new, more powerful machines. These came from the two surviving Canadian diesel manufacturers: General Motors and Montreal Locomotive Works. Both GM and MLW were producing the "second generation diesel" designs of their parent companies in the United States. CP orders for new power were limited until 1965 when the company purchased its first SD40 3000-hp road diesels and in subsequent years ordered the MLW equivalent, the C-630s. Early problems with the designs of the first SD40s (notably wheel-slip controls and turbo-charger failures) led CP to order equivalent MLW power in 1967. In the meantime, Alco, MLW's parent, withdrew from the locomotive building business and MLW in Canada was on its own. MLW introduced a redesigned line of high horsepower diesels and designated the models M-630 and M-636. The 3000-hp M-630s were to be important components of new coal train services.

The initial design problems of the SD40s were soon rectified while problems with the MLWs compounded with age. The net result was that after 1972 the CPR concentrated its new orders on the SD40-2, the successor to the SD40. These two types of 3000-hp road diesels came to dominate all main line traffic on the CPR through British Columbia by the mid-1970s. Individually, these units had nearly twice the horsepower of the first generation diesels and offered other improvements in electronics, fuel consumption, maintenance and controls. The CPR became so impressed by the SD40s and SD40-2s that by the mid-1980s, over 500 were in use.

The lower Fraser Canyon is blanketed with new snow but the fall is insufficient to impede traffic. A mixture of power—an SD40, two MLW M-630s and a GP9R—eases toward the siding at Spuzzum on December 18, 1971.
—ROBERT D. TURNER

Increasingly through the early 1970s, first generation diesel power was reassigned from main line freight duties to wayfreights that handled switching along the line, yard service, and branch line operations. In this scene at Chase from July 1973, a GP9R and an H16-44 roll along the flat valley lands of the South Thompson with little effort on a wayfreight.
—ROBERT D. TURNER

Not only were the locomotives changing during the 1970s but so too was the rolling stock. Larger and more specialized cars, particularly grain and potash hoppers, coal and sulphate gondolas, and flatcars for containers and truck trailers, were coming into increasing usage. The long trains of once-familiar boxcars, like those shown passing at Lytton on May 4, 1971, would be gradually replaced. The westbound, at left, was an extra powered by two SD40s and an H16-44 while the eastbound was a long train of empty grain cars. —ROBERT D. TURNER

Gradually, the diesels first used to replace steam power were retired. In British Columbia, the Baldwin and Fairbanks Morse units, ordered from the Canadian Locomotive Company, were retired in increasing numbers in the late 1960s and early 1970s. Their places were taken by General Motors GP7 and GP9 diesels no longer needed in main line service. In the mid-1970s, however, the surviving units were retired very rapidly from road service and scrapped. General Motors FP7s and FP9s also were retired from freight service or transferred to passenger duties. Most of the surviving units were sold to VIA in 1978.

A most dramatic change in operations occurred in the late 1960s when a renewed development of the Crowsnest area coal fields began. The coal was destined for export to Japan and it was to be shipped in record quantities over at least a 20-year period. To produce and transport the coal at competitive prices, new technologies in mining and transport had to be developed and implemented. They would be vastly different from those used in the past. Most of the coal was to be recovered from surface mines using the latest and largest in earth-moving equipment. The coal was then to be transported by dedicated unit trains to the Coast for shipment, via bulk carrier capable of carrying 100,000 tons or more, to Japan. These trains were not the first unit train operations in British Columbia but they introduced the technology on a vastly larger and more sophisticated scale than ever before.

The mines were developed by Kaiser Resources Limited (later a part of B.C. Coal which was in turn renamed Westar Resources) and the CPR subsidiary, Fording Coal. Mines were located in the Crowsnest near the long-established mining communities of Fernie, Michel and Natal. However, for the new developments, the towns of Michel and Natal were completely phased out. A new community, known as Sparwood, was developed and most vestiges of the depressed, run-down mining towns of an earlier generation became history. To reach the Fording operations, tracks were extended up the Elk River Valley a distance of 33.8 miles (54.4 km) and were in use in 1972.

At first, proposals were made to ship the coal through the United States over a new branch line that would have connected with the Burlington Northern in Montana. Eventually the coal would have been re-routed back to B.C. for shipment from a coal port to be developed at Roberts Bank south of Vancouver. The charter of the Kootenay & Elk Railway, which was controlled by Kaiser Resources, was to be used for this branch line. However, the proposal met with strenuous opposition from the CPR and other interests who insisted that the coal be routed over Canadian carriers. Their arguments were persuasive and the scheme to use the BN did not progress.

However, to use the CPR meant that heavy upgrading of the route to the Coast would be required. The main line was in excellent condition, but the route south of Golden required extensive reconstruction of bridges and tracks to permit the operation of the heavy unit trains.

At the Pacific Coast end of the line, major construction was required to develop an adequate docking facility at Roberts Bank for the bulk carriers that were to transport the coal to Japan. The terminal was built by Westshore Terminals. Connecting the new port to the main line of the CPR at Mission involved the construction of new trackage and the improvement of existing lines in the Fraser Valley. The existing bridge over the Fraser at Mission was used and from there a new 2-mile (3.2-km) long CP-CN interchange track was built between Riverside on the CP's Mission Subdivision and Page on the CN's Yale Subdivision. From there CN trackage was used to a connection with the B.C. Hydro Railway at Livingstone. Over seven miles (11 km) of B.C. Hydro trackage, upgraded and equipped with CTC (central-ized traffic control) for the coal train service, was used through to a point named View. From there, the B.C. Harbours Board Railway built 23.3 miles (37.5 km) of new trackage (later transferred to the B.C. Railway) to Roberts Bank.

The operation of the trains was itself quite complicated and required new locomotives and rolling stock and the introduc-tion of new equipment, computer facilities and staff training, to facilitate the movement of the long trains. The final, refined plans called for the coal to be shipped in 88-car (10,000-ton, or 10 160-tonne) trains. To move these trains over the mountains efficiently, locomotives were to be oper-ated at the head end and also in the middle of the trains. The latter units were to be controlled from the leading unit by radio using a device called Locotrol. The mid-train units were referred to as "slave units," with the control devices carried in a Robot car. This type of operation is more complicated than it would first appear because, for example, when a train is over one mile (1.5 km) long and in mountain-ous country, the front end of a train may be over the summit and heading downgrade, while the back end is still labouring uphill. This sort of situation complicates the throttle applica-tions and braking in the diesels. Considerable experimenta-tion and experience was required to refine fully this method of operation. An additional requirement on the diesels was a low throttle control, called "Pacesetter," that permitted the units to operate at a low, constant speed (0.50 to 0.75 miles or 0.80 to 1.2 km per hour) through the loaders near the mines. The speed controls were programmed to provide for the increasing weight of the train as the loading operation prog-ressed. At Roberts Bank, the trains were dumped one car at a time in a rotary dumper. There, the train was moved ahead mechanically by a device known as a "Mule" as the dumping proceeded.

Rolling stock for the trains comprised specially-designed gondola cars of 105-ton (106.7-tonne) capacity. These were developed under the supervision of Anthony Teoli, Engineer

The unit trains began at loading facilities like the one near Sparwood shown above. Special cars were built from retired B-units to house the remote control equipment for the slave units. —BOTH ROBERT D. TURNER

The Unit Trains

The big MLW diesels were impressive, powerful units. These M-630s were thundering eastbound through the tunnels just north of Yale in the Fraser Canyon in 1971. —ROBERT D. TURNER

of Car Equipment, at Montreal. The cars were a particularly efficient design and, weighing 53,000 lbs (24 000 kg), they had an excellent weight-to-capacity ratio. The standard cars were each equipped with a rotary coupler at the rear end so that they could pass through the rotary dumper for unloading without needing to be uncoupled. Additional cars were fitted with two rotary couplers because the locomotives and Robot cars were not fitted with this type of equipment. In operation, it became very important to see that no two cars with two rotary couplers were run together because the cars could move too freely from side to side around the axis of the couplers. Harmonic vibrations could develop in the train during normal train movements and cause derailments. Other features of the coal gondolas included tapered sides and ends and the bottoms of the cars were rounded and low-slung — just one foot (30 cm) above the rails. These features facilitated rapid unloading and produced a low centre of gravity (and consequently greater stability) for the cars.

Locomotives used on the trains in the first years of operation were MLW C-630 and M-630 units. However, as these designs gave increasing problems in maintenance and as programs of regional standardization were introduced, they were replaced by General Motors SD40 and SD40-2 units and the MLW units were transferred to the East. The Locotrol, Pacesetter devices and other special equipment for unit train service were removed from the MLW's and reinstalled in GM units during the mid-1970s.

The operations began with three (soon increased to six) 88-car trains which were capable of moving a total of 6,000,000 tons (6 096 000 tonnes) of coal annually. The first train left Sparwood for Roberts Bank on April 28, 1970. The overall return distance for the trains was 1,403 miles (2258 km) and it was hoped that a complete cycle could be run in 72 hours. However, in practice 82 hours proved to be more reasonable and in the summer, due to maintenance requirements on the line, the time was lengthened to 92 or 110 hours. As more and more trains were added to the route, the times were lengthened so that in the 1980s, the 110 hour cycle has been typical. Loading time is about two and one half to three hours, while unloading can be accomplished in about two hours.

The locomotive requirements for the trains varied over the route due to the reduced tonnage ratings of the diesels in the mountains. The problem areas were between Golden and Chase over the Selkirk and Monashee ranges. The operations during the first year of service were different from the procedures adopted later. At first, four units on the head end of the train powered it from Sparwood to Golden where they were cut off and used to take a returning empty train through to the mines. These units had the Pacesetter equipment needed for the low-speed loading operations. At Golden, four new units were put on the head end and four slave units were added (about 39 cars behind the leading units). At Beavermouth (after 1974, Rogers), the diesel consist was supple-

What might the masons building the abutments for the original cantilever bridge at this site have thought if they had known that their work routinely would support 10,000-ton trains 100 years later? Satisfaction, surely. Proving the strength of the old structures, a loaded coal train of 112 cars (over 14,500 tons or 14 730 tonnes) rolls across the Fraser and on down the canyon into the rain and mists. —ROBERT D. TURNER

278

The long coal trains ended their journey from the Crowsnest Pass at the new "superport" of Roberts Bank. The port was built at the end of a long causeway near the mouth of the Fraser River, south of Vancouver.

Roberts Bank

The coal gondolas, shown when new and clean, were designed to be moved through a rotary dumper by a mechanical device known as a mule, shown at right.

The coal port was designed for the rapid handling of the coal from the trains to bulk carriers for shipment to Japan. Stockpiles were built up to ensure continuous loading of the ships. As unit train service expanded, the port was enlarged with additional trackage, dumping equipment, coal storage space and ship docking facilities. All three photos were taken on September 1, 1972.—ROBERT D. TURNER

mented by three manually controlled pushers working about 15 cars ahead of the caboose. The pushers ran only as far as Stoney Creek where they were cut off and then run back light to Beavermouth. There, they waited for the next westbound coal train. Two of the slaves were cut out at Revelstoke (where the diesels were fueled) and two head end units were dropped off later at Chase. The remaining four units (two head end units and two slaves) pulled the train through to Roberts Bank and back to Chase without additional assistance. The units that were dropped off at Chase and Revelstoke were used as required for the empty eastbound movements.

It was found, however, that as the operation grew, more flexibility was required and, beginning in August 1971, additional units were equipped with both Locotrol and Pacesetter controls. With these modifications, it was no longer necessary to restrict units to the Sparwood-to-Golden section of the operation. Moreover, the slave units could be run over the entire route from the loading facilities to Roberts Bank. Operations of a typical 88-car train during the 1970s took the following pattern:

Sparwood to Golden, 223.7 miles (360.0 km)
2 - 3000-hp units on the head end
2 - 3000-hp units behind the 36th car

Golden to Beavermouth, 28 miles (45 km)
4 - 3000-hp units on the head end
2 - 3000-hp units behind the 36th car
    (at Golden two units were cut in behind the head end diesels)

Beavermouth to Stoney Creek, 14.1 miles (22.7 km)
4 - 3000-hp units on the head end
2 - 3000-hp units behind the 36th car
4 - 3000-hp manually controlled "Pusher" units behind the 52nd car
    (the pushers were cut out of the train at Stoney Creek and run back light to Beavermouth.)

Stoney Creek to Chase, 141.5 miles (227.7 km)
4 - 3000-hp units on head end
2 - 3000-hp units behind the 36th car
    (Same consist as Golden to Beavermouth; at Chase, the third and fourth head end units were cut off)

Chase to Roberts Bank, 289.5 miles (465.9 km)
    Same as from Sparwood to Golden

Roberts Bank to Sparwood, 696.8 miles (1121.4 km)
    Same as from Sparwood to Golden

The operation of the coal trains and other heavy tonnage movements led to the accumulation of extra units at Chase and when several sets of diesels had been dropped off there, they were added to the front of a convenient freight and run back to Revelstoke. This operation, like the pushers based at Beavermouth, was expensive and, as described later, a target for improved efficiency.

Ideally, the trains were well spread out on the circuit so that there would be an efficient use of power and loading and

Leaving the great barrier of the Selkirks behind, a coal train begins the long descent to Revelstoke on a cold March morning in 1978. Four SD40-2s are on the point and two slave units are back in the train. —ROBERT D. TURNER

Crews still change at North Bend in the Fraser Canyon and at the other traditional division points on the system. But the locomotives will not be changed, except for extra power being added where required.—ROBERT D. TURNER

The great weight of the loaded westbound trains resulted in locomotives accumulating at Chase where the extra power was dropped off. If regular eastbound movements did not need the engines, they were periodically run back to Revelstoke on the head of a convenient freight. That is what happened on May 7, 1978 when 10 units (including one GP38) and a robot car were run back to Revelstoke on this eastbound. That is 28,000 horsepower on the train.

—ROBERT D. TURNER

unloading facilities. A typical distribution of the trains during the first years of operation would have been:

Train 1, leaving Sparwood, westbound.
Train 2, between Golden and Beavermouth, westbound.
Train 3, at Kamloops, westbound.
Train 4, leaving Roberts Bank, eastbound.
Train 5, leaving Spences Bridge, eastbound.
Train 6, between Golden and Sparwood, eastbound.

With experience and more export contracts, the unit train operations grew and became routine on the CPR in southern British Columbia. Production in the coal fields increased, with five major loading facilities being established. Four are on the Fording River Subdivision north of Sparwood: Fording (Fording Coal); Line Creek (Crows Nest Resources); and Greenhills and Elkview (Westar Resources, formerly B.C. Coal, and originally Kaiser Coal). The fifth, close to Crowsnest Pass, is located at the Byron Creek Collieries near the original site of Corbin and ships coal mainly to the East.

Train lengths were increased from the initial 88 cars to 91, 104, 108 and then to 112 cars. The location of diesel units in the trains was modified and the number required was increased as the number of cars grew. The pusher consist working up to Stoney Creek grew to six units (18,000 hp) for the coal trains and five units were often used on other heavy (13,000-ton, or 13 200-tonne) bulk commodity trains.

A typical movement from the 1980s of a 112-car (14,672-ton, or 14 906-tonne) train was as follows:

Fording to Golden
3 - 3000-hp units on head end
2 - 3000-hp units behind the 46th car

Golden to Rogers
4 - 3000-hp units on head end
2 - 3000-hp units behind the 46th car

Rogers to Stoney Creek
4 - 3000-hp units on head end
2 - 3000-hp units behind the 46th car
6 - 3000-hp manually controlled "Pusher" units behind the 81st car

Stoney Creek to Revelstoke
    Same as Golden to Rogers

Revelstoke to Roberts Bank and return to Fording
    Same as Fording to Golden

(Note that the position of power consists could vary up to three car lengths from the positions indicated above.)

When one considers that one SD40-2 is approximately equivalent in tonnage rating (pulling power) to one of the T1 Selkirk steam engines, the size of these trains and the increased capacity of the line is clear. It would have been impossible to handle this type of tonnage with steam power of the type used in the 1940s and 1950s.

281

The aging equipment inherited by VIA brought a legacy of streamlined elegance. The photo above captures No. 1 in the Selkirks with four locomotives and 20 cars rolling west along the Illecillewaet River on August 20, 1983. The rock retaining wall dates to the 1890s. At left, the late afternoon sun catches the stainless steel sides of the former CPR cars as the *Canadian* winds downgrade beside the Kicking Horse River, just west of Field, on August 5, 1985.
—DAVE WILKIE; ROBERT D. TURNER

VIA and the *Canadian*

The *Canadian*, eastbound in the lower Kicking Horse Canyon near Glenogle on July 8, 1986, flanked by the vertical stratigraphy of the Rockies. —ROBERT D. TURNER

On board

Vignettes of the *Canadian* passing through Field. Winter travel is often quiet; the warmth of the train inviting in a snow-covered landscape. In summer the conductor was faced with standing room only.—ALL ROBERT D. TURNER

The experienced hand of G. E. Pushie guided VIA's *Canadian* through the Rockies in January 1984 and imperceptibly brought the train to a halt at Field. Also in the cab of the F-unit were Bob Gray and Louie Ursocchi. Gordie Hendricks worked in the cramped kitchen of the dining car.

The RDC run on Vancouver Island was the CPR's last local
service in British Columbia. Tied to promises made in the
original land grant agreements to operate the railway
continuously, and with the determined support of many Island
residents, the E&N passenger service endured despite petitions
for abandonment. Becoming part of VIA's system, the trains
gradually grew in popularity. Sunday service was added,
summer traffic volumes required a second RDC, and a new
station was built in Victoria.—ALL ROBERT D. TURNER

The scene above shows the RDCs southbound high over
Arbutus Creek on August 21, 1984.

The E&N Dayliner

Scenery and a personal touch made the
E&N service special. Where else would a
Christmas traveller find candy canes for the
children or learn that a second generation
E&N engineer like Don or Al MacLachlan
is at the throttle?

John Mahy, conductor on the *Railiner* (as VIA calls its RDCs), above at Victoria in 1985, and at right, helping summer passengers board the train at Parksville in 1983.

Parksville station in winter with the water tower still standing in the distance. January 4, 1985.

Typical of freight operations in the 1980s on the Victoria Subdivision, Extra 8827 North has only eight cars as it crosses Niagara Canyon on June 13, 1986. —DAVID WILKIE

The main line north of Victoria is depicted in another mode in January 1969 as two Baldwins piloted the *Dayliner* northbound through Langford. Late perhaps, but still running when all other means of travel were blocked by snow. —ROBERT D. TURNER

On the Esquimalt & Nanaimo

The late 1970s and the 1980s were years of decline for the E&N. Log hauling on the Lake Cowichan Subdivision (shown at right) ended in 1981 and the line was abandoned two years later. Increasingly, businesses centralized distribution in Vancouver and trucked products on the Island. Freights out of Victoria declined to three a week. Recession hurt other major shippers. Local stations closed as the business of the line was run mainly from Vancouver.

—ROBERT D. TURNER

The line between Port Alberni and Nanaimo, with traffic dominated by forest products, remained the backbone of the E&N's business. This eastbound (Work Extra 8835) had 43 cars as it crossed an arm of Loch Arkaig at the summit of the Port Alberni Subdivision on June 25, 1986. —DAVE WILKIE

The Kettle Valley-Kootenay Lines

High over the Kettle River at Cascade, Extra 3094 West rolls on towards Grand Forks in late afternoon sun between rain showers in July 1986. Four nearly new GP38-2s lead the train of empty woodchip cars and flatcars for the mills of Grand Forks and Midway. —ROBERT D. TURNER

After the abandonment of the Coquihalla Pass line and the trackage between Penticton and Midway, all rail traffic to and from the southern Okanagan, Princeton and Merritt had to be routed through Spences Bridge. Even the Kettle Valley Division itself had disappeared; the trackage was incorporated into the Canyon and Kootenay divisions. The train at left is a 35-car eastbound extra with units 3005 and 8835 and caboose running along the Nicola River to Merritt on August 22, 1983. —DAVE WILKIE

Westbound through Tulameen, a freight from Penticton to Merritt eases over a low pile trestle surrounded by swimmers in July 1982. —ROBERT D. TURNER

On June 2, 1981 three units wind along the course of McRae
Creek climbing eastbound towards Farron at the summit
of the line between Grand Forks and Castlegar.

—ROBERT D. TURNER

Castlegar's unusual station was built inside the wye at the junction of the main line of the Kootenay Division and the branch line from Trail. At noon on June 1, 1978, a crew had just come in from Midway and was taking a break for lunch and to check in at the station for orders. —ROBERT D. TURNER

Freights meet at South Slocan. On the main line, a heavy train from Trail and Castlegar passes through the wye on its way to Nelson. The train at left has come in from Slocan City to the north. Woodchip cars were spotted in the small yard for another crew to switch over to the pulp mill at Castlegar while this crew will couple its train to the caboose of the Trail extra for the remainder of the run into Nelson.
—ROBERT D. TURNER

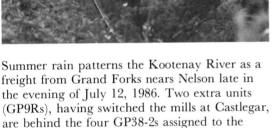

Summer rain patterns the Kootenay River as a freight from Grand Forks nears Nelson late in the evening of July 12, 1986. Two extra units (GP9Rs), having switched the mills at Castlegar, are behind the four GP38-2s assigned to the crew coming in from the west. —ROBERT D. TURNER

Top to bottom right

Nelson's beautifully maintained 1899 station is home for the Kootenay Division headquarters. However, increasing centralization of diesel servicing has reduced the importance of the city to the CPR since the closure in the mid-1970s of the diesel shops. —ROBERT D. TURNER

Montreal Locomotive Works (Alco design) S-4 No. 7110 was assigned to the Nelson yards in 1973. Most MLW yard units were retired by the CPR by the mid-1980s. —ROBERT D. TURNER

CLC power, once almost synonymous with CPR train services in the Kootenays, was replaced by GM locomotives. These H16-44s and the two trailing C-Liners, shown passing through McConnel westbound for Trail with 39 cars on August 1, 1973, were all scrapped by 1975.
—MICHAEL WILKIE

Elko was one of the last train order stations on the CPR in British Columbia. In this photo, the operator is handing up orders to the conductor of an eastbound freight heading towards the Crowsnest in March 1980. —ROBERT D. TURNER

Through the Crowsnest

Crowsnest remains an important point on the CPR. It is the division point between the Kootenay and Alberta South divisions. Snow still covers the yards in this scene from March 1982 as a coal train rolls past the crew's boarding house and five SD40-2s (four of them Union Pacific units) idling in the background. Just as the Spokane International provided an important gateway between the CPR and American lines radiating from Spokane during the early 1900s, it continues to do so in a modern role with run-through trains using pooled UP-CP motive power. The lower photo shows CP Train No. 979 led by three Union Pacific units passing through Moyie on April 3, 1978. —ROBERT D. TURNER; DAVE WILKIE

Lasers & Spike Mauls

Maintenance of trackage has changed dramatically on the CPR. During the steam era, section crews, often living at remote stations, patrolled and maintained sections of line as short as eight miles. Gradually mechanization took over and the sections were phased out and combined. By the 1980s, track maintenance was the responsibility of highly mechanized track gangs moving from place to place as required.

The crew shown in these photographs from September 1985 was working north of Spillimacheen in the Rocky Mountain Trench on the route of the heavy coal trains. The equipment they used incorporated lasers which were used by the tamping machine to guide the alignment of the rails. Coming along behind, the men drove the odd spike in traditional fashion. Bringing up the rear was another tamper which completed the work. Laser guided tampers are more than a generation away from the handcars and prybars of the steam era section men or from the technique of the somewhat legendary B&B foreman from the Kettle Valley who, reputedly, after walking out onto the middle of a large wooden trestle and jumping up and down, pronounced it safe for heavier locomotives.

—ALL ROBERT D. TURNER

The traditional 40-foot (12.2-m) bolted-together sections of rail have given way on the main lines to welded lengths up to one quarter mile (400 m) or more in length. Onsite welding—thermite welding—is a routine procedure. This crew, working near Spuzzum in the Fraser Canyon on July 8, 1982 is welding a replacement section of rail. The pot shown in the upper photo contains the chemical reaction producing the weld. Grinding down the joint is hard work even with modern equipment. The process takes about two hours for each weld.—BOTH ROBERT D. TURNER

Diesel Reflections

Top and bottom inside right
The tug and barge service on Slocan Lake connecting the isolated branch line to Nakusp became the last remnant of the once-important B.C. Lake & River Service. In September 1974 the train has been loaded onto the barge at Rosebery, shown at right, and the tug *Iris G.* will take the barge to Slocan City. There, as shown in the lower photo, the CLC diesel will unload the train and run on to Nelson.
—ROBERT D. TURNER

Upper right
Baldwin DRS4-4-1000 No. 8001, one of the CPR's first road diesels, was called into snow plow service on the E&N in January 1969. The plow is shown in Victoria.—ROBERT D. TURNER

Middle right
The General Motors GP9R and GP7R were highly successful and versatile diesels. Photographed at Revelstoke in 1973, 8838 is a GP9R built in August 1959 while the second unit, 8410, is a GP7R dating to March 1952. It was the second GP7 acquired by the CPR.
—ROBERT D. TURNER

Lower right
Traffic to and from the Sullivan Mine at Kimberley has been an important source of tonnage since the turn of the century. On October 26, 1985, a freight led by CP Rail and BC Rail diesels (the latter on lease), crosses the St. Mary's River on the Kimberley Subdivision.
—ROBERT WHETHAM

The late evening sun catches a northbound coal train as it winds along the Columbia River near Invermere in the beautiful Rocky Mountain Trench in the early 1970s. Nicholas Morant, who has recorded the CPR in many moods and settings, was the photographer. —CPCA

Winter is coming to the high country as the ridges have their first dusting of new snow. It is late September 1985 and an eastbound freight is winding its way up the Field Hill between the Spiral Tunnels. The photograph was taken from the lookout on the Trans-Canada Highway. A few minutes later, the same train passed Summit Lake just west of the Great Divide.

—ROBERT D. TURNER

With a background of Cathedral Mountain and Mount Stephen, a freight composed mostly of piggyback and container equipment makes the final assault on the summit of the Rockies in September 1985. —ROBERT D. TURNER

The seasons change quickly. Snow will soon dominate the landscape and require the use of the plows. The scene at left is less than two miles distant from the fall setting and shows Snow Plow Extra 5671 clearing the line at 2:10 p.m. on February 2, 1982. —DAVE WILKIE

The time-honoured position of operator is all but gone from the CPR. The operator handled train orders relayed along the line by telegraph, telephone or radio but, by 1986, only a few important junctions and major terminals had train order offices. Centralized traffic control (CTC), radios and computers had taken over. Closed in the 1980s was Spences Bridge where Judy Pulley worked in October 1981.
—ROBERT D. TURNER

The station clock still hangs in the yard office at Field but most of the traditional steam era features have long since gone. On July 8, 1986, the operator, Rod Van Vlack, works a computer terminal, the telegraph key long obsolete. At left is Vern Shipp, the crew caller. Crews working at Field have to be aware of the time zone change: Mountain Time to the east, Pacific Time to the west. To avoid confusion, the station clock has two hour hands. Pocket watches might also be fitted with an extra hand to make sure of the times. —ROBERT D. TURNER

Along the Main Line

Entering the broad vista of the Fraser Valley, a westbound freight heads onto double track at Ruby Creek on March 30, 1978.
—JOHN C. ILLMAN

CP Rail and CN Rail trains parallel each other east of Spences Bridge on November 8, 1985, while below, west of Spences Bridge, trains pass on June 10, 1983. —ROBERT D. TURNER; NANCY J. TURNER

At Spences Bridge, the main line crosses the Nicola River where it meets the Thompson. This freight was westbound on July 2, 1972.
—ROBERT D. TURNER

Above: Notch Hill. An eastbound container train takes the old main line downgrade to Salmon Arm on June 7, 1985.

Two photos, lower left: A snow plow extra winds down through the Selkirks on November 6, 1985, and a unit train slows for a meet along the Illecillewaet in May 1978.

Below: Both dynamic and train brakes were in use on this westbound descending the Field Hill on September 10, 1980.

—ALL ROBERT D. TURNER

VIA's *Canadian* climbs towards the Great Divide above the
Spiral Tunnels on August 6, 1985.

The heavy concentration of power required for the unit coal trains and other traffic movements over Rogers Pass was far from desirable from an operational and economic standpoint and the railway began a search for alternatives. Moreover, traffic projections suggested that by the mid-1980s, the capacity of the main line over the Selkirks would have been reached, thus precluding any significant increase in traffic. This situation was bad from the perspective of the railway and the national economy as a whole. An appreciation of the growth in westbound traffic can be gained from comparing the tonnages of grain, coal and total traffic over the line between 1965 and 1980. Coal grew from 1.0 to 10.5 million short tons (0.9 to 9.5 million tonnes) while grain increased from 2.9 to 4.2 million short tons (2.6 to 3.8 million tonnes). Total traffic increased from 6.7 to 22.5 million short tons (6.1 to 20.4 million tonnes) — over 300 percent. Forecasts projected a further doubling of these tonnages by the late-1980s, although the recession of the early 1980s slowed these growth rates significantly. Electric operations for the entire main line between Calgary and Coquitlam and for the coal train route between Golden and Sparwood were considered as one possibility for increasing line capacity and reducing the need for helpers. Studies were carried out during the 1970s that included the construction of a short section of overhead electric wiring, or catenary, near Ross Peak, B.C. However, the capital costs of electrifying the main line coupled with uncertain economic conditions suggested that other alternatives were more feasible.

Grade reductions, with the continued use of diesel power, were seen, initially at least, as the most cost effective approach. Four areas were identified as problems. These all had ascending grades over one percent. The reductions included a new route over Notch Hill and realignments east of the Great Divide near Lake Louise at Stephen, and at Clanwilliam, on the Shuswap Subdivision, west of Revelstoke.* All three of these projects resulted in new westbound tracks being built on separate alignments so that not only were the grades reduced but the routes were double tracked in the process. The sections were signalled for operation in either direction to provide maximum flexibility in train movements. The cost of these revisions, when completed, was $46,000,000. However, the fourth major target, and the most difficult, was the climb up the eastern face of the Selkirks over Rogers Pass. For this bottleneck, a new tunnel was planned under Mount Macdonald. Coupled with new trackage, nine bridges and a second tunnel, the new tunnel was developed to reduce the westbound gradient and eliminate the need for helpers while at the same time effectively double-tracking the main line

---

* The Notch Hill revision, completed in 1979, reduced the westbound ruling grade, compensated for curvature, from 1.9 to 1.0 percent and required 11 miles (nearly 18 km) of new trackage. The Clanwilliam revision, also com-

Grade Revisions and the Mount Macdonald Tunnel

A major goal of the new line through the Selkirks was to eliminate the expensive and time-consuming pusher operations. Six units (all 3000-hp SD40-2s) were required on this westbound grain train crossing Mountain Creek in July 1986. The new right-of-way is visible, lower right.

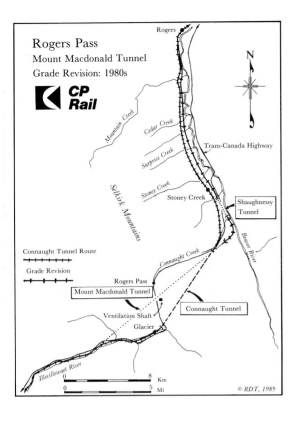

Rogers Pass
Mount Macdonald Tunnel
Grade Revision: 1980s

CP Rail

N

Mountain Creek
Cedar Creek
Surprise Creek
Rogers
Trans-Canada Highway
Stoney Creek
Stoney Creek
Selkirk Mountains
Shaughnessy Tunnel
Beaver River
Connaught Creek
Connaught Tunnel Route
Grade Revision
Rogers Pass
Mount Macdonald Tunnel
Ventilation Shaft
Connaught Tunnel
Glacier
Illecillewaet River

0   8   Km
0   5   Mi

© RDT, 1985

The enormous project of lowering the westbound main line through the Selkirks required two major tunnels, the Mount Macdonald (9 miles; 14.5 km long) and the Shaughnessy (one mile; 1.6 km long), extensive viaducts and bridges, and long sections of concrete retaining walls. The east portal of the Mount Macdonald tunnel is shown in the upper photo (taken in September 1985) while the east portal of the Shaughnessy is illustrated below as concrete work progressed in July 1986. A feature of the longer tunnel is the ventilation system needed to purge the tunnel of diesel exhaust. It required central ventilation shafts (located near the summit of Rogers Pass) and a series of five fans as well as two doors to control and regulate the flow of air. Each fan has a capacity of 400,000 cubic feet (37 160m³) of air per minute. By the co-ordinated use of the fans, the central ventilation shafts and the system of doors, the eastern half of the tunnel can be purged while a train is still proceeding through the western half. The maximum planned train speed through the tunnel is 30 miles (50 km) per hour. —BOTH ROBERT D. TURNER

over the Selkirk Mountains and significantly increasing its capacity.† Allowing for maintenance and other constraints on traffic, the capacity of the main line on a sustained basis was considered to be 15 trains in each direction every 24 hours. On the completion of the tunnel, the capacity could be increased to 19 trains a day or an increase of over 25 percent. Further improvements to the main line through double tracking and line modifications would increase capacity to 24 westbound trains per day. The construction of a new route under Rogers Pass for loaded westbound trains was approved by the Canadian Transport Commission on March 9, 1982.

The route diverged from the main line near Rogers at Mile 63.10 and climbed towards Rogers Pass on a steady 1.0 percent grade to Stoney Creek where it entered a one mile long (1.6 km) tunnel, named the Shaughnessy Tunnel, which passed under the Trans-Canada Highway. West of this tunnel, the line crossed Connaught Creek and a short distance later entered the new, nine-mile long (14.5-km) tunnel under Mount Macdonald. This tunnel, with a ruling grade of 0.7 percent, passed 300 feet (90 metres) under the Connaught Tunnel and 840 feet (256 metres) under Rogers Pass. From the east portal in Cheops Mountain, new track carried the line back to the original main line approximately 3.4 miles (5.5 km) west of Glacier. In 1982, the project was estimated to cost over $550,000,000; however, further increases were anticipated. The 2.6 percent compensated grade leading up to the Connaught Tunnel and the need for extra helpers would be eliminated for westbound traffic. The company described this area as "the most restrictive remaining capacity constraint on CP Rail's main line between Calgary and Vancouver."

Preliminary work, engineering and environmental studies were carried out through the early 1980s as the design process was refined. Hearings and further research were required as approval from the Canadian Transportation Commission and Parks Canada was sought for various stages in the construction. Actual construction began in mid-1984 with completion scheduled for 1988. William C. Van Horne and

† The use of helpers caused significant delays to all traffic. Typically, at least 20 minutes were required to switch in the units at Rogers and then 45 minutes to one and one half hours were needed to push the train to Stoney Creek. There, an additional 20 minutes were needed to remove the helpers and a further 20 to 25 minutes required for them to run back light to Rogers. In total, the operation could take up to two and one half hours for each train movement over the pass.

pleted in 1979, reduced the ruling grade from 1.6 to 1.0 percent with the construction of 4.5 miles (7.25 km) of track. When these grade reductions were completed, the extra units previously run to Chase were cut off the trains at Revelstoke and run back to Golden as traffic conditions required. The Stephen revision, completed in the summer of 1981, required 5.5 miles (slightly under 9 km) of new construction and reduced the grade there from 1.9 to 1.0 percent (compensated).

The new Stoney Creek Bridge takes shape in September 1985. —ROBERT D. TURNER

Against the snow-covered peaks of the great barrier of the Selkirks, a westbound freight crosses Surprise Creek and climbs towards the Connaught Tunnel in September 1985. The first snows have come to the high country but the warm afternoons have melted all traces from the forests of the lower slopes. —ROBERT D. TURNER

Epilogue

Light ground fog and snow give the Golden station a ghostly image in this late night photograph from March 1981. Few early stations survived the CPR's centennial as active railway structures but Golden's was one that did. —ROBERT D. TURNER

James Ross would certainly approve and envy the technology that permits railway construction under the mountains rather than over them.

The location of the railway through the heart of Glacier National Park complicated the work since particular efforts were made to minimize the impact of the project on the natural environment of the park. These included high standards of waste water treatment, revegetation of disturbed sites, careful site selection for access roads and camp facilities, and the monitoring of erosion and stream sedimentation. With a project of the magnitude of the grade revisions through the Selkirks, the task of limiting environmental damage is not an easy one. The relationship between the CPR and the National Park has always been a close one because it was the original main line over Rogers Pass that made the beauty of the Selkirks accessible and visible to so many people. The park has always been a mixture of wilderness area and transportation corridor since its creation in 1886 but the balance is a delicate one that requires attention to concerns that, 100 years ago, the construction workers would not even have contemplated.

Once this enormous project is completed, it and the other realignments and track improvement works will have produced a double tracking of most of the CPR main line between Golden and Kamloops and the major barrier of the mountain grades will have been virtually eliminated.

In the 100 years since the completion of the CPR through British Columbia, the railway has changed greatly and so too has the country through which it passes. The railway itself has evolved from a frontier-era transcontinental with a sometimes tenuous service through a wilderness of mountains and canyons to a modern transcontinental system of enormous capacity and reliability. This change required the efforts of thousands of people in many professions. Shrewd and capable management by Stephen, Van Horne, Shaughnessy, Beatty, Coleman, Crump, Sinclair and their successors was essential but so too were the efforts of the section men, labourers, conductors, dispatchers, operators, engineers, brakemen, porters, waiters, track patrolmen, civil engineers, contractors and a host of others. A company like the CPR is seldom better than the people it employs and the railway drew on men and women of particular ability and dedication. The role of the people on the job cannot be lost in the attention directed to the corporation as a whole or to the technology of its operations.

Physically the railway has seen enormous changes. Just in the steam era, the wood-burning 4-4-0s of the 1880s gave way to a generation of 2-8-0s, 4-6-0s, and early 4-6-2s and 2-8-2s. These in turn were overshadowed by new Pacifics and Mikados and heavier power including 2-10-0s, 2-10-2s, 2-10-4s and the Royal Hudson 4-6-4s. Freight rolling stock evolved from small capacity wooden cars to steel cars with three or four times the capacity. Passenger cars changed from ornate wooden tributes to the car builder's art to steel cars of the streamlined era. But these were just the beginnings of the changes. Diesels and radio-communications revolutionized the nature of the railway and the lives of the people working on it. Containers and specialized freight equipment such as the rotary dumping coal gondolas have toppled the box car from its place of complete dominance of the freight car fleet of the 1950s. Individual trains now operate through the mountains by the hour with tonnages that would have taxed the daily capacity of line at the end of the steam era.

The introduction of centralized traffic control, radios and modern communications has eliminated the need for many small stations all along the line. Mechanized maintenance equipment has replaced innumerable section crews and track workers. The track and roadbed have changed too. Rail size and strength have grown dramatically and on the heavily-trafficked routes, welded rails have replaced short, bolted-together sections of steel. Crushed rock has replaced navijack, pit-run ballast. More dramatically, grade revisions and tunnels have so changed the profile of the original line that the worst sections of mountain railroading were eliminated in the early 1900s and subsequent improvements have meant enormous improvements in productivity.

The CPR has evolved as part of a much larger economic and social system. The transportation components of this system have been constantly changing with improvements in roads and highways and air travel. Perhaps no change is more striking than the decline of passenger trains on the railway. After 1967, service on the main line was reduced to but one daily train and after the formation of VIA, it was no longer operated by the railway itself. Traffic on the branch lines has dwindled, and the Kettle Valley and Kootenay divisions no longer form a through route from the Coast to the Kootenays. The Railway Post Offices are gone as are the leisurely local passenger services that were the link for many small communities to the rest of the world. Where once the railway was the economic and social focus of many communities, a symbol of progress and prosperity, it is now largely unnoticed and just a part of the industrial transportation system.

Despite this almost continuous change that has characterized the CPR, and in particular its main line operations, there are still some aspects of the system that have escaped, to a degree at least, the rapidity of change. Perhaps more correctly, they have survived despite the changes. Tug and barge service still continues on Slocan Lake, a small passenger train still winds its way along the eastern shore of Vancouver Island, and local freights — peddlers — still switch mills in the Kootenays and on Vancouver Island. Sadly, such services are not always economic, and their chances of long survival can be dependent only on subsidy or the prospect of better economic times.

Rolling west through Leanchoil, a grain train carrying the harvest of the Canadian prairies is a symbolic subject on which to end. The great distances and mountain barriers have always been a part of Canada's story. Inescapably, they will continue to be. So too will the CPR, as long as railway technology is a competitive form of transportation. It is an evolving technology, no longer the centre of public attention, but its importance for the foreseeable future is immense, as is its enduring fascination. —ROBERT D. TURNER

The trends towards reductions of branch line services and to a concentration on bulk commodities and intermodal container systems are well established. So too are reduced manpower requirements and mechanization. The CPR will be a dominant presence in the transportation system of British Columbia for years to come and the investments in grade revisions underway in the 1980s suggest that its importance will only increase.

*   *   *

On November 7, 1985, Lord Strathcona and Mount Royal, the great grandson of Donald A. Smith, using a spike maul, drove a spike at Craigellachie to commemorate the centennial of the completion of the Canadian Pacific Railway. R. S. Allison, President of CP Rail, sitting on a mechanized track spiking machine, drove a second spike to signify the entry of the railway into its second century. It was a misty, cold morning in the mountains near Eagle Pass just as it had been 100 years before. So much had changed, yet the overriding purpose of the railway as a system for bridging the vast distances of the country was still fundamentally the reason for the continuing presence of the CPR in the mountains of British Columbia.

East of the Great Divide. The climb over the vast ranges of the Rockies and the Selkirks lies behind and ahead stretches a thousand miles of prairie and the granite backbone of the Canadian Shield. Now the trains roll across the country with a routine, unremarked frequency.

A hundred years ago, a sometimes faltering system was just beginning. In one hundred years there have been profound, unforeseen changes both in the CPR, and in the country it serves. The certainty of the next century is that the changes, ever more rapid, will be even more profound and certainly less predictable.

—ROBERT D. TURNER

Royal Hudson 2860 was restored for summer operation on the B.C. Railway.
In March 1978, it travelled across Canada bringing steam back to the Kicking Horse Canyon. —LANCE CAMP

314

Sources

Notes on References

In compiling *West of the Great Divide*, I have relied on many, varied sources including the recollections of a number of people who worked for, travelled on, or photographed the CPR and the Great Northern in a variety of capacities. I have avoided footnoting but I hope the following notes and the bibliography will give any reader anxious to probe further a general account of the documents and printed sources I have drawn on most. Normally the sources of direct quotations are included in the narrative. For simplicity, I have abbreviated the more common sources, including: *The Railway & Shipping World* (*R&SW*), *Canadian Railway & Marine World* (*CR&MW*), *Poor's Manual of Railroads* (*Poor's*), *The Inland Sentinel* (*Sentinel*), Victoria's *The Daily British Colonist* and later, *The Daily Colonist* (*Col.*), *The Victoria Daily Times* (*Times*) and institutions as noted in the acknowledgements. Where books are collections of papers, the papers are noted here; normally only the volume itself is cited in the references. Significant incidents usually were reported by several of the newspapers; in the notes that follow only representative, or particularly detailed accounts are noted.

There have been several general histories of the CPR, including those by Innis (1923) and Gibbon (1935), and most recently W. Kaye Lamb's *History of the Canadian Pacific Railway* (1977). In addition, Roger Burrows has produced *Railway Mileposts: British Columbia*, Vol. 1 (1981) and Vol. 2 (1984), that provide great detail on the routes and structures of the CPR (and also the GN/BN) in British Columbia. These are highly recommended as general references and field guides. Other general references include Berton's *The National Dream* (1970) and *The Last Spike* (1971); Dempsey's *The CPR West, The Iron Road and the Making of a Nation* (1984), a compilation of excellent papers presented in 1983 in Calgary; Lavallée's *Van Horne's Road* (1974) and *Canadian Pacific Steam Locomotives* (1985); Dean and Hanna's *Canadian Pacific Diesel Locomotives* (1981); Sanford's *McCulloch's Wonder* (1977); and McKee and Klassen's *Trail of Iron* (1983). There are also a number of pictorial works that illustrate many facets of CPR operations in British Columbia, including the series of booklets by Bain (1978-1985), which also provide detailed captions, and the books by Riegger (1981) and Hungry Wolf (1979, 1983).

Published material on the Great Northern is more restricted but includes Albro Martin's biography of James J. Hill (1976) and volumes by Wood and Wood (1979) and Burrows (1984). The Great Northern's corporate papers, which include much early material, are preserved by the Minnesota Historical Society in St. Paul. GN construction and development in British Columbia was covered extensively in *R&SW* and *CR&MW*.

Public and employee (operating) timetables, published schedules in newspapers, special instructions, issues of the *Official Guide*, publicity literature and other material published by the railway companies themselves have been particularly useful and have been consulted throughout. References in the text to specific operations, passenger services and scheduling are based on official published sources. In addition, CPR *Division Information Books* for the sections treated were valuable references, as were limited circulation CPR publications such as *Haulage Capacity of Locomotives* (1916, 1926 and 1941), *General Train and Interlocking Rules* (KVR, E&N and CPR, various dates).

A particularly useful source of material has been the early newspapers of the province. These include *The Inland Sentinel* (Emory, Yale and Kamloops), *The Mainland Guardian* (New Westminster), *The British Columbian* (New Westminster), *The Kootenaian* (Kaslo), *The Kaslo Claim*, *The Nelson Daily Miner* (originally *The Miner*), *The Daily News* (Nelson), *The Ledge* (New Denver), *The Kootenay Mail* (Revelstoke), *The Revelstoke Mail*, *The Daily Colonist* (Victoria), *The Victoria Daily Times*, *The Vancouver Daily World*, *The Vancouver News-Advertiser*, *The Truth* (Donald), *The Golden Era*, *The Golden Star*, *The Port Moody Gazette*, *The Midway Dispatch*, *The Nicola Herald*, *The Phoenix Pioneer*, *The Courier* (Cranbrook), *The Creston Review*, *The Penticton Herald*, *The Trail Creek News* and *The Province* (Vancouver).

Several unpublished sources were also useful, including the Premier's papers (PABC), particularly the McBride papers (PABC), Department of Railways papers (PABC), papers of the Crow's Nest Pass Coal Company (Glenbow-Alberta Institute), the Great Northern papers (including Canadian subsidiaries) noted previously, files from Canadian Pacific's corporate archives, Joseph Hunter papers on the E&N Railway (PABC), Fraser Bucham and Ira Barr papers (PABC), and the recollections of W. H. Holmes on Fraser Canyon construction (CVA).

West of the Great Divide does not explore the political and economic background of the CPR. nor does it relate in detail the problems with the surveys; these are all well covered by British Columbia (1880), Fleming (1877, 1878, 1879), Innis (1923), Gibbon (1937), Berton (1970, 1971, and 1972), Gilbert (1965) and Lamb (1977).

Chapter 1, the story of construction and the early years of operations, drew on a number of sources. Fleming's survey reports (1877-79) provide details on the various route options and Martin (1976), Lamb (1977) and Berton (1970) all reflect on the decisions leading to the final selection of the route for the CPR. Lavallée's *Van Horne's Road* (1973) is an exceptionally detailed treatment of the construction period through to the first years of operation. The railway lands are treated in Cail (1974), Taylor (1975), Lamb (1977), CPR *Annual Reports* and in B.C. *Sessional Papers* (1883, 1886). Construction under Onderdonk was reported extensively in *The Inland Sentinel*, which moved with the railway from Emory to Yale and then to Kamloops. Nearly every issue during the construction period contained progress reports, tenders for contracts and other details. Also useful are the Onderdonk albums (PABC), which give a detailed pictorial record of the construction. The notes of W. H. Holmes (1936) gave insights into the construction at Yale in 1880. Gerry Wellburn provided correspondence and documents from his private collection. *Engineering*'s series on the CPR (see particularly parts 18 and 19) provided a description of the route through British Columbia. Part 19 (Sept. 5, 1884) includes engineering drawings and a complete discussion of the Cisco Bridge crossing and other features of construction. The role of the Chinese was unfortunately poorly recorded in accounts or diaries from the 1880s, but is described by Berton (1971), Morton (1973), Lee (1983) and Roy (1984). In addition, there were many references to the Chinese in the *Sentinel* and other papers of the era, but these usually reflect a strong anti-Chinese bias. Material on the broader history of the Chinese in B.C. was drawn from Wickberg (1982). Government reaction to the destitute condition of the Chinese is summarized in the report of November 21, 1885 (*Sessional Papers*, 1886:347). Construction from the East is recorded in the recollections of engineers Secretan (1924) and Bone (1947). Further material is from the *Engineering* articles (1884), Muckleston (1905) and Ramsay (1884). The *Sentinel* also covered work from the East under Ross (cf. Jan. 29, 1885). Particularly useful is the paper by Regehr (1984) "Letters from End of Track," which gives many details of construction and the problems faced by Ross. A correspondent for Montreal's *Gazette* (PABC clippings) provided a lengthy discussion of construction and development, in August 1884, along the line through the Rockies.

Construction leading up to the last spike was recorded in the *Sentinel*, with further details in Vaughan (1920). Sandford Fleming's recollections were published in Wheeler (1905). Reports on the completion of the line and subsequent events were frequent (cf. *Times*, November 7, 1885, *Col.*, November 8, 10, 12, 15, 19 & 22, 1885). The first through freight was reported on Nov. 24, 1885, as were notices of the possible closing of the line. On Jan. 21, 1924, the *Colonist* published an interview with Dugal (Duke) McKenzie, a locomotive engineer who was at Craigellachie and worked the line in the early years. Similar extensive coverage was devoted to the arrival of the first train at Port Moody (cf. *Times*, July 5, 1886, *Col.* July 6, 1886 (quoted), *Sentinel* July 8, 1886 and *The British Columbian* July 7, 1886). The extension to Vancouver the next year and land grant details are described in Cail (1974) and Lamb (1977). For the agreement with the province, see B.C. *Sessional Papers*, 1886:460-61. For the arrival of the first train, see *The Daily News-Advertiser* and *Col.*, May 24, 1887, and for background on the shipping connections, see Hacking and Lamb (1976) and Turner (1977, 1981c). The Bellingham Bay & British Columbia is described in Jukes et al. (1951).

Snow sheds were described by Muckleston (1905) and Lavallée (1974) and in *Engineering News* (January 21, 1888: 38-39 and *Supplement* December 14, 1889). The incidents described in the section *At War With Winter* are based on reports in the *Sentinel* as noted, March 5, 1887 for the buried plow train (see also *Times*, March 3, 1887) and November 11, 1897 for the accident of November 6. Other reports on the blockage of the line were in the *Sentinel* (March 19 and 26) and *Times* (March 4). The following section of anecdotes is based on reports from *The Truth* as noted, except for the account of the burning of the *Atlantic Express* which was based on reports in *The British Columbian* (July 14, 1887) and the official report quoted by Lavallée (1974). The second incident was reported in *The Truth* of June 2, 1888.

Throughout the section *Hotels, Chalets and the National Parks*, CPR promotional literature was consulted extensively. Examples include the 1903 booklet *Banff and The Lake in the Clouds in the Canadian Rockies*, both eastbound and westbound annotated timetables from the 1890s and early 1900s, *The New Highway to the Orient* (various issues from the 1890s) and the booklet *The Challenge of the Mountains*. A brief but helpful report on hotel development appeared in *R&SW* (Mar. 1902:99). The company publications *Canadian Pacific Facts and Figures* (1937 and 1946) and *Factors in Railway and Steamship Operations* (1937) provided general information. Particularly helpful were Hart's *The Selling of Canada, The CPR and the Beginning of Canadian Tourism* (1983), Kalman (1968), McKee and Klassen (1983), Robinson (1973), Martin (1980) and Hart (1984). Two papers on Glacier House were consulted: Marsh's *A History of Glacier House and Nakimu Caves* (1979) and Longstaff's "Historical Notes on Glacier House" (1947) (PABC).

Material on the development of the National Parks is included in the above, as are the papers in Nelson and Scace (1968), particularly Scace's "Banff Townsite: An Historical-Geographical View of Urban Development in Canadian National Parks," J. I. Nicol's "The National Park Movement in Canada" and Robert Craig Brown's "The Doctrine of Usefulness: Natural Resource and National Park Policy in Canada, 1887-1914." Quotations from House of Commons Debates are from May 3, 1887 (pp. 232 and 233). Services in the Kootenays are based on Turner (1984).

Rotary snow plow development, critical to the CPR, and snow fighting equipment in general, are described by Best (1966), H. H. Vaughan (1913), who was assistant to the vice president of the CPR in charge of motive power, W. H. Winterrowd, Chief Mechanical Engineer of the CPR (1920), and an unattributed paper (BCPM) titled "Snow Fighting Equipment". Marpole's letter is from CPCA, as were construction records. Interviews with Perley McPherson and Gordon Fulkerson provided operational information and insights.

Fraser Valley floods of 1894 were noted by Lamb (1977), all of the regional papers during the period, and in B.C. *Sessional Papers* (1895). The dispute over the standard of construction on the Onderdonk contracts and general improvements to the main line are both noted in Lamb (1977), *Annual Reports* for early 1890s, and in Vaughan (1920). An undated clipping (PABC) elaborates on the arbitration proceedings. Much of the reconstruction work which proceeded through the 1890s in B.C. is documented in photographs in the PABC and in regular reports in *R&SW* after 1898 (cf. February 1899:41-42). The hydraulic filling of the approaches to Mountain Creek bridge was described in detail in *R&SW* (December 1898:269-270). Branch line construction and expansion in the Okanagan is based on Morkill (1954), Turner (1984), and *Poors*. Vancouver's station of 1898 is described in *R&SW* (November 1898:235, June 1899:172-173) and in Martin (1980).

The story of the slide at Rogers Pass in 1899 was developed from accounts in the *Revelstoke Herald* (cf. February 1 and 4, 1899), *The Daily News-Advertiser* (February 2, 1899), Woods (1984), Pugsley (1973), clippings and photographs from the PABC and the notes (unpublished) of Jack McDonald. Facility relocations were noted in *R&SW* (August 1898:154; September 1898:183) and shown in plans of the yards (BCPM and CPCA).

Field Hill operations and procedures are drawn from Yeats (1985) and CPR special instruction and timetables for the Field to Stephen line. The incidents noted are based on accounts in Carter (1910), Parks Canada (1985) and district newspapers (cf. *Sentinel*, February 2, 1889; *The Golden Era*, August 4 and 11, 1894, the latter having inquest testimony; *The Kootenay Mail*, August 1894; *The Golden Star*, January 22, 1904; *Sentinel*, January 26, 29, 1904; and *The Revelstoke Herald*, January 29, 1904). An incomplete copy of a memorandum by T. H. Crump dated October 21, 1940 (CPR Public Relations and Advertising office, Vancouver) also provided background on incidents relating to the Field Hill.

Chapter 2 develops the story of the main line and coastal operations between the turn of the century and World War I. References to the coastal steamships are based on Hacking and Lamb (1974) and Turner (1977). The E&N Railway section is based on Turner (1973), with additional material from the Hunter, Barr and Bucham papers (PABC) and reports in *R&SW* and *CR&MW*. The Land Grant note is derived from British Columbia (1880), Cail (1974), Taylor (1975), legislation as noted, and a copy of the E&N contract (BCPM). The roster is based on many sources, including the papers noted above, the B.C. Dept. of Railways papers, Dept. of Mines *Annual Reports*, Lavallée (1985), CPR mechanical department records and drawings, newspaper reports, Baldwin and Schenectady builders' lists from the Railway & Locomotive Historical Society, correspondence with Gerald M. Best and interviews with E&N staff, including the late Bob Brown. *Improvements to the Main Line* was compiled from descriptions in *CR&MW*; see particularly: September 1907:641, 643 re Palliser Tunnel; September 1907:666 re Revelstoke Bridge; November 1907: 809 re Vancouver Terminal development; and *Annual Reports*. The development of the Mallet locomotives is explained in Lavallée (1985), (the articulated locomotive) and reports in *CR&MW*, including August 1909:557-561; September 1909:657; April 1910:250-269; June 1910: 455-457; January 1912:4-5; March 1912:103-106. The simple machine was described in May 1912:219-220.

The Spiral Tunnels section was derived from reports in engineering journals including: J. E. Schwitzer, "Reduction of the Kicking Horse Pass Grade on the CPR," *CR&MW*, October 1909:710-713 and other *CR&MW* reports in September 1909:655; January 1911:11-15 and *The Canadian Engineer*, August 26, 1915:293-296. Carter (1910), Lamb (1977) and Marsh (1984) provide further background. The new rotary snow plows were described in the papers by Winterrowd (1920) and an anonymous paper (BCPM). The story of the Rogers Pass disaster was based on a recorded interview with Bill LaChance by Imbert Orchard (PABC), an edited version of which appears in Turner (1981a), an original letter by John Anderson (Urquhart coll.), newspaper reports in the Revelstoke *Mail-Herald* (particularly March 5, 9, 10, 16, 19 and 23, 1910 which include inquest testimony), Woods (1983), and Pugsley (1973). Details of the slide at Wellington, Washington are from Martin (1976) and Wood and Wood (1979).

The Connaught Tunnel project was described in *The Canadian Engineer*, April 23, 1914:621-624 and August 26, 1915:293-296; *The Contract Record* (undated CPCA); and in *CW&MW*, particularly April 1913:119; October 1913: 485; November 1913:524; February 1915:50-51; June 1914:

254-255; March 1916:86; May 1916:169-172 and is detailed by Marsh (1985). The ventilation system is described in *CR&MW* in September 1917:339-340 and salvage of the old line is noted in December 1917:457-459. Lining the tunnel is outlined in February 1921:57-59 and in *Railway Review*, March 14, 1925:491-497. Most of these reports were written by or based on information provided by J. G. Sullivan, Chief Engineer, Western Lines, CPR. A most thorough discussion of the project was written by A. C. Dennis (1917) and presented to the American Society of Civil Engineers. This paper was published along with subsequent discussions by other prominent engineers, including J. G. Sullivan.

Details of first train movements are from CPR memoranda. The note on Glacier House is based on Marsh (1979), Woods (1983), and the article by Longstaff (PABC). Development of Vancouver's terminals is from Turner (1981c), Martin (1980), *CR&MW*: July 1912:344-345; August 1912:394-395; December 1912:596-597; April 1913: 162; February 1914:63-64; June 1914:253.

General conditions during the war are outlined by Innis (1923), Gibbon (1935) and Lamb (1977) and noted in the *Annual Reports*, while CPR steamship services are described in Turner (1981c) and Musk (1981). These sources also provide material on the silk trains, as do Kirkpatrick (1937), Lafortune (1981) and a compilation of documents and aural history interviews by Ruth Chambers (PABC) on the trains. Background on Bill Miner, the train robber, is from Anderson (1968) and a robbery report in *The Express Gazette* (1904).

Chapter 3 describes the expansion of the CPR and Great Northern across southern British Columbia. Aside from the general corporate histories, publications relating to these operations include: Fahey (1965), Affleck (1973), Sanford (1977), Riegger (1981), Doeksen (1981), Kennedy (1983), Turner (1984), Burrows (1984), and a few papers published in the regional historical society reports. Construction was well documented in *R&SW*, *CR&MW* and the local newspapers, which generally were established in the communities before the railroads were built. The construction of the C&K and the development of the steamboat services is based on newspaper reports, Affleck (1973) and Turner (1984). Van Horne's comment is from the *Sentinel* (October 29, 1892). Corbin's involvement and the N&FS is documented by Fahey (1965), and reports in *Poors* give operational and corporate details.

Early mining development is reported in the Dept. of Mines *Annual Reports* and in *The British Columbia Mining Record*. The background on the K&S is from Hearn (1959), Hearn and Wilkie (1971), Lavalle (1972), the Great Northern papers K&S files (MHS), *Poors*, *The Kaslo Claim*, *The Kootenain* and other district newspapers.

The development of the railroads into Rossland and Trail is based on Turnbull (1964), Fahey (1965), Lamb (1977), Kennedy (1983), Turner (1984) Burrows (1984), CPR *Annual Reports* and *Poor's*. Mining development was recorded in the Dept. of Mines *Annual Reports*, *The British Columbia Mining Record*, Wilson (1913), Fowler (1939) and local newspapers as noted. CPR expansion through the Crowsnest Pass draws on the same sources, in addition to the commission of inquiry reports by Dugas et al. (1898) and Clute (1899), and reports in *R&SW*, particularly: March 1898:15; May 1898:67; April 1899:114-115; May 1899:129-132 (by J. L. Davidson); and May 1900:141-143.

Moir (1947) provides personal recollections of Crowsnest and Kootenay area construction.

For the reconstruction of the C&W and its extension west to Midway see LeRoy (1912 and 1913), Kennedy (1983) and *R&SW*, particularly June 1898:97-98; May 1899:139; June 1899:173; September 1899:267; October 1899:292; November 1898:237; December 1898:267-268; April 1899:112-113; December 1899:350-351; August 1900: 225-229; and September 1900:262-264 (the last two by H. B. Smith, B. C. Government inspector).

Great Northern expansion into the Kootenays is treated in the general sources noted for the C&W and Crowsnest Pass lines of the CPR. In addition, from the GN papers (MHS), the KR&N and Kaslo & Lardo-Duncan files were particularly valuable. KR&N sternwheelers are treated in Turner (1984) and were described in *The Kaslo Claim* and *The Kootenain*. See also *R&SW*, September 1898:181-82; April 1899:117; and August 1901:230-231.

Martin's biography of James J. Hill (1976) was essential, and Lamb's *History of the Canadian Pacific Railway* (1977) provided further insights into the competition between the two lines and the background of corporate decision making. Photographic records provided additional information on GN operating practices and equipment assignments, as did interviews with Ken Merilees and Norman Gidney. Victoria & Sidney history is well covered in Hearn and Wilkie's *The Cordwood Limited* (1966) and in Harvey (1960) and Turner (1973).

The development and construction of the Kettle Valley Railway and its predecessors, which is presented in the next five sections of this chapter, is treated in detail in Sanford (1977) and Burrows (1984) and pictorially in Doeksen (1981) and Riegger (1981). The political backgound to McBride's railway policy is explained by Roy (1980). Other sources include: the McBride papers (PABC), Brown (1981), Statutes of B.C., *Poor's*, Dept. of Railway papers (PABC), community newspapers, and CPR *Annual Reports*. I have relied heavily on construction reports from *R&SW* and *CR&MW*, including May 1901:155-156 (KRVR); June 1901:175 (M&V); August 1901:235; September 1901:277; November 1901:334 (KRVR); February 1902:58 (KRVR); April 1902:126 (KRVR); January 1904: 5-6 (NK&S); July 1905:285 (NK&S); December 1905:567 (M&V); April 1912:181; January 1914:21; February 1914: 80-81; March 1915:94; August 1915:303; August 1916:317; and December 1917:471.

Articles by McCulloch (n.d., 1965) and Macorquodale (1949, 1961) provided further background, as did interviews with Arthur Stiffe, Perley McPherson and Gordon Fulkerson. The incidents involving the KRVR and the GN were reported in *The Midway Dispatch* (cf. June 23, September 1, and November 17, 1902). Great Northern expansion is discussed in the sources noted above as well as in GN *Annual Reports*, Martin (1976), Wood and Wood (1979), and Middleton and Keyes (1980). Construction reports from *R&SW* and *CR&MW* included June 1898: 100; July 1898:122-123; April 1901:115; June 1901:178-179; July 1905:287; December 1905:569; July 1906:383; January 1910:29; April 1911:347; and November 1912:559. Additional material came from Department of Mines *Annual Reports*. GN (VV&E) arrangements with the Canadian Northern are noted by Regehr (1976) and in reports in *CR&MW*.

Background on Corbin's involvement with the Spokane International is based on Fahey (1965). Further material came from *Poor's*, *CR&MW* (December 1916:494), Ehernberger and Gschwind (1968), and correspondence with Lawrence Shawver. CPR timetables, advertising material, Lamb (1977) and Dubin (1964, 1974) were consulted regarding the through passenger service over the SI. The section on the coal mining lines in the Crowsnest Pass drew on Dowling (1915), Burrows (1984), *Poor's*, Fahey (1965), Scott and Hanic (1974), *CR&MW*, Strachan (1928), Department of Railway files (PABC), and Crow's Nest Pass Coal Co. papers (Glenbow). Particularly helpful were the Department of Mines *Annual Reports*, and special publications and an article in the *British Columbia Mining Record* (February 1899:17-23). The concluding section on the GN was summarized from the sources noted for the GN lines, timetables and press reports.

Chapter 4, which describes the modern steam era on the CPR, was based on the general sources noted, interviews with CPR employees and both published and unpublished documents relating to operations, ranging from timetables to dispatchers' records. Details of railway employees returning from military service are from *CR&MW*. Construction along Kootenay Lake is from *Annual Reports*, *CR&MW* (March 1929:133; July 1929:430; November 1930:701) and reports in Nelson's *Daily News* announcing the opening of the line in December 1930 and January 1931. Information on improvements on the main line was based on regular reports in *CR&MW* and division information books.

The new locomotive types are best described in Lavallée (1985), CPR locomotive diagram books and *CR&MW* articles, such as November 1910:373-375 (ST8, 4-6-0); March 1910:166-175 (N3a, 2-8-0); May 1914:205-207 (P1b, 2-8-2); March 1917:91-92 (R2b, 2-10-0); November 1923: 513-516 (G3c, 4-6-2); and September 1929: 564 (T1a, 2-10-4). The comments on passenger train developments were based on timetables, *Annual Reports*, Dubin (1964, 1974) and Wagner (1983). *CR&MW* articles featuring passenger rolling stock included: July 1919:378; September 1924:435-436; August 1926:404; June 1929:356-358; and September 1929:541-544. CPR hotels and related enterprises were also discussed in *CR&MW*, and a summary history is provided by Mathews (1937).

The background to the Crystal Gardens is detailed in Berton et al. (1977). Expansion of shipping services is derived from Hacking and Lamb (1974), Turner (1977) and detailed reports on Pier B-C in *CR&MW* (May 1924:224; July 1924:342; and October 1926:513-516). CPR steamship terminals are described in the article "Canadian Pacific Docks in North America," in CPR (1937). Descriptions of the tunnel under Vancouver are in *CR&MW* February 1931:86; March 1931:141; May 1932:237-238 and September 1932:451-454.

The section on operational problems in the mountains is based on published accounts of the incidents, photographs and recollections by employees. The Palliser wreck of October 20, 1921 was reported in the *Times* (October 21, 1921) and *The Revelstoke Herald* (October 27, 1921). The July 11, 1928 explosion of the pusher engine was described in *CR&MW* (August 1928:469), and in *The Revelstoke Review* (July 18, 1928). The collapse of the Surprise Creek bridge was detailed in *The Revelstoke Review* on January 30, 1929, as were the collision at Lauretta and the death of engineer Pat McLaughlin. The February 6, 1929 edition carried further details, reports of the coroner's jury and information on the bridge reconstruction. Reopening of the main line was described on Feb. 20. The blockage of the Connaught Tunnel and the reconstruction of Twin Butte Creek bridge were discussed by F. W. Alexander in *The Engineering Journal* (August 1932:383-386). Photographs of several of these incidents are in the PABC and BCPM. An interview with Harry V. Davis added insights into several engineering problems on the Mountain Subdivision, including those noted above and the winter problems of 1935. These were outlined in *The Revelstoke Review* on January 25 and February 1, 1935. The disaster of March 2, 1936 dominated *The Revelstoke Review* of March 6, 1936 and included extensive coverage of the inquest.

The Depression Years and *The War Years* were based on many sources, notably Lamb (1977), *Annual Reports*, timetables, interviews with employees, and the sources noted regarding locomotives. Details of the experimental Selkirk (No. 8000) and its tests were recorded in *CR&MW* in May 1931:292-294 and October 1932:495-497, the latter by H. B. Bowen, Chief of Motive Power and Rolling Stock. Further details came from Lavallée (1985) and interviews with Walter Paffard, Wally Huffman, and Bruce Davies. Background on operations also came from the studies on the economics of dieselization, CPR (1947, 1950 and 1952) which considered the patterns of traffic.

Operations in the Mountains During the Steam Era was based on the paper "Operating Trains in the Rockies" by H. C. Taylor (1937), who was Superintendent of Transportation, Western Lines; an article "Mountain Railroading" by A. E. Mimms, Chief Engineer, Munitions Dept., Office of Motive Power & Rolling Stock, in the *Kelowna Courier* (April 26, 1945); detailed notes of and interviews with Walter Paffard, retired Assistant Superintendent, Revelstoke Division; and the CPR Research Department's study on the economics of using diesels on the Laggan and Mountain subdivisions (1950). CPR employee and public timetables, locomotive roster material in Lavallée and Brown (1951), Lewis (1984), and Lavallée (1985) and the detailed treatment of the present day main line in Burrows (1981) were also consulted.

Additional locomotive data were provided by the CPR specification books *Classification and Dimensions of Locomotives* (1935 and 1945), *Summary of Equipment* (1929) and *Haulage Capacity of Locomotives* (1915, 1926 and 1941.) Interviews with the late Wally Huffman, engineer on these subdivisions, Arthur Dawe and Arthur Urquhart provided further material on operational practices as did a review of the extensive photographic records available for this period.

Similar sources were consulted for the section on the steam era on the Esquimalt & Nanaimo. Further background came from interviews with the late Bob Brown, the late Ted Robson and A. L. Robinson. Dispatchers' train sheets gave complete daily pictures of train movements and were the basis for the detailed descriptions provided. Traffic patterns and other details of carload movements were from the CPR Research Department's dieselization study (1947), as were the description of passenger train operations and the outline of the available locomotives at the time of conversion to diesels on the Island. General E&N references include Turner (1973) and Baird (1985).

Kettle Valley Division and Kootenay Division steam operations drew on similar sources to the two preceding sections. Additional details came from Sanford (1977),

Riegger (1981), Doeksen (1981-85), Kennedy (1983), Turner (1984) and Burrows (1984). Again, I was privileged to talk to former employees on the lines including Perley McPherson, Bill Curran, Gordon Fulkerson and Gib Kennedy. The CPR's dieselization study for the Kettle Valley and Kootenay divisions (1952) provided great detail on operational practices and traffic patterns. Reference to photographic collections, both public and private, was most helpful.

Chapter 5, which includes the diesel era, the post war development of the CPR and further material on the Great Northern, was developed from a varied range of sources. The background on dieselization came from an overview of the change from steam reported, debated and detailed in periodicals such as *Trains* and *Railway Age*. Further material on the CPR and its development during this period was derived from Lamb (1977), Dean and Hanna (1981) and *Annual Reports*. The dieselization of the E&N was studied in detail by the Research Department in 1947 and the report provided the basis for the discussion in this section. Articles in the *Times* and *Colonist* described the transition on the Island. The later history of the E&N Baldwins and the passenger service comes from Dean and Hanna (1981), personal observations, photographic records, and hearings before the CTC (e.g., 1983) regarding terminating the service. Again, I was assisted by employees at various times including Doug Smith, Don MacLachlan, Dominique Coumount, John Mahy, Hugh Miller and Walter Paffard.

Dieselization of the main line between Calgary and Revelstoke also was preceded by a thorough study by the Research Department (1950), which proved invaluable to me. Walter Paffard, then a road foreman of engines, also provided many insights into the process and technical aspects of main line dieselization on these divisions. The dieselization of the Kettle Valley and Kootenay divisions was studied by the CPR's Research Department in 1952 and this report was invaluable for describing the transition from steam to diesel across southern British Columbia. Further material came from Sanford (1977), Riegger (1981), Doeksen (1981-85), Kennedy (1983), Turner (1984), Burrows (1984) and interviews with CPR employees, timetables, operating instructions and related material.

The post-war developments in passenger services brought great changes to travel in British Columbia. Published sources included Dubin (1964) and Wood and Wood (1979). The background on the *Canadian* came from Dubin (1964), Lamb (1977), Wilson (1980), Nelligan (1982), Wayner (1983), and numerous press releases from CPR (Vancouver Public Relations and Advertising offices) including the inaugural run press kit. Timetables and publicity material gave more background. I have also travelled frequently in the Budd-built equipment. The changes to passenger services on the E&N and Kettle Valley were documented by CPR press materials, timetables and *Annual Reports*. The end of passenger service on the Kettle Valley and Kootenay divisions was covered extensively by the regional papers including *The Penticton Herald* (January 16-18, 1964), and *The Courier* (Cranbrook) of January 22, 1964. Further details were included in Dewdney (1964) and Sanford (1977).

The Evolving Railway and the Unit Trains was based on extensive CPR press material, timetables, Lamb (1977), Dean and Hanna (1981), and notes and interviews with Walter Paffard and other CPR and B.C. Coal employees, still working or retired. I have also been able to photograph the unit coal train operations since their inception. The section outlining the grade revisions and the new Mount Macdonald Tunnel draws on CPR press material, and the extensive briefs prepared by CP Rail for the Rogers Pass grade revision project (cf. 1982 and 1983). Tours of the project provided further insights into the construction process and environmental protection program.

—R.D.T., *December 1985*

Steam power: 3716 climbing to Eholt and at rest.
—ROBERT D. TURNER

320

BIBLIOGRAPHY

The following references include the major published sources. Articles, usually anonymous, from engineering journals, are noted through the source discussion. Additional references to CPR coastal, trans-Pacific and inland shipping services are included in the bibliographies of Turner (1977, 1981c, 1984).

Affleck, E. L. 1973. *Sternwheelers Sandbars and Switchbacks.* The Alexander Nicolls Press, Vancouver, B.C.

Affleck, E. L. 1973. *The Kootenays in Retrospect.* (Vol. 1-4). The Alexander Nicolls Press, Vancouver, B.C.

Anderson, Frank W. 1968. *Bill Miner, Train Robber.* Frontier Book No. 7, Frontier Publishing Ltd., Aldergrove, B.C.

Atkins, C. P. 1973. "Canadian Pacific Selkirks," *Loco Profile.* No. 35. Profile Publications, London, England.

Bain, Donald. 1978-1985. *Canadian Pacific in the Rockies* (Vol. 1-10). British Railway Modellers of North America, Calgary, Atla.

Baird, Ian. 1985. *A Historic Guide to the E&N Railway.* Heritage Architectural Guides, Victoria, B.C.

Barnwell, R. 1906. "Economic Use of Western Coal," *Proceedings of the Meeting of Western Lines Officials Held at Field, B.C.* CPR, Montreal, Que., pp. 102-110.

Beebe, Lucius and Charles Clegg. 1957. *Steamcars to the Comstock.* Howell-North, Berkeley, Ca.

Berton, Pierre. 1970. *The National Dream. The Great Railway 1871-1881.* McClelland and Stewart Ltd., Toronto, Ont.

Berton, Pierre. 1971. *The Last Spike. The Great Railway, 1881-1885.* McClelland and Stewart Ltd., Toronto, Ont.

Berton, Pierre. 1972. *The Great Railway Illustrated.* McClelland and Stewart Ltd., Toronto, Ont.

Berton, Pierre, Carolyn Smyly, Terry Reksten, Alastair Kerr, Martin Segger, Stuart Stark and Reynold Knowlton. 1977. *The Crystal Gardens. West Coast Pleasure Palace.* Crystal Gardens Preservation Society, Victoria, B.C.

Best, Gerald M. 1966. *Snowplow. Clearing Mountain Rails.* Howell-North Books, Berkeley, Ca.

Blakemore, W. 1903. "The Future of the Coal and Coke Supply of the Interior of British Columbia," *The Mining Record.* 10 (January): 461-464.

Bone, P. Turner. 1947. *When the Steel Went Through. Reminiscences of a Railroad Pioneer.* Macmillan of Canada, Toronto, Ont.

British Columbia. 1880. *Papers in Connection with the Construction of the Canadian Pacific Railway, between the Dominion, Imperial, and Provincial Governments.* Government Printing Office, Victoria, B.C.

British Columbia. 1883. "Papers Relating to the Island Railway, the Graving Dock, and the Railway Lands," *Sessional Papers,* Legislative Assembly, Victoria, B.C.

British Columbia. 1886. "Papers Relating to Dominion Lands within the Province," *Sessional Papers,* Legislative Assembly, Victoria, B.C.

Brown, Kevin M. 1981. *The Quintette Tunnels on the Coquihalla Subdivision of the Abandoned Kettle Valley Railway.* Heritage Conservation Branch (Unpub.), B.C. Prov. Government, Victoria, B.C.

Burrows, Roger G. 1981. *Railway Mileposts: British Columbia. Vol. 1: The CPR Mainline Route from the Rockies to the Pacific.* Railway Milepost Books, North Vancouver, B.C.

Burrows, Roger G. 1984. *Railway Mileposts: British Columbia. Vol. 2: The Southern Routes from the Crowsnest to the Coquihalla.* Railway Milepost Books, North Vancouver, B.C.

Cail, Robert E. 1974. *Land, Man, and the Law. The Disposal of Crown Lands in British Columbia, 1871-1913.* University of British Columbia Press, Vancouver, B.C.

Caine, W. S. 1888. *Trip Round the World in 1887-8.* George Routledge and Sons, London, England.

Cairnes, C. E. 1934. *Slocan Mining Camp, British Columbia.* Memoir 173, Geological Survey, Dept. of Mines, Ottawa, Ont.

Canadian Pacific Railway. 1881-1984. *Annual Reports.* CPR and CP Ltd., Montreal, P.Q.

Canadian Pacific Railway. 1891. *The Canadian Pacific. New Highway to the Orient.* Canadian Pacific Railway, Montreal, P.Q. (also later editions)

Canadian Pacific Railway. 1906. *Proceedings of the Meeting of Western Lines Officials Held at Field, B.C.* Canadian Pacific Railway, Montreal, P.Q.

Canadian Pacific Railway. 1937. *Factors in Railway and Steamship Operation.* General Publicity Department, Canadian Pacific Foundation Library, Montreal, P.Q.

Canadian Pacific Railway. 1937. *Canadian Pacific Facts and Figures.* General Publicity Department, Canadian Pacific Foundation Library, Montreal, P.Q.

Canadian Pacific Railway. 1946. *Canadian Pacific Facts and Figures.* Department of Public Relations. Canadian Pacific Foundation Library, Montreal, P.Q.

Canadian Pacific Railway. 1947. *A Study of Possible Economies & Advantages by using Diesel-Electric Locomotives on the Esquimalt and Nanaimo Railway*. Department of Research Report, No. 13-7. CPR, Montreal, P.Q.

Canadian Pacific Railway. 1950. *An Application Study on Diesel-Electric Locomotives Calgary to Revelstoke*. Department of Research Report, No. 23-50. CPR, Montreal, P.Q.

Canadian Pacific Railway. 1952. *An Application Study of Diesel-Electric Locomotives for the Kootenay and Kettle Valley Divisions*. Department of Research Report, No. 30-52. CPR, Montreal, P.Q.

CP Rail. 1982. *Rogers Pass Brief*. Environmental Assessment and Review Process Hearings, April 1982. CP Rail, Montreal, P.Q.

CP Rail. 1983. *Rogers Pass Project: Submittal to Federal Environmental Assessment Review Office, June 1983*. (J. Fox, Vice-President Engineering, Special Projects, CP Rail). CP Rail, Montreal, P.Q.

Chapman, Peter. 1981. *Where the Lardeau River Flows*. Provincial Archives of British Columbia, Sound Heritage Series No. 32, Victoria, B.C.

Chodos, Robert. 1973. *The CPR. A Century of Corporate Welfare*. James Lewis & Samuel, Toronto, Ont.

Clute, R. C. 1899. "Report of Mr. R. C. Clute on the Commission to Inquire into the Death of McDonald and Fraser on the Crow's Nest Pass Railway," *Sessional Papers (No. 70)*. Ottawa, Ont.

Dean, Murray W. and David G. Hanna. 1981. *Canadian Pacific Diesel Locomotives*. Railfare Enterprises, Montreal, P.Q.

Dennis, A. C. 1917. "Construction Methods for Rogers Pass Tunnel," *American Society of Civil Engineers, Transactions*, Paper No. 1390. (also including commentary by J. G. Sullivan and others) pp. 448-497.

Dempsey, Hugh A. (Ed.) 1984. *The CPR West. The Iron Road and the Making of a Nation*. Douglas & McIntyre Ltd., Vancouver, B.C.

Dewdney, Kathleen S. 1964. "A Farewell Trip on the Kettle Valley Railroad," *Okanagan Historical Society*, 28th. Report.

Doeksen, G. 1981-1985. *Railways of Western Canada* (Vol. 1-4), Published by the author, Montrose, B.C.

Dolmage, V. 1934. *Geology and Ore Deposits of Copper Mountain, British Columbia*. Memoir 171, Geological Survey, Dept. of Mines, Ottawa, Ont.

Dowling, D. B. 1915. *Coal Fields of British Columbia*. Memoir 69, Geological Survey, Dept. of Mines, Ottawa, Ont.

Dubin, Arthur D. 1964. *Some Classic Trains*. Kalmbach Publishing Co., Milwaukee, Wn.

Dubin, Arthur D. 1974. *More Classic Trains*. Kalmbach Publishing Co., Milwaukee, Wn.

Dugas, C. A., Frank Pedley and John Appleton. 1898. "Report of the Commissioners in Re: Crow's Nest Complaints," *Sessional Papers (No. 90A)*. Ottawa, Ont.

Ehrenberger, James L. and Francis G. Gschwind. 1968. *Smoke Along the Columbia*. E. & G. Publications, Cheyenne, Wy.

Esquimalt & Nanaimo Railway. 1914. *The Timber, Agricultural and Industrial Resources of Vancouver Island British Columbia*. E&N Railway, Victoria, B.C.

Fahey, John. 1965. *Inland Empire. D. C. Corbin and Spokane*. University of Washington Press, Seattle, Washington.

Fleming, Sandford. 1877. *Report on Surveys and Preliminary Operations on the Canadian Pacific Railway up to January 1877*. MacLean, Roger & Co., Ottawa, Ont.

Fleming, Sandford. 1878. *Reports and Documents in Reference to the Location of the Line and a Western Terminal Harbour*. MacLean, Roger & Co., Ottawa, Ont.

Fleming, Sandford. 1879. *Report in Reference to the Canadian Pacific Railway*. MacLean, Roger & Co., Ottawa, Ont.

Fowler, S. S. 1939. "Early Smelters in British Columbia," *British Columbia Historical Quarterly*, Vol. 3(3): pp. 183-201.

Fraser Valley Rehabilitation Authority. 1949. "Interim Report," *Sessional Papers*, Legislative Assembly, Victoria, B.C., Vol. 2: pp. 9-24.

Gibbon, John Murray. 1937. *The Romantic History of the Canadian Pacific*. Tudor Publishing Co., New York, N.Y.

Gilbert, Heather. 1965. *Awakening Continent, The Life of Lord Mount Stephen, Vol. 1*. Aberdeen University Press, Aberdeen, Scotland.

Hacking, Norman R. 1947. "British Columbia Steamboat Days, 1870-1883," *British Columbia Historical Quarterly*. 11(2): pp. 69-112.

Hacking, Norman R. and W. Kaye Lamb. 1974. *The Princess Story. A Century and a Half of West Coast Shipping*. Mitchell Press, Vancouver, B.C.

Haldane, J. W. C. 1900. *3800 Miles Across Canada*. Simpkin, Marshall, Hamilton, Kent & Co. Ltd., London, U.K.

Harris, Cole. 1983. "Moving Amid the Mountains, 1870-1930," *BC Studies*. No. 58, pp. 3-39.

Hart, E. J. 1983. *The Selling of Canada. The CPR and the Beginnings of Canadian Tourism*. Altitude Publishing Ltd., Banff, Alta.

Hart, E. J. 1984. "See this World Before the Next. Tourism and the CPR," in Dempsey (ed.), *The CPR West*. Douglas & McIntyre Ltd., Vancouver, B.C.

Harvey, R. D. 1960. *History of Saanich Penninsula Railways*. Queen's Printer, Victoria, B.C.

Hearn, George R. 1959. *Narrow Gauge in the Kootenays.* Vancouver Island Railway Historical Association, Bulletin No. 1, Victoria, B.C.

Hearn, George and David Wilkie. 1966. *The Cordwood Limited. A History of the Victoria and Sidney Railway.* The British Columbia Railway Historical Association, Victoria, B.C.

Hearn, George and David Wilkie. 1971. "The K&S Railway," *Canada West,* 3(3): pp. 9-16.

Horetzky, C. 1880. *Some Startling Facts Relating to the Canadian Pacific Railway and the North-west Lands, also a Brief Discussion Regarding the Route, the Western Terminus and the Lands Available for Settlement.* Free Press, Ottawa, Ont.

Hungry Wolf, Adolf. 1979. *Rails in the Canadian Rockies.* Good Medicine Books, Invermere, B.C.

Hungry Wolf, Adolf. 1983. *Canadian Railway Scenes. Vol. 1.* Good Medicine Books, Invermere, B.C.

Hyde, Henry M. n.d. "Sitting Up With the Mountain Division," *Technical World Magazine,* pp. 138-144.

Innis, Harold A. 1971. *A History of the Canadian Pacific Railway.* University of Toronto Press, Toronto, Ont.

Jukes, Fred, Philip Van Wyck and Bruce B. Cheever. 1951. "The Bellingham Bay & British Columbia Railroad Company," *Bulletin, Railway & Locomotive Historical Society.* No. 84: pp. 7-24.

Kennedy, W. Gibson, 1983. *Canadian Pacific's Rossland Subdivision.* British Railway Modellers of North America, Calgary, Alta.

Keys, Norman C. Jr. and Kenneth R. Middleton. 1980. "The Great Northern Railway Company: All-time Locomotive Roser, 1861-1970," *Railroad History.* No. 143 (Autumn): pp. 20-163.

Kirkpatrick, W. M. 1937. "Steamship Freight Problems," in General Publicity Department, *Factors in Railway and Steamship Operation,* Canadian Pacific Foundation Library, Montreal, P.Q.

Koch, Michael. 1971. *The Shay Locomotive, Titan of the Timber.* World Press, Denver, Co.

Lafortune, Jean. 1981. "Silkers Had Top Priority Across the System; God Help the Railroader Who Delayed One," *Canadian Pacific Railway News.* 11(2): pp. 6.

Lavallée, Omer. 1972. *Narrow Gauge Railways of Canada.* Railfare Enterprises Ltd., Montreal, P.Q.

Lavallée, Omer. 1974. *Van Horne's Road.* Railfare Enterprises Ltd., Montreal, P.Q.

Lavallée, Omer. 1985. *Canadian Pacific Steam Locomotives.* Railfare Enterprises Ltd., Montreal, P.Q.

Lavallée, Omer S. A. and Robert R. Brown. 1951. "Locomotives of the Canadian Pacific Railway Company," *Bulletin, Railway & Locomotive Historical Society,* No. 83: pp. 7-93.

Lee, David. 1983. "Chinese Construction Workers on the Canadian Pacific." *Railroad History,* 148 (Spring): pp. 42-57.

LeRoy, O. E. 1912. *The Geology and Ore Deposits of Phoenix, Boundary District, British Columbia.* Memoir No. 21, Geological Survey, Dept. of Mines, Ottawa, Ont.

LeRoy, O. E. 1913. *Mother Lode and Sunset Mines, Boundary District, B.C.* Memoir 19, Geological Survey, Dept. of Mines, Ottawa, Ont.

M.P. (anonymous). 1886. *A Winter Trip on the Canadian Pacific Railway.* John J. Banks, Imperial Library, Cheltenham, England.

MacBeth, R. B. 1924. *The Romance of the Canadian Pacific Railway.* The Ryerson Press, Toronto, Ont.

Macorquodale, Ruth McCulloch. 1949. "Andrew McCulloch and the Kettle Valley Railway," *Okanagan Historical Society,* 13th Report. pp. 71-82.

Macorquodale, Ruth McCulloch. 1961. "Andrew McCulloch, Civil Engineer," *Okanagan Historical Society,* 25th Report.

McCulloch, Andrew. n.d. *The Kettle Valley Railway Notes.* (memorandum) CPR Superintendent's Office, Penticton.

McCulloch, Andrew. 1964. "Railway Development in Southern B.C. from 1890 on..." *Boundary Historical Society,* 4th Report, pp. 37-50.

MacDonald, Norbert. 1977. "The Canadian Pacific Railway and Vancouver's Development to 1900," *BC Studies,* No. 35, pp. 3-35.

McKee, Bill and Georgeen, Klassen. 1983. *Trail of Iron. The CPR and the Birth of the West.* Glenbow-Alberta Institute / Douglas & McIntyre, Vancouver, B.C.

Marsh, John S. 1979. *A History of Glacier House and Nakimu Caves, Glacier National Park British Columbia.* Canadian Recreation Services, Peterborough, Ont.

Marsh, John S. 1984. "The Spiral and Connaught Tunnels," in Dempsey (ed), *The CPR West.* Douglas & McIntyre Ltd., Vancouver, B.C.

Martin, Albro. 1976. *James J. Hill and the Opening of the Northwest.* Oxford University Press, New York, N.Y.

Martin, J. Edward. 1980. *Railway Stations of Western Canada.* Studio E. Martin, White Rock, B.C.

Mathews, H. F. 1937. "Canadian Pacific Hotels," in General Publicity Department, *Canadian Pacific Facts and Figures.* Canadian Pacific Foundation Library, Montreal, P.Q.

Mattison, David. 1985. *Camera Workers. The British Columbia Photographers Directory 1858-1900.* Camera Workers Press, Victoria, B.C.

Middleton, Kenneth R. and Norman C. Keyes, Jr. 1980. "The Great Northern Railway Company: Predecessors and Fully-Controlled Subsidiaries." *Railroad History*, No. 143 (Autumn): pp. 8-19.

Moir, George T. 1947. *Sinners and Saints.* published by the author, Victoria, B.C.

Morkill, George H. 1954. "The Shuswap & Okanagan Railway," *Okanagan Historical Society*, 18th Report. pp. 47-50.

Morris, Keith. 1928. *The Story of the Canadian Pacific Railway.* William Stevens Ltd., London, England.

Morton, James. 1973. *In the Sea of Sterile Mountains. The Chinese in British Columbia.* J. J. Douglas, Ltd., West Vancouver, B.C.

Muckleston, H. B. 1905. "A Short Description of the Canadian Pacific Railway Through the Selkirks," in A. O. Wheeler, *The Selkirk Range*, pp. 422-429.

Musk, George. 1981. *Canadian Pacific. The Story of the Famous Shipping Line.* David & Charles, Newton Abbot, England.

Nelligan, Tom. 1982. *VIA Rail Canada: The First Five Years.* PTJ Publishing Inc., Park Forest, Ill.

Nelson, J. G. and R. C. Scace. 1968. *The Canadian National Parks: Today and Tomorrow.* University of Calgary, Studies in Land Use History and Landscape Change, National Park Series, No. 3, Calgary, Alta.

Parks Canada. 1985. *The Kicking Horse Times.* Parks Canada, Ottawa, Ont.

Pugsley, Raymond E. 1973. *The Great Kicking Horse Blunder.* The Author, Vancouver, B.C.

Ramsay, G. G. 1884. "Over the Rocky Mountains by the Canadian Pacific Line in 1884," *MacMillan's Magazine*, No. 301 (November): pp. 120-129.

Regehr, T. D. 1976. *The Canadian Northern Railway.* Macmillan Company of Canada, Toronto, Ont.

Regehr, T. D. 1984. "Letters from End of Track," in Dempsey (ed.), *The CPR West.* Douglas & McIntyre Ltd., Vancouver, B.C.

Riegger, Hal. 1981. *The Kettle Valley and Its Railways.* Pacific Fast Mail, Edmonds, Wa.

Robinson, Bart. 1973. *Banff Springs, The Story of a Hotel.* Summerthought, Banff, Alta.

Roper, Edward. 1891. *By Track and Trail. A Journey Through Canada.* W. H. Allen & Co., London, England.

Roy, Patricia E. 1980. "Progress, Prosperity and Politics: The Railway Policies of Richard McBride," *BC Studies*, No. 47: pp. 3-28.

Roy, Patricia E. 1984. "A Choice between Evils, the Chinese and the Construction of the Canadian Pacific Railway in British Columbia," in Dempsey (ed.), *The CPR West.* Douglas & McIntyre Ltd., Vancouver, B.C.

Sanford, Barrie. 1977. *McCulloch's Wonder, The Story of the Kettle Valley Railway.* Whitecap Books, Ltd., West Vancouver, B.C.

Sanford, Barrie. 1981. *The Pictorial History of Railroading in British Columbia.* Whitecap Books, Ltd., Vancouver, B.C.

Schofield, Stuart J. 1915. *Geology of Cranbrook Map-Area, British Columbia.* Memoir 76, Geological Survey, Dept. of Mines, Ottawa, Ont.

Scott, David and Edna H. Hanic. 1974. *East Kootenay Saga.* Nunaga Publishing Co., New Westminster, B.C.

Secretan, J. H. E. 1924. *Canada's Great Highway: From the First Spike to the Last Spike.* Thorburn & Abbott, Ottawa, Ont.

Shaw, Charles Aeneas. 1970. *Tales of a Pioneer Surveyor.* Longman Canada Ltd., Toronto, Ont.

Soole, G. H. 1937. "Field and the Big Hill," in General Publicity Department, *Factors in Railway and Steamship Operation*, Canadian Pacific Foundation Library, Montreal, P.Q.

Strachan, Robert, W. J. Dick and R. J. Lee. 1928. "The Coal Mining Industry of Western Canada," *Second (Triennial) Empire Mining and Metallurgical Congress, Proceedings*, Part II, pp. 192-402.

Stevens, G. R. 1973. *History of the Canadian National Railways.* Collier Macmillan Canada Ltd., Toronto, Ont.

Taylor, H. C. 1937. "Operating Trains in the Rockies," in General Publicity Department, *Factors in Railway and Steamship Operation.* Canadian Pacific Foundation Library, Montreal, P.Q.

Taylor, W. A. 1975. *Esquimalt and Nanaimo Rly. Land Grant. The Railway Belt and Peace River Block.* Surveys and Mapping Branch, Department of Lands, Forests and Water Resources, Victoria, B.C.

Turnbull, Elsie G. 1964. *Topping's Trail. The First Years of a Now Famous Smelter City.* Mitchell Press, Vancouver, B.C.

Turner, Robert D. 1973. *Vancouver Island Railroads.* Golden West Books, San Marino, Cal.

Turner, Robert D. 1977. *The Pacific Princesses. An Illustrated History of Canadian Pacific's Princess Fleet on the Northwest Coast.* Sono Nis Press, Victoria, B.C.

Turner, Robert D. 1981a. *Railroaders. Recollections from the Steam Era in British Columbia.* Provincial Archives of British Columbia, Sound Heritage Series No. 31, Victoria, B.C.

Turner, Robert D. 1981b. *The Princess Marguerite. Last of the Coastal Liners.* Sono Nis Press, Victoria, B.C.

Turner, Robert D. 1981c. *The Pacific Empresses. An Illustrated History of the Canadian Pacific's Empress Liners on the Pacific Ocean.* Sono Nis Press, Victoria, B.C.

Turner, Robert D. 1984. *Sternwheelers and Steam Tugs. An Illustrated History of the Canadian Pacific Railway's British Columbia Lake and River Service.* Sono Nis Press, Victoria, B.C.

Vaughan, H. H. 1913. "Rotary Snow Plows, Their History, Construction, Etc.," *Canadian Railway & Marine World*, March, pp. 101-105.

Vaughan, Walter. 1920. *The Life and Work of Sir William Van Horne.* The Century Company, New York, N.Y.

Wayner, Robert. 1983. *A Century of De Luxe Railway Cars in Canada.* Railfare Enterprises, Ltd., Toronto, Ont.

Wheeler, A. O. 1905. *The Selkirk Range.* Government Printing Bureau, Ottawa, Ont.

Wickberg, Edgar (Ed.). 1982. *From China to Canada. A History of the Chinese Communities in Canada.* McClelland and Stewart Ltd., Toronto, Ont.

Wilson, Alfred W. G. 1913. *The Copper Smelting Industries of Canada.* Mines Branch (No. 209). Canada Department of Mines. Government Printing Bureau, Ottawa, Ont.

Wilson, Dale. 1980. *From Abbey to Zorra via Bagdad. Canadian Pacific Railway Passenger Services in the 1950s.* Nickel Belt Rails, Sudbury, Ont.

Winterrowd, W. H. 1920. "Snow Fighting Equipment," *Canadian Railway & Marine World*, Sept. pp. 469-475; Oct. pp. 525-529; Nov. pp. 581-588.

Wood, Charles and Dorothy Wood. 1979. *The Great Northern Railway. A Pictorial Study.* Pacific Fast Mail, Edmonds, Wa.

Woods, John G. 1983. *Snow War. An Illustrated History of Rogers Pass Glacier National Park.* National and Provincial Parks Association of Canada, Toronto, Ont.

Yeats, Floyd. 1985. *Canadian Pacific's Big Hill. A Hundred Years of Operation.* British Railway Modellers of North America, Calgary, Alta.

On the Field Hill: 1201 in July 1986; Train No. 2 in September 1952.—ROBERT D. TURNER; RAILWAY NEGATIVE EXCHANGE

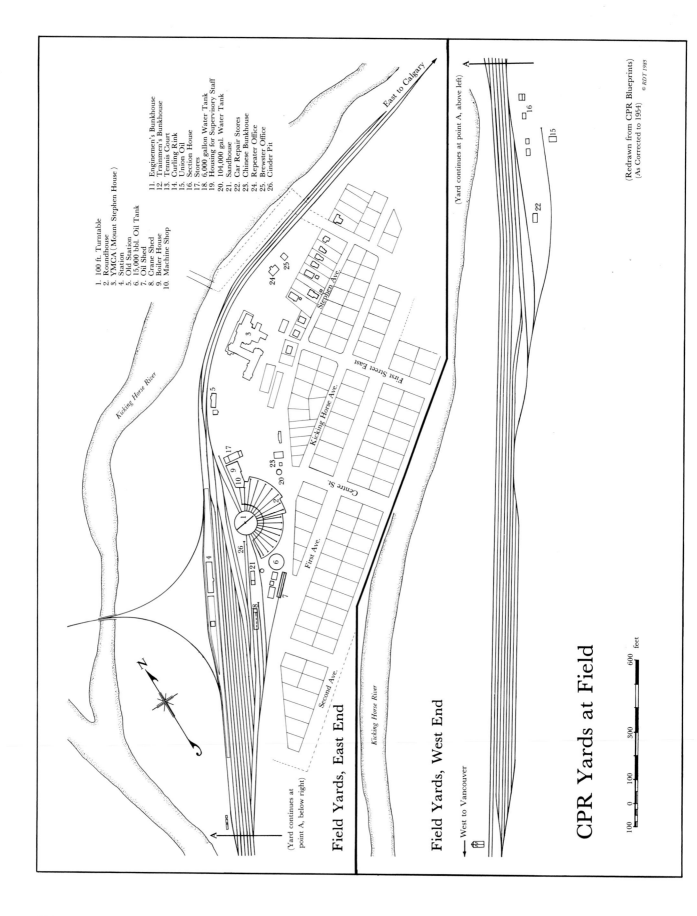

CPR Yards at Field

Field Yards, East End

Field Yards, West End

1. 100 ft. Turntable
2. Roundhouse
3. YMCA (Mount Stephen House)
4. Station
5. Old Station
6. 15,000 bbl. Oil Tank
7. Oil Shed
8. Crane Shed
9. Boiler House
10. Machine Shop
11. Enginemen's Bunkhouse
12. Trainmen's Bunkhouse
13. Tennis Court
14. Curling Rink
15. Union Oil
16. Section House
17. Stores
18. 6,000 gallon Water Tank
19. Housing for Supervisory Staff
20. 104,000 gal. Water Tank
21. Sandhouse
22. Car Repair Stores
23. Chinese Bunkhouse
24. Repeater Office
25. Brewster Office
26. Cinder Pit

East to Calgary

West to Vancouver

Kicking Horse River

Kicking Horse River

Stephen Ave.

First Street East

Kicking Horse Ave.

Centre St.

First Ave.

Second Ave.

N

(Yard continues at point A, below right)

(Yard continues at point A, above left)

(Redrawn from CPR Blueprints)
(As Corrected to 1954)

© RDT 1985

100   0   100   300   600
                                feet